Hanna-Barbera

THE RECORDED HISTORY

Hanna-Barbera

THE RECORDED HISTORY

From Modern Stone Age to Meddling Kids

GREG EHRBAR

Foreword by Tim Matheson

A Personal Note by Leonard Maltin

University Press of Mississippi / Jackson

The University Press of Mississippi is the scholarly publishing agency of the Mississippi Institutions of Higher Learning: Alcorn State University, Delta State University, Jackson State University, Mississippi State University, Mississippi University for Women, Mississippi Valley State University, University of Mississippi, and University of Southern Mississippi.

www.upress.state.ms.us

This book makes reference to various HANNA-BARBERA copyrighted characters, trademarks, marks, elements, and registered marks © and ™ Hanna-Barbera.

The University Press of Mississippi is a member of the Association of University Presses.

Library of Congress Cataloging-in-Publication Data

Names: Ehrbar, Greg, author. | Matheson, Tim, 1947– writer of foreword. | Maltin, Leonard, writer of personal note.
Title: Hanna-Barbera, the recorded history : from modern stone age to meddling kids / Greg Ehrbar, Tim Matheson, Leonard Maltin.
Description: Jackson : University Press of Mississippi, 2024. | Includes bibliographical references and index.
Identifiers: LCCN 2024013344 (print) | LCCN 2024013345 (ebook) | ISBN 9781496840981 (hardback) | ISBN 9781496851857 (trade paperback) | ISBN 9781496851864 (epub) | ISBN 9781496851871 (epub) | ISBN 9781496851888 (pdf) | ISBN 9781496851895 (pdf)
Subjects: LCSH: Hanna, William, 1910–2001. | Barbera, Joseph. | Hanna-Barbera Productions—History. | Hanna-Barbera Cartoons. | Hanna-Barbera Singers. | Animated television programs—United States—History and criticism. | Animated films—United States—History and criticism. | Animated television music. | Cartoon characters—United States--Songs and music.
Classification: LCC NC1766.U52 H36335 2024 (print) | LCC NC1766.U52 (ebook) | DDC 338.7/6179145340973—dc23/eng/20240507
LC record available at https://lccn.loc.gov/2024013344
LC ebook record available at https://lccn.loc.gov/2024013345

British Library Cataloging-in-Publication Data available

publication supported by a grant from

The Community Foundation for Greater New Haven

as part of the Urban Haven Project

For my wife, Suzanne,

the very heart and soul of this book

Contents

Foreword

Tim Matheson

In *Hanna-Barbera, the Recorded History*, Greg Ehrbar takes us behind the scenes of the birth of the television animation giant Hanna-Barbera. The journey of these two pioneers, Bill Hanna and Joe Barbera, is fascinating and heartfelt. Their passion to find a way to bring animation affordably to television and to continue to expand the scope of the work that they produced were the drivers of their long careers.

I was fortunate enough to be a part of this wonderful company and community when I was chosen by Joe Barbera to play the voice of Jonny Quest. I was fifteen years old. For the next three years in a variety of shows, I was introduced, educated, and invited into the community of incredibly talented voice actors. I was also able to wander through the cubicles of the animators who were producing the hand-drawn cels (no computer animation back then) and to understand how lengthy the process was to produce the characters and scenes for their TV shows.

As I look back on those years at Hanna-Barbera, I realize now that it was a "Golden Age" and a unique part of television history. I consider myself fortunate and proud to have been a small part of the Hanna-Barbera empire. This book takes us into their journey and into the lives of Bill Hanna and Joe Barbera, two wonderfully talented and kind-hearted stalwarts of television animation.

Tim Matheson is a two-time Emmy-nominated actor/director whose career spans generations of hit television series from *Bonanza* and *The West Wing* to *Hart of Dixie* and *Virgin River*. His films include *National Lampoons Animal House*, Steven Spielberg's *1941*, and *Yours, Mine and Ours*. He voiced Hanna-Barbera's Jonny Quest, Jace of *Space Ghost*, Sinbad Jr., and Young Samson.

A Personal Note

Leonard Maltin

I don't have one of those memory banks that can pinpoint what I was doing every day of my life, but I do know where I was at 6:00 p.m. on September 28, 1958: perched in front of my family's black-and-white television set, eagerly awaiting the debut of a brand-new half-hour cartoon program called *The Huckleberry Hound Show*. It had been promoted for at least a week leading up to its debut and now here it was, with a catchy, upbeat theme song and action to match: "The biggest show in town is Huckleberry Hound / For all you guys and gals . . ." This fast-paced opening even incorporated the sponsor, Kellogg's cereals, a name I knew well, and its emblematic characters.

Even at the age of seven (going on eight) I understood that this was a Big Deal, an all-new half-hour consisting of three separate cartoon shorts. That night I was introduced to Huck (whose appealing southern-inflected speech was provided by the great Daws Butler), Yogi Bear and his little pal Boo-Boo, and a pair of mice named Pixie and Dixie, whose perennial antagonist was named Mr. Jinks.

It was love at first sight—and sound. As Yogi Bear's popularity soared, he earned a half-hour show of his own, which I tuned in and thoroughly enjoyed. This was followed by another spin-off series, *Quick Draw McGraw*, which boasted yet another catchy title tune. I later learned that the man who provided all that music was named Hoyt Curtin. The lyrics were written by none other than Joe Barbera, one-half of the producing and directing team of Hanna-Barbera.

By the time *Magilla Gorilla* came along in 1964 I'd had my fill of Hanna-Barbera's shows, which were slavishly following a formula that wore out its welcome. At the ripe old age of twelve, I had moved on to Jay Ward's Rocky and Bullwinkle. I also became curious to know more about the history of animation. I came to learn that Hanna and Barbera had created Tom and Jerry when they were working at MGM in the 1940s and were pioneers when it came to producing cartoons for television on a tight budget. Propelled by youthful moxie I mounted a high horse and decried their use of so-called limited animation. With the passage of time, I came to appreciate what they actually accomplished, entertaining kids while keeping animation alive in Hollywood and providing a lifeline to countless veterans of the business. I even became friendly with Joe Barbera.

Fade out, then fade in circa 1995. When Rhino Records released a CD of vintage H-B theme songs I played it while driving and found myself singing out loud along with the likes of Huckleberry Hound and Quick Draw McGraw, somehow remembering all the lyrics. I hadn't seen an episode of those series since the early 1960s, but those cartoons made a deep and lasting impression on me, and millions of others. I'm so glad that Greg Ehrbar has done this deep dive into H-B audio history to set the often-forgotten record straight (pun intended). No one is more qualified to tell the story.

Leonard Maltin is one of the most recognized and respected film critics and authors of our time. His best-sellers include the *Movie Guide* series, *Of Mice and Magic*, and *The Disney Films*. His television career includes thirty years on *Entertainment Tonight* and regular appearances on Turner Classic Movies. His prestigious USC film classes have become a fixture for over two decades.

About This Book

**It was Hanna and Barbera's sense of timing, the point of
view, the attitude, that definitely set those cartoons apart.
There was personality in these characters and the cartoons
themselves. It was their unique "voice" that came through . . .**
—ANIMATION HISTORIAN JERRY BECK

Some of the biggest moments in life are the littlest, nicest things.

One evening long ago, my dad came home from work carrying a shopping bag
from the Grand Way department store.

"I know how much you like these records, son," he said. "So on the way home
from work, I bought you this one. No special reason."

Dad didn't know what a bad day I had at school that day. He turned it all around
with his act of kindness and his awareness of what made me happy. He gave me
a brand-new Hanna-Barbera "HBR Cartoon Series" Record—*Pixie and Dixie with
Mr. Jinks Tell the Story of Cinderella*. I played it over and over again, memorizing
it completely. I used it as a comedy monologue in junior high school. In college, I
gathered a group of actors to perform the script. I continue to quote its wry and
unique humor.

Decades later, I found a second copy of this album and gave it to one of its two
stars, whom I called "Lovely Lady June" Foray. (The other star was Paul Frees.) June
had given her only copy of the LP to a friend. She was delighted to have it again.
I had taken my father's loving deed full circle. Now, through this book, I hope to
continue what Dad, June, and countless good and talented people gave to others.

This is the story of the partnership of Bill Hanna and Joe Barbera in the thirties, their creation of Tom and Jerry, and the establishment of Hanna-Barbera
Productions. It continues through their developments in television animation to
movies and live-action—the changes, challenges, milestones, and memories, right
up to Hanna-Barbera projects in the twenty-first century.

The author, his father, Harold F. Ehrbar (far right), and Fess Parker (*Davy Crockett, Daniel Boone*).

Your "guides" through this saga are the music, voices, sound effects, and especially recordings created and inspired by Hanna-Barbera and its people. Bill Hanna and Joe Barbera established a "voice" from the moment they formed their partnership. They and their associates were able to bring an extraordinary range of entertainment to life. The sounds were part of the unparalleled success. From an Academy Award–winning *Tom and Jerry* cartoon or an Emmy-winning *Huckleberry Hound Show* episode to a beloved *Flintstones* episode or *Scooby-Doo* mystery, every work is steeped in audio artistry as well as visual mastery.

Hanna-Barbera's music was nonstop from the start. In the virtual dialogue vacuum of vintage Tom and Jerry cartoons, Scott Bradley's scores seemed to speak to the audience like an offscreen character. Hanna-Barbera TV cartoons brought a wave of catchy, iconic themes known in dozens of languages, as well as unmistakable musical background cues. There have been cartoons with original "book" musical scores, some cowritten by Hanna, Barbera, composer Hoyt Curtin, and major names from Broadway

and Hollywood. H-B character voices set precedents in entertainment history, beloved and revered by the public and within the industry. Artists like Daws Butler, Janet Waldo, Don Messick, June Foray, John Stephenson, Alan Reed, Mel Blanc, Scatman Crothers, and Allan Melvin fortified or established their status. How many studios have sound effects so inextricably connected with them? George Jetson's air car. Fred's tippy toes. The Jet Screamer solar swivel. Perhaps only Lucasfilm sounds from Ben Burtt and his team can claim the same iconic level.

Even Hanna-Barbera's harshest critics—especially in the later years—can concede some admiration for the H-B music, scripting, sounds, and vocal work that lend support to the visuals.

Here for the first time is a comprehensive Hanna-Barbera history told through the prism of the "animation behind the animation." These were the auditory elements that created a sense of motion through sound. From it sprang a vast and vivid body of recorded work, some by familiar names and others that might be surprising. Please know that there

One of many Hanna-Barbera recordings that continues to delight and inspire.

is no requirement for prior listening to any of the recordings mentioned, though perhaps the discoveries described within might encourage seeking some of them out.

Every possible step was taken to make this book as accurate and comprehensive as possible. With numerous facts on every page, there are bound to be omissions and "Boo-Boos" in addition to Yogis. Facts were verified as much as possible and feasible, but there will be suppositions and educated guesses marked as such. The author appreciates your kind understanding.

Each chapter covers a general region of history. Because Hanna-Barbera produced such a monumental amount of work, the precise chronology shifts slightly, but generally stays within the same few years.

Most of the Hanna-Barbera productions in this book are part of the precious memories of times,

places, and people. Some are truly extraordinary works of art, and others might have missed the mark but are still interesting parts of the whole story. The main goal was to entertain with the best work possible given each set of circumstances, material, and time frame.

For those who have brought these creative works into existence, I can only hope this book can "yabba-dabba-doo" everyone justice.

Hanna-Barbera

THE RECORDED HISTORY

William Hanna and Joseph Barbera created two of the most enduring animated characters during the heyday of theatrical shorts.

Chapter 1

TOM AND JERRY AND BILL AND JOE

I had studied music for years and years before I ever got into the cartoon business. And knowing music and notes and then determining the number of drawings for each note and so forth and so on, I soon . . . got into timing and directing animation.
—BILL HANNA, *TOM AND JERRY SPOTLIGHT COLLECTIONS* DVD

They came from opposite sides of the United States, but William Denby Hanna and Joseph Roland Barbera might as well have come from different planets.

Hanna was an outdoorsman instilled with a rock-solid work ethic. He had a natural gift for structure and timing that translated perfectly from engineering and construction to animation and production. Barbera was a street-smart artist/writer from Brooklyn who learned early to be self-reliant, confident, and resourceful.

During Hanna's youth in Melrose, New Mexico, and Compton, California, young Bill relished his time on construction sites with his father, a structural engineer. There he learned the values of organizing a project and working with a crew.

The artistic talents of his mother and sisters inspired him to pursue a creative field. "They imparted to me a great appreciation of rhythm, timing, and imagery," Hanna wrote in his memoir, *A Cast of Friends*. His love of music and innate sense of timing would prove to be lifelong. He decided against studying piano, but one of his favorite pastimes was writing verse. The Great Depression made some decisions for him. Sidelining the arts, Hanna joined his father in the construction of Hollywood's landmark Pantages Theater.

Hanna's sister happened to be dating an employee of Leon Schlesinger, whose company made titles for the Warner Brothers studio and expanded into animated cartoons. Schlesinger had just hired two animators, Hugh Harman and Rudolf Ising. "Rudy" worked with Walt Disney during his Kansas City days and in the early Hyperion era. At Warner, Harman and Ising's new Merrie Melodies cartoons would promote songs from the Warner studio catalog and compete with Disney's hit Silly Symphony cartoons. They followed a similar format, featuring popular songs rather than classic and public-domain music.

Hanna eagerly started at the bottom, soaking up every aspect of animation production. He kept the studio tidy and washed the ink and paint off each of the finished "cels" (sheets of illustrated celluloid that, when placed over background art, created one or more frames of animation). Ising eventually allowed Hanna to participate in story development.

"I also began writing little songs that Harman and Ising began to incorporate into the early Looney Tunes and Merrie Melodies cartoons," Hanna wrote. "These lyrics were actually progressions of the whimsical little verses I had begun composing as a boy, never thinking at the time that they would ever lead to anything beyond maybe a family greeting."

When Warner opened its own cartoon department, Hanna remained with Hugh and Rudy when "Harman-Ising" (the name having a musical sound) became an independent studio, distributed through RKO-Radio Pictures.

▲▼▲▼

As much as Bill Hanna enjoyed mathematics and applied its principles creatively to music and verse, Joe Barbera loathed math. Calculating tax figures in a New York bank job, he restlessly counted each eternal minute. Lunchtime was his chance to dash to magazine publishers to drop off his clever on-panel gag cartoons. Nighttime meant art classes at Pratt Institute. He dreamed of cartooning or writing a Broadway show. Barbera was encouraged when *Collier's* magazine bought some of his cartoons. Upon seeing Walt Disney's 1929 Silly Symphony cartoon, *The Skeleton Dance*, he became enthralled with cartoons that could move.

"And that is how I came to write my first and only fan letter," he wrote in his autobiography, *My Life in Toons*.

Walt Disney personally answered the letter, saying he would visit Barbera the next time he was in New York. Sometimes dreams that come true are better than the original wishes. Joe would have happily quit his bank job, but the meeting slipped Walt's mind.

In retrospect, he believed the course of events was better for all concerned. "And I humbly thank God for that providence," he said.

Barbera broke into animation at the Fleischer Studios, home of Betty Boop and Popeye, inking and painting cels. Like Bill Hanna, Joe forged lifelong friendships with artists like Carlo Vinci (eventually an animator on *The Flintstones* in 1960) and Dave Tendlar (who worked on *Charlotte's Web* in 1973). Barbera recalled the Fleischer pay and working conditions as "Dickensian," which drove him back to working at the bank. Due to the Depression, the bank let him go.

A friend told Barbera that New York's Van Beuren Studios was hiring an animator, whose most popular characters were two cartoon men named Tom and Jerry. The term "Tom and Jerry" was originally associated with a traditional British holiday concoction combining cognac and rum with a batter mixture. Many a household kept a Tom and Jerry punch bowl and glass set (even the kitchen in Walt Disney's office has one). The Van Beuren cartoon duo used the names at first, but years later, they were renamed Dick and Larry because of the cat and mouse cartoon stars that eclipsed them. Even further into the twentieth century, a young folk/pop duo, inspired by the cat and mouse characters, called themselves "Tom and Jerry" before performing under their real names, Simon and Garfunkel.

The Van Beuren studio lost its RKO-Radio Pictures distribution deal to Disney and eventually folded. No matter the levels of his later success, Barbera could never shake the emotional jolt of being a part of a group in a seemingly permanent, physical place one minute, and then being tossed outside of it all the next. He landed another job at Terrytoons, run by the notoriously parsimonious Paul Terry. Later best known for Mighty Mouse and Heckle and Jeckle, at the time Terrytoons produced the Aesop's Fables series.

Animation was beginning to gain momentum in the film industry, especially on the West Coast, where artists were increasingly needed. Barbera made a modest living at Terrytoons, but Disney was luring animators to California with higher salaries. Terry convinced Barbera to stay until a mishap occurred. The young animator was handed a larger paycheck by the business manager. Joe was delighted at the apparent raise and stunned when the manager abruptly took the check back, returned with a smaller check, and blamed it on a clerical error. Barbera had enough and headed west.

▲▼▲▼▲▼

By the time Joe Barbera found himself working face-to-face with Bill Hanna in the cartoon studio of Metro-Goldwyn-Mayer in 1937, Hanna had already directed his first cartoon. The 1936 musical fantasy *To Spring* is about little gnomes who create seasonal colors as they sing a song written by Hanna. Harman-Ising Productions had since moved from Warner to MGM, and Hanna, now a producer/director, moved with them. In just a few years, Hanna and Barbera experienced the precarious life of the animation business.

"I would have been happy to spend the rest of my life working there producing cartoons for the Harman-Ising studio," Hanna recalled, but MGM canceled its contract with Harman-Ising. They overextended their abilities to produce enough cartoons on time and within budget—a lesson the young Hanna had already learned after years at his father's side in the construction business.

Executive Fred Quimby was hired from MGM's short films unit to administer the cartoon studio and enlisted several of Hollywood's up-and-coming animation talents to get it going, including Friz Freleng from Warner and Bill Hanna, who reluctantly moved on from Harman-Ising. Quimby acquired the rights to a popular comic strip called "The Katzenjammer Kids" to ignite the fledgling studio. It was a tone-deaf misfire, filled with Teutonic dialect just as the war with Germany was brewing in Europe. "Friz became so disenchanted with this series," Hanna wrote, "that he shortly thereafter left MGM and rejoined Warner Bros."

Quimby's concession to finally give up on "The Katzenjammer Kids" meant his MGM cartoon studio units, whose directors now included Tex Avery, had to come up with a hit series. Getting to know each other over their drawing desks and sharing stories of studio instabilities, Hanna and Barbera saw the warning signs of possible dismissal. A successful new character cartoon was vital to keep them employed.

▲▼▲▼▲▼

During a brainstorming session, Hanna and Barbera mentioned their idea of a cat-and-mouse chase. It was immediately shot down as trite, irrelevant, and done to death. They pursued the idea on their own anyway.

"Quimby was so desperate he didn't stop us," said Barbera, who recalled that, in addition to new characters, the duo came up with a way to present their cartoon that was new to the industry. Instead of presenting standard storyboards, they made a film with selected animation within the drawings. It was not a traditional cartoon by the standards of the day but would run the length of the finished film. The process was a more effective way to convey the personalities of the characters, the poses, the gags, and the reason the concept worked—beyond just "another cat and mouse cartoon." In doing this, Hanna and Barbera created two standard entertainment techniques: what would be called "limited animation," and what is today called an "animatic," used for presentations and as a motion picture "skeleton," within which rough sections are replaced with finished ones.

The test film enabled MGM execs to understand what they were seeing and they approved it. However, the animation department initially took the characters for granted. Rudy Ising authorized full production of *Puss Gets the Boot* and was credited as director, but he had no real participation or interest. According to Barbera, "He was never in the room." The film was given no departmental love, so it became the work of Hanna, Barbera, and the animation team alone. *Puss Gets the Boot* was a smash, playing for months in several theaters.

The animation studio acted as if nothing special had happened. Instead of recognizing Hanna and Barbera's success and asking them to create more Tom and Jerry cartoons, Quimby told them to stop. "We don't want to put all our eggs in one basket," he told them.

None of this changed until influential Texas theater owner Bessa Short contacted Quimby. She was startled that no additional cartoons starring the cat and mouse team were on their way, since they had been such a hit with theatergoers. "When are we going to see another one of those delightful cat and mouse cartoons?" she wrote to Quimby. Suddenly, Bill and Joe were assigned to make more cartoons with the cat, who was named Jasper. The mouse was not named in the actual cartoon. Hanna referred to "Jasper and Jinx" as the names he and Barbera worked with when they created the first cartoon. According to Barbera, neither he nor Hanna came up with the names "Tom and Jerry." A contest among the personnel resulted in those names being pulled out of a hat. Fifty dollars were awarded to animator John Carr.[1]

▲▾▲▾▲▾

Tom the cat and Jerry the mouse quickly ascended to the "A"-list of characters alongside Mickey Mouse, Bugs Bunny, and Woody Woodpecker. The MGM animation studio was on a roll, breaking Walt Disney's eight-year streak of Best Animated Short Cartoon Academy Award wins with 1940's *The Milky Way*, directed by Rudy Ising (and coproduced with an uncredited Bill Hanna the same year as *Puss Gets the Boot*).

Tom and Jerry won the first of seven Academy Awards in 1944 with the WWII-themed *The Yankee Doodle Mouse*. It was the greatest number of Oscars given to any continuous characters, including Bugs Bunny and Mickey Mouse. Tom and Jerry tied with Walt Disney's Silly Symphony series for seven total Oscar wins, but Tom and Jerry cartoons earned thirteen nominations to the Silly Symphonies' nine.

Walt Disney appeared on the Oscar stage to accept his statuettes, something directors Hanna and Barbera could never do despite Tom and Jerry's wins. Producer Fred Quimby accepted them and kept them. Academy rules specified the producers as recipients in that category, not directors. Now that the cartoons were hits, Quimby had his name placed prominently in the credits. One afternoon when Quimby had left his office, Hanna, Barbera, and the other people who *really* made those seven cartoons crept into his office to take photos with the Oscar statuettes.

There has been much discussion about the enduring popularity of Tom and Jerry. The thrill of the chase as well as the dysfunctional bond between these particular "frenemies" has timeless appeal. Hanna and Barbera were partners with no enmity, but by all reports, complete opposites. Colleagues, historians, and enthusiasts marveled at Barbera's knack for story and characterization and Hanna's impeccable animation timing.

▲▾▲▾▲▾

The success of MGM cartoons was due in large part to composer Scott Bradley. His innovative piano flourishes and violin strokes could express bewilderment, guile, or any number of expressions. Characters and specific actions were given leitmotifs that were often theirs for the entire MGM series.

Like many studios, MGM amassed its own library of sound effects, some gathered from live-action films and others created for animation. Bradley's technique was to work the music around the sound effects, whenever possible building the score up to the impact points, then halting to allow the action and effect to become its own punctuation. This is commonplace in modern scoring but unusual in the days of on-the-nose music synchronization called "Mickey Mousing" (as it began with Mickey during the dawn of sound when the novelty was fresher).

"We do the same thing in comedies today that Scott Bradley did so many years ago," said Hollywood composer Christopher Lennertz (*Supernatural, Lost in Space*). "We lead right up to when the actor's going to drop the punchline and you stop, let him drop it on his own, then we come in and 'tell' everybody, 'Okay, here we go now it's time to laugh.' That is still the technique, seventy years later, that we all use."

The music of Scott Bradley and the MGM Orchestra was as precision timed as Hanna's execution of the gags from the story artists and Barbera's storyboards. Bradley's music was not the savvy, sarcastic music that Carl Stalling created and Milt Franklyn sustained to perfection at Warner Brothers. That was because MGM, and Tom and Jerry cartoons, in particular, required a different approach. Bradley's score acted as a third character, communicating directly with the audience. He developed a distinct blueprint for scoring animation which he often discussed in lectures and essays. Bradley took great pride in scoring animation and believed it had an importance that would only increase with time.

▲▼▲▼▲▼

In the 1940s, there were no soundtrack recordings made of any MGM animation with Scott Bradley scoring. That would not happen until the twenty-first century.

The very first Hanna-Barbera recording ever released was *The King Who Couldn't Dance* on Columbia Records in 1945. It was a 78 rpm record with a storybook narrated and sung by the multitalented Gene Kelly. The record was adapted from Hanna and Barbera's landmark live-action/animated sequence in the MGM musical *Anchors Aweigh*, directed by George Sidney.

The film transitions into animation when Kelly's character tells a fanciful tale about a sailor in a magical kingdom where music and dancing are forbidden. The sailor confronts the king, who passed the law because he couldn't dance and mandated that no one else was permitted, either. The sailor teaches him by singing and dancing "The Worry Song" by Sammy Fain and Ralph Freed.

Assistant choreographer Stanley Donen (who later codirected *Singin' in the Rain* with Kelly) came

up with the idea. He thought the story would work best by placing Kelly in an animated environment. Combining animation with live-action was nothing new, even in the forties, but never before was such an intricate blend attempted. Walt Disney had taken the technique to its technical limits a year earlier in *The Three Caballeros*, in which Donald Duck cavorted at a beach party and Aurora Miranda made a city seem to dance. In the silent days, he gained prominence with the "Alice Comedies" featuring a live-action girl and cartoon creatures. Years earlier, animation visionary Max Fleischer combined live and animated elements in his "Out of the Inkwell" series.

"Gene said the MGM studio didn't believe it could be done," said his widow, Patricia Ward Kelly, in an interview with author/music historian Will Friedwald. "They didn't think it was possible and that's why they sent Gene over to talk to Walt Disney." Barbera believed it was because Fred Quimby did not want a special project to distract from their main job of making lucrative Tom and Jerry short cartoons.

One of the biggest animated stars up to that time was Mickey Mouse, but Donald Duck gained enormous popularity (along with Bugs Bunny and Popeye) during WWII. Kelly and Donen would have been happy with Mickey or Donald.

Walt Disney's abrupt dismissal of Gene Kelly is an urban legend that Patricia Ward Kelly is determined to dispel. "One bit of mythology, just to correct," she said, "that Gene went over and asked Walt Disney if he would do the animation with him and that Disney said something like, 'No, Mickey Mouse will never dance with MGM and you,' . . . It's not true."

The recollections of Hanna and Barbera themselves were recorded decades later and reflect their outlooks and personalities. Hanna's 1996 autobiography reads subtly, "Walt Disney declined," but adds nothing of rancor either way. Joe Barbera's 1996 book says that "Walt turned him down flat," which does not confirm the rumor (might inadvertently reinforce it) and is not a firsthand account.

The most concrete evidence of what Walt Disney *would not* have said or done exists in the cooperation he afforded two other MGM films. The 1934 MGM musical comedy *Hollywood Party* showcases an animated Mickey Mouse with Jimmy Durante, plus custom color animation provided by Walt Disney Studios. The same year, MGM released Hal Roach's musical fantasy *Babes in Toyland* (aka *March of the Wooden Soldiers*) starring Laurel and Hardy. It also includes a live-action Mickey Mouse helping to save the village (with a costumed simian interpreting the role) as well as the music and images of the Three Little Pigs.

▲▼▲▼

Hanna, Barbera, and Quimby were not present at the Walt Disney meeting, but Kelly was there and never forgot it. "Gene said that Walt Disney actually loved the idea of Gene dancing with the animated figure," said Ms. Ward Kelly. "But he was too busy with all the war effort and really over-committed. Walt Disney said, 'I will call them and endorse it for you and tell them it is a really great project and should go ahead.' So he did do that. Hanna-Barbera was under the MGM umbrella and so he went with Hanna and Barbera and loved both of them."

Hanna and Barbera were thrilled to work on the sequence with Jerry (and a cameo by Tom). The combined talents of Kelly, Hanna, and Barbera were uniquely suited to the process. Like Hanna, Kelly's technique was based on timing, precision, and musical instinct.

Patricia Ward Kelly explained,

You connect it to musical beats. You can connect the movement of the camera and the placement for the mouse [to] your placement for yourself . . . to make sure that's all in sync with the musical beats. That's what allowed Gene to do these things that were so extraordinary. He understood that the studio did not understand it, the camera operators didn't understand it, and in fact had no musical talent, so that's why Gene had his assistants behind the camera operators counting

out the musical beats and telling them when to move the camera and when to stop and when to dolly and when to pan.

Either Hanna or Barbera was always on the set, Barbera having worked out the storyboards and Hanna planning the timing for the animation production. Like the Oscar-winning special effects in Walt Disney's 1964 musical fantasy *Mary Poppins*, "The King Who Couldn't Dance" sequence employed some of the earliest and most state-of-the-art techniques of its day. "We used a device Max Fleischer had invented, now outmoded, called a rotoscope," wrote Barbera. "This enabled the animator to trace over the live-action footage *frame-by-frame*. Tedious? You bet."

The filmmakers may also have had the good fortune that artist/inventor Ub Iwerks had just developed a more effective way to combine film images for Walt Disney's *The Three Caballeros* (1944). Iwerks's optical process was more convincing than Hollywood's earlier rear-screen projection system which placed live actors in front of projected images.

Animation authority J. B. Kaufman, author of *South of the Border with Disney: Walt Disney and the Good Neighbor Program*, describes the moment in the timeline.

At a point when a lot of that work on *Three Caballeros* was done, Ub Iwerks finished and unveiled his two-head optical printer, which made combination shots exponentially easier; it was a major development. And it coincided with the making of combination shots for "La Pinata" (i.e. Donald, Joe, and Panchito flying their sarape through Mexico, dancing with Carmen Molina, etc.).

Far more intricate and complicated combinations could now be accomplished with relative ease. At the same time, they went back to "Baia" and used the optical printer to matte even more effects into the combination shots they'd already made. The optical printer was the real breakthrough. It also appears that the timing of the production of *Anchors Aweigh* coincided neatly

The first recording to result from the teaming of Bill Hanna and Joe Barbera was originally released in a hardcover storybook edition.

with the finish of the production of *Three Caballeros*. I don't know whether or not Iwerks actively cooperated with MGM on their film; I've never pursued that, but the timing is pretty convenient.

The "lookit me, I'm dancin'!" exclamation of Jerry as the King could just as well be attributed to the confident, assured Kelly and his acute attention to cinema as well as dance. The animation talents of Ed Barge, Michael Lah, Ken Muse, Ray Patterson, Barney Posner, and Irv Spence (most of whom worked with Hanna and Barbera for many years), along with the MGM filmmakers, created an animation/live-action combination that would not be equaled until *Mary Poppins* in 1964 and *Who Framed Roger Rabbit* in 1988.

▴▾▴▾▴▾

Columbia Records' adaptation of *The King Who Couldn't Dance* was produced by Hecky Krasnow, a creative pioneer of the children's and holiday recording industry. He was responsible for one of the all-time best-selling records, "Rudolph, the Red-Nosed Reindeer." Krasnow convinced an initially reluctant Gene Autry to record the "kiddie" tune. Autry needed no further coaxing to follow the hit with the original versions of "Frosty the Snowman" and "Peter Cottontail" for Krasnow. His daughter Judy Gail Krasnow, who chronicled her father's groundbreaking career in the book, *Rudolph, Frosty, and Captain Kangaroo*, recalls the recording session for *The King Who Couldn't Dance*.

"Gene Kelly was truly a nice guy," Krasnow said. "As I wrote in my book, he made my mother's day when he danced with her. It was brief, but nevertheless, it happened. I have the record to this day."

Broadway and recording industry legend Lehman Engel wrote and conducted original background music for the record. Engel became one of the pillars of the Columbia label, particularly for his landmark recordings of Broadway musical scores. He also founded the prestigious BMI Lehman Engel Musical Theater Workshop, whose illustrious songwriting participants include Alan Menken (*The Little Mermaid*, *Beauty and the Beast*), as well as Kristen Anderson-Lopez and Robert Lopez (*Frozen*, *Finding Nemo: The Musical*).

Slipping in and out of rhyming verse, Kelly's audio narration on the record goes beyond the film script to add verbal descriptions of the visuals. The book is illustrated with composites of a photographed Kelly combined with spot-color illustrations, perhaps supplied by Hanna and Barbera's animation unit. The fantasy world is described as "painted," a clever way to convey the nature of the animated settings in a storybook-friendly way. Two uncredited actors accompanied Kelly and a full orchestra for the New York session. The voice of King Jerry in the *Anchors Aweigh* film is Sara Berner, a veteran of hundreds of radio shows and cartoons, telephone operator Mabel Flapsaddle on *The Jack Benny Program*, and the mother buzzard in the Warner Bros. cartoon, *The Bashful Buzzard*.

During the time *Anchors Aweigh* was released to theaters, children's records were nearing the height of their popularity. Under the innovative direction of Alan W. Livingston, Capitol's line of children's records starring Bozo, Looney Tunes, Woody Woodpecker, and others were charting as best sellers. Children's records were so popular that they ascended the pop music charts as well as in the children's category (e.g., the RCA Victor version of Walt Disney's *Cinderella*, which was number one on both charts in 1950). Some of the biggest movie stars of the mid-twentieth century recorded records for kids, from Lionel Barrymore and Jimmy Stewart to Gloria Swanson and Loretta Young.

The King Who Couldn't Dance was reissued by Columbia on several vinyl LP compilations, and on CD by DRG Records. "The Worry Song" soundtrack version first appeared on the Rhino Records CD, *Gene Kelly at Metro-Goldwyn-Mayer: 'S Wonderful* (R2-72434, 1996).

▲▾▲▾

Tom and Jerry made their second feature film appearance in the 1953 musical, *Dangerous When Wet*, starring Esther Williams, champion swimmer and queen of the musical water extravaganzas. In a seven-and-a-half-minute sequence, her character falls asleep reading a Tom and Jerry comic book called "Pearl Divers." She dreams of underwater adventure with the cat and mouse team, including a shark chase and the lure of a romantic singing octopus (whose design suggests Hanna-Barbera's 1965 character, Squiddly Diddly).

While the combination of Esther Williams with Tom and Jerry did not require the complex physical interaction of the dance between Gene Kelly and Jerry, the Williams sequence had further challenges. Williams's performance is entirely submerged, as opposed to being on a dry stage. This required meticulous planning because all of her actions with Tom and Jerry would be executed as swimming moves. The story requirements also gave Williams greater opportunities for underwater acting beyond her trademark smile of recognition at the movie audience.

Dangerous When Wet was one of a handful of MGM films that did not have a soundtrack album. Some recording artists released cover versions of the songs by Johnny Mercer and Arthur Schwartz. The animated portion was not set apart as its own standalone story the same way as "The King Who Couldn't Dance" in *Anchors Aweigh*. In this case, the sequence made direct reference to music, characters, and story elements already established in the movie.

There was no special "Worry Song" created for this animation as there had been for *Anchors Aweigh*. Two songs were interpolated into the cartoon score. "In My Wildest Dreams," the love theme assigned to costar Fernando Lamas in the live-action film, was lampooned by the octopus character. A family of fish spoofs the peppy family of Williams's character in the film.

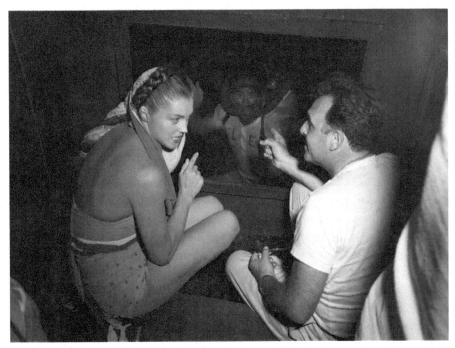

Two friends of Tom, Jerry, Bill, and Joe—director George Sidney and aquatic movie star Esther Williams—on the set of the MGM musical *Jupiter's Darling*. Photograph by Bruce Mozert. Courtesy of State Archives of Florida, MOZ00596.

Delightful as the underwater sequence is, the fact that it does not stand on its own outside the context of the feature could be the reason that a story record was not produced. One of the signature songs, "I Got Out of Bed on the Right Side," was not released in soundtrack form until the age of CDs when Rhino Records included it on a boxed set of music from the "That's Entertainment" films.

Scott Bradley interpolated the "I Got Out of Bed on the Right Side" melody into several shorts. Bradley also worked the tune into some MGM cartoon scores, including both "Over the Rainbow" and "We're Off to See the Wizard" in the 1948 Tom and Jerry short, *The Truce Hurts*. This was a priority for in-house animation studios attached to large film companies. Early Warner Brothers cartoons were intended to promote record and sheet music sales in their publishing divisions, so these tunes were showcased or folded into the scores. The same was true with Paramount and its Famous Music Company catalog.[2]

Anchors Aweigh provided Hanna and Barbera with a key ally in director George Sidney, as well as his father, MGM executive Louis K. Sidney. The younger Sidney called upon the animation unit for projects outside short subjects, including the opening sequence for his 1946 musical *Holiday in Mexico*, starring Walter Pidgeon and Jane Powell.

Director/screenwriter Richard Brooks also called upon the Hanna and Barbera unit to create an animated sequence for the 1955 Glenn Ford/Sidney Poitier classroom drama *The Blackboard Jungle*. In the sequence, Ford is able to engage his English class in an ethics discussion by running the ending of an animated "Jack and the Beanstalk" film on a 16mm projector. The cartoon lightens the extreme tension, as the majority of young delinquents greet the cartoon with smiles and laughter—not unlike the classic sequence in Preston Sturges's *Sullivan's Travels* (1941), in which a chain gang laughs along to a Walt Disney Pluto cartoon played in an African American church. Hanna and Barbera's animation in *The Blackboard*

▲▼▲▼▲▼

Jungle allows Ford's character to break through the students' resistance to learning. It is a key turning point in the film, which is also known for making Bill Haley's "Rock Around the Clock" a hit song.

▲▼▲▼▲▼

Gene Kelly returned to Hanna and Barbera to work with them on a sequence in *Invitation to a Dance*, Kelly's 1956 *Fantasia*-like trio of dialogue-free dance segments. The third and final segment, "Sinbad the Sailor," was the most ambitious and lengthy theatrical animation and live-action sequence attempted by Kelly, Hanna, and Barbera up to that time. The highly stylized segment was highlighted by two sequences often excerpted for later compilations. One was a dance between Kelly and a serpent (modeled in live-action by Kelly's longtime collaborator Carol Haney). The other was Kelly's encounter with the palace guards, including a classic Vaudeville "chain dance" in which the dancer's ankles synchronize as if connected.[3] Unfortunately, these efforts were contained in a film that was met with mixed reactions and limited success. The experimental *Invitation to a Dance* also suffered from a multiyear delay and a changing studio system.

MGM's soundtrack album was limited to the first two sequences of *Invitation to the Dance*, "Circus" and "Ring around the Rosy," perhaps because they were created for the feature. There was no room on the LP disc to add "Sinbad the Sailor," adapted from Rimsky-Korsakov's classic *Scheherazade Suite*. With so many versions of this classical piece available, the decision may have been to omit this segment.

▲▼▲▼▲▼

The postwar demand for children's records made it possible for almost every well-known story, rhyme, song, and especially popular character to make their way into shellac, Bakelite, or the emerging vinyl records. Tom and Jerry were so popular—not just on the screen but on the merchandise shelves—that they recorded more albums without speaking than many artists who do. Bill Hanna's immortal vocal effects ("AAAAAAA!" "EWWW!" "YEEEEOWWW!") do not appear on the Tom and Jerry MGM records, but they continue to be reused in current Tom and Jerry shorts and features.

Just as on Capitol's impressive line of children's records featuring Looney Tunes/Merrie Melodies characters, the violence is toned down but not eliminated (on records, for example, Elmer Fudd and Yosemite Sam use guns loaded with gumdrops). Tom still slides into walls, but the sonic results are milder yet amusing, like the "tah-ting" of a bell for example. The records have a certain prescience to Tom and Jerry's softer relationship in later cartoons, cooperating as partners, encountering special characters, or visiting places outside their home. Still, lots of chases and action material are packed into these brief discs.

Thirteen Tom and Jerry story records were released by MGM between the years 1950 and 1952. The first title, packaged with a book, was called *Tom and Jerry at the Circus*, written by Irving Townshend with music by Curtis Biever. This two-record set differs from the other Tom and Jerry recordings in narration and approach. It is narrated by character actor Francis DeSales, usually cast in films and TV episodes in an administrative or professional role. Since this is a record for kids, actor DeSales is allowed the latitude for more whimsy (and merry singing) than when playing a surgeon in *Jailhouse Rock* or the district attorney in *Psycho*. The adventure takes Tom and Jerry throughout the circus so the children listening can learn about the various animals. The text is written in the style of Tom and Jerry storybooks and comics, so Tom and Jerry have speaking lines the same way Donald Duck had more lucid conversations in print. DeSales reads all the text and varies his voice for the characters, so the effect is more informal and that of a grownup reading to a child.

▲▼▲▼▲▼

Accomplished film and radio actor Bret Morrison narrates all the other MGM Tom and Jerry records. Morrison was a well-known personality when these records were first released, as radio's popular crime fighter "The Shadow." Orson Welles originated the dual role of Lamont Cranston and the Shadow, but Morrison enjoyed the greatest longevity on the weekly series. While the presence of Tom and Jerry was incentive enough for a consumer to buy these records, the presence of a celebrity like Bret Morrison added to the perceived product value. As a singer, Morrison trilled a few country-style bars as Farmer McDonald for *Tom and Jerry on the Farm*.[4]

Like *Tom and Jerry at the Circus*, a deluxe two-record treatment is provided for the adaptation of *Johann Mouse*, from the 1953 widescreen Oscar winner placing Jerry in the home of Strauss with the curious tendency to waltz in a trance when music is played. Morrison narrates *Johann Mouse* with a vaguely European accent in the manner of Hans Conried in the theatrical cartoon.

"There are a number of things that can be recommended here," said *Billboard* magazine in its May 23, 1953, review of *Johann Mouse*. "First of all, it's Tom and Jerry. Finally, and far from least, it's a clever blending of a good story and good music—Strauss waltzes. One disadvantage is that it's a two-record set, but [a 45 rpm extended-play disc] fills the bill nicely here." (78 rpm discs were just starting to become passé by this time and a 7-inch extended-play 45 could hold twice as much as one 10-inch 78.)

Almost all of the MGM record stories were written by Elmer Gregory with music by Leroy Holmes. Julliard trained, Holmes started with big bands and orchestras for such names as Benny Goodman and Gordon Jenkins before joining MGM's Hollywood film music department. His name became more prominent in MGM's New York record division, where the Tom and Jerry records were produced.[5] Rather than duplicate Scott Bradley's cartoon scores, Holmes created original themes and custom scoring to match the action (an exception to this is Johann Strauss II's "Tritsch-Tratsch-Polka"). Like other children's records

Actor Bret Morrison, who narrated almost all the Tom and Jerry records, was best known as "The Shadow" on radio.

of this time, there was ample budget to afford rich orchestrations. Records like this were usually done with the narrator (and whatever cast there was) and the orchestra all at once, like a radio broadcast, stopping only for each side of each record.

Several of the recorded Tom and Jerry story titles suggest actual Tom and Jerry shorts but are originals created for records like *Tom and Jerry Meet Robin Hood* (no relation to the 1958 theatrical short *Robin Hoodwinked*). Some stories are largely musical, such as *Tom and Jerry and Old MacDonald's Barnyard Band*. Others are dream based, like the aforementioned Robin Hood disc. *Tom and Jerry and the Rocket Ship to the Moon* might have made an interesting cartoon. In this adventure, moon cats are tiny and moon mice are giants.

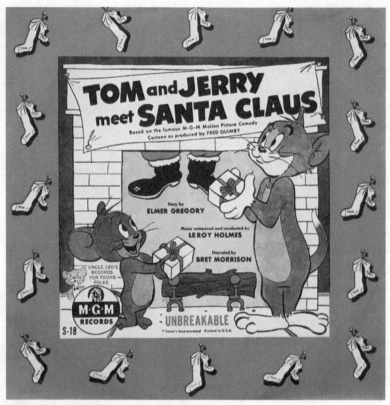

One of the fully-orchestrated Tom and Jerry stories available on MGM Records during their theatrical days.

Other titles in the series include *Tom and Jerry Meet Charlie the Choo Choo Train*; *Tom and Jerry and the Fire Engine*; *Tom and Jerry in the Wild West*; *Tom and Jerry Down on the Farm*; *Tom and Jerry Meet Santa Claus*; *Tom and Jerry Find Aladdin's Lamp*; *Tom and Jerry and the Texas Rangers*; and *Tom and Jerry and the Tugboat*.

The MGM Tom and Jerry records do not mention Hanna and Barbera on their labels or covers, but they do credit producer Fred Quimby, who retired three years later.

▲▼▲▼

Hanna and Barbera found themselves running the MGM animation unit, where movie stars strode just outside the doors. Future stars were also plentiful. A young Jack Nicholson would regularly wheel in the MGM coffee and Danish cart, appreciating the words of encouragement he received from Bill Hanna.[6]

For almost two decades, Tom and Jerry were counted among the MGM studio stars, having scored in shorts, guest appearances in features, and a stack of records. "We were shocked," said Hanna. "I think the both of us felt this was where we were set up for the rest of our lives. Everything was going great. And all of a sudden—it closed."

Hanna and Barbera were put in the position of telling the staff that everyone was dismissed, themselves included. Fortunately, most would soon be employed at the company Hanna and Barbera created.

Chapter 2

RUFF AND REDDY GET H-B SET

It's all about the music.
—DAWS BUTLER ON VOICE ACTING

Television became the medium of choice in the fifties. Movie ticket sales were down as people enjoyed free entertainment at home. The US Supreme Court ruled that movie studios were not permitted to own theaters, nor could they exercise exclusivity in where their films were shown or other unfair trade practices like "block booking" to force weak films in with strong ones. To lure people back into theaters, extravagant spectacles, widescreen formats, and sensory gimmicks like 3-D and "Smell-O-Vision" were attempted. In the early days of moviegoing, a short cartoon was rarely treated as the main draw, but rather as a pleasant segment within an overall theater program of one or two features, newsreels, trailers, and perhaps live-action short films.

Some industry leaders anticipated a change in the wind and prepared early. Walt Disney and his brother Roy knew early that the precarious future of short theatrical cartoons made it imperative to move into feature-length animation and/or live-action. Comedy producer Hal Roach also transitioned from comedy shorts into features.1

Like almost all emerging entertainment platforms, TV required lots of material. Distributors snapped up old cartoons and live-action film packages, often for lower prices than the material would later be worth. The prevailing mindset did not anticipate the future value of material perceived as irrelevant old junk that would never be watched again. The time and expense of creating animation had to change if it was to continue in any appreciable manner. New animation for TV had to be made faster and at a lower cost while retaining its value and appeal.

Hanna and Barbera were not alone in knowing the future was on the small screen. Lower-cost animation was nothing new, even by the fifties. Most of the fully animated theatrical films had become stylized in the wake of UPA Studio. The UPA blend of sleek, angular designs and bold splashes of color with unconventional music and dialogue captured awards and praise. Disney, MGM, and other studios dabbled in the trend. The theatricals were still richly animated with varied backgrounds and fluid movement but were a step closer to what would eventually reach home TV sets.

Paul Terry had been cost-cutting for years with his low-rent theatrical Terrytoons. In the fifties, Terry's nephew, Alex Anderson, tried to interest him in TV cartoons. Terry was supportive but would not touch TV because his cartoons were distributed by 20th Century Fox, another major studio vehemently opposed to television.

With college friend Jay Ward, Anderson came up with *Crusader Rabbit* in 1950, considered historically to be the first animated series for television, though its extremely stilted movement is different from what Hanna and Barbera would later develop. A year later, Ward and Anderson began pitching *The Frostbite Falls Review*, which reached TV as *Rocky and His Friends* in 1959, in the wake of *The Huckleberry Hound Show*'s immense success with all ages.

Amid prestigious features like *Lady and the Tramp* and *Sleeping Beauty*, Disney also produced modest but no less memorable limited animation for educational films and TV. Among the most memorable examples are the 1955 *Mickey Mouse Club* titles with repeating cycles and simplified character designs, and commercials created in-house for such clients as Peter Pan peanut butter and Ipana toothpaste.

▲▼▲▼▲

Joe Barbera pitched television animation as much as possible to the major studios. Had MGM retained the animation staff, the company could have benefited from the new form being developed by Hanna and Barbera. Narrow vision, lower risk, and the lure of short-term gain persuaded the MGM brass to resist. They were led to think that there were enough newly finished Tom and Jerry cartoons to last for two more years. Repeat bookings of old cartoons seemed to do as well as new ones, at least for a while. There was little or no foresight as to the eventual depletion of the existing shorts, just as there was insufficient con-

sideration of transitioning into TV animation, titles, commercials, or any other profit-making enterprises. Joe Barbera also found it difficult to convince any other Hollywood decision makers.

"We were turned down by everybody," Joe Barbera told author/historian Leonard Maltin in an extensive 1997 interview for the Academy of Television Arts and Sciences. "First of all, they said 'You cannot make cartoons for television for a profit. It's too expensive. There was no money . . .' 'TV' was a bad word. On the lot at MGM, [you weren't] supposed to even talk about it."

There were, however, some executives who did see the potential for what Hanna and Barbera could deliver, but they kept a low profile. "L. K. Sidney wanted to do animation commercials for the features," said Barbera. "We did one on *Scaramouche* and we did one on *Pat and Mike* [both in 1952] with Spencer Tracy . . . and they loved them. But he wouldn't tell anybody that we did them. It was weird."

Hanna and Barbera's animated *Scaramouche* trailer was one of a handful of Hollywood movie trailers that did not include any clips it promoted.[2] Instead, the *Scaramouche* trailer featured a suave animated version of MGM's Leo the Lion. This cartoon version of Leo was used in advertising and industry announcements in the thirties and forties. For the *Scaramouche* trailer, he was dressed in eighteenth-century French garb, swashbuckling through various comic escapades. Leo's design bears a physical resemblance to future characters like Lippy the Lion and Loopy De Loop. The animation is fluid in spots but is done with many still poses and an economy of action.

"We also did another thing while we were working there," Barbera told Maltin.

An agent contacted us that was handling *I Love Lucy* . . . We did the title figures, kind of stick figures, and we did a commercial I believe. Here's the irony: Quimby called us down. He says, "Fellas, you wanna see the best stuff in animation . . . watch *I Love Lucy*!" And you wanna tell him, "Look, you dummy! We did it! We've been trying to sell you on doing it! We did that!" But we didn't say a word about it.

MGM did not give any notice of the animation department closing and termination of its staff. "They just said they were discontinuing production," Bill Hanna told Jerry Beck in *Animation Magazine*. However, Hanna and Barbera were able to buy some time because the staff had several new cartoons in production. "We had six months to decide what we were going to do, which was a real blessing."

Action was taken for the future. According to Don Yowp on his Hanna-Barbera history website, yowp-yowp.blogspot.com, *Ruff and Reddy* dated back to May 1956, a few months before the MGM animation layoff. The characters were copyrighted by a company called Shield Productions, owned by Bill Hanna, animator Mike Lah, and design artists Don Driscoll and Don McNamara. Animator Dick Bickenbach told animation historian Mike Barrier that there was work done on *Ruff and Reddy* material during the final week of the MGM animation department. On July 7, 1957, H-B Enterprises entered the world.

▲▼▲▼▲▼

Ruff and Reddy, a deceptively low-key series, established the model for many animated series of today that use "arcs" over a period of episodes. The "buddy premise" reflected almost all of Hanna-Barbera's most popular and resonant works. The cartoons have a jaunty, lightly irreverent attitude that was the genesis of how H-B would appeal to kids and adults. Barbera made sure the stories had the kind of adventure and melodrama that he enjoyed in the cliffhanger serials of his youth.

Instead of a new six-minute animated film roughly every month for $65,000 per short, H-B was now presenting NBC with fifty-two cartoons running roughly three minutes (not counting recaps and themes) for $2,700 per episode. The results could have been disastrous in less capable hands, but critics and the public were pleased. Three seasons were produced,

bringing the episode total to 156, an exhaustive number compared to the output at MGM—and this was just the beginning. Because their new process of "limited" or "planned" animation cut the number of drawings drastically, Hanna and Barbera recognized the importance of the soundtrack immediately. The music, sound effects, and voices were essentially part of the momentum to compensate for the reduced appearance of action on screen.

"Voices make or break a cartoon that relies heavily on character and dialogue, and this is especially true of cartoons made for television, which is as much a verbal medium as it is a visual medium," Barbera wrote. "Casting a single character frequently meant auditioning sixty, seventy, even eighty voices."

Radio broadcasting was also fading as audiences turned to television for comedy, variety, and drama with televised programming. Veteran radio actors were as eager to find new creative opportunities as animation artists.

Hanna and Barbera's first coup was casting Dawson "Daws" Butler. He gave Reddy a southern drawl similar to one he used for years for Tex Avery and Walter Lantz characters. Butler began his career in stage revues and radio (his first break was in a local contest) making his first big mark through comedy records with animation voice veterans Stan Freberg and June Foray. Hit discs like "St. George and the Dragonet" and "Little Blue Riding Hood" brought a bit of well-deserved attention to the actors that cartoons had not. Butler and Foray were also frequent performers on Capitol's children's records. He and Freberg also created a sensation with the satiric puppet TV show *Time for Beany*, sparked with a sly humor that made it a favorite show of Albert Einstein and Groucho Marx.

The *Ruff and Reddy* budget allowed for just two actors. Hanna and Barbera knew Butler from MGM voices; Butler in turn suggested Don Messick for Ruff the cat. It was a gesture of Butler's benevolence that was well known among his contemporaries. Hanna and Barbera had known of Messick when the actor filled in for Bill Thompson as Droopy in several car-

One of animation's greatest and most beloved actors, Daws Butler, greets fans at the 1976 San Diego Comic-Con. Butler was beloved by colleagues, fans, and those he mentored. Photo by Alan Light. (CC-BY-2.0, Wikimedia Commons.)

The Ruff and Reddy Show yielded the very first Hanna-Barbera theme song. "When we were working on the storyboards, I decided to indulge my fondness for writing verse and try to come up with some catchy lyrics for the theme song for our new show," Hanna recalled. "Although I didn't give it much thought at the time, it was to set the pattern for my writing the theme song lyrics for Hanna-Barbera cartoon shows for the next thirty years."

Hanna called Hoyt Curtin, who composed jingles for advertising and scores for films. Both Hanna and Barbera immediately recognized his strength for what are now called "earworms," catchy tunes that won't be forgotten.

Curtin told the story in an interview with Michael Mallory, author of the book, *Hanna-Barbera Cartoons*:

We did some Schlitz Beer commercials and they came out fine, I never thought anything. You know, another job. And then the phone rang and it was Bill and Joe on the phone. And they had a

toons. For *Ruff and Reddy*, Messick gave the Professor Gizmo character a voice similar to that of Droopy, though Messick generally tried to avoid direct impressions. According to *The Magic Behind the Voices* by Tim Lawson and Alisa Persons, one of Messick's first big breaks was working for Bob Clampett, though not in cartoons. On the recommendation of Joan Gardner (*Santa Claus Is Comin' to Town*, *Valley of the Dinosaurs*, *Mr. Magoo's Christmas Carol*) he was given a puppeteer role in the short-lived series *The Adventures of Buffalo Billy*, *Thunderbolt the Wondercolt*, and *The Willy the Wolf Show*.

"Daws and Don did what professional voice actors still do, they act," explained Bob Bergen, the voice of Porky Pig and numerous other voices for Warner, Disney, and many other studios. "They don't just do funny voices, they developed the characters just as fully as any actor would. If you watched them before the recording mike, you saw them going through the physical motions and facial contortions of the parts they played."

Don Messick's H-B start with *Ruff and Reddy* led to voicing Scooby-Doo, Papa Smurf, and countless others.

▲▼▲▼

The Randy Van Horne Singers included such major Hollywood vocalists as Marni Nixon and Thurl Ravenscroft, who soloed in several H-B projects.

lyric. They said: "We want you to write a song for this lyric, and we're going to make an animated television show." So I wrote down the lyrics over the phone, and about five minutes later I called back and sang it to them. And there was this hideous silence, and I thought, Oh boy, I've el-bomb-oh-ed. But no, that wasn't it, they were just in shock or something. [They said:] "Could you get an orchestra together and record that?" "Yeah." "Could you do it tomorrow night?" "Yeah." And that was the way we started, and that was the way we kept going for years.

The *Ruff and Reddy* theme was as unpretentious as the cartoon. A few woodwinds and percussion play under a simple vocal. The arrangement is so sparse it briefly becomes a capella. The remaining music in the series was from preexisting music libraries, which provided

hundreds of comical and dramatic cues for films, radio, and television. Some of the same background cues could be heard on completely different programs (e.g., a suspense cue often used on *The Adventures of Superman* was also heard on *The Honeymooners*).[3]

This was the first of several beloved Hanna-Barbera themes sung by The Randy Van Horne Singers. Van Horne was a vocal director and arranger who assembled some of Hollywood's greatest singing voices for TV, movies, commercials, and his record albums. Many in his group enjoyed renown, including Marni Nixon (singer for Deborah Kerr in *The King and I*, Natalie Wood in *West Side Story*, and Audrey Hepburn in *My Fair Lady*) and Thurl Ravenscroft (The Haunted Mansion, *How the Grinch Stole Christmas*). The group worked with numerous artists such as Dean Martin, Nat "King" Cole, Esquivel, and Mel Tormé.

Curtin and Van Horne worked extensively in advertising so it's likely Curtin selected the group for the cartoon. They sang on H-B cartoons for the first half of the sixties. As the group began to disband, some continued to record for H-B in other capacities as part of other studio vocal groups.

▲▼▲▼▲

At first, the *Ruff and Reddy* pilot film was not given a warm welcome. There was a disappointing screening for the notoriously ruthless and abrasive head of Colulmbia Pictures, Harry Cohn (whose comment was "Throw them out!"). Fortunately, New York producer Roger Muir saw the potential. Muir was well versed in the genre as he also produced the *Howdy Doody* children's show.

When the *Ruff and Reddy* cartoons were first introduced to TV, they did not air by themselves or within a Hanna-Barbera-produced half-hour series. They were "eased in" by adding them to a then-familiar format, a hosted live-action children's show. A new *Ruff and Reddy* cartoon was presented at the beginning and the end of each half hour. Screen Gems cartoons from Columbia's library would serve as filler.

Jimmy Blaine was a familiar name to audiences as a radio and TV announcer as well as a game show host when *The Ruff and Reddy Show* first appeared on Saturday morning on December 14, 1957. Blaine entertained, informed, and interviewed guests, in addition to singing and joking with puppets performed by Rufus Rose and Bobby (Nick) Nicholson.

Hanna, Barbera, and their team must have been aware that MGM's Tom and Jerry merchandise was still prominent on store shelves long after they were producing new cartoons. Even most of the Tom and Jerry/Bret Morrison story records were reissued on several LP records between 1955 and 1958. It must have been very exciting for H-B Enterprises to have similar plans for their own properties this time around. Ruff and Reddy generated its own line of books, puzzles, toys—and, of course, a record or two.

The year 1958 also ushered in an album starring characters created by Hanna and Barbera's new company. *Ruff and Reddy: Adventures in Space* was the first H-B recording produced for long-playing (LP) records. Hanna-Barbera TV productions worked well on records from the start because of the strong audio elements needed to support the animation. The first thirteen dialogue soundtracks of *Ruff and Reddy* were combined with no need for additional narration, making the transition virtually seamless. One could easily enjoy the record with no knowledge of *Ruff and Reddy* cartoons. The producer of the LP was Hecky Krasnow, producer of *The King Who Couldn't Dance* recording in 1945.

A songwriter and composer as well as producer, Krasnow created production music cues, also known as "library," "needle drop," or "stock" music. "Television adopted the radio strategy of using 'canned' music in the vast majority of shows," Jon Burlingame explains in *Music for Prime Time*, which details the history of production music and its creators. Only in the rarest instances were early television programs actually graced with original music. The term "canned music" refers to prerecorded selections, chosen for special purposes (whether source music, meaning origination on a radio, record player, or another obvious source; or as dramatic cues, designed to evoke suspense, create romantic moods, bridge disparate scenes, or otherwise enhance the on-screen action). Hanna-Barbera used such production cues extensively in their early cartoons.

Among the composers who specialized in such music were Bill Loose, John Seely, Jack Shaindlin, Harry Bluestone, Phil Green, Emil Cadkin, Geordie Hormel, and Spencer Moore, as well as composers well known for their recordings and film work, like Laurie Johnson, David Rose, Nelson Riddle, Les Baxter, and Fred Steiner. The selections even included "The Happy Cobbler," composed by record producer Hecky Krasnow.

Ruff and Reddy: Adventures in Space was the first in a series of Hanna-Barbera albums for the fledgling Colpix label. The first record company run by

Serialized episodes of H-B's first TV series were edited into a complete album

Columbia Pictures, Colpix launched a variety of recordings based on their film and TV products as well as pop music and other general interest titles. The Hanna-Barbera children's releases were a prime asset in establishing Colpix in the marketplace, as were hit singles like "Blue Moon" by the Marcels and "Locomotion" by Little Eva.

Colpix released the *Ruff and Reddy* LP with two front covers, both identical in design and artwork. The difference is the text. The second version gives more prominence to the actors and producers, emphasizing the text, "starring Daws Butler and Don Messick" and "produced by Bill Hanna and Joe Barbera." The back cover stayed the same, with photos of all four people. Subsequent Colpix/Hanna-Barbera albums also credited the main cast and producers.

▲▼▲▼▲▼

Production music was a staple of early television. Budgets did not allow lavish orchestrations and, at the time, musicians' unions allowed a limited amount of prerecorded music to be used. One could visit a music facility or postproduction studio, listen to categorized music selections, and purchase them on contract for limited use. Sometimes the production cue used for a TV theme became so identified with a show, the studios bought exclusive rights to the cue and its alternate versions and it became the official theme, often modified in successive seasons. This was the case for a cue like "Toy Parade" becoming the theme for *Leave It to Beaver*. Two Screen Gems shows, *Donna Reed* and *Huckleberry Hound*, premiered in 1958, using the same cues from the Capitol Hi-Q library. The cue that became the *Donna Reed* theme can be heard at the beginning of the Yogi Bear cartoon, "Tally Ho Ho Ho."

Hanna-Barbera's contracts for "needle-drop" music were for broadcast, but not for commercial recordings. The music on the *Ruff and Reddy* Colpix album was original, post-scored accompaniment played on the organ by the aforementioned Nicholson. He had already been employed by *Ruff and Reddy* producer Roger Muir on *The Howdy Doody Show* as several characters, most famously Bob Keeshan's replacement as Clarabelle the Clown. The same year as *Ruff and Reddy*, Nicholson also pioneered early TV animation—of sorts—with the Miami-based series *Colonel Bleep*, for which dissolves and cuts served as movement from one image to another. The only song on the Colpix *Ruff and Reddy* album is the TV theme, never played completely but interpolated into the spoken word sections like the accompaniment to a silent movie.

▲▼▲▼▲▼

The success of *The Ruff and Reddy Show* and H-B Enterprises led to a second recording license with the prestigious Golden Records label in New York, which sold millions of six-inch yellow plastic 78 rpm and black 45 discs for children. The Golden catalog included several popular cartoon characters. Most Golden Records were "cover versions," performed by a different cast of actors in place of the original cartoon voices.

This was common in the entertainment business and was fully approved by licensed contract partners. The entertainment business relied heavily on cover records of popular tunes. When a new song had hit potential, a record company immediately considered which artists would cover it. A venerable pop standard like "Stardust" could fill a room with its various recorded versions on records and sheet music. True, a hit song or performance was certainly associated with a specific film, show, or artist, but this was less of an issue in the early twentieth century.

The same was true with cartoon characters. Walt Disney was the voice of Mickey Mouse from the twenties to the forties. He passed the baton to Jimmy

Macdonald with the release of *Fun and Fancy Free* in 1947, who was "officially" followed by Wayne Allwine in the eighties. During those years, there were several "unofficial" actors in the role of Mickey on fully authorized, "official" Disney products. These include Stan Freberg, Alan Young, and Peter Renaday (aka Renoudet). Long before Hanna-Barbera Productions existed, there had been multiple voices for Popeye, Olive Oyl, Porky Pig, Woody Woodpecker, and other classic characters in various cartoons. Cartoon voice acting had not yet become the recognized art form it is today. One of the people who brought attention to the art and the artist was Mel Blanc, the voice of Bugs Bunny and many other Warner Brothers animated stars. Blanc received "voice characterizations" billing in short cartoons, unusual in its day. Blanc's talent made the voice work as integral to the development and identity of the characters as the visual aspects, something that would be crucial to successful television animation.

"He shaped almost all the studio's cartoons, even the few in which he didn't participate," wrote Jaime Weinman in *Hammers, Anvils and Dynamite: The Unauthorized Biography of Looney Tunes*. "Before Blanc, most cartoon voices were done by anyone available, or someone around the studio . . . With Blanc as the primary voice artist, the studio had someone who could give extra dimensions to characters before the animation even started; this encouraged the animation crew to match the energy of Blanc's line readings."

▲▼▲▼▲

Arthur Shimkin started as a freelance writer who realized that there was a market for a recorded offshoot of the popular Little Golden Books, first published in 1942. He established Little Golden Records in 1948 as a way to market small, inexpensive, high-quality children's records.[4]

Little Golden Records' "in-house" talent included oboe player Mitch Miller, who was the first musical director, and arranger/conductor Jimmy Carroll. They established a distinctive Golden sound and

A 1941 trade ad for radio actor Gilbert Mack (*CBS Mystery Theater*), who voiced characters from Hanna-Barbera's first three TV series on Golden Records.

style. Miller and Carroll also worked at the Columbia label, where they influenced the careers and music of such stars as Tony Bennett, Rosemary Clooney, and Johnny Mathis. Miller and Carroll's early Golden Records featured a quartet called The Sandpipers, consisting of Dick Byron, Bob Miller, Ralph Nyland, and vocal contractor Mike Stewart. The four were seen on the popular Milton Berle variety show as "The Men of Texaco." They are sometimes confused with an easy-listening pop group also called The Sandpipers, best known for the hit "Guantanamera."

In addition to their house artists, Golden sometimes enlisted popular celebrities like Jimmy Durante, Diahann Carroll, Bing Crosby, and Danny Kaye for children's recordings. They also signed lucrative licenses with media companies to create records featuring TV and film characters. New York–based Golden Records produced most of their recordings in the Manhattan area, but also Los Angeles depending on the budget, talent, and scope. Since Colpix was already contracted to do a *Ruff and Reddy* soundtrack

album, Golden opted to produce six "cover" songs economically in New York with their regular talents rather than produce the songs in Los Angeles with Daws Butler and Don Messick. Butler himself recalled to author Keith Scott that he and Messick were contracted to Colpix Records.

The first actor to play the early Hanna-Barbera characters for Golden Records was Gilbert Mack. A seasoned New York stage, radio, and early TV actor, Mack worked with the finest talent in the business well into the late 1970s. According to the limited press coverage of his participation in the Hanna-Barbera Golden Records, he studied the voices as thoroughly as he could and took the job very seriously. Before a videotape or disc could easily play several cartoons for reference, it's impossible to know whether he had access to 16mm films or simply waited for the shows to air. Approximating the distinctive, familiar character voices of multiple actors was a formidable task. It was not one that earned fame, acclaim, or very much remuneration.

Songs from Ruff and Reddy (1959) included: "Professor Gizmo," "Harry Safari," "Ubble Ubble," "Killer and Diller," "Salt Water Daffy," and the theme song. It was released on a 45 rpm EP disc. The *Ruff and Reddy* theme and the "Professor Gizmo" song were available on a single 45 or 78 rpm record. (All six were later included on the Golden album *Quick Draw McGraw and Huckleberry Hound*.) The Ruff and Reddy songs appear in the Golden catalog after other Hanna-Barbera titles, but they sound as if they were recorded first. The voice of Golden's "house female vocalist" Anne Lloyd and The Sandpipers are present on these tracks, but Golden was making changes behind the scenes at this point and no subsequent Golden-Hanna-Barbera songs include these artists.

If the Walt Disney Studios' history seems to be a throughline in this story, it is by design. Hanna-Barbera Productions' historical trajectory had several creative and business parallels with Disney, but they took on different manners and tones. Bill Hanna and Joe Barbera thought they had it made with the success of their creations, Tom and Jerry, but they didn't own the rights. Ruff and Reddy were Hanna-Barbera–owned characters. The initial loss of the rights to Oswald the Lucky Rabbit necessitated the creation of Walt Disney's signature character, Mickey Mouse. Ruff and Reddy marked the starting point that helped prove Hanna and Barbera could make animation viable for television.

Joe Barbera quickly learned that, in the fast-moving world of TV, one couldn't sit back and savor the success of one hit. He had to hustle more characters and projects on the air, and fast. Some of Joe's colleagues chuckled about his favorite idea for improving any cartoon: "Let's try a dog."

Chapter 3

HUCKLEBERRY HOUND GOES TO COLLEGE

~~~~~~

**Not since Mickey Mouse, Donald Duck, and Pluto ventured
into the movies a quarter of a century ago has such a delightful company of characters been created.**
—LARRY WOLTERS, *CHICAGO TRIBUNE*, SEPTEMBER 29, 1958

After the success of *Ruff and Reddy*, much was learned as Hanna-Barbera moved ahead. The new studio strengthened some aspects and abandoned others. Serialization was among the first formats to go. Cliffhangers worked fine for movie matinees and soap operas, but stand-alone stories were more flexible for H-B's purposes. These cartoons need not be dependent on one another for continuity and could be placed anywhere needed.

Ruff and Reddy opened the door for subsequent television animation throughout the industry. H-B Enterprises created a system of providing original animation programming on the scale needed for television, with the needed quantity at a feasible price. They drew upon a top resource of artists from the early days of cartoons and encouraged newcomers. Barbera worked with writers like Mike Maltese, Warren Foster, and Charles Shows to apply their experience in creating stories and gags for short films to the second Hanna-Barbera TV series.

Premiering in the fall of 1958, *The Huckleberry Hound Show* was the first completely animated thirty-minute cartoon series made for TV. Earlier cartoons could either be run with a live-action host or puppets; mixed in with unrelated cartoons and live-action shorts; or combined in a half hour at the whim of local TV stations. *Huckleberry Hound* was a full program consisting of an opening theme song, "bumpers" (short animation between segments and commercials), and a closing theme, all brand new. Except for Kellogg's and other commercials, nothing was to be added or removed during the initial syndication run. The newly christened Hanna-Barbera Productions created the series (though some segments still carry the H-B Enterprises banner) at the former Chaplin Studios on LaBrea Avenue in

The Chaplin Studio became home to Hanna-Barbera Productions, A&M Records, and most recently the Jim Henson Company.

the past. They made assets out of elements like long pauses, shrewd edits, memorable poses, and off-screen action that was funnier because it was not seen, etc. The voices, music, and sound effects were part of what "moved" the animation.

▲▼▲▼▲▼

Each of the three cartoon segments of *The Huckleberry Hound Show* was strong enough to stand on its own. Together they were a powerhouse. Tying the three cartoons together were "interstitial" gags that wrapped around the segments. Only in these portions did the characters interact together outside their own segments. It was a potent way to further endear them to viewers. A catchy theme song, more fully animated and rapidly edited than the three cartoon segments, promised the home audience lots of fun and merriment. This was another technique Hanna-Barbera created—the "sixty-second sell," as it were—that H-B and all the other studios put to effective use for decades afterward.

The Pixie and Dixie series was Hanna and Barbera doing what they knew worked best, a cat-and-mouse premise. The big difference was the twist of clever dialogue between two sharp mice and a beatnik Brando-like "method" cat named Jinks, whose "I hate meeces to pieces" established another H-B element, the quotable character line.

Hollywood (later A&M Records and the Jim Henson Company).

Huckleberry Hound brought a new level of comedy to TV animation. In a short time, it set the stage for clever shows that went further in pace and edge, particularly the cartoons of Jay Ward. Daws Butler and Don Messick were given great freedom by dialogue director Barbera to enhance the way they interpreted each line, extending syllables and transforming even the simplest sentences into gags that didn't exist on the storyboards. Butler's years with Stan Freberg, Capitol Records, and on stage were called into play.

"It's an understatement to say Daws Butler was part of the success of the early Hanna-Barbera cartoons," opined Don Yowp. "Since the animation wasn't—and couldn't be—as intricate as the old theatricals airing on TV in the late '50s, Bill and Joe had to rely on design and, especially, the soundtrack. They were fortunate enough to hire the best TV cartoon voice in history (Daws) and two of the best writers in cartoon history (Mike Maltese and Warren Foster) to put words in Daws's mouth."

Hanna's talent for animation timing, Barbera's acumen for storytelling, and a team of outstanding creatives did more than just compensate for a lack of animation. They made the limits work for them by emphasizing everything else they had used in

Yogi Bear had trouble behaving himself, so like his descendant Bart Simpson, he instantly clicked with those who dreamed of thwarting authority and delighted in seeing it done with the wit and creativity of Bugs Bunny.

Visually, the cartoons were designed to look good in black and white as well as in color. Hanna-Barbera filmed the cartoon portions (not the intros) in more expensive color knowing that they would be more valuable that way in the future. This was also the case with another Kellogg-sponsored series, *The Adventures of Superman*, and the narrative portions of Walt Disney's anthology series. Kellogg's was a prominent force in the emergence of Hanna-Barbera, along with Columbia/Screen Gems. Kellogg's featured the H-B characters on their most popular cereal boxes, touted special mail-in offers and premiums (in "specially-marked boxes"), and assumed a portion of the syndication costs to air *The Huckleberry Hound Show* on local stations.

Huck and his fellow characters became sensations, not just within the series, but through merchandise and in popular culture. Unlike the snappier Ward or Warner characters that are credited with animated comedy, the more understated cartoons in *The Huckleberry Hound Show* were, in their day, hailed as breakthrough entertainment for their wily sense of satire, as well as their positive influence on kids. It became a genuine critical darling, embraced by the intelligentsia just as Mickey Mouse cartoons in the early days. Numerous college campuses elected Huckleberry Hound as their mascot, holding weekly meetings to watch the show. His show shared the same kind of devoted adult (and celebrity) following as *Kukla, Fran and Ollie*, *The Soupy Sales Show*, and particularly *Time for Beany*.[1]

"As it turns out, there was more than the 'occasional' adult tuning in," wrote Don Yowp on his blog. "Several universities held Huck Hound Days. A bar and grill in Seattle was named for him. Employees at an aircraft plant made him the company mascot, to give you a few examples."

The *New York Times* said,

> The true home of *Huckleberry Hound*, however, is in a maze of corridors of three loosely connected buildings here, where Charlie Chaplin once made silent films . . . The motto of the House of *Huckleberry* is that children can understand a great deal more than adults realize. No script is "written down" to the child's level . . . Some connoisseurs of cartoon shorts think Huckleberry Hound and his friends have done the business a good turn.

▲▼▲▼▲▼

Television sets in bars and lounges were tuned to *The Huckleberry Hound Show* every afternoon and early evening. The physical proof is a record album that seems unfathomable today yet fits within the comedic and pop culture context of the late fifties and early sixties.

Huckleberry Hound for President (1960) is physical evidence of the sophisticated level at which these characters were historically perceived. It is an ensemble comedy album with a droll style, unlike the typical "kiddie" disc. A wry satire, the album was akin to films such as *Will Success Spoil Rock Hunter?* or the stories of James Thurber. It was produced and distributed by Golden Records, but it was not specifically made for children, so it was released on their "AA" label for more general, teen and adult interest titles such as cartoonist Walt Kelly's equally sophisticated *Songs of the Pogo* and the actor Gabriel Dell's lurid *Famous Monsters Speak*.

Huckleberry Hound for President now serves as a time capsule of the Madison Avenue advertising world of the early sixties. Writer/director Sascha Burland played Huck and Yogi. He composed the mid-sixties theme to the game show *What's My Line?* and devised Alka-Seltzer's "Whatever Shape Your Stomach's In" campaign, the music for which was made into an album and single by The T-Bones. Another Burland claim to fame is The Nutty Squirrels, a smooth jazz knockoff of Alvin and the Chipmunks, whose modest success was a song called "Uh-Oh." Burland's cowriter on "Stomach" and "Uh-Oh" was jazz musician/composer/singer Don Elliott. Elliott arranged and performed on several Golden Records of the late fifties/early sixties, including children's versions of *Peter Gunn* and *77 Sunset Strip*.

The cast includes Mort Marshall (*Tennessee Tuxedo*), Herb Duncan (*The Milton the Monster Show*), and Joe Silver (*Raggedy Ann & Andy: A Musical Adventure*). Rendered in mock seriousness, the LP follows a story similar to a Dell comic book sold through Kellogg's cereals for the "Huckleberry Hound for President" promotional campaign. Radio star Gracie Allen, TV marionette Howdy Doody, and other personalities

This sophisticated satire aimed at older audiences exemplifies the appeal of *The Huckleberry Hound Show* to college students.

had run mock presidential campaigns in the past, but the Huckleberry Hound satire took specific aim at television, as it was a crucial factor in the Kennedy/Nixon campaign.

The album is evidence of the fact that Huckleberry Hound was indeed an intellectual icon in that the record begins in a bar, where his show is running on the TV screen, as it did in real-life bars. Actor Mason Adams (Charlie Hume on the series *Lou Grant* and longtime voice of Smucker's Preserves) plays an ad executive and bar patron named Bert. The bartender is Harry, a reference to "Bert and Harry Piels," of a long-running beer campaign featuring comedians Bob and Ray. Bert opens and closes the album, asking for seltzer and peanuts.

As snippets of the actual *Huckleberry Hound Show* soundtrack theme are heard, they are interrupted by campaign announcements (the complete soundtrack

theme was not released on a vinyl album until the 1980s). Burland's Yogi (which unlike Butler's Yogi is a nuance-free imitation of Art Carney's Ed Norton right down to the "Va-va-va-voom!") talks Huck into the campaign (as in the comic book), then takes him to an advertising agency. This is Stan Freberg territory, much like the kind of humor the writer/performer presented on his CBS radio show a few years before this album.

Burland shares his love/hate relationship with the advertising industry on this album, skewering the various conceits of its archetypical grand schemes. The exec assigns two Tin Pan Alley songwriters to cook up a snappy new campaign jingle. Here the material feels like filler as they rattle off numerous historic (and public domain) presidential campaign songs. The LP finale is a brassy parody of Hanna, Barbera, and Shows's theme song as if it is being created for a glitzy

TV promo. Huck gives a humble, *Meet John Doe* speech in which he admits he knows nothing about being a president and walks off the program.

The director mutters, "First Jack Paar does this to me, now him!" and then we are back in the bar with Mason Adams asking for more peanuts. This refers to an on-camera walk-off by the renowned late-night talk show host, who was known for having his heart on his sleeve. There are also a few coy references to Huck's home studio: he claims his birthplace as "Barbera, California in Hanna County" and mentions Tom and Jerry as "two friends who sorta helped me grow up."

Huckleberry Hound for President had to have been difficult to market and distribute properly. On the cover, Huck and Yogi are pictured smaller than they might have been seen on most children's records, but they are surrounded by other Hanna-Barbera characters and other campaigners wearing Huckleberry Hound masks. Even if a record store placed it in the comedy section, adults might not think it was as savvy as it is unless they heard it. Like the TV series itself—as well as *Rocky and Bullwinkle*, *The Muppet Show*, and *Animaniacs*—this album was for everyone if they were fans of Huckleberry Hound willing to give it a listen. Writer Frederick Weigand recalls:

Huckleberry Hound for President was one of my favorite albums when I was young, despite the fact that I didn't understand the majority of the gags or even much of the plot. This is one album that got better as I got older. It took several listens for me to get a sense of what the story was all about, beyond of course the main points. It also took some getting used to different voices for Huckleberry and Yogi. The musical scenes with Irving and Dimitri provide some valuable and little-known information about various campaign songs of the past. But I think the adult humor worked, even for a kid, because not understanding all of the gags told me that this was not written down to my level, so I respected it. The album builds to a grand finale with a full-scale production number with the "Huckleberry Hound" theme reworked as a

campaign song. And the ending is almost identical to the comic book version, with Huck finally backing down from the campaign.

▲▼▲▼▲▼

Howl Along with Huckleberry Hound and Yogi Bear (1960) is Sascha Burland's other album for Golden. This production is more clearly a children's record, albeit with humorous nods to adults. Burland was spoofing sing-along albums, particularly the best-selling "Sing Along with Mitch" series by Mitch Miller and the Gang. By this time Miller was a TV personality with a hit CBS series (with former Golden personnel including arranger Jimmy Carroll and bass singer Mike Stewart). Miller is credited with introducing singer Leslie Uggams on his series. A few years later, Hanna-Barbera would spoof Miller's series as "Hum Along with Herman" on a *Flintstones* episode called "The Flintstone Canaries."

Burland sounded very little like Daws Butler, but he knew it and all but admitted it right on the album cover. Assuming he wrote the tongue-in-cheek liner notes, he offers a disclaimer: "With apologies to Daws Butler, Mitch Miller, Norman Luboff, Lawrence Welk and Blue Barron," the last four names known for popular vocals and instrumentals that encouraged singing along.

Howl Along with Huckleberry Hound has a Stan Freberg influence as *Huckleberry Hound for President* does, this time in the handling of comedy with song. Burland's Huck deals with the discontented jazz musician named Orville that suggests Peter Leeds's cool cat in Freberg's "Banana Boat Song," Huck is constantly needled by Orville, who mutters, "This is the last time I do a kiddie record, man." Yogi Bear pops up on side two to handle the sound effects.

In the manner of David Seville and the Chipmunks, most of the songs are comically disrupted. The gags include whistling with mouthfuls of crackers, spewing projectile watermelon seeds during "The Children's Marching Song," and a train wreck during "I've Been Working on the Railroad."

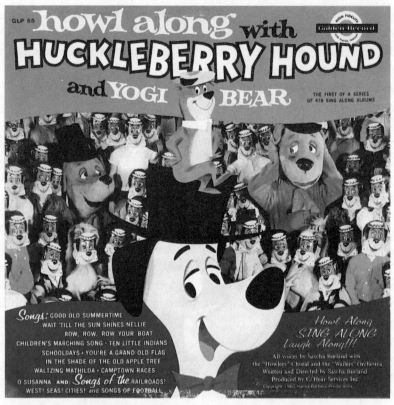

The masks worn on this album cover for *Howl Along with Huckleberry Hound* are like the one Audrey Hepburn donned in *Breakfast at Tiffany's*.

Popular culture so perceived Huckleberry Hound as "cool" and as part of the "smart set" that no less than Audrey Hepburn, one of Hollywood's most stylish stars, tried on a Huckleberry Hound mask during a romantic shopping spree scene in the hit film *Breakfast at Tiffany's*. Perhaps it was done for the sheer absurdity, but with so many other cartoon character masks in the scene to choose from, it seems more likely that the Huck selection was a current, "in" choice for the elegant Ms. Hepburn to grace her face. Either way, Huck had arrived in his first feature film appearance, if in a convoluted manner.

▲▼▲▼▲▼

Huckleberry Hound: The Great Kellogg's TV Show was the first Colpix album featuring soundtracks from the series. Prominent on the front cover is a box

of Kellogg's Corn Flakes on one of the railroad cars carrying the cast of the show. This "product placement" surely assisted with the album's budget. The record itself contains three stories selected to play especially well in audio. This marks Daws Butler's debut on vinyl as a storyteller, relating three adventures of Yogi, Pixie, Dixie, and Mr. Jinks. In his narration as Huck, Butler creates the impression that he's sharing fun folktales rather than recounting cartoon synopses.

The organ music on the Colpix LP is similar to that of the *Ruff and Reddy* disc, but a bell sound is added for the Pixie and Dixie story. Instead of using any of the cartoon themes, there is one original background theme for each of the three selected 1958–1959 cartoon stories (all of which are correctly identified on the album cover but renamed on the record label). Having post-scoring for the entire

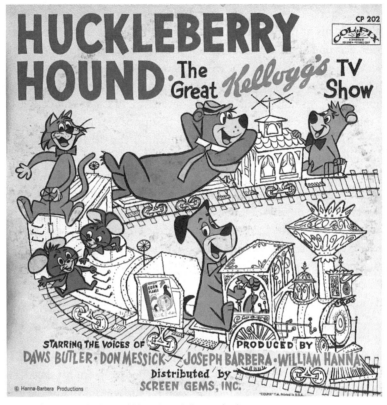

Daws Butler narrated the first Huckleberry Hound album as the character.

album allows for some comic emphasis the cartoons themselves could not afford. In the cartoons, still dependent on stock production music, there is only so much synchronization to the action possible. The record gives the organist an occasional chance to add flourishes. In "Be My Guest Pest" (aka "Yogi Bear and the Missing Eley-Phint") for example, there are little flairs each time the characters repeat the running gag, "What kind of elephant? Striped? Checkered? Polka-dotted?"[2]

▲▴▾▴▾▾

Stand-up comedian and actor Andy Griffith is often cited as an inspiration for Huck's persona, but Hanna-Barbera artist Scott Shaw also suggests deadpan comedian George Gobel as an inspiration. Daws Butler explained the actual origin in 1987:

My wife is from North Carolina and I would go down there when I was on leave from the Navy and so forth. There was a neighbor next door, a veterinarian, and he talked the way Huckleberry Hound did. And I didn't get to do it until several years later when I got out of the service and so and so. [speaking in dialect] But ah mean he had the kind of voice just like that, he wuz easy. I'd come home on leave, ya know, I wanna see mah wife, her name was Merdis. He'd say, "Hi Daws. Come on over'n sit down and let's talk a little bit." And I'd say, "Well I'm gonna go over and see Merdis first," and he'd say, "Well c'mon back. We'll jest talk. I'd like to know what's goin' on with you." And it was just wonderful, just comfortable.

Daws Butler had previously done this kind of character in Lantz and MGM theatrical cartoons, but they were never the lead characters. The impact of experiencing these characters daily at home, rather than by chance in a theater, was one of the earliest forms of appointment television.

The ascendance of Hanna-Barbera coincided with the rise of television, teen pop music, and youth culture in general. There was no question that Disney was the top name in animation, but television changed the way audiences, particularly kids, related to the characters. Before video, cable, and streaming, seeing classic Disney animation on TV was a rare and carefully parceled treat. A new or reissued Disney animated feature was a major event. Cartoons on early local stations were usually the earliest theatrical shorts. To 1958 audiences, *The Huckleberry Hound Show* reflected UPA's crisp, modern cartoon look and current advertising. Many adults saw the verbal aspects as a plus as it reduced the cartoon violence, which was an issue even then. The daily routine of seeing and hearing brand-new cartoon characters every day of the week created a bond between the audience *and* the characters that never existed in popular culture before.

Master animator Nik Ranieri (*Who Framed Roger Rabbit, The Little Mermaid, Beauty and the Beast*) credits Hanna-Barbera as much as Disney for creating bonds that last a lifetime. "I've always loved Disney animation, it became part of my career," he said, "but when I was growing up in Canada, Hanna-Barbera cartoons were probably more of an influence on me. They were there more often for me, while the Disney ones were always far away, few and far between."

Viewers forged a connection with cartoon characters at home in a way they never could in theaters. Even Hanna-Barbera may not have fully realized the impact of their visuals and sound elements. The voices, music, and effects were as germane to this new phenomenon as any other aspect.

▴▾▴▾▴

Huckleberry Hound/Yogi Bear Movie Wheels is a very odd creation that was covered in the *Sunday Herald* of Bridgeport, Connecticut, with the headline, "Newest Thing in Records: Huckleberry Hound and Yogi." It proclaimed Movie Wheels as an "innovative new phase of the record business." Surely not by coincidence, Movie Wheels were launched by Bridgeport resident Lou Lewis and Paul Kwartin of Westport.

"Suppose the record is about 'Huckleberry Hound,'" the story reads. "The child playing this holds the envelope which has in one corner a built-in, revolving device that shows the 'Hound' pictures by dialing. The other side of this particular record is 'Yogi Bear and His Friends.' With this also is a series of pictures, making the new product a kind of music to listen to while dialing."

The *Huckleberry Hound/Yogi Bear Movie Wheels* set was a "space-age" version of the read-along book and a cross between a toy and a record (children's records were often also sold in toy departments). There was only one other Movie Wheels release, starring Felix the Cat, another limited animation syndicated TV star, rebooted from his days as an early silent character. Felix was played by his original TV voice, Jack Mercer, also the longtime voice of Popeye the Sailor. Mercer also voices Yogi Bear for Movie Wheels and other characters, presumably because this was an East coast production. Announcer Jim Sparks plays Huck. Remarkably, snippets of the actual soundtrack themes from the 1958 versions of Huck and Yogi cartoons open each story (like the Presidential album, it may be because an excerpt is less costly to license than the whole selection).

This product is just one indication of how quickly Yogi was gaining ground with Huck in popularity. Donald Duck began to eclipse the less-flawed Mickey Mouse in the 1940s, though not with the same lightning speed as in the wild west of early television. All three cartoons within *The Huckleberry Hound Show* enjoyed great success in their first few years and were each featured on various forms of merchandise, a key point of success in animated characters. A film or series can be a hit, but if it doesn't move "stuff," it's not as viable in business terms. With the guidance and encouragement of Screen Gems sales and mar-

A Movie Wheels story was enjoyed by playing the record and rotating the picture wheel inside the cover.

keting executive John H. Mitchell, Joe Barbera was emerging as a master pitchman as well as a fount of ideas and development.

Over the years, Huckleberry Hound settled comfortably into his stature as a classic H-B character. His more sophisticated, elite status was left behind as Hanna-Barbera sprinted into an increasing number of projects and rival cartoons sprang up. To survive the competition that they helped make possible, they had to build on the elements resounding with the public. Bolstering Yogi's fame was one of many strategies. The creative team turned to more good-natured satires of westerns, detective shows, and family comedies to get fresh products and new concepts on the air.

Chapter 4

QUICK DRAWS AND LOOPY LOOPS

~~~~~~

I was going to sue the Yogi Bear program for using my name until somebody reminded me Yogi isn't my real name—it's Lawrence.

—YOGI BERRA, BASEBALL LEGEND AND NON-SEQUITUR MASTER

Once the *Ruff and Reddy* cartoons and *The Huckleberry Hound Show* forged a lucrative trail of opportunities for television programmers, sponsors, and producers, additional made-for-TV animation was soon to follow. The year 1959 saw the debut of *Rocky and His Friends* during ABC's daytime schedule. This highly revered animated TV series from Jay Ward and Alex Anderson was based on the aforementioned *Frostbite Falls* concept developed in the early fifties.

An original episode of *Rocky and His Friends* contained thirty minutes of animation divided into segments, like *The Huckleberry Hound Show*. Two Rocky and Bullwinkle adventures bookended the show, told in the serialized manner of Ruff and Reddy. The remaining segments told self-contained stories. General Mills, archrival of Kellogg's, supported the half hour with a portion of ads devoted to its products, also primarily breakfast cereals. Kids had been exposed to such sponsored programming since radio and early television, including *The Adventures of Superman*, the *Mickey Mouse Club*, and *Howdy Doody*. Local children's show hosts also sold every kid-tempting item from toys to lollipops.

The Rocky and Bullwinkle series was produced by Ward with Producers Associates of Television, led by executive Peter Piech. He was one of the earliest initiators of outsourcing animation to other countries, not because of a lack of artists but to save money. It would be over a decade before Bill Hanna would bend to the same pressure as H-B was overwhelmed by multiple series, specials, and feature film projects.

The cartoons within *Rocky and His Friends* episodes, including *Fractured Fairy Tales* and *Peabody's Improbable History*, took satire and irreverence a step beyond the comparatively subdued adventures of Huckleberry Hound and his friends.

Rocky's umbrella of cartoons, later adding segments like *Dudley Do-Right of the Mounties* and *Aesop and Son*, became best known under the umbrella title *The Adventures of Rocky and Bullwinkle*. However, Ward and company were fiercely independent, often tangling with the powers that be at General Mills. The cereal giant sought an alternate supplier of programs using the same outsourced animation facilities.

The result was the sarcasm-free Total TeleVision (TTV) cartoons from New York, starting with *King Leonardo and His Short Subjects* and most successfully with *Underdog*. Charming and more kid oriented, they also ran in syndication for decades. Like the Ward cartoons, the TTV segments were run constantly by General Mills, often in combination with their more acerbic Ward "relatives." When Ward and TTV did not have this corporate support with such series as *George of the Jungle* and *The Beagles*, their shelf life was much shorter.

Both Ward and TTV cartoons were dependent on the power of their writing and voice work as well as the delightful visuals. The original cast partnered with head writer Bill Scott and musical director Dennis Farnon to create a highly regarded cast album for Golden Records.

▲▼▲▼▲▼

The Quick Draw McGraw Show (1959) was another three-cartoon half hour sponsored by Kellogg's. Quick Draw is a dim-witted lawman horse with a burro sidekick named Baba Looey. *Snooper and Blabber* spoofed detective films and TV shows. *Augie Doggie and Doggie Daddy* shorts were the warmest of the three, with a gently surreal approach. The positive response to Huckleberry Hound's slightly satirical touch must have been a green light to go a little further in the Quick Draw cartoons, all of which (according to Don Yowp's research) were written by a master of sly wit, Warner Bros. story artist Warren Foster. He and other writers would continue to weave satire into episodes of *The Flintstones*, *Top Cat*, and *The Jetsons*.

Colpix's *Quick Draw McGraw* soundtrack album (1960) followed the same format as the Huckleberry

Hound album. Daws Butler narrates as both Quick Draw and Baba Looey. To the credit of Colpix Records producer Hecky Krasnow, each successive Hanna-Barbera release saw production improvements. Hanna-Barbera provided additional resources, and (perhaps due to strong H-B record sales) Screen Gems allowed for a slightly higher budget, especially for music. The disc contains one story for each of the three cartoons: Augie Doggie in "In the Picnic of Time"; Snooper and Blabber in "The Slippery Glass Slipper";[1] and Quick Draw in "El Kabong Strikes Again."

Colpix was still unable to utilize the genuine cues heard in the cartoons. The Quick Draw LP eschews the single organist underscore for one single library cue, "Cockeyed Colonel" by David Buttolph, from the production music library of Sam Fox Film Rights, Inc. It plays at the start of each story and the end of the album, and that's it. Colpix also used "Cockeyed Colonel," plus a few others, on the TV dialogue soundtrack album of *Dennis the Menace*.

The *Quick Draw* album also introduces the animation voice work of Doug Young to records, in several supporting roles. Young was a veteran of radio and live performing who, like Don Messick, was hired on Daws Butler's recommendation to Barbera when there was talk of bringing in some new vocal sounds.

▲▼▲▼▲▼

Yogi Bear and Boo-Boo was the first soundtrack LP filled with authentic music cues from Hanna-Barbera cartoons. The cues were placed over the dialogue in the final mix. This was preferable, and more costly, rather than just a simple "pick-up" of the finished soundtrack which would have resulted in abrupt edits.

Colpix producer/writer/editor Howard Berk narrates this album. Berk scripted some of television's biggest prime-time series, including *The Rockford Files*, *Mission: Impossible*, and *Columbo* (including the famous "By Dawn's Early Light" episode with Patrick McGoohan and Madeleine Sherwood). For Colpix, he wrote, narrated, and/or edited albums like the TV soundtrack to *Dennis the Menace*, *A Treasury of*

Yogi and Boo-Boo's first album appears on screen during "The Telephone Hour" in the 1963 film *Bye Bye Birdie*.

Great Stories with actor Larry Storch, and the movie soundtrack to *The Three Worlds of Gulliver*.[2]

Inside jokes are always fun to spot or hear in Hanna-Barbera cartoons. In "The Buzzin' Bear," Yogi is flying a helicopter at one point. The previous pilots are rangers named Bill and Joe. "H-B" could show up on businesses, movie cameras, trucks, or license plates.[3]

Here Comes Huckleberry Hound offers listeners the best of all possible worlds for a Hanna-Barbera TV soundtrack recording. This was the first Colpix album with background Hanna-Barbera soundtrack music by Hoyt Curtin in addition to dialogue tracks. Though it does not include *The Huckleberry Hound Show*'s main title theme song, the album does include three "sub-themes." These are the short music cues heard over the title cards of each cartoon segment. Huck's sub-theme is an instrumental of his favorite tune, "Clementine."

All three stories came from season three (1959–1960) when the music changed from library music to Hoyt Curtin: *Huck, The Giant Killer*; *The Pony Express Rider* (aka *Pony Boy Huck*); *Rah, Rah, Bear*; and *Heavens to Jinksy* (a reworking of the 1949 *Tom and Jerry* short, "*Heavenly Puss*," in which Tom faces losing his nine lives unless he is kind to Jerry).

▲▼▲▼▲

Hanna-Barbera's Loopy DeLoop cartoons are especially significant for musical reasons. Just as other studios (including MGM, which ended up reviving Tom and Jerry with directors Gene Deitch and Chuck Jones) were cutting back on theatrical cartoon budgets, Columbia was paying only slightly more on Loopy theatricals than the costs for H-B's TV animation, a portion of which was spent on new music. Thus

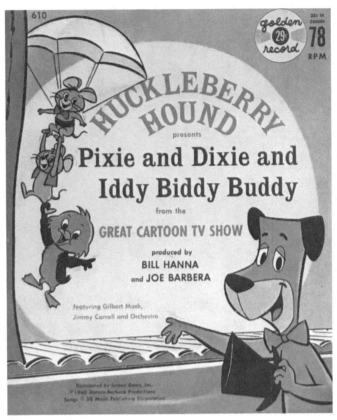

Iddy Biddy Buddy/Yacky Doodle appeared in Huck, Quick Draw, and Yogi's TV series.

Loopy DeLoop became the first cartoon series with custom-made cues composed by Hoyt Curtin. These cues were the basis for H-B's in-studio music library for the editors to reuse in scoring its productions for the next several years and occasionally beyond.[4]

Loopy's film career lasted from 1959 to 1965, almost as long as the partnership between H-B and Columbia/Screen Gems. The time span offers a "mini-history" of the studio's subtle variations in style and reflects changes in voice casting as the studio was producing various series. Loopy was special in that he appeared only on the big movie screen, but it kept him from "bonding" with regular TV viewers in the magnetic manner of Yogi Bear, Huckleberry Hound, Super Snooper, Blabber Mouse, and Quick Draw McGraw.

Golden Records starred all five of the above characters to "present" Loopy on an extended-play 45 rpm disc called *Yogi Bear Introduces Loopy DeLoop*. The label had already used this technique of "leveraging" popular characters by "presenting" *The Quick Draw McGraw Show* characters through Huckleberry Hound and Yogi Bear. This was done through cover art and text to make it seem that well-known H-B characters were presenting new ones.[5]

On the *Yogi Bear Introduces Loopy DeLoop* EP, Yogi introduces Loopy verbally on the record in addition to the "presents" notation on the cover. Since Loopy was not a TV character at the time, this may have been done to further a connection between the characters.

Written by frequent Golden scribes Bill Kaye and Paul Parnes, the EP presents a studio version of the Loopy theme with lyrics never heard in the cartoons. Loopy then tells his version of "Little Red Riding Hood" with a parody of "Bicycle Built for Two" as "Grandmama." After befriending Red Riding Hood

Golden Records often used star characters to "present" newcomers like Loopy DeLoop, the only H-B character created for theatrical shorts.

and her grandmother, Loopy prepares a gourmet dinner for them (with wine from the provinces). It's a more positive conclusion than those found in most Loopy cartoons, which often conclude with his rejection. Additional song parodies round out the mini-album, reusing earlier Golden material and public domain songs. Sascha Burland again produces and provides voices with Don Elliott. In an unusual move for most recordings, this one ends with Huck promoting his Golden LP, *Howl Along with Huckleberry Hound.*[6]

▲▼▲▼▲▼

Quick Draw McGraw and Huckleberry Hound: TV's Favorite Cartoon Stars may not have offered the original TV voices, but it contained nineteen tracks with lots of lyrics, the highest number of Hanna-Barbera

character songs on one LP record up to that time and for many years afterward.

"The audiences who saw the finished cartoons thought they were just getting voices," Barbera wrote. "What they were really getting were characters."

Barbera's comment reflects his many years in theatrical cartoons more than what he and Bill Hanna did to change the perception with their TV work. Even they may have been unaware that they were creating an unprecedented attachment between cartoon characters and the actors who voiced them. Hanna, Barbera, and the staff involved with recordings were fully aware of when voices were substituted. Golden and subsequent nonoriginal cast records were fully approved by the studio. However, they may not have anticipated the reaction of a record-buying public who expected Daws Butler and Don Messick. Listeners were left to puzzle out reasons for the substitu-

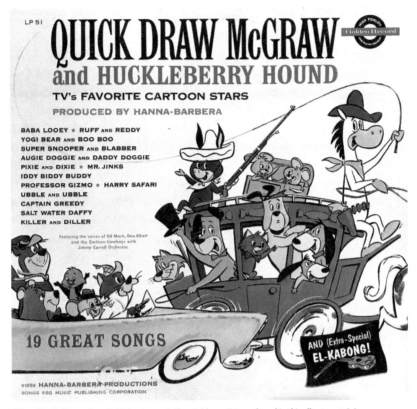

Gilbert Mack, Jimmy Carroll's Orchestra, and other Golden artists are heard in this album containing more Hanna-Barbera character songs than any other vinyl LP.

tion, seek satisfactory similarities (there were a few), or accept it as another interpretation.

The last option was a little easier for some of the theme songs. Of all the Golden renditions, the "Pixie and Dixie" song is the most faithful to the original, and the soundtrack version did not appear on commercial recordings until the 1990s. On the album, all the major characters from the two series get a chance to sing, with a few minor characters worked into the lyrics.

Gil Mack took the roles very seriously, rehearsing each voice as carefully as possible. It was a daunting task when facing the interpretations of voices of two different actors, attempting to match their style and timbre, sometimes within the same track. The six earlier Golden Ruff and Reddy songs, rendered in a slightly different Golden musical style, round out the album.

Some listeners have decided that Golden and other "off-brand" renditions are unacceptable. This speaks to the audio dynamism of Hanna-Barbera cartoons. Records produced by legitimate labels like Golden without the original voices were fully licensed and authorized, carrying the Hanna-Barbera name on the albums, singles, and EPs. RCA, Columbia, Capitol, Disneyland, and other labels also released cover versions of their own properties as well as studio versions of material made by other companies.

It's interesting to note that Golden Records was one of the licensees to display the possessive "Bill Hanna and Joe Barbera's" on their H-B titles instead of "Hanna-Barbera's" or "Hanna-Barbera Presents." On Colpix, they were credited as "Produced by Bill Hanna and Joe Barbera" and later "William" and "Joseph." With the studio still young, perhaps they were experimenting with ways for "branding" their names. Golden's use of "Bill and Joe" may have been intended to create a more approachable relationship with audiences the way Walt Disney was relating to viewers each week on TV and through his signature imprint. Hanna and Barbera appeared in photographs on early record albums, as did the voice artists.

Huck and Quick Draw's series were big hits, sustaining a "cool factor" among young adults and professionals. "A poll at Yale University last season proved them to be the most popular TV characters at this Ivy League institution," reported the *Chicago Tribune* on November 13, 1960. A learned society at Pasadena asked that the shows be shifted to a later hour so the membership could watch. In two short years, Huck and Quick Draw also became famous in far-flung outposts of the world. Down in the Antarctic's Bellinghausen Sea sits a tiny island that bears the name of "Huckleberry Hound."

Marketing exec John H. Mitchell once again helped initiate an even more pivotal project, the Hanna-Barbera series that permanently revolutionized the entertainment industry. It would transform their upstart venture into one of the biggest and most successful animation studios in the world.

Chapter 5

THE FLINTSTONES ROCK THE WORLD

~~~~~~

Yabba Dabba Doo! That was a ride and a half!
—*APOLLO 7* ASTRONAUT WALLY SCHIRRA FROM HIS SPACECRAFT TO
HOUSTON MISSION CONTROL, OCTOBER 1968

Animation in the form of a prime-time half-hour situation comedy began when *The Flintstones* premiered on Friday, September 30, 1960, at 8:30 p.m. Eastern time on the ABC-TV network. The entertainment landscape was forever changed.

"The show was the first full-length animated narrative (previous TV cartoons were three separate seven-minute segments—think Yogi Bear—in a half-hour program)," animation historian Jerry Beck told writer Michael Coate. "It was the first animated sitcom on a major American TV network. It was the first TV cartoon aimed at adults."

The Flintstones set additional precedents in animation beyond television. Some theatrical cartoons had already been produced that ran roughly thirty minutes, like the Fleischer studios' three Popeye Technicolor specials and the "Mickey and the Beanstalk" segment in 1947's *Fun and Fancy Free*. No extended-length cartoon series with the same characters and settings had ever sustained more than a few installments.

It was a mammoth assignment for the young studio. A typical TV sitcom of the day required at least a dozen episodes per season, often more. Just the first season of *The Flintstones* required Hanna-Barbera to produce twenty-eight films of about twenty-five minutes each without titles and commercials—the equivalent of nine animated feature films or 116 short cartoons. Most notably, the half-hour sitcom form presented challenges beyond simply making the cartoon longer by adding extraneous material. When the short cartoon form transitioned to animated features, much more than simple gags were necessary to fill out the extra time. The TV sitcom format also demanded commercial breaks, bumpers, theme songs, and other conventions of the still-new medium.

In his autobiography, Bill Hanna referred to *The Honeymooners* as one of the best sitcoms on television. He and Barbera hired Herbert Finn, one of Jackie Gleason's writers, to create scripts for *The Flintstones*. The premise had earlier roots in the radio comedy *The Bickersons* and in several Laurel and Hardy films in which the duo hatches get-rich-quick schemes or tries to outthink their wives, most notably in *Sons of the Desert*. A stone-age setting was used to clever effect by MGM director Tex Avery and some artists later employed by H-B in the cartoon, *The Shooting of Dan McGoo*.

Before the stone-age concept was set, the Hanna-Barbera staff considered numerous families that might be amusing in cartoon form—from hillbillies to pilgrims—but it was a musical device that helped move the needle. Barbera recalled that one factor in choosing cave people was a drawing of a "Stoneway" piano, a play on the Steinway. These visual and spoken puns instantly set *The Flintstones* apart.

▲▼▲▼▲▼

As *Snow White and the Seven Dwarfs* was for Disney, *The Flintstones* was vital to the survival and eventual expansion of Hanna-Barbera as a company and by extension, the animation industry. Walt Disney found it necessary to move into animated (and later live-action) features. Unlike the majority of short cartoons, features were the main attraction on a theater bill and a competitor alongside other features. The main attractions received the most attention from the press and the public. The potential for merchandising a feature was enormous, as was the potential for reissues. *The Flintstones*, as a network prime-time series, was also at the center of attention in the press, more than any daytime short cartoons could ever be.

Screen Gems president John H. Mitchell was most aware of this. As the president of Screen Gems during its heyday, he led such series as *The Donna Reed Show*, *Bewitched*, *Hazel*, *I Dream of Jeannie*, *The Flying Nun*, and *The Partridge Family* to success at the networks and into lucrative syndication. Mitchell was the person who encouraged Hanna-Barbera into prime time. "He was relentless," Barbera said, "He wouldn't let up."

The Flintstones was publicized as the first "adult" TV cartoon. That was especially true of its first two seasons, which focused more on issues between the two couples. However, it was an inversion of what worked well on *The Huckleberry Hound Show* (and later, *The Muppet Show*). This time H-B had a cartoon sharp enough for adults to compete in prime time that was also a family show kids loved.

It was a major success, changing the perception of animation among the public and within the entertainment industry. Cartoons had taken a serious downturn in theaters (Disney films also had to make production changes within tighter budgets in a changing marketplace). *The Flintstones* opened up a market beyond daytime for cartoons. All three networks began preparing prime-time shows (in addition to the few existing shows like *The Bugs Bunny Show* and *Rocky and His Friends* revamped as *The Bullwinkle Show*, all of which were made up of short segments).

As the Stoneway piano inspired Barbera, another musical implement became the very first "modern stone-age gadget" introduced in the series. In the fifth episode aired, "Fred's Split Personality," a little bird's needle-sharp beak was placed into the grooves of a crudely cut stone record. Before playing the record, the bird addressed the home audience and said, "I hate opera!" thereby setting the stage for hundreds of creatures dispensing one-liners before taking care of business.

▲▼▲▼▲▼

Hanna-Barbera's essential, effective implementation of audio was used to its fullest from the beginning of *The Flintstones*. In the episode "The Swimming Pool" (expanded from the original short pilot film) Barney Rubble plays bongos to a jazz version of a Hoyt Curtin music cue that would become "Meet the Flintstones" in the third season.

In the short pilot mentioned above, Fred Flintstone was voiced by Daws Butler; Barney was either

IF YOUR CHILD WATCHES *Saturday Morning* TV,
MOST OF THE MUSIC HE HEARS
WAS COMPOSED AND CONDUCTED
BY

FLINTSTONES
YOGI BEAR
SUPER FRIENDS
TOM AND JERRY
QUICK DRAW McGRAW
THESE ARE THE
    DAYS
EMERGENCY PLUS
    FOUR
DEVLIN
KORG
ADDAMS FAMILY
BEANIE AND CECIL
WHEELIE

SCOOBY DOO
JETSONS
HONG KONG PHOOEY
HUCKLEBERRY HOUND
VALLEY OF THE
    DINOSAURS
JEANNIE
SPEED BUGGY
GRAPE APE
MAGILLA GORILLA
GOOBER
WAIT 'TIL YOUR
    FATHER GETS HOME

HOYT CURTIN
SOUNDTRACK MUSIC

Composer Hoyt Curtin was responsible for music heard in hundreds of Hanna-Barbera cartoons.

Butler or Bill Thompson (sources vary on this); Betty Rubble was June Foray; and Wilma was played by Jean Vander Pyl, a role she would play for life.

Bill Thompson—best known as the voice of MGM's Droopy character, Disney's White Rabbit, Mister Smee, and Ranger Woodlore—was cast as Fred with several episodes recorded. Barbera's ear for voices was as acute as Hanna's for music, and he felt that Thompson was unable to sustain Fred's gravelly voice, later casting him numerous times in cartoons, most notably as Touché Turtle.

According to Charles "Chas" Butler, his father, Daws, was characteristically supportive when Alan Reed was cast as Fred Flintstone instead of him or Thompson. "Dad thought it was inspired casting," said Chas. "He admired talent and was okay with it. He was appreciative of being chosen for the test film."

Alan Reed's long career on stage and in motion pictures, including *The Postman Always Rings Twice*

and *Breakfast at Tiffany's* (the film with Huckleberry Hound's "cameo" as well as voice work by Mel "Barney" Blanc). Reed personally felt that on-camera stardom eluded him, but *The Flintstones* afforded him a rare immortality. Through Fred, he was able to incorporate a variety of his skills and experiences in both comedy and drama. Fred could be a serio-comic character when needed, even in the series' more whimsical seasons, given to regret his impulsive behavior and lost opportunities. Reed could also use previous radio and animation voices, such as Falstaff Openshaw of *The Fred Allen Show* (Allen was a lifelong friend) and the Russian accent he used in Walt Disney's 1955 classic *Lady and the Tramp*, which was his first animation work though he also tested for 1951's *Alice in Wonderland*.

Reed suggested at the outset that this series should not be voiced in the extreme "cartoony" style, but should be more grounded in natural speech, a

Alan Reed, seen here in 1956's *Time Table*, originated the role of Fred Flintstone with Jean Vander Pyl as Wilma, Bea Benederet as Betty, and Mel Blanc as Barney.

Mel Blanc easily voiced more classic "star" cartoon voices than any other actor.

form of voice acting unusual in animation at the time but widely employed today in prime-time cartoons.

▲▼▲▼▲▼

Mel Blanc is probably the single most lauded voice actor of all time, particularly since his work is recognized as pivotal to the success of the Warner Brothers cartoon studio. His role as Barney Rubble is a substantial achievement in itself. For the first several months of *The Flintstones* on ABC, Blanc was finding Barney's character. The tone was more nasal and closer to Blanc's speaking voice. Gradually it deepened to the more familiar, goofier tone. His experience in radio was likely a factor in creating a complementary voice to play against that of Reed.

The most unsung of the cast is also one of the finest actors of radio and animation: Bea Benederet, who added sharp comedy and sure-fire support to many a radio series, including *The Jack Benny Program*, *My Favorite Husband*, and later on TV's *The Burns and Allen Show* and *Petticoat Junction*. Her performance of Betty was difficult to equal. Scripts increasingly gave

Betty less to do (Benederet herself was given only one episode focusing on Betty called "Old Lady Betty"). In the nineties, B. J. Ward brought a fresh approach to the role by adding a fine singing voice in addition to acting chops.

▲▼▲▼▲▼

Actor/comedian Jackie Gleason, who created and starred in *The Honeymooners*, is said to have considered taking legal action about the similarity of *The Flintstones* to his program but reportedly decided against upsetting children and families by suing Fred Flintstone. Gleason himself was sued about *The Honeymooners* by *The Bickersons* sitcom creator Philip Rapp due to their similarities and the case was settled out of court. As noted earlier, the concepts were predated by Laurel and Hardy's husband-and-wife comedy films. Some personalities like Phil Silvers gave little weight to such things, perhaps deciding that somehow it widened their fan base, just as a new *Saturday Night Live* impression revives young interest in a famous person. *The Flintstones* eventually took

This Golden LP introduced "Meet the Flintstones" and a variety of music cues used on the TV series.

on a life of its own, branching out into stories and comedy styles beyond *The Honeymooners*, keeping in tune with how television and its audiences were changing in the sixties. Within its 166 original episodes, one can find sly satire, pop culture references, guest stars, publicity stunts, social commentary, current events, and the kind of songs that kids would sing together at school and adults would hum at work the following Monday.

Every season included several musical showpieces, some informal and some full-scale spectacles that required prerecorded vocals and additional orchestrations. The first tune written for *The Flintstones* was "The Car Hop Song" from the first season episode "The Drive-In." Viewers familiar with the song know it better as "Here We Come on the Run with a Burger and a Bun" sung by Ginny Tyler and Nancy Wible as Gwen and Daisy (otherwise known as "Charlie and

Irving"). Like most H-B theme songs, the "Car Hop Song" was composed by Hoyt Curtin with lyrics by Bill Hanna and Joe Barbera. Songwriting by the team would continue throughout their partnership.

▲▼▲▼▲▼

Eight songs were included on one of the finest Hanna-Barbera records, *Songs of the Flintstones*, released in 1961 on the Golden label. Most tie-in records are mere offshoots of their film or series, but this had an ongoing influence on the show's entire run and Hanna-Barbera's musical legacy.

The format of the LP takes shape in either short comic adventures or informal exchanges about their lives. These lead up to songs in which they share a verse. Betty Rubble, who didn't get her own Flintstones vitamin until the public demanded it from the manufacturer, is the only character on the LP who gets a solo song.

Golden's *Songs of the Flintstones* introduced one of the most well-known and beloved theme songs in television history. The unabashed joy of "Meet the Flintstones" was exemplified in John Hughes's comedy feature *Trains, Planes, and Automobiles* when Steve Martin and John Candy try to lead a busload of travelers in a sing-along. Steve Martin's character croons "Three Coins in the Fountain" to silence. After a beat, Candy's character sings "Meet the Flintstones," which everyone seems to know. Cut to a high-level exterior of the bus in the city with the sound of the voices still joyfully singing.

On the Golden LP, "Meet the Flintstones" is sung by Jean Vander Pyl and the actors who became the original voices of Fred (Alan Reed); Barney (Mel Blanc); and Bea Benederet (Betty). However, when this album was released in 1961, this was not the theme song to *The Flintstones*.

For the first two seasons and two episodes of the third, an instrumental called "Rise and Shine" played over the titles as Fred rushed home from work each evening. On the album, the cast sings the tune with lyrics. Hanna always preferred theme songs that set up the premise and characters as much as possible within sixty seconds, so that may have had something to do with the replacement "Meet the Flintstones" (as well as his being the lyricist)!

When *The Flintstones* went into syndicated reruns, "Rise and Shine" was replaced with "Meet the Flintstones" and was not seen until three decades later. Hanna-Barbera writer and historian Earl Kress located the footage and restored it to the correct episodes.

▲▼▲▼▲▼

Another contribution from the *Songs of the Flintstones* album to the TV series is a substantial amount of reusable music cues. Six out of the eight tracks on the album contain music beds that, without the vocals and dialogue, were used countless times on Flintstone episodes and occasionally on other Hanna-

Barbera cartoons. The two most repurposed music beds come from "I Flipped" and "Split Level Cave."[1] The other songs include "Dino the Dino," with Mel Blanc also voicing "barks" of the Flintstones' pet; "Dum Tot Song," in which the couples encounter a little boy who lost a nickel in a gum slot. Without the vocal, this becomes an elegant piano piece connecting to a music bed (heard exactly that way in the episode "Social Climbers"). "Split Level Cave," describing all the "modern conveniences" they enjoy in the suburbs of Bedrock, is a treasure trove of music cues and a great example of the process Hoyt Curtin developed in advertising and film, then perfected at Hanna-Barbera. The music works well in its entirety yet provides the editor with ample options to break at various points. The aforementioned "Car Hop Song" caps off the album, exactly as heard on the TV episode with Tyler and Wible, with a different context than on the TV episode. On the LP, the foursome goes for a drive, and his stingy refusal to tip a car hop inspires Wilma and Betty to perform the song in car hop uniforms to make Fred and Barney "feel small" (depicted literally on the TV episode).

Songs of the Flintstones was the first "in-house" Hanna-Barbera record album, created and executed by the studio. It was a plum project for Golden Records' Arthur Shimkin and undoubtedly bears the personal touch of Hanna and Barbera. Golden issued several single 45 rpm and 78 rpm records with material from the LP. The theme was also reissued in 1972 on a compilation called *Cartoon Favorites* after Golden was renamed Wonderland Records.

▲▼▲▼▲▼

Beyond the cast album and in addition to original songs, the use of license-free public domain songs was common practice as far back in cartoon history as Fleischer's Screen Songs and Disney's Mickey Mouse and Silly Symphony shorts. The episode "The Hot Piano" features one of the most memorable Flintstone parodies in which Wilma is serenaded by "Happy Anniversary," sung to the tune of Rossini's

"William Tell Overture" (also familiar as *The Lone Ranger* theme).

The first guest star on *The Flintstones* was music related. Songwriter, singer, and occasional actor Hoagy Carmichael is a significant name in the music canon known as the Great American Songbook. His songs spanned decades of stage, film, and recordings, especially the song that granted him immortality, "Stardust." It is this song for which Fred claims ownership in the episode "The Hit Songwriters." Fred's mangling of the words and music is one of many masterful Alan Reed performances.

Carmichael's appearance signaled the series' first elaborate production number, "Yabba Dabba Doo," written for the show by Carmichael and sung by him with the cast. He introduces the tune by saying, "The words to this song were written by my friend Barney Rubble, who created the lyrics from a title suggested by his best friend, Fred Flintstone." This is as good a way as any to describe how Bill and Joe came up with ideas for themes and original songs for their shows. The "Yabba Dabba Doo" sequence is distinguished by more fluid animation, more varied backgrounds, fast cuts, and unique layouts. The pacing and detail of these set pieces would occur periodically in H-B series and features. The music recorded for them was most likely produced separately from the music cues. Often these "set pieces" were given special attention and assigned to specific creative teams.

▲▼▲▼▲▼

Depending on the project, Alan Reed did his own singing for Fred—on the Golden Records LP, in "The Hit Songwriters" episode, and when he sang opera in "The Split Personality." In other instances, another vocalist would do his singing.

When Fred sings "When the Saints Go Marching In" (in "Hot Lips Hannigan") and "Listen to the Rockin' Bird" (in "The Girls' Night Out") in a cool, hip voice, the singing is provided by Duke Mitchell. Mitchell was a nightclub performer and producer. In the early fifties, Mitchell was in a comedy act that toured as

the "Dean Martin-type" to Jerry Lewis clone Sammy Petrillo. The duo starred in the basement-budget feature *Bela Lugosi Meets a Brooklyn Gorilla* and skirted lawsuits from the real Martin and Lewis. On his own, Mitchell enjoyed success among the Hollywood elite, and either vacationing or performing in Palm Springs may have connected him to Joe Barbera, who enjoyed visiting the popular resort area and mingling among show business movers and shakers.

In the episode "The Twitch," Jerry Wallace was the singing voice of "The Bedrock Twitch" for both Alan Reed and Hal Smith, who was the speaking voice of guest character Rock Roll. Wallace was a studio singer and stage performer who briefly teamed coincidentally with comedian Red Coffey (aka Merle Herman Coffman). Hanna and Barbera hired Coffey to voice Little Quacker for MGM Tom and Jerry cartoons and Yakky Doodle for their own *Yogi Bear Show*. Due to Coffey's touring schedule, actor and public speaker Jimmy Weldon became Yakky's second and longest-running voice. Weldon was a popular Los Angeles TV personality for his *Webster Webfoot* children's show.

▲▼▲▼▲▼

The phrase "Yabba Dabba Doo" is as familiar outside *The Flintstones* as Bugs Bunny's "What's Up Doc?" and Charlie Brown's "Good Grief!" According to Alan Reed's autobiography (and contrary to most public accounts including those of Reed himself), there is more detail to the story of the catchphrase. As Reed explained in his book:

At the outset, I realized that here was an opportunity to promote what is known as a "catchphrase" in the world of show business. In the early days of radio, the airwaves were full of them . . . I brought this thought to Joe Barbera who produced and directed *The Flintstones*. When he agreed, I volunteered to find the right words. Inasmuch as Fred was an exuberant character, I thought I'd try to find a phrase that could be used to express excitement or glee. I started with the first word that popped into my mind the old cowboy expression, "Yahoo!"

For the next few days, my wife must have thought I'd gone off my rocker as I went around the house uttering the strangest sounds, like "Yahoodle doodle!" "Doodle-dee-dodo!" "Dabble-Dee-Doo-Roo!" Finally, I hit on "Yabba doo," and I felt I was close but it needed a little something more. I added the middle "dabba" and my brain-child was born. "Yabba dabba doo!"

With this polished gem at the ready, Reed entered a *Flintstones* recording session. Joe Barbera recalled:

> I'm up in the booth and I'm marking my script, and they're down on the floor with the microphone and they're marking their scripts . . . Alan Reed yells out, "Hey Joe!" and I said, "Yeah?" and I'm marking away. He says, "It says 'Yahoo!' here." I said, "Yup." He says, "Can I say, 'Yabba dabba doo?'" I say, "Yup."

▲▼▲▼▲▼

In addition to the Golden Records cast album, a TV soundtrack of *The Flintstones* was released by Colpix Records in 1961. "The Snorkasaurus" and "The Big Bank Robbery" episodes are presented on the disc with limited narration by Alan Reed as Fred. (He also adds a line about Barney being swallowed by a giant fish because it was a visual gag.)

The dialogue is almost music-free with generic sound effects not necessarily from the H-B editors. The "Rise and Shine" begins and ends each story, with a "mini-finale" on side two. This was incorporated into the studio cue library and was edited into the "Peek-a-Boo Camera" episode. When the ants invade Wilma and Betty's camp lunch, the "Colonel Bogey March" is heard on the TV episode. This was a familiar melody and a surefire gag because the hit film *The Bridge on the River Kwai* was fairly recent. The album

omits this music, probably for licensing reasons. The overall production is light on music and sound effects, but the solid gold writing and performances are certainly worth hearing on their own.

Entertainer Jerry Mann is given his biggest *Flintstones* showcase in "The Snorkasaurus," as a Phil Silvers–like Dino that would thereafter be a vocal effect by Mel Blanc rather than a speaking voice. Mann's vocal history with Hanna and Barbera dates back to their Tom and Jerry days. His stage work on the road made his animation credits (he also does an excellent Ed Wynn in the same episode) sporadic but welcome.

There was a general atmosphere of mutual respect and admiration on the part of the professionals involved in *The Flintstones* that set the tone for future projects at the studio, large and small. One of the most dramatic examples of camaraderie occurred in 1962 when Blanc was in a devastating automobile accident, leaving him bandaged and unable to speak, which was alarming for a person who made a living with his voice.

Until Blanc was able to speak, Daws Butler filled in as a favor, free of charge so he would not be taking work away from a colleague. Once he was well enough to play Barney again, Hanna-Barbera set up the recording equipment in his home so that Reed, Vander Pyl, and Benederet could gather in his room and record *The Flintstones* together.

▲▼▲▼▲▼

The same year as *The Flintstones* soundtrack, the label also released the first Hanna-Barbera album to include all three crucial elements of voice, music, and sound effects. *Mr. Jinks, Pixie and Dixie* presented four cartoon soundtracks from *The Huckleberry Hound Show*, narrated by Huck himself. Hoyt Curtin's music cues and the H-B sound library could all finally be heard on vinyl.

H-B's various characters continued gaining momentum, not only through television and merchandise but through "personal appearances."

Narrated by Alan Reed, *The Flintstones* soundtrack album includes "The Snorkasaurus" and "The Big Bank Robbery."

Instantly recognizable costumed characters toured the countryside and eventually abroad, from shopping malls to business meetings.

Yogi Bear repeated animation history by following in the webbed footsteps of feisty, irascible Donald Duck, who during the mid-twentieth century surpassed the more polished Mickey Mouse. Hanna-Barbera's easygoing nice guy Huckleberry Hound became eclipsed by the more flawed, easily tempted rule-breaker Yogi. In 1961, the breakout bruin was given Hanna-Barbera's first spinoff series, *The Yogi Bear Show*. Cindy Bear and Ranger Smith were redesigned and given more prominence.

To backfill Yogi's space on *The Huckleberry Hound Show*, Hokey Wolf (Butler) joined the half hour. Doug Young, another actor recommended by Butler to voice Doggie Daddy in 1959, was cast as Hokey's adoring pal Ding-A-Ling. Two new cartoons were created to round out *The Yogi Bear Show*, soon to be fan favorites. Diminutive Yakky Doodle duck was based on one of Hanna and Barbera's go-to cute characters back at MGM and later at their own studio, where he was sometimes called "Itty Bitty Buddy." This time he was paired with bulldog protector Chopper. Chopper's voice was Vance Colvig (son of Pinto Colvig, voice of Goofy, Grumpy, and the original Capitol Records Bozo). Hapless adversary Fibber Fox was played by Daws Butler, inspired by one of the most popular humorists of the comedy record and *Ed Sullivan Show* era, Shelley Berman.

The third cartoon yielded an erudite, theatrical pink mountain lion named Snagglepuss. He was one of Daws Butler's signature voices and provided more catchphrases and memorable wordplays than almost any other H-B character ("Exit, stage left!" etc.) thanks to writers Maltese, Shows, Foster, and

Cecil Roy, who voiced Casper the Friendly Ghost and many other characters, plays Cindy Bear on the Golden album, *Songs of Yogi Bear and All His Pals*.

The 1960s brought a new "house sound" to Golden Records. With some exceptions, the musical director of their albums and singles was Jim Timmens, also a composer at Terrytoons and an audio editor.[2] Timmens's unmistakable jazz style of woodwinds, guitars, vibraphone, percussion, and mellow chorus was a contrast to Golden's boisterous big band/Broadway-based Mitch Miller–Jimmy Carroll sound. Timmens's records did not sound like Curtin's music except when his light jazz style lent itself to themes like *Yogi Bear* without the big brass.

Frank Milano was a radio, television, and cartoon voice actor who specialized in animal imitations. His most notable TV series was the early live children's variety show, *Rootie Kazootie*. For Golden Records, his performance of the classic Little Golden Book, *The Poky Little Puppy* (for which he narrated, barked, and sniffed), was available for decades. Milano's jaunty Yogi interpretation leans more toward Daws Butler than purely Art Carney. When a good actor must reproduce a beloved figure, it can be a daunting challenge, but if done with affection, respect, and spirit, it can be appreciated on its own merit for the effort.

Frank Milano is joined on the LP by Cecil Roy as Cindy Bear, a veteran New York voice actor whose work was largely uncredited like many of her peers on both coasts. Roy was one of the voices of Casper the Friendly Ghost and countless other roles in a wide age range.

▲▼▲▼▲▼

particularly Butler, who enjoyed free reign to ad-lib. The voice of Snagglepuss was a little too close for comfort to suit Bert Lahr, who played the Cowardly Lion in *The Wizard of Oz*. Litigation resulted in a "voice by Daws Butler" disclaimer added to Kellogg's commercials. Such action was unusual in the animation industry, but Lahr's strongest case applied to advertising because a voice that could be mistaken for his was endorsing a product.

▲▼▲▼▲

Little Golden Records were released to introduce *The Yogi Bear Show* characters. Even Ranger Smith is given a solo, singing "Before Yogi" on side two of Golden's *Yogi Bear* TV theme single, and part of the album *Songs of Yogi Bear and All His Pals*.

Songs of Yogi Bear and All His Pals was a multipurpose album, allowing Golden to release all of its songs on various single records. An elaborate LP-size book and record set with lyrics was also issued for a brief time.

Some earlier cuts with Gil Mack, Don Elliott, and the Jimmy Carroll Orchestra were also included, like "Blabbermouse" from the 1959 *Quick Draw McGraw and Huckleberry Hound* LP. This is an instance of the songwriters having little information about the character to write about beyond the name and general premise, as film examples were sparse to nonexistent and VHS tape samples, DVDs, or emailed files were in the future. Style guides might have a few sentences, and if they were lucky, a storyboard. An established character made it easier because materials were already available with character information to research. For the "Blabbermouse" song, Snooper's sidekick is given a rapid-fire style and uses the speedy speech to tell a short mystery. He did not have this personality in the cartoons, but what if Golden didn't have the details? The kids did, but not necessarily the licensees. Nevertheless, it is a funny song with a fine comic flair by Gil Mack, sans the TV Blabber's lisp. None of these reasons can fully address the varying reactions of kids to these records at the time. The circumstances as to prep materials, contracts, and budgets were of no concern to children. Some kids were more disappointed than others to hear vocal imitations. They sold in the millions, which could not have happened had there not been some repeat business.

Many of Golden's musical renditions of Hanna-Barbera themes and character ditties offered another benefit to event planners. When the costumed characters made appearances at stores, theaters, or other public events, even though they could not speak, the records allowed them to dance and sing. All the

venue required was a public address system, a few Golden Records, and a phonograph to put together a little show. The comparative vocal accuracy of the Golden performances would have seemed unimportant considering the noise levels and the fact that the costumed characters were also a variation on an animated representation.

The number of Hanna-Barbera characters featured on Golden's *Songs of Yogi Bear and All His Pals* 1961 LP is an indication of the steady increase in characters and the rapid rise of Hanna-Barbera Productions in only a few years. On January 6, 1962, Yogi's birthday was celebrated by characters from his series, plus characters from the *Huckleberry Hound* and *Quick Draw McGraw* shows. *Yogi's Birthday Party* was a special half-hour segment aired as the final first-run episode of *The Yogi Bear Show*. It could be considered Hanna-Barbera's first TV special, or as a "very special episode," because it was directly attached to the series. It closed with an original "Happy Birthday Yogi" song by the voice cast and The Randy Van Horne Singers.

The studio was not immune to setbacks. Their next big project pushed the new TV animation form even further. Instead of high ratings, there were lessons to be learned.

Chapter 6

TOP CAT'S BIG CITY BLUES

~~~~~~

The theme song had one of my favorite lines in it: "Close friends get to call him T.C., provided it's with dignity."

—BOB DYLAN

For their second prime-time animated sitcom, Hanna-Barbera pushed a bit beyond the boundaries of *The Flintstones*. Some critics felt *The Flintstones* had not delivered fully on its "adult" promise. Barbera chalked some of that up to marketing. Their second series, *Top Cat*, featured a lovable gang of anthropomorphic felines living in a New York City alley.

Top Cat links to comedian Phil Silvers and his *Sgt. Bilko* TV series. It even converted one of *Bilko*'s most popular cast members into animated form: Maurice Gosfield as the childlike Benny the Ball. The *Top Cat* characters and stories were also reminiscent of the lovable New York street rogues of Damon Runyon's short stories and the series of films starring the Bowery Boys/East Side Kids.

To this ambitious move of animating a larger regular cast of characters for *Top Cat* was added a more complex and expensive musical score with a string section. *The Flintstones*' scoring emphasized tactile instruments like xylophones and percussion (in addition to tubas and bassoons, which historian Earl Kress surmises Hoyt Curtin might have chosen to represent Fred).

Musically, *Top Cat* came along at a perfect time. "The period from 1957 to 1965 was the golden age of jazz, or jazz-influenced, movie and TV scores," wrote music historian and biographer Gary Giddins in his essay, "Sweet Smell of Success: The Fantastic Falco." "Suddenly, music directors with a background in jazz and even true jazz composers were taken on by the studios: Johnny Mandel, Duke Ellington, Miles Davis, John Lewis, Henry Mancini, Pete Rugolo, Van Alexander, Eddie Sauter, Benny Carter, Andre Previn, Lalo Schifrin, Quincy Jones, and others, plus great jazz improvisers, who appeared in nightclub scenes or soloed invisibly on soundtracks."

Hoyt Curtin gave the *Top Cat* cues a Gershwin flavor. Interpolating a classical composer's signatures into musical scoring is practically a tradition in Hollywood animation and live-action filmmaking. Not only is it still acceptable, but it can also win Oscars. It would be four years after Curtin brought *Top Cat*'s innovative jazz and blues sound to prime-time animation that Vince Guaraldi presented his own brand of piano jazz in *A Charlie Brown Christmas* to perpetual and well-deserved acclaim.

www

One of the *Top Cat* leads would become a fixture of the studio: John Stephenson, who gave a Cary Grant lilt to Fancy-Fancy. One of Stephenson's longest-running voices was that of Fred Flintstone's boss, Mr. Slate, after a few initial shifts in the actor and character. Stephenson was also the announcer over Bill Hanna and Joe Barbera's animation for the early titles of *I Love Lucy*. New to H-B was actor/singer Leo DeLyon in the role of slow-witted Brain and Beatnik Spook. One of DeLyon's many talents is imitating musical instruments, a gift put to use on the soundtrack for Walt Disney's *The Jungle Book* (1967) for the scat singing and vocal effects of several characters, particularly the White-Haired Monkey, in the King Louie sequence. Also new was Marvin Kaplan, an actor of remarkable comic and dramatic range. Kaplan was capable of performing roles without his distinctive Brooklyn accent, but it was perfect for Choo-Choo, a well-read romantic, the intellectual of the gang. "I always figured Choo-Choo was the one in Top Cat's group who went to City College," Kaplan quipped.

Because of the number of characters per episode, most of the actors "doubled," handling more than one role per episode. While the entire cast dabbled in this to some degree, DeLyon and Stephenson did the greatest number of incidental voices, in addition to Hanna-Barbera regulars like Bea Benederet and Daws Butler and newcomers including Herb Vigran and Walker Edmiston.

Allen Jenkins played Officer Dibble, the long-suffering voice of authority. Dibble is no match for T. C.'s rapid-fire finagling, but while he threatens to "run them all in," there is a neighborhood kinship among

them. On several occasions, they might solve a problem for Dibble or miss him when he is replaced. Jenkins is one of the most ubiquitous golden-age movie actors. Easily recognizable in hundreds of golden-age Hollywood films and TV shows, often as an authority figure, he gives Dibble a grounded, genuine quality.

The *Top Cat* cast worked from two microphones, several leaning into one or the other. This was the system for recording TV voices, much like radio comedy and drama, and it would serve both Hanna-Barbera, the actors, and the audiences well.

▲▼▲▼

Hollywood character actor Michael O'Shea was originally cast as Top Cat. After several episodes were recorded, Joe Barbera decided to cast a different voice. With his ear for the "music" of dialogue, Barbera decided that O'Shea's approach to the character and his chemistry with the cast wasn't working. According to Earl Kress, Barbera thought O'Shea wasn't getting the comedy of the character. The first four episodes were rerecorded after Arnold Stang was chosen as the new Top Cat. Stang had years of experience in animation, most often for Paramount's Famous Studios, voicing Herman in the Herman and Katnip cartoons. When he began the *Top Cat* sessions, Stang was baffled by the vocal direction since he was primarily known for lovable milquetoast roles, though Katnip was a tough, streetwise mouse.

"The character that I ended up playing was completely unlike what I had been identified with," Stang told Kress in an interview. "The one thing that Alan [Dinehart, the associate producer] seemed to do more than anything else, and Joe suggested it a couple of times . . . was to be 'more Arnold Stang' and I kept saying, 'Well, you sure that's what T. C. is supposed to be?' 'Yes, that's what we want.' So I ended up doing myself again which has been very effective for me other times, you know."

The resulting voice was a lower, smoother, and more self-assured sound than Stang had ever done. It's not Herman, but it's not the usual Stang. In addi-

Popular character actor and *Top Cat* star Arnold Stang in the 1951 NBC series *The Great Talent Hunt*.

Jay Ward's cartoons were also highly satirical and loaded with dialogue, but their speech was kooky and exaggerated. The pace was frenetic. Children might not get the sharp digs, but they'd laugh at the silliness. Despite *Top Cat*'s setting in a New York alley (called "Hoagy's Alley" after *Flintstones* guest star, Hoagy Carmichael), his sly attitude toward the world tended to be more elegant and polished, even if sometimes it was all in his own mind.

The *Top Cat* story lines didn't break new ground, but it had snappy dialogue and character-driven humor comparable to the sharpest live-action sitcoms. It gave voice acting greats like Don Messick, Hal Smith, and Jean Vander Pyl some of the sharpest repartee ever written for Hanna-Barbera.

▲▾▲▾

Slightly edited and minus the theme song except as background music, the two episodes on the *Top Cat* soundtrack album (1962) offer a gangster caper and a romantic farce. "The Unscratchables" (a twist on the hit Desilu series *The Untouchables*) brings criminals, action, and danger to the alley. Herschel Bernardi plays one of the menacing gangsters with Jean Vander Pyl very amusing as the boss's faux-stylish girlfriend, Fifi. All the characters get a few minutes of groove time. "Top Cat Falls in Love" is a comedy of errors with T. C. going to extremes to spend time with a lovely nurse, to the point of faking a rare Arctic disease contracted by eating stale blubber burgers.

The soundtrack album offers several examples of *Top Cat*'s need for balance between the verbal and visual. Because there is no narration, a few scenes are missing information that might make the gags and situations funnier or clearer. In "Top Cat Falls in Love" for example, T. C. enters a hospital waiting area unaware that it's a maternity ward. In the actual cartoon, the TV audience sees the sign. Album listeners cannot, so they are left to eventually figure out that the expectant fathers are talking about babies, while T. C. thinks they're bachelors waiting for their lady friends to finish their shifts. Album

tion to his appearance with Kaplan and Jonathan Winters in the 1963 comedy classic, *It's a Mad, Mad, Mad, Mad World*, playing Top Cat gave Stang lifelong fans. He continued getting mail and messages until he passed away in 2009.

▲▾▲▾

Following a hit that was on its way to becoming a phenomenon is nearly impossible. *Top Cat* is fondly regarded today when viewed on its own merits and not for how it performed at 8:30 p.m. against *The Joey Bishop Show*. Hanna-Barbera was still experimenting with the animated sitcom form. Barbera was concerned that many TV sitcom writers wrote too much dialogue and did not understand the need for visuals. By the very nature of its premise, *Top Cat* would have been a highly verbal TV series, animated or not. T. C. was a verbal character with a lot of gabby sidekicks.

For the *Top Cat* soundtrack album, the two selected episodes were rich in witty dialogue and the chemistry of recording actors as an ensemble.

narration could have clarified the situation faster.[1] *Top Cat* scripts tended to be wordy (as are many in television animation), but they are also savvy and sharp-tongued, perhaps too much so to connect with the widest possible prime-time audience needed to satisfy the sponsors.

Top Cat was one of several 1961 animated hopefuls on the prime-time network schedules. The success of *The Flintstones* in the 1960s prompted all three networks to get animated comedies into prime time, including *The Alvin Show* (the first animated version of David Seville and the Chipmunks) on CBS and a reworked version of *Rocky and His Friends* called *The Bullwinkle Show* on NBC. After one season, only *The Flintstones* remained. *Top Cat* attempted to reach beyond what people expected from an animated sitcom, at least in sound and verbal tone, based on what Hanna and Barbera were experimenting with in 1961.

What worked and what did not, especially about the amount of dialogue vs. cartoon action, was a learning experience that affected almost all subsequent H-B cartoons.

Top Cat enjoyed a second life on Saturday morning TV. A respectable amount of merchandise continued over the ensuing decades, whether the series was readily available or not. The series had developed enough of a following to justify an ongoing presence. *Top Cat* and the gang also became popular throughout the world. In Great Britain, the title was changed to "Boss Cat," because "Top Cat" was a brand of cat food. T. C.'s name remained the same within the episodes.

▲▼▲▼▲▼

In 1962, Hanna-Barbera produced three new five-minute syndicated cartoon series to compete with the cartoons flooding the marketplace from other studios. Five-minute cartoons were appealing to viewers, flexible for local stations, and lucrative for producers. If a station's movie had an irregular running time, a cartoon could be added at the end, saving time in editing the movie. Five-minute cartoons could round out hours and half hours of miscellaneous cartoons. Live children's shows could easily find places for them. Hundreds of such cartoons poured out of studios around the world in the early sixties. King Features had sold Popeye, Beetle Bailey, Krazy Kat, and Snuffy Smith cartoons with tremendous success, as did Trans-Lux with Felix the Cat and the Mighty Hercules, and UPA with Mister Magoo and Dick Tracy.

Hanna-Barbera's *Touché Turtle*, *Wally Gator*, and *Lippy the Lion and Hardy Har Har* were the studio's first stand-alone, five-minute cartoons. They could be run together for a half hour or mixed in with other programming. The studio produced sixty-five episodes of each of the three new cartoons.

A series of Little Golden Records were released with the three theme songs. Like other Golden versions lacking original casts, they did offer additional lyrics, though sometimes curious ones. In the *Touché Turtle* cartoon, the theme has few lyrics but instead is augmented with exciting Hoyt Curtin action music as Touché fights assorted adversaries. The records presented more complete music and lyrics, published by Screen Gems Music and written by Barbera and Hanna, arranged and conducted for Golden by Jim Timmens. The *Lippy the Lion and Hardy Har Har* single includes two theme verses not heard on the TV version. Especially fascinating is the Golden version of the *Wally Gator* theme song. Author and pop culture expert Tim Hollis elaborates:

> The "new" lyrics that appear on the H-B Little Golden Records often sound like someone knew nothing about the characters, even though they're sometimes credited to Bill and Joe themselves! In that way, they're a lot like the earliest H-B Little Golden Books, which also seem at odds with the characters and their personalities.

The LGRs seem to go out of their way to make the characters seem more like the animals they really are, like having Augie Doggie wagging his tail, Snagglepuss threatening to eat someone, or Super Snooper proving he's a cat by meowing. But I think the dumbest lyric of all is "Wally Gator, where did you get that walk? Wally Gator, where'd you ever learn to talk?" Like talking animals aren't an everyday occurrence in that world. I don't think I'm the first to point out that the actual Wally Gator TV theme is off-kilter since the lyrics talk about a swamp and the animation shows him zooming through the Everglades in a motorboat, while the whole series takes place in a zoo.

Golden's *Wally Gator* record also states that "People by the dozen take advice from you / The town begins a-buzzin' every time you leave the zoo," both of which are far from accurate.

Any number of reasons could have contributed to anomalies within Golden's licensed work. Creative teams were limited to such input, so the writers, art directors, actors, and composers were limited to what they received from the West coast—and how much might have changed in the cartoons between the time they made the records and the shows were finished.

For example, a merchandising kit for these three cartoons might have been limited to basic descriptions offering little more than Wally Gator as a fun-loving alligator who escapes from the zoo in search of wild hijinks; Touché Turtle as a small but brave hero who fights fantastic foes with his sheepdog sidekick, Dum-Dum; and Lippy the Lion and Hardy Har Har as a fast-talking hobo lion and his sad-sack hyena sidekick on the road to fun-filled adventures.

There were no reference tapes, DVDs, streaming codes, or digital files, making it even more challenging to accurately capture the qualities of the cartoons. Golden might have been shipped story lines, art, color guides, storyboards, film reels, and maybe even audio recordings for reference. To get the records in stores on time, this information may have had to be

Golden Records offered original songs about H-B characters and some themes with additional lyrics not heard on TV.

sent months before the cartoons were finished. Any number of changes could have occurred, so there were bound to be inconsistencies and inaccuracies.

▲▼▲▼▲▼

In 1962, Yogi starred on an LP called *How to Be a Better-Than-the-Average-Child without Really Trying*. The title spoofs the 1961 Broadway musical *How to Succeed in Business without Really Trying*, a top-of-mind hit when this album was released. As a rule, the packaging of children's records sells to parents through the cover art and liner notes first and the actual recording second. Even if kids did not get the joke, the parents were reading the cover and making the purchase. The "How to Succeed" and "Without Really Trying" phrases, were a clever hook for an

album that used Yogi and his friends to teach kids basic rules about good habits and behavior. Popeye and Olive Oyl were given a similar assignment in an earlier Golden LP about health, safety, friendship, and manners.

Yogi's *How to Succeed* album, along with several concurrent Little Golden Records with Hanna-Barbera characters singing about keeping your city clean and staying safe, made sense for heroic types like Huckleberry Hound and Quick Draw McGraw. For the most part, Yogi's original cartoon persona was that of a lovable rascal. Here he and Boo-Boo are heard as both teachers and students. This causes some confusion in the script, especially when Boo-Boo complains about having to follow rules on one track, then talks about why rules are important on the next without any transition. (Eleven years later,

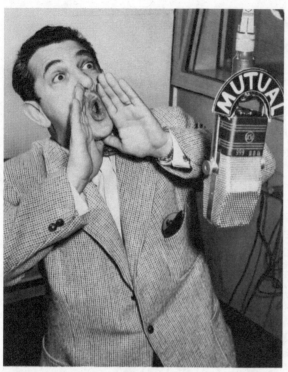

New York TV personality and voice actor Frank Milano voices several *Yogi Bear Show* characters for Golden Records.

parental pressure groups would encourage "prosocial" messages on Saturday morning TV and Yogi Bear would again be on his best behavior for *Yogi's Gang* on ABC.)

As Yogi, Frank Milano sounds as if he refined his interpretations of the characters; since the *Songs of Yogi Bear* LP, perhaps benefiting from accessing additional cartoon broadcasts. Cindy is played in this case by New York studio singer Dottie Evans, whose work can be found on many children's records for Columbia, RCA, and the famous "Singing Science" series with Tom Glazer. The album also contains the LP debut of Golden's versions of the themes for Top Cat, Wally Gator, Lippy and Hardy, Touché Turtle, and Dum-Dum, as well as the dog-biscuit-loving hound, Snuffles, one of Joe Barbera's favorite recurring characters.

Yogi was the title and subject, in vocal style if not by lyrics, of a 1960 novelty record released by Shell Records, a record label owned by a New Jersey dentist.

"Three frat brothers at Adelphi University on Long Island formed a group called the Ivy Three," Don Yowp explained. Ivy member Charles Koppelman (aka Charlie Cane) cowrote a song called "Yogi." It was also recorded by Georgie Young and the Rockin' Bocs on the Swan label, but the Ivy Three's version hopped on the charts at number 80 on August 8 and peaked at number 8 eight weeks later. London Records bought the song and released it overseas.

"Other than the quasi-Daws Butler impersonation (which sounds more like Art Carney's Ed Norton) in the chorus and the arbitrary shout of 'Hey, Boo Boo!' the song has absolutely nothing to do with Yogi Bear or any cartoon characters," continues Don Yowp. "The lyrics involve a yogi, as in the transcendental meditation kind." Though this may have been intended to avoid copyright violation, the Ivy Three left no doubt which "Yogi" they meant in August 1960, when they lip-synched the "Yogi" record on Dick Clark's *Saturday Night Beechnut Show* accompanied by a generic costumed bear. No other kind of "yogi" was in sight.

▲▼▲▼

Chapter 7

JETSON JAZZ

A Crazy Thing!

Today "The Jetsons" stands as the single most important
piece of 20th-century futurism.
—MATT NOVAK, *SMITHSONIAN MAGAZINE*

Fifty years after *The Jetsons* premiered on network prime-time TV in 1962, *Smithsonian* published an article called "Why the Show Still Matters," including a partial list of *The Jetsons'* ongoing influences. One is the name itself. "Jetsons" is part of the English language, equating with the most imaginative, colorful, innovative, and sometimes outlandish examples of futuristic vision.

The Jetsons is, at its most basic, a 1960s prime-time network sitcom that needed to conform to the conventions of its specific circumstances to get sponsored by Scotch Tape. Some merely note similarities between *Blondie* and *Hazel*. Others have dismissed it on a surface level by focusing on the "typical" sitcom story lines, completely missing the effectiveness by which those elements kept the twenty-four episodes airing, almost uninterrupted, since the original run. That is far from typical.

George, Jane, Judy, Elroy, Rosie, and Mr. Spacely may be the main characters, but the star of the show is really where they live and the possibilities of what people might achieve, without the usual dystopian consequences of such fiction. Generations of viewers never stop watching because they want to visit them and their world. *The Jetsons* do not suffer the science-fiction trope of paying a terrible price for technology. More often than not, technology is annoying or tiresome. Pressing too many buttons makes fingers hurt and "three-hour work days" are "exhausting." Their complaints comment on the human tendency to take creativity, conveniences, and comforts easily for granted, no matter how fantastic they seem at first. Computers and robots could be a threat, but they were transparent and had weaknesses. One of the series' most "love-to-hate-able" robotic bureaucrats, the brown-nosing Uniblab, is a caricature of human office politics.

▴▾▴▾▴▾

As a work of creative art, *The Jetsons* came about at the best possible time, perhaps for all time. The year 1962 combined postwar promise, space-age anticipation, DuPont's "better living through chemistry," Ray Bradbury's "I Sing the Body Electric," the stylish elegance of *The Dick Van Dyke Show*, and the winsome whimsy of *The Donna Reed Show*. It was the height of Kennedy's "Camelot" era. While civil rights, international issues, and atomic disasters were making news, the Kennedy era created a perception of hope for the future. This was reflected in the 1962 Seattle World's Fair (which inspired many of *The Jetsons* designs). It was also a popular subject for Walt Disney, whose Sunday night TV program presented lively documentaries directed by Ward Kimball that encouraged the NASA moon project. Disneyland was allowing its guests to "walk through the future" with such attractions as the Monsanto House of the Future in Tomorrowland. Even the Disney theme park concept itself fast became a much-imitated blueprint for city planning. Disneyland's monorail was the first in the US, but it was not the last. "People Mover" systems appeared in several cities outside the Disney gates.

Nevertheless, when most people refer to futuristic vision, they say something like, "That's right out of *The Jetsons*." Not everyone was able to visit Disneyland between 1957 and 1967 and tour the House of the Future. The Seattle and New York World's Fairs only retain a few buildings. Epcot in Florida no longer designates the front section of its park as "Future World." *The Jetsons* made the future accessible at a time in history when its look and its outlook were almost completely in tune. Anyone with access to a TV could visit when the series premiered, and it is even easier today. It was the essence of what twentieth-century science fiction and fantasy had promised and predicted—a funny, jazzy, beautifully designed living theme park where everyone could defy gravity—zooming into homes on a regular basis.

That was among the strongest Hanna-Barbera distinctions: accessibility, proximity, and familiarity. H-B made repetition and exposure a bonding strength. Other studios soon figured it out, but few had the elements in place to duplicate the success.

▴▾▴▾▴▾

When Joe Barbera sold the "flip side" of *The Flintstones* to ABC as *The Jetsons*, the studio was at an artistic point when new creative talent was blending with some of the finest talents of the classic animation industry.

"It was the most exciting time in the world to be there," recalled writer/director Tony Benedict, who helped develop the character of Astro through his writing of all the episodes featuring "Reorge Retson's roggie."

"Ideas were coming in at a rapid pace," said Benedict. "Joe loved working with stories. I would go in to see him, either alone or with other artists like Willie Ito, and we would pitch story ideas. We felt like the sky was the limit."

ABC was finally ready to try something new for the network—color television. *The Flintstones* and *Top Cat* were filmed in color, but they were broadcast in black and white (all of Hanna-Barbera's TV cartoons were filmed in color to keep them fresh in the event of color TV). Sunday, September 23, 1962, *The Jetsons* became the first color program broadcast on the ABC network. The competition was Walt Disney himself, hosting his top-rated *Wonderful World of Color* on NBC. Family favorite *Dennis the Menace* was a hit on CBS, with lovable *Lassie* as a strong lead-in (these two were still in black and white). *The Jetsons* was expensive to produce and ABC was the number three network. Placing the series on the highly competitive Sunday night schedule suggests expectations of nothing less than total success. There was a massive publicity buildup with merchandise already on shelves in anticipation.

▴▾▴▾▴▾

George O'Hanlon's many TV credits included the sitcom *The Life of Riley*.

Pyl as Rosie, Daws Butler as Elroy, Don Messick as Astro, and Mel Blanc as boss Spacely.

"It isn't just that you read lines and skip over things," said Penny Singleton of the Jetson sessions with Joe Barbera. "He makes you pay attention and each word is very important. You have your pacing, your timing, and he's absolutely fantastic."

Becoming the voice of Judy Jetson opened up a new world for Janet Waldo, who had been acting on camera for many years since her days in radio and had never done animation until this point. Waldo was a popular juvenile lead on radio and in films during the postwar era. Media icon Ozzie Nelson encouraged her to develop the "eeeeeooouuu!!" squeal and bubbly teen personality when she played Emmy Lou on radio's *The Adventures of Ozzie and Harriet*. This came in handy when she starred in the radio sitcom, *Meet Corliss Archer*. *I Love Lucy* fans know her as Ricky's adoring teenage neighbor, Peggy.

The actors originally selected to voice George and Jane Jetson were comedian Morey Amsterdam (best known as Buddy Sorrell on *The Dick Van Dyke Show*) and Pat Carroll (Prunella in Rodgers and Hammerstein's 1965 *Cinderella*, Ursula in Disney's 1989 *The Little Mermaid*). Whether it was a contractual legal/network/sponsor issue or a case of second thoughts by Barbera, they did not play the roles, and a legal settlement was reached.

George and Jane were ultimately played by George O'Hanlon and Penny Singleton. O'Hanlon, a writer and character actor well known to theatergoers as "Joe McDoakes" in sixty-three comedy shorts, worked with Hanna and Barbera on the 1958 Tom and Jerry cartoon *Vanishing Duck*. Singleton was beloved as Blondie in twenty-eight Columbia Pictures films based on the Chic Young comic strip, with Arthur Lake as Dagwood. O'Hanlon and Singleton joined the ranks of Hanna-Barbera actors who performed their voices for most of their lives, along with Jean Vander

The joyous Janet Waldo began her spectacular animation acting career as Judy Jetson.

ORIGINAL TV SOUNDTRACKS!

the JETSONS

COLPIX RECORDS

STARRING THE VOICES OF   GEORGE O'HANLON · PENNY SINGLETON · JANET WALDO · DAWS BUTLER · MEL BLANC · HOWARD MORRIS · DON MESSICK AND JEAN VANDERPYL

PRODUCED BY
JOSEPH BARBERA
WILLIAM HANNA

DISTRIBUTED BY
SCREEN GEMS, INC.

HI FIDELITY   CP 213

Howard Morris's unforgettable "Eep-Opp-Ork" is among the highlights of the TV soundtrack album.

"I loved doing radio, it's my very favorite kind of acting," said Waldo. "After a while, I noticed that Joe Barbera was always going around the table at script readings to see who could do various extra voices. Jean Vander Pyl [Rosie] was always so great at it. I got to be Mr. Spacely's secretary and several other people. I had no idea this could be a career and decided it was for me."

▲▼▲▼▲▼

The 1962 Colpix album of *The Jetsons* was the last Hanna-Barbera TV soundtrack for the label. The first two episodes, "Rosie the Robot" and "A Date with Jet Screamer," were ideal for audio and Colpix includes elements not possible on *The Flintstones* or *Top Cat* albums—complete dialogue, sound effects, original songs, and background music that work beautifully without narration. Only the theme song is missing. A "lift" of the finished audio from a track and releasing it on a recording might seem simple, but it is not easy to do either legally or at high quality. It took Colpix years to get to this point after being restricted to partial elements due to music rights, contracts, budgets, and so forth.

"Rosie the Robot" opened the series and the album, providing general information about the Jetsons and their world. They live in a three-bedroom apartment, George is a digital index operator, and Jane's age is thirty-three. Spacely barely knows George in this episode and meets his family for the first time (even though he knows Jane's age and mentions it when he meets her, which seems odd). Rosie the Robot maid is introduced in an archetypical sitcom "boss invites himself to dinner" story line. Spacely is incensed at George's extravagance in getting a maid but her delicious dessert changes his mind.

The second episode, "A Date with Jet Screamer," includes two Curtin-Hanna-Barbera songs, "The Swivel" and "Eep Opp Ork," played by some of Hollywood's best musicians in a segment that was directed especially for the series by UPA artist Bobe Cannon. This is the only Colpix Hanna-Barbera album to include original songs, which incurred some cost, even though the theme could not be negotiated. Actor/director Howard Morris also made his animation debut as hyperkinetic pop star Jet Screamer. His entrances are accompanied by a fast musical swirl that builds to a high-pitched stab. The sound effect, called the "Jet Screamer," is considered among Hanna-Barbera's all-time most famous.

"I was so inspired by just watching Howard at work," recalled Waldo. "He could just let himself go, completely, with that 'Baby, baby, baby!' thing! It was a kind of acting that was so new and exciting to me!"

▲▼▲▼▲▼

Hanna-Barbera discovered early that the one-minute show open was crucial, not only to grab viewers but encourage them to return for more fun. The animation and effects were more elaborate and accelerated in theme visuals.

The Jetsons theme sequence opens with a dash through a colorful galaxy toward the Earth, presumably filmed using multiplane animation camera equipment, a very pricey move for H-B. The earth shatters, followed by a cut underneath the Jetson's car, which zooms them away into the skyscape of their optimistic future.

With so much to see and hear, too many lyrics would have stood in the way. The simple lyrics (performed by The Randy Van Horne Singers) introduce the main characters as they begin their futuristic day. In one minute, warmth, comedy gags, cuteness, thrills, and fantasy are communicated, along with the enticement to watch again and again. Van Horne's

group returned to sing the theme. Among the group was Betty Jane "B.J." Baker, a popular Hollywood session soloist. As the singing voice of Jane Jetson, Baker stopped the "Miss Solar System" pageant with "Won't You Come Home, Phil Spacely?" She also belted out "When You're Smiling" as Betty Rubble (with Mel Blanc as Barney), and sang the "Rockenspiel Jingle" as "Happy Housewife" Wilma. Baker was married to Disney composer Buddy Baker (after following Ava Gardner as the second of Mickey Rooney's eight wives) and was the singing voice of Nancy Kwan in 1961's *Flower Drum Song*.

▲▼▲▼▲▼

By its nature, Hanna-Barbera's futuristic prime-time series seemed to invite experimentation in every aspect. In an interview with Jon Burlingame, Hoyt Curtin recalled that Bill Hanna also loved jazz, and gave him a lot of freedom. "I thought jazz fit in everything, and it really does because jazz is joyous," Curtin said. He also told Burlingame that Hanna said, "We'll put the pictures on it. You make it happy."

Curtin went beyond the traditional big band, adding electronic and organ music played in a lighthearted manner. The music cues and most of the sound effects are predominantly humorous and upbeat.

Some of the most iconic sound effects in history were created for *The Jetsons*. Like the eager young animators forging new paths, both young and veteran editors sat with seemingly endless strips of 35mm magnetic film tracks and set new standards in animation sound as they went along.

"Most of the time, we would choose music and the effects based on how we could make each other laugh," said Tony Milch, an editor who went from sound editing on Hanna-Barbera cartoons to feature films like *Elf* and *The Fugitive*. Because the future innovations created for *The Jetsons* did not exist (or hadn't happened yet), Tony and his colleagues had to figure out how they might sound. Tony's assembled tools and materials were simple "found items" which were usually unlikely sources for the sounds that continue to make imaginations soar.

"I made the Jetson library of original-for-the-series sound effects entirely by myself," Milch recalled. "I then placed them in the sound effects library to subsequently be used by myself and my colleagues when cutting sound effects for *The Jetsons*."

The iconic flying bubble car sound effect started with a toy belonging to Tony's child. "You're actually hearing several things at the same time in the sound effect," he said:

I used a squeaker duck that we recorded at different speeds. I went into a studio to record all the sounds I could get out of an air compressor, and things like that. The trick was how I played them back and combined them. I didn't have a mixing board available to me, but the company did have a VSO—a variable speed oscillator—and two quarter-inch tape machines, one in mono and the other a two-track. With a VSO, it was possible to vary the timing of the power from 60 cycles per second, which is normal in the U. S. When applied to an electric motor, the VSO allowed me to vary the speed of the motor and, in turn, vary the speed of the capstan thus slowing or speeding up the audio.

Then I "mixed" the two tracks of one tape machine and re-recorded to the other mono machine. From there, it was like orchestrating musical instruments. You can arrange them, vary them, fast, slow, and so on, to create a variety of sound effects. So, for example, by varying the speed of the two-track machine by means of the VSO while simultaneously varying the output levels, I created the "pass-by" Doppler sounds of the Jetson cars.

▴▾▴▾▴

To add to the merchandise mix, Hanna-Barbera contracted with Golden Records for a Jetsons record album without the original cast, to be produced at a fraction of the cost of the TV music. In recording parlance, when a popular film or stage entity is done without the original cast, the album is called a "studio cast." In pop music this is similar to sound-alike "cover versions" of hits by pop stars or live touring "cover bands." Most times these artists are just as professional and talented as the people they are "covering." For example, the aforementioned Marni Nixon sang brilliantly on Disney's "second cast" album of *Mary Poppins* in the Julie Andrews role—and she was also in the movie itself singing for the animated geese.

Since Colpix was releasing a soundtrack album, it was unlikely that Golden would do an original cast LP, even though both had been done for *The Flintstones*. Much had changed in the record business over the past few years. The market share of children's records was getting smaller and operating costs were always increasing. Even Disneyland Records' output in the early sixties was different in scope than its more lavishly mounted productions of the fifties.

For Golden's *The Jetsons* LP, Arthur Shimkin and musical director Timmens cast Herb Duncan as George and Elroy. Duncan was a veteran of stage and commercials and would go on to voice New York–based cartoons for Hal Seeger and Rankin/Bass. (*Mad Magazine* fans may have heard the flexi-disc of "Gall in the Family Fare" upon which he plays Mike Stivic.) While his Elroy voice is passable, his take on George is quite good. George Jetson's character voice was close to the natural speaking voices of both Duncan and George O'Hanlon.

The premise is an interview with the Jetson family for children on Mars. Writer Fay Winter is credited with Hanna and Barbera for all the material. One might assume that Bill and Joe had less time for this album than for *Songs of the Flintstones* as their workloads were already expanding. The album includes nine songs (and a few notes from the theme song) rendered in Golden's signature early sixties warm jazz sound of musical director Jim Timmens (who would soon work for Joe Barbera's old studio, Terrytoons). Purists may immediately feel distanced in

Golden Records released *The Jetsons* song album featuring New York actors from TV, commercials, and the stage. [blue cover]

The alternate front cover for Golden's Jetsons LP. [red cover]

Huckleberry Hound and the Ghost Ship was the first of two original album productions starring the classic Hanna-Barbera "universe," written and performed by Daws Butler and Don Messick with Doug Young.

that respect, but there was no point in Golden trying to emulate a full orchestra. Instead, it's as if this small cast has gathered at a smart Manhattan supper club to entertain sophisticated *Jetsons* devotees in an original musical revue set to a small combo. The characters are played in a casual, down-to-earth manner that would be right at home in a small theater by actors between busy gigs.

If "Push Button Blues" had been sung by a young Carol Burnett on TV during her breakout on *The Garry Moore Show*, it might have been hailed as a comedy triumph instead of just a cute little song on the Jetsons Golden LP. Rose Marie Jun, one of the leading New York session singers, sings for Jane and Judy. Because of her perfect pitch and phrasing, Jun was also a popular choice for Broadway songwriters to sing demos for some of the greatest shows of all

time. (Please keep in mind that Penny Singleton is also not Jane's singing voice on the TV show either, it is B. J. Baker.)

There is an earnest quality that makes the Golden version one of the most congenial of the cover versions. When competent actors, writers, and directors do the best they possibly can with very limited budgets, resources, and patchy information, it shows respect for the material with an earnest attempt to capture the spirit of the series. Two different cover designs graced this LP. Golden released six songs on a 45 rpm EP and two songs each on two Little Golden Records.

▲▼▲▼▲▼

Quick Draw McGraw and the Treasure of Sarah's Mattress was the second album to star characters from various Hanna-Barbera cartoons in a single story.

The Jetsons was the final Hanna-Barbera TV soundtrack for the label. But also in 1962, Colpix released two albums that were "firsts." To many people, they are also "two of the finest." *Huckleberry Hound and the Ghost Ship* and *Quick Draw McGraw and the Treasure of Sarah's Mattress* were the first audio recordings of original stories combining Hanna-Barbera characters. In this case, they originated from *The Huckleberry Hound Show*, *The Yogi Bear Show*, and *The Quick Draw McGraw Show*.

The characters had appeared together in comics, puzzles, and storybooks, but of course, their original voices were not heard. Several appeared together in the syndicated *Yogi Bear's Birthday* TV special, also in 1962, but not in the same large number. It was not until 1972 that they would have a "reunion" in *Yogi's Ark Lark* on the *ABC Saturday Superstar Movie*,

the pilot film that sold the 1973 series *Yogi's Gang*. However, the 1962 Colpix recordings were a bit truer to the early personalities of the characters.

These albums were personal favorites of Daws Butler. He and Don Messick wrote the scripts for both records in addition to performing voices. An avid writer since his youth, Butler loved wordplay and the chemistry of actors capable of good ad-libs. These albums were a twice-in-a-lifetime for Butler, Messick, and Doug Young. These would be the only two non-soundtrack record albums Doug Young recorded for Hanna-Barbera. He was a key actor for the studio, versatile enough to sustain a long career, but it was necessary for him to leave the California area.

▲▼▲▼▲

Each recording is done in the manner of a classic radio adventure blended with Hanna-Barbera cartoon comedy. *Huckleberry Hound and the Ghost Ship* finds Huck, Yogi, Boo-Boo, Hokey Wolf, Ding-a-Ling, Mr. Jinks, Pixie and Dixie out to sea aboard the *Black Swan*. After Mr. Jinks disappears, his pals are moved to sing a back-handed tribute to their pal ("He wasn't half-bad, only ninety percent.").

"I can still sing that 'Poor Jinksy' song!" said Daws's son Chas, launching into an impromptu chorus. "They were a really good trio of actors working together, no doubt about it. Those are the only albums that have all three of them together. He and Don wrote those themselves. And they're written so well."

In addition to the a capella song, Butler and Messick add an amusing verse in the spirit of Edward Lear and Lewis Carroll ("Clean sheets! Clean sheets!"). It's surely no accident that Yogi says, "Mysteriouser and mysteriouser!" The H-B stars are joined by supporting characters that include some of Butler's other familiar voices, even one he seldom used for records or Hanna-Barbera. Inspired by character actor Charles Butterworth the voice is best known as Captain Crunch, as well as assorted Fractured Fairy Tales authority figures for Jay Ward. Butler, Messick, and Young play a total of thirteen roles.

"*Huckleberry Hound and the Ghost Ship* is probably my favorite Hanna-Barbera character record," said actor/writer Joe Bevilacqua, who was mentored by Butler in voice acting. "Daws and Don were the heart and soul of these characters. The story is everything that Daws loved to write about—comedy, adventure, mystery—and to have his best friends beside him is a treasure we will have forever."

Quick Draw McGraw and the Treasure of Sarah's Mattress is a mystery set at Doggie Daddy and Augie Doggie's recently acquired Tarantula Ranch. After rejecting job applicants Snagglepuss ("I beg to differ. I'm a differ-beggar!") and Chief Crazy Coyote, Quick Draw is hired as foreman. Two husband (and treasure)–hunting ladies, voiced by Butler and Messick, check in around the same time strange, scary noises have been heard in the shadows. Snooper and Blabber are brought in to investigate, though Quick Draw insists he is the hero around there.

Augie Doggie, Doggie Daddy, Snagglepuss, Baba Looey, Super Snooper, Blabber Mouse, and the others discover what Scooby-Doo and Mystery Incorporated would learn hundreds of times—that the ghosts are not genuine but actually deceptions to scare people away from a treasure hidden by one Sarah Bellum in her mattress. But then, the real treasure is really on the record.

▲▼▲▼▲▼

Following in *Top Cat*'s tracks, *The Jetsons* series moved to Saturday morning television, where Hanna-Barbera's future seemed to be beckoning. Prime time was not a dead issue by any means, however. *The Flintstones* was still a hit on Friday nights. Experience taught Joe Barbera that there had to be more shows in the immediate future to keep the studio going and hopefully growing. The next move was to be even more ambitious and costly. Another H-B landmark, this project would set the standard for epic spectaculars for generations.

Chapter 8

JONNY QUEST AND ANN-MARGROCK

~~~~~~

The opening titles had pterodactyls and machine guns and mummies and robot spiders and this really cool music, and the first time I saw that I just about exploded.
—BRAD BIRD, DIRECTOR OF *THE INCREDIBLES* FILMS AND *MISSION: IMPOSSIBLE—GHOST PROTOCOL*

To continue operating and expanding, Hanna-Barbera needed to create new characters and series that built on successes and moved into new areas. This meant new approaches to what they did well and branching into new areas, like live-action.

One of Hanna-Barbera's first live-action films was *The Story of Dr. Lister*, produced for the Warner-Lambert Company. A twenty-eight-minute educational film telling the story of Dr. Joseph Lister (Richard Ney of MGM's *Mrs. Miniver*) and the development of antiseptic medicines and the solution named for him: Listerine (originally a topical antiseptic). The twenty-five-minute film was released to theaters and includes breaks for commercial TV broadcasts. Its veteran Hollywood cast includes David Frankham, Lloyd Bochner, John Archer, Wanda Hendrix, Sean McClory, and John Hoyt. *The Story of Dr. Lister* has slick production values resembling prime-time dramas of its era. The stodgy, point-driven script might be a minus for fun seekers, but a plus for the corporate sponsors.

Hanna-Barbera would produce many live-action and animated industrial and educational films from this point, under the supervision of *Flintstones* story editor Arthur Pierson, a former rehearsal director for Cecil B. DeMille and Ernst Lubitsch.

▲▼▲▼▲▼

The Flintstone family added new pages to their history in 1963 when Wilma and Fred became the first couple in the history of American animation to become expectant parents. Wilma sported a maternity outfit and there was no talk of storks. Naturally, it was designed to keep the show fresh and sell merchandise. Hanna-Barbera rarely put on airs when it came to the realities of why animation was developed, sold, and sustained. Merchandise was a major part of why a property arrived, departed, or was given prominence over another. Actually, in the early planning stages of *The Flintstones*, Fred and Wilma already had a son. Some of the books and comics reflect this, including the "Cave Kids" books with a little boy resembling the Ubble-Ubble character from *Ruff and Reddy*. In the TV series, Wilma was originally going to give birth to a son. "We were all set to introduce a baby boy when someone at the Ideal Toy Company told us that little girl dolls sell more than boy dolls," Barbera recalled. Upon hearing Ideal's comment, Barbera unflinchingly declared the Flintstone baby a female.

Though the animated blessed event could not match the headline-making birth of Little Ricky on *I Love Lucy*, few TV births had been so heavily publicized. Alan Reed, Jean Vander Pyl, Mel Blanc, and Bea Benederet recorded a series of radio spots as part of a nationwide contest campaign to guess the weight and gender of the wee bairn that led up to the airdate of the episode ("The Dress Rehearsal," aka "The Blessed Event"). (A similar contest was launched when Hoppy the Hopperoo debuted in 1964.)

There have been conflicting accounts as to whether Jean Vander Pyl was expecting or had given birth just before recording Pebbles first scene for the broadcast in February 1963. Her three children were older. Her fourth, Roger DeWitt Jr. (voice of Peter in 1982's *Heidi's Song*) was born in October 1963, so she would have been expecting in February. What is certain are the tears she and Reed shed during the scene and her desire to voice Pebbles. She recalled the script meeting in the *Asbury Park Press*: "[Barbera] said, 'Now, who's going to do the baby here?' The *minute* those words were out of his mouth, I said, 'I want to do the baby! She's Wilma's baby and she should sound like Wilma!'"

All four *Flintstones* actors could, on occasion, seamlessly step outside the comic tone of the series. In the episode that introduces "Little Bamm-Bamm," Mel Blanc and Bea Benederet's performances as Barney and Betty are realistic and touching. Hurt by Fred's insensitive bluntness about their not having their own child, they share a few private moments, consoling each other and hoping things will change. This is one of several sequences that created the believability of Hanna-Barbera's new animated sitcom form. The connection to the weekly home audience was something that had not been accomplished in previous TV cartoons and was impossible in the sporadic scheduling of animated features and shorts. Suddenly viewers could become attached to a cartoon TV family just as they had loved the Ricardos and the Petries while visiting them in a hand-drawn world where odd things could happen.

Pebbles dolls flew off the shelves, along with other related products. Even Golden Records brought the genuine Fred to their label again to celebrate—not a sound-alike. On a lovely 1963 Little Golden Record, *Lullaby of Pebbles* (aka *Pebbles' Lullaby*), Alan Reed does a one-man show in miniature as Fred struggles to feed, change, and serenade Pebbles while Wilma is away. Reed even provides baby cries! The single record was also issued on an EP with selections from 1961's *Songs of the Flintstones* LP.

Writer Mark Evanier recalled visiting the May Company department store in Los Angeles as a child when the once-mighty retail chain was promoting the new Pebbles dolls by inviting shoppers to visit the "electronic Fred Flintstone in person":

It was a very good likeness about five feet high. His mouth opened and closed, not particularly in sync with a constantly repeating voice recording—Fred welcoming us to the May Company and wishing us Happy Easter. His right arm went up and down. My mother took a photo of me next to him but, damn it, the pictures didn't come out. A day or two later, they trucked the Robot Fred over to the local ABC studios and I saw it "perform" on the morning cartoon show hosted by Chucko the Birthday Clown. The voice didn't work and

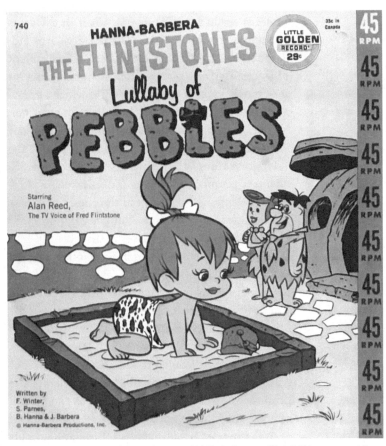

Alan Reed recorded a warm, lighthearted tune in which Fred takes care of little Pebbles, even providing the baby's cries.

The May Company department stores invited shoppers to meet an electronic Fred Flintstone during a promotion of Pebbles dolls.

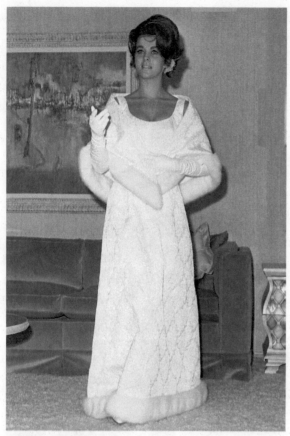

Ann-Margret models the Jean Louis gown she wore to the Presidential Inaugural Ball not long after her appearance as Ann-Margrock on *The Flintstones*. *Los Angeles Times* Photographic Collection, Department of Special Collections, UCLA. (CC-BY-4.0.)

stones is easily a memorable highlight in the association of Columbia, Screen Gems TV, George Sidney, and Hanna-Barbera. Sidney, still a copresident of Hanna-Barbera, directed Ann-Margret in the hit 1963 movie version of *Bye Bye Birdie*, which became a showcase for the multitalented young performer. Viewers can spot Hanna-Barbera plush toys in various scenes of *Bye Bye Birdie*. During the song, "The Telephone Hour," the Colpix *Yogi Bear* soundtrack album is propped up in a young lady's room. Animated telephone wires melt at the end of the song. When Dick Van Dyke sings "Put On a Happy Face," he draws animated happy faces in the air.

Ann-Margret participated in *The Flintstones* voice session with the cast, so Jean Vander Pyl was able to create the Pebbles voice so "Ann-Margrock" could fuss over her in person. Two original songs were fully orchestrated for the episode, "The Littlest Lamb" and "I Ain't Gonna Be a Fool No More." "Ann-Margrock Presents" was scheduled to air later in the fall, but ABC requested that Hanna-Barbera accelerate the production so it could be promoted as the season opener. The studio, as it would so often, complied with the request, resulting in an episode that holds together quite well and still receives press attention and positions on various "best of" lists.

▲▼▲▼▲▼

the moving arm kept stopping and starting, and Chucko (who was a pretty funny guy) kept warning Fred that if he didn't talk, ABC would cancel his prime-time show. I assume that robot is long since gone but I'd give about a year's pay to have it in my living room.

▲▼▲▼▲▼

One of the story opportunities that Pebbles provided for *The Flintstones* was adding heart to the popular Hollywood trope of the "big star that arrives in town and loves the fans but wants to relax from the glamorous craziness and, by the way, is *so* nice in real life." The guest appearance of Ann-Margret on *The Flint-*

To keep Hanna-Barbera Productions alive and thriving, the studio had to find ways to make its animation processes work effectively in a wider range of storytelling forms and genres. Development began on their first half-hour adventure series in 1961. As kids, both Bill Hanna and Joe Barbera thrilled to action-packed adventure novels, comics, movies, serials, and radio programs of the '30s.

Children's radio programs of the early twentieth century offered comedies, westerns, and fairy tales, but the predominant genre was action-packed adventures set in exotic locations. Several would, in part, provide the groundwork for major Hanna-Barbera cartoons: *I Love a Mystery* for *Scooby-Doo, Where Are*

You? and *Jack Armstrong* for *Jonny Quest*. To tackle a project with a very different approach than situation comedy and "funny animals," Hanna-Barbera hired comic book artist Doug Wildey to adapt *Jack Armstrong* for animation. When the *Jack Armstrong* rights proved unavailable, Wildey developed the principal characters and distinctive look for *Jonny Quest*. Bandit was added (though Wildey reportedly resisted) to provide humor and youthful appeal. As mentioned earlier, Barbera was known to be fond of adding a lovable canine into the concepts of either new or existing cartoons.

A *Jonny Quest* orchestration could require over twenty musicians, almost double the usual for which Curtin usually composed unless it was a big production number. Special mention should also be given to arrangers and orchestrators like Jack Stern, who often worked with Curtin on his H-B scores. The theme from *Jonny Quest* is extremely (and deliberately) difficult to play, especially for the trombone. Curtin wrote the *Jonny Quest* theme in a specific manner to challenge his trombone players, who had been complaining about not having interesting things to play. "I wrote that *Jonny Quest* theme in a killer key," he told Jon Burlingame. "And I knew the hardest place to play is all of the unknown, odd positions [on the slide trombone]. It was in E flat minor, just murder, and they killed themselves because nobody wanted to make a mistake. I just sat in the control booth watching these guys, their blood pressure going up. I just about fell down laughing!"

Tim Matheson was the original voice of Jonny Quest, with Mike Road as Roger "Race" Bannon and Danny Bravo as Hadji. John Stephenson was heard as Dr. Benton for several episodes before Don Messick was recast in the role. Joe Barbera's "ear" for voices indicated that Stephenson was too similar in tonal quality to Mike Road. (Stephenson certainly was at no loss for more work at Hanna-Barbera as the voice of Fred Flintstone's boss, Mr. Slate, and countless other characters.)

"When Joe Barbera cast the voices in a cartoon, it was like creating a musical ensemble," said renowned

Seen here on NBC's *The Virginian*, Tim Matheson's Hanna-Barbera voices include Jonny Quest, Young Samson, and *Space Ghost's* Jace.

artist and historian Stacia Martin. "Wilma Flintstone is an alto, Fred is the bass, Betty is a soprano and Barney is a baritone. On *The Jetsons*, George is kind of a tenor, while Jane is an alto, Judy is a soprano, with Elroy a squeaky sort of baritone. You don't have a bass until Mr. Spacely shows up."

There is a reason for the abrupt "button" edit at the end of the theme as heard in the show (when Mike Road says, "*Jonny Quest!* Brought to you by . . ."). The entire piece of music ran 110 seconds to accompany the spectacular pitch film that Barbera used to sell the series to ABC and its sponsors. The tail end of the original composition was actually heard over the title card with the iconic three-note blast that was parodied by composer Michael Giacchino in the Pixar short film, *Jack-Jack Attack*.

▲▾▲▾▲▾

"The music to me is most important," said Doug Wildey in an interview. "It can either make a scene or kill it. What I wanted for the *Jonny Quest* theme music was to do the same job that other shows' music had done—on *Maverick*, *77 Sunset Strip*, and on and on, you could remember the music. What I wanted was heavy drums, jazz drums. Hoyt Curtin was the musical director and did a fine job."

The same must be said about Ted Nichols, who took up the main Hanna-Barbera baton in 1964. Between July and November of that year, both he and Hoyt Curtin were composing and recording music for *Jonny Quest*. Nichols, a former Disneyland Dapper Dan park performer, was composer for documentaries and religious films as well as choir director for the same church Bill Hanna attended. The two were introduced and Nichols accepted Hanna's invitation to write cues for *Jonny Quest*. Soon the H-B sound editors were requesting more. "The Quest theme was already written, so I used its motifs to compose the rest of the cues," said Nichols to Jon Burlingame. "That led to Bill and Joe asking me to become their musical director the following spring, and from there until 1972 . . . coming from a jazz and big band background, I felt right at home." Nichols did not recall ever meeting Curtin. During the music preparations for *Jonny Quest*, they worked on alternate recording sessions with most of the same musicians.

In the essay, "The Mystery of the Music Men," accompanying the long-overdue 2016 *Jonny Quest* soundtrack album, Jon Burlingame deciphers the cryptic circumstances surrounding Hoyt Curtin's "sabbatical":

Why Curtin left is unclear. He never discussed it publicly, although he did boast in the pages of *Variety* (in November 1964, about the time he left) about the financial success of his "other" career in music for advertising. And he did acknowledge in our interview that, during the early years of Hanna-Barbera, the corporate policy was to only credit Hanna and Barbera as composers, thus denying Curtin (and, most of his time there, Nichols) "cue sheet" credit which would have entitled them to royalties for their

work. By the time Curtin returned to Hanna-Barbera in 1972, the policy apparently changed, and today Curtin is co-credited (with Hanna and Barbera) with many of the classic themes that he composed, including *The Flintstones*, *The Jetsons*, and *Jonny Quest*.

Ted Nichols's fondly remembered contributions to the dynamic scoring of *Jonny Quest* and the Hanna-Barbera sound are evidenced by his subsequent work on almost every Hanna-Barbera background score of the late sixties. He was perfectly adept at comedy and the "big" brassy studio house sound, but his skill in action-adventure cues was especially fortuitous for Hanna-Barbera during this period and would add immeasurably to *Space Ghost*, *The Herculoids*, *Frankenstein, Jr.*, *Shazzan*, and many others.

▲▼▲▼▲▼

Hoyt Curtin and Ted Nichols are credited as musical directors for several reasons, among them the fact that the studio's rapid pace and workload required contracting additional composers, orchestrators, and arrangers. This practice is still quite common in the industry and it keeps freelancers working and can assist young composers on their path. *Jonny Quest* benefited from at least a third known composer, Jack de Mello.

"Dad met Bill Hanna in Hawaii and they struck up a friendship," recalled his son, Jon. "Bill told Dad that they needed music. He invited Dad to write some for them when he was in Hollywood."

Like Curtin and Nichols, de Mello's background was the big band sound, but he specialized in music of the South Sea islands. He wrote cues for *The Flintstones*, *The Jetsons*, *Jonny Quest*, and the *Magilla Gorilla* and *Peter Potamus* shows. It was purely an uncredited, work-for-hire deal. According to Jon, creating the music freelance without credit was not a big deal to Jack. He loved what he did, and wrote very fast (even during conversations). "When we would watch something like *Ricochet Rabbit*, I would point to the screen and say, 'That is your music playing now, isn't it, Dad?' and he would nod."

Clues to some de Mello H-B cues can be theorized by listening to a regionally released album he produced called *The Adventures of Coconut Willie and Pukahead*. The LP contains six tales of Polynesian lore set to cues also heard in Hanna-Barbera cartoons starting in 1964 with the *Magilla* and *Potamus* series.

▲▼▲▼▲▼

None of the *Coconut* cues are heard on *Magilla Gorilla and His Pals*, the final Hanna-Barbera LP album released by Golden Records. Instead, like Golden's *Songs of the Flintstones*, the music under the vocals also doubled as cartoon cue music. This is the first commercial recording to offer a Hanna-Barbera theme song from the TV soundtrack. This album makes full use of the tune, using it three times, including a vocal by Magilla himself (Allan Melvin).

The format is similar to *Songs of the Flintstones* in that each of the characters chats informally, though Magilla is aware of the listeners while the Flintstones and Rubbles were not. Magilla introduces the stars of the two companion cartoons in his show: Ricochet Rabbit with Droop-A-Long (Don Messick and Mel Blanc) from their comical western adventures; then Punkin' Puss with Mush Mouse (Allan Melvin and Howard Morris), a hillbilly Tom and Jerry. All five sing about themselves and tell the kind of jokes that might have appeared in one of those "101 Funniest Kids Jokes" books.[1] On side two of the record, each sings their partner's song in the third person with more jokes, followed by a little party for them all.

Magilla Gorilla and His Pals has every indication of being an in-house Hanna-Barbera production from start to finish. The format was almost identical to what would be the format on Hanna-Barbera's forthcoming "Cartoon Series" records, right down to tracks that separate and stop in one track, then resume in the next with a slight snippet still audible from the previous track. Hanna and Barbera, once again informally called "Bill" and "Joe," are given

writing credit. No musical director is mentioned, so it could have been Curtin, Nichols, de Mello, or another freelancer.

Hanna-Barbera's last Little Golden Record, *The Presidential Campaign Songs of Yogi Bear & Magilla Gorilla*, showed how the character hierarchy at the studio had changed. Huckleberry Hound was no longer a candidate. The single contains a song for each candidate, performed by a male studio chorus and Jim Timmens orchestra. The Magilla vs. Yogi campaign was merchandised on other items in 1964, including slides for Kenner's Give-A-Show Projector.

▲▼▲▼▲▼

The end titles of *The Magilla Gorilla Show* credit "Magilla for Sale" to Nelson Brock. This is likely to be advertising copy and jingle writer N. B. Winkless Jr. of the Leo Burnett Company (the agency for Kellogg's). On-screen credits being subject to a myriad of circumstances, coupled with the complex issues of music rights and ownership, the theme song was later credited to Hanna, Barbera, and Curtin. There are no music credits on *The Peter Potamus Show*. He and his companion cartoons seemed in the shadow of Magilla and pals. There were no Breezly and Sneezly records about being a polar bear and a seal foraging through an Arctic military base; no discs featuring goofy medieval guards Yippee, Yappee, and Yahooey; and not a single song from the time-traveling star, Peter Potamus and his simian sidekick, So-So.

The *Magilla Gorilla* and *Peter Potamus* shows were launched at the same time with Ideal Toys as a backer. But to the public, Magilla seemed to have the edge on publicity and presence. *Here Comes a Star* made it very clear that Magilla was the luminary referred to in the title. Hosted by *You Bet Your Life* announcer George Fenneman, this twenty-five-minute promotional film was Hanna-Barbera's humble but earnest answer to Walt Disney's 1941 scripted "behind-the-scenes" docu-comedy, *The Reluctant Dragon*.

Here Comes a Star also features the recently constructed Hanna-Barbera building. It still stands at

Protected by the Los Angeles Conservancy, the Hanna-Barbera building continues to gleam in the California sun at 3400 North Cahuenga Boulevard.

3400 Cahuenga Boulevard in North Hollywood and is protected as a historical landmark by the Los Angeles Conservancy. Hanna in particular spoke fondly of this building in his biography, *A Cast of Friends*. Supervising the construction must have brought back memories of Hanna and his father working together when building the Pantages Theater. Seeing its completion was proof of the success of the entire staff in a highly tangible form. The duo would joke about switching off the lights illuminating each other's name on the "Hanna-Barbera" sign at the top of the building at night so only his own would be seen. (They claimed the order of names was originally determined by a coin toss.)

Portions of *Here Comes a Star* may have been staged, but the studio's state of bustling activity was actually happening. The same year that Magilla Gorilla and Peter Potamus made their bow on television, Hanna-Barbera was readying its first feature-length animation for the big screen.

Chapter 9

MOVIES, GUEST STARS, AND ROCK 'N' ROLL

~~~~~~

It, uh, gives me great pleasure to award this prize to one of the nicest, warmest, most young-at-heart couples I ever knowed.

—JAMES "JIMMY DARROCK" DARREN,
THE FLINTSTONES EPISODE "SURFIN' FRED"

To keep the staff working and avoid layoffs between each animated series, the studio maintained a flow of ongoing assignments like one-shot films, merchandise, specials, and features.

Before Columbia released Hanna-Barbera's first theatrical feature, *Hey There, It's Yogi Bear* on July 3, 1964, Hanna-Barbera began generating publicity and merchandise internally and in partnership with various companies. It had proven effective, especially with family films, to release some merchandise, books, and comics several months ahead of the release date. Kids often enjoyed knowing the entire story and looked forward to seeing it unfold on the big screen.

Yogi's "old sponsor buddy," Kellogg's, offered a seven-inch long-playing music and story record by mail order. *Music and Story from Hey There, It's Yogi Bear* would be the first of many Kellogg's direct mail record offers featuring Hanna-Barbera and other makers of kid-friendly entertainment. It was mailed in a square manila envelope proclaiming its contents with a picture of Yogi. The thrill of receiving such a package cannot be measured in mere cornflakes. The record opens with a special arrangement of the title song. Yogi (Daws Butler) greets listeners directly and introduces Cindy Bear (Nancy Wible, filling in for film voice Julie Bennett), Boo-Boo, and Ranger Smith (Don Messick). With Marty Paich's score in the background, the effect is that of a short radio promo, in which most of the ending is teased.

The lush look of the finished feature, particularly the early sequences, was another result of the infusion of talent from theatrical studios after the short cartoon business all but dried up and Disney met with disappointing box-office results for the premiere of 1959's *Sleeping Beauty*. Among these top artists were

Kellogg's Cereals offered this story record of Yogi's first movie by mail.

Willie Ito, Jerry Eisenberg, Iwao Takamoto, Charles Nichols, Dan Gordon, Dick Bickenbach, Ron Dias, Harry Holt, George Kreisl, Grant Simmons, Ed Aardal, Dick Kelsey, and an uncredited Friz Freleng.

▴▾▴▾▾

Like *Bye Bye Birdie*, the musical soundtrack of *Hey There, It's Yogi Bear* reflects the Columbia empire of the 1960s. Released on Colpix Records, it features one of their most popular recording stars. When Yogi croons the romantic ballad, "Ven-E, Ven-O, Ven-A," his voice is that of James Darren, star of Columbia's *Gidget* movies (and later, of TV's *The Time Tunnel*). As a gag, gondolier Boo-Boo says, "Gee Yogi, you sound just like James Darren." On the other side of the US, Columbia/Screen Gems' music department in New York was coming up with hit songs for their record label, films, and TV series. One of the young composers toiling away in the cubicles alongside Carole King and Neil Diamond was David Gates, who wrote the "Hey There It's Yogi Bear" song long before he found fame with the pop group Bread ("Baby I'm-a Want You," "Make It with You").

The lead speaking voices did not sing the songs, however, thus the soundtrack album does not feature Butler, Bennett, or Messick. The use of "ghost singers" was common in live-action; in animation, it is still frequent—and sometimes publicized—in animated features such as *Aladdin* (Brad Kane and Lea Salonga for Scott Weinger and Linda Larkin); *Pocahontas* (Judy Kuhn for Irene Bedard) and *Mulan* (Lea Salonga for Ming Na Wen and Marni Nixon for June Foray). Off-screen singing is a technique dating back to the early days of sound film. Trained, proven singers could sight-read sheet music in seconds and lay down vocal tracks in perfect pitch. It not only saves time and money, but when done well it can enhance a film, score, and an actor's presentation the way expert lighting, photographic effects, second units, stunts, dialogue looping, and editing can, all of which are a filmmaking tool rather than an on-set reality.

"The decision depends on the vision of the filmmakers," said Jackie Ward, who sang "Like I Like You" for Cindy Bear and dubbed Natalie Wood's singing in the film *Inside Daisy Clover*. "They want every aspect to serve the role and the film. If they feel the singing does not do that, they bring in a studio singer." The "ghosts" also "fill in" certain notes and help create "guide tracks" for non-singers. *The King and I* star Deborah Kerr realized and celebrated the fact that Marni Nixon's singing was an extension of her performance. Kerr was magnanimous enough to insist Nixon get proper recognition. The two performers worked together on the songs, and on the film set, in hopes of changing the perception of musical film acting.

The "ghost" of Captain Von Trapp sings for Yogi Bear in his movie. It's Bill Lee, the "male Marni Nixon" who sang for movie leads such as John Kerr in *South Pacific*, Tom Drake in *Words and Music*, and most famously, Christopher Plummer in *The Sound of Music*. Boo-Boo's singing voice, Ernest Newton, is also the voice of Pierre, one of the Audio-Animatronic birds that host The Enchanted Tiki Room in the Disney parks.

▲▼▲▼▲▼

In addition to the usual commercial spots for "Hey There, It's Yogi Bear" sent to radio stations, Columbia also provided LP promo discs with public service announcements. Called *Yogi Bear Speaks for Summer Safety*, it featured Daws Butler offering helpful tips, which by coincidence kept Yogi top of mind during the season of his film's release. The record used the same label art as Kellogg's seven-inch story record.

Yogi's singing voice for "Ven-E, Ven-O, Ven-A" was James Darren, seen here with fellow Colpix artist Shelley Fabares ("Johnny Angel") on *The Donna Reed Show*.

Hey There, It's Yogi Bear allowed Hanna-Barbera to launch its first "book" musical score for a film, using songs to advance and complement the story and as leitmotifs to suggest characters and recall emotions within the underscore. Cindy Bear's "Like I Like You" is an upbeat example of the "I Want" song, a musical theater device in which the main character, usually female, declares her aspiration near the beginning of the show. Once again blending experience with youthful enthusiasm, Hanna-Barbera hired Oscar-winning songwriter Ray Gilbert to work with newcomer Doug Goodwin. The young songwriter was working as a music copyist when he sought the opportunity through his friend, Friz Freleng. "Bill and Joe called Friz in . . . to help them in putting the first feature together *Hey There, It's Yogi Bear*, and *The Man Called Flintstone*," he recalled in a DVD documentary interview. "I told Friz that I would like to present a song to Bill and Joe, to maybe write the songs for the feature and Friz said, 'Sure! Do it!'"

One of the songs was almost the title of the film: "Whistle Your Way Back Home," sung in the second half of the film by Yogi, Boo-Boo, and Cindy, then reprised for the final fade-out. In another scene, a vocal group identified only as "Jonah and the Wailers" provided one of the most memorable sequences with both their performance and the animated staging of "St. Louie."

The expansive arrangements are the work of Marty Paich, considered one of the best in the business. Paich arranged and conducted for such stars as Frank Sinatra, Barbra Streisand, Sarah Vaughn, Linda Ronstadt, and Sammy Davis Jr. He would return to Hanna-Barbera soon for *Alice in Wonderland*, *The Man Called Flintstone*, and other projects. Colpix Records producer Jack Lewis, who had also produced the soundtracks for *Lawrence of Arabia* and *Dr. Strangelove* for the label, was renowned for his experience in jazz; he worked with greats like Duke Ellington, Nina Simone, and Zoot Sims.

Colpix was aware of how one of its major competitors, Disneyland Records, marketed its soundtracks and scores. The *Yogi* soundtrack jacket text included the words "All the Songs from the Motion Picture" on the album. This was a phrase almost exclusive to the Disneyland label. Columbia made sure the music from the Yogi feature score was given as much exposure as possible on vinyl. Colpix released a single with peppy instrumentals from the film by Billy Costa of "Yogi's March" (from the background score) and "Whistle Your Way Back Home." Golden Records' contribution was 2 *Songs from Bill Hanna and Joe Barbera's "Hey There, It's Yogi Bear" and Many Other Songs of Yogi, Huck, and Quick Draw*. It was a compilation of previously released Hanna-Barbera character tunes, plus the "Hey There" title song and "Ash Can Parade," and a few that had not yet been included on LP like "Snuffles" and "Huck, Yogi & Quick Draw Safety Song." Kapp Records included "Ash Can Parade" in an album called *Marching Along Together* by the Do-Re-Mi Children's Chorus, a popular New York vocal group

assembled by Richard Wolfe with a distinctive sound emphasizing harmonica, accordion, and children with brassy, stage-like delivery.

▵▾▵▾▵▾

Sixties-era television programs set in the present day were either showcasing or spoofing the rise of rock-and-roll music. The "modern stone age" was as ready to rock as the futuristic world of *The Jetsons*, within the comfy confines of early sixties TV. *The Flintstones'* prehistoric premise assured that none of its music could truly be out of date. Stone-age "little bird" record players and jukeboxes were just as likely to play rock and roll as classical. Hanna-Barbera often created composites for musical styles and pop stars. Before The Beatles, some pop music characters had elements of Elvis Presley. Dance crazes invoked the song styles of Chubby Checker.

Columbia's "Gidget" movies and the Annette Funicello/Frankie Avalon "Beach Party" movie craze were among the inspirations for the Colpix single *Makin' with the Magilla* by singing star Little Eva ("Locomotion"). Arranged by Carole King and produced by Gerry Goffin, it was written by Ed Justin, Jack Keller, and Tony Powers, and it was played on the soundtrack of a cartoon with the same title. A costumed Magilla danced with a model on the single's picture sleeve photo. Diagrams on the back cover explained how to do this "new dance," created by the Fred Astaire Dance Studios franchise.

▵▾▵▾▵▾

The world of Hollywood was the subject of an original 1965 album by Hoyt Curtin featuring the musicians and singers he worked with on Hanna-Barbera music with arrangements by Jack Stern. *Hollywood Directory: Songs about Hollywood* is an eclectic blend of instrumentals and vocals. Some were released before, others were originally music cues, and one became a theme song. They cover a variety of styles (though rooted in jazz), one reason being that they were cre-

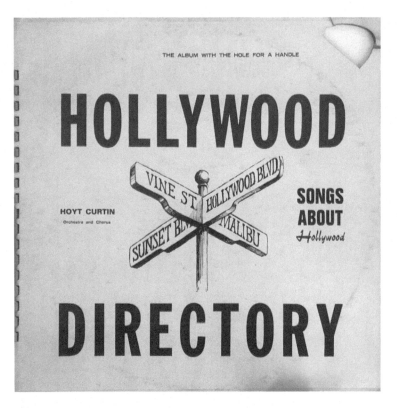

Hoyt Curtin released this album of instrumentals and vocals featuring Hollywood's finest session artists with some tracks connected to Hanna-Barbera cartoons.

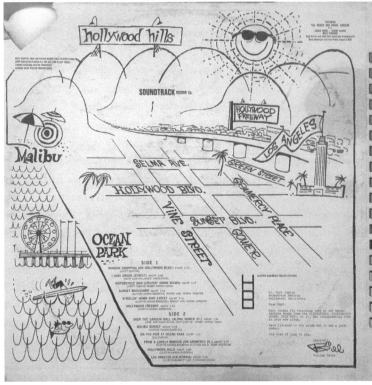

Daws Butler managed to spoof both Lorne Greene's "Ringo" and The Beatles' drummer in one novelty single.

ated and recorded at different times. There is an air of playful satire to the album, beginning with the jacket, proclaiming it as "The only record album with a handle." To make it resemble a directory, a comb binding is threaded into the jacket spine. Hand-drawn maps and oddball song titles add to the whimsy.

Curtin's "I Love Green (Street)," fondly remembered by its soloist, Jackie Ward (the singing voice of Cindy Bear), is a straight-faced spoof of bluesy chanteuse songs, in which the lady isn't too upset because she finds another love, which makes everything seem green—and she loves green. Bobby Adano sings of a supposed tough guy who still has to "stand in line and ask permission just to take a look at his transmission." Adano also croons Vegas nightclub-style to Curtin's jazz version of the nursery rhyme, "Over the Garden Wall," adding "Along Gower Street." Two

instrumentals, "Sunset Boulevard" and "Malibu Sunset," suggest the Henry Mancini sound.

Another two songs are the full-length cues with Top Cat origins: "From a Lonely Window" and the instantly recognizable "Strolling Down Vine," which the H-B editors used for Nurse LaRue in the episode, "Top Cat Falls in Love." Two tracks date back to the early Flintstone days on what is perhaps the first record released by Hanna-Barbera, two novelty instrumentals by "Fred Flintstone and His Orchestra." The single appeared on "B-H Records" (Barbera-Hanna) with a distinctly stone-aged look to the label and Hanna-Barbera art on the picture sleeve.

Neither instrumental has the typical Hanna-Barbera sound. Rather, they have the kooky weirdness of bandleader Raymond Scott's most famous works. "Quarry Stone Rock" is a tribute to the first half of Scott's "Powerhouse." Each is laden with the studio's sound effects.

Hollywood Directory had the potential of being a "turntable hit" in AM radio terms. Not so much a charting song, it could have been a flexible (and potentially profitable) record to play as a lead-in to news breaks because most of the tracks can fade easily at any time. Two previously released as "Fred Flintstone and His Orchestra" were retitled. "Quarry Stone Rock" was changed to "Hollywood Freeway" (the busy thoroughfare also known as the "101" behind the H-B studio). "A Night in Bedrock Forest" became "Hollywood Hills." Either way, the titles fit the tracks.

Hollywood Directory's "finale" is "Los Angeles," a paean to the city and its sites sung to the schmoozy lounge hilt by guitarist Billy Strange. The arrangement, resembling "Meet the Flintstones," has all the exuberance of Hanna-Barbera's brassiest, splashiest themes and production numbers.

Hollywood Directory was released independently on a label called Soundtrack Records, which may have been created by Curtin as a way to showcase his services to the entertainment industry as he went out on his own into the rest of the 1960s. A note on the Hanna-Barbera letterhead appears in the bottom right corner of *Hollywood Directory*.

Dear Hoyt,
    Many thanks for recording some of our Hanna-Barbera songs from the FLINTSTONES, HUCKLEBERRY HOUND, YOGI BEAR, et al, and incorporating them into your album.
    Have listened to the album and it has a great sound.
    The best of luck to you.
    Sincerely,
    [Bill]
    Bill Hanna

▲▼▲▼▲▼

Colpix released its final Hanna-Barbera title in 1965, a year before the label was converted by Don Kirshner into Colgems Records and struck gold with The Monkees. Yogi was pictured as Uncle Sam on the cover of *Wake Up, America!* with the subtitle "It's Time for Physical Fitness . . . Keep Trim with Yogi Bear and His Friends."

Multitalented actor, writer, live TV pioneer, and film historian Chuck McCann plays every role, from Yogi and Boo-Boo to Huck, Mr. Jinks, and Cindy. Hearing the album in stereo is quite impressive as one can forget that only one person is always speaking. McCann's credits are countless, but some of the well-remembered voices he created are Sonny and Gramps of the Cocoa Puffs commercials, and several voices for *DuckTales*, *The New Adventures of Winnie the Pooh*, and a former Epcot character called "Dreamfinder" based on actor Frank Morgan.

This is the second album to position Yogi and friends as self-improvement coaches, the first being Golden's 1962 *How to Be a Better Than Average Child*, but *Wake Up, America!* leans more toward making adults smile, though not as heavily as A. A. Records' 1960 campaign satire, *Huckleberry Hound for President*. The songs, a mix of originals and parodies, are credited to Hanna, Barbera, and Sylvia Parnes (wife and writing partner of frequent Golden songwriter Paul Parnes). The album has a slightly bigger sound than Golden, with an orchestra arranged and conducted by veteran jazz saxophonist Al Cohn (jazz producer Jack Lewis also helmed this disc). Being the last Colpix LP, and involving material from creatives usually associated with Golden Records, *Wake Up, America!* appears to be a way for the various partners to wrap up the loose ends and use the last available materials.

▲▼▲▼▲▼

Throughout the network prime-time run of *The Flinstones*, the series made good use of its connections with Screen Gems Television and George Sidney, who continued to direct Hollywood movies with big stars. One of these was a 1960 comedy called *Who Was That Lady?* starring Dean Martin, Janet Leigh, and Tony Curtis (when the latter two were a married couple).

That year, Curtis was one of the stars who contributed cameos to Sidney's musical comedy pastiche, *Pepe*, a showcase for Mexican comedian Cantinflas, and a tie-in to Columbia's film and TV stars. Hanna-Barbera had produced animation for the film that was unused. The connections again brought a movie star to Bedrock in "The Return of Stony Curtis," one of the most memorable (and saucy) *Flintstones* episodes. Jean Vander Pyl expressed her disappointment that Curtis himself was not available for the voice session, since guest stars usually attended.

Hanna-Barbera had an active role behind the scenes of Screen Gems' *Bewitched* more than a year before Elizabeth Montgomery and Dick York voiced their characters in a *Flintstones* episode called "Samantha." The studio created the titles for the classic fantasy sitcom, both in color and black and white. (The *Bewitched* theme song was cowritten by Jack Keller, who also coauthored "Makin' with the Magilla").

"We had to create a different set of titles when *Bewitched* went from black-and-white to color," said background artist Ron Dias, whose career ranged from Disney's *Sleeping Beauty* in the '50s to Hanna-Barbera in the '60s and '70s, to *The Chipmunk Adventure* in the '80s and *Beauty and the Beast* in the '90s. "All the cels and backgrounds were painted in varying gray shades for the first two season titles. They were a different set of cels and backgrounds when they were in color." Hanna-Barbera continued to modify the various changes in the theme, station breaks, and bumpers, including the casting of Dick Sargent as the second Darrin.

"Elizabeth Montgomery was an avid artist, and at one point in her life, dreamed of being an animator," explains Montgomery's biographer, Herbie J Pilato. "She was a little disappointed when she first saw the *Bewitched* titles because she was expecting something on the level of *Fantasia*. But of course, this was not done under the same circumstances. I'm sure she has since appreciated what they did. She eventually produced the show and Hanna-Barbera animated her name in sparkling letters at the beginning of the later episodes."

The Flintstones and Rubbles welcomed many a faux celebrity and fictional character to Bedrock in the forms of Rock Quarry, courtesy of John Stephenson's spot-on Gary Cooper impression ("I miss the ah-duw-lay-tion."). Others included Gary Granite (Cary Grant), Daisy Kilgranite (Dorothy Kilgallen), and Perry Gunite (Perry Mason). In the episode "Happy Housewife," Wilma Flintstone's lessons on being a TV personality included Loretta Young's elegant swirls through doorways and Dinah Shore's "mwah" kisses to the home audience.

▲▼▲▼

The most unlikely person to pop up on *The Flintstones* has to be Swedish comedian/musician Owe Thörnqvist. In 1962, he released a novelty single called *Wilma!* in which he crowed, "Yabba-dabba-dabba-dabba-dabba-dabba-DOOOO! Aye, aye, aye Vilma!!!" and so forth. The long arms of H-B's business affairs department reached across the mighty seas bearing lawsuit threats.

Using only his powers of silly humor, Thörnqvist contacted Hanna and Barbera (and/or members of the Flintstone creative team). They thought his wild performance of the song was funny. Even funnier was his preposterous explanation of the origin of "yabba-dabba-doo" in Sweden, and his claim that "Wilma" had already been a popular name for countless Swedish women. There were lots of laughs and no lawsuits. Instead, they commissioned an English version (he also performed a version in Swedish for the final soundtrack). "The Swedish Visitors" episode was written and produced because of Owe Thörnqvist's goofy song, forever preserved in the exquisite amber of *Flintstones* eternity. Yogi Bear and Boo-Boo also made a cameo appearance.

Other existing songs were also acquired for use as Bedrock continued to rock. Two songs from the Imperial Records album, *Tell 'Em I'm Surfin'* by the Fantastic Baggys were rerecorded for James Darren's guest spot in "Surfin' Fred." The tunes, "Wax Up Your Boards" and "Surfin' Craze," were written by P. F. (Phil) Sloan and Steve Barri, who founded and fronted the band. James Darren's voice performance is unique among guest stars. He adds a slight edge, playing an exaggerated version of his public persona. "Jimmy Darrock" is a character as well as Darren himself, with a street-smart attitude from his south Philadelphia youth. He sings the songs as a surf rocker rather than a teen idol crooner.

The Beau Brummels were one of the many bands influenced by The Beatles' early Liverpool sound. Their 1964 Rock and Roll Hall of Fame hit "Laugh, Laugh" was worked into the *Flintstones* episode, "Shinrock a' Go-Go," as heard on the original record. The episode spoofed (and promoted) ABC's popular teen dance show with the voice and likeness of its host Jimmy O'Neill(stone). "Laugh, Laugh" appeared on the LP, *Meet the Beau Brummels*. Hanna Barbera added a *Flintstones* touch to their second album, *Volume 2: Tell Me Why / Don't Talk to Strangers*. On the back cover, the band members are depicted Flintstone-style in H-B studio-created art.

▲▼▲▼▲▼

Huckleberry Hound and Daws Butler also entered the pop music fray as Huck "Ringo" Hound on a single released by Merri Records featuring the novelty tune, "Bingo Ringo." Butler's only solo single as Huck, "Bingo Ringo," crosses Ringo Starr of The Beatles with Lorne Greene's 1964 hit ballad in one spoof in which a lone drummer enters a western town. It was written by longtime Las Vegas pianist Tommy Deering and arranged by Ernie Freeman.

Freeman's career spans the history of mid-century big band, R&B, and traditional pop. He played piano for Dinah Washington and Dorothy Dandridge; formed a combo that hit the top ten with the song "Raunchy" and appeared in the film *Rock Around the Clock*; and arranged Dean Martin's "Everybody Loves Somebody" and Petula Clark's "This Is My Song." His arrangements also won him Grammys for Simon and Garfunkel's "Bridge over Troubled Water" and Frank Sinatra's "Strangers in the Night," the song that ends

with "doo-bee-doo-bee-doo . . ." But that's another chapter.

"Bingo Ringo" was produced by Hanna-Barbera and released with Huck's favorite tune, "Clementine," preserved on side two. The cover art and typography are similar to the "Fred Flintstone and His Orchestra" single. It was released by Merri Records, a small Los Angeles label founded by Ned Hertzstram. According to Don Yowp, Hertzstram was a former WW2 prisoner of war who became a pianist and songwriter also associated with a Los Angeles label named Fink Records.

▲▼▲▼▲▼

Hanna-Barbera's successful advertising partnership was celebrated on the cover and inside label of a promotional disc called *A Kellogg Concert of Best Cereal Sellers—The H. O. T. Tunes for 1965*. On the front cover, Kellogg's mascot Tony the Tiger is seen in detail, conducting an orchestra of a silhouetted Huckleberry Hound, Quick Draw, Baba Looey, Pixie, Snagglepuss, and Yogi Bear (plus a character named "Hillbilly Goat" who represented Kellogg's Stars Cereal). The record's label is framed with line drawings of characters from Hanna-Barbera (Huck, Yogi, Quick Draw, Snagglepuss); Kellogg's (Tony, Toucan Sam, Hillbilly Goat, Sugar Pops Pete); and Walter Lantz (Woody Woodpecker).

There is no direct Hanna-Barbera material on the recording, but it connects through the 1937 song, "Good Morning, Good Morning," which was interpolated into early H-B cartoon show themes as the announcer mentioned Kellogg's. Written by Sam Coslow, it was licensed by Kellogg's from Famous Music, a division of Paramount Pictures and first sung by Martha Raye in the movie *Mountain Music*. Paramount animation departments (also named Famous for several years) used Famous songs to sell sheet music and enhance the cartoons, thus "Good Morning, Good Morning" also popped up in the Popeye short, *Protek the Weakest*.

Between Beatles concerts in the '6os, the Kellogg's jingle inspired John Lennon to write a song that would end up on the album *Sgt. Pepper's Lonely Hearts Club Band*. As he told biographer Hunter Davies, "I often sit at the piano, working at songs, with the telly on low in the background. If I'm a bit low and not getting much done, then the words on the telly come through. That's when I heard 'Good morning, Good morning.' It was a Corn Flakes advertisement." A friend of Lennon's, Micky Dolenz of The Monkees, attended the *Sgt. Pepper* recording sessions where he heard "Good Morning, Good Morning" for the first time. He used an excerpt of the song at the open of a Monkees TV episode he directed, "The Frodis Caper." *The Monkees* prime-time series was sponsored by Kellogg's and was rerun on Saturday mornings amid cereal commercials and Hanna-Barbera cartoons.

Another familiar Kellogg's jingle, the "Snap! Crackle! Pop!" Rice Krispies jingle was written by the aforementioned Burnett agency staffer H. B. Winkless Jr. and was sung by "The J's with Jamie" a vocal group popular in commercials and on Columbia Records.

▲▼▲▼▲

By 1965, Hanna-Barbera stepped away from licensing characters, music, and stories to record companies. The company had all the resources to start its own label. Hanna-Barbera would take a unique approach to its records, just as it had in animation for television. While benchmarked on successful business models and inspired by storytelling and musical forms, the "HBR" logo came to signify records that were fun, sharp, offbeat, and consistently smarter than the average disc.

Chapter 10

ENTER, STAGE LEFT

Hanna-Barbera's Record Company

I was out layin' down a little rubber on the freeway when I
zigged where I should-a zagged and wound up in Woodsville.
Then there was this great, big, old, fat, kooky bearosaurus
who kept ad-libbing, "Somebody's been sleeping in my Hollywood bed," and like that. Then when they found me sacked
out in their pad, like wow! It was hairy and scary!

—GOLDI-ROCKS (ALAN REED) FROM THE ALBUM,
THE FLINTSTONES: FLIP FABLES

Hanna-Barbera Records was front-page news. "We plan to go into all phases of the record business," said Bill Hanna on the cover of *Billboard* magazine on December 26, 1964. "We have our own recording facilities and are completely equipped to move ahead in that field. We feel our characters, as we have them now and as we continue to develop them, will make good merchandisable material for the kiddie and adult market."

Don Bohanan left his position as marketing director at Liberty Records to begin 1965 as head of the new Hanna-Barbera label. "Bill Hanna didn't merely want Yogi Bear recordings," wrote entertainment industry authority Kliph Nesteroff in his examination essay, *From Wall of Sound to Huckleberry Hound: The Vinyl Side of Hanna-Barbera*. "That was part of it, of course, but he asked Bohanan if he could capitalize on the 1960s youth movement. Bohanan brought in Larry Goldberg of Ultima Records to guide Hanna-Barbera into the pop music field."

Hanna-Barbera Productions was ideally suited to fold almost full-service recording into the production of cartoons and live-action films into the operation at 3400 Cahuenga. A golden age of voice talent was walking the studio halls, entering H-B's booths to provide their acting talents for animation, and now they would be

Two Raymond Scott–inspired instrumentals by Hoyt Curtin were released on the "B-H" (Barbera-Hanna) label.

working on records as well. It made sense to schedule both on days when the actors were scheduled for session work.

▲▼▲▼▲

Everything on the records was new except two exclusive elements sure to delight any Hanna-Barbera enthusiast. The story albums would be scored with signature studio sound effects. And no new scores were needed because six years' worth of outstanding, unmistakable music cues by Hoyt Curtin, Ted Nichols, Jack de Mello, and perhaps other freelancers, were part of the package. Any series with a sufficient budget for new music would result in additional cues for the studio cue library. B-H Music was an early studio publishing company; Anihanbar Music came along in the mid-sixties for the publishing of cues

and many of the songs released on the new label. An amalgam of "Hanna," "Barbera," and "animation," the name Anihanbar can be seen on music listings for many years after HBR existed.

Like its studio, Hanna-Barbera Records went from zero to sixty, rapidly launching brand-new character-based records while at the same time aggressively promoting rock, country, folk, and instrumental songs to radio stations on singles. Records had to be on the shelves, ready to compete with the other labels within a few weeks. Just as the time and budget restraints of television animation necessitated, Hanna-Barbera Cartoon Series Records developed its own production process. The voice tracks were edited exactly like soundtracks for Hanna-Barbera TV cartoons by the same staff, including editor Tony Milch.

"We transferred the half-inch dialogue tape to 35mm magnetic film," Milch said. "Then we chose

Don Bohanan (*center*) came from Liberty Records to head the new Hanna-Barbera label with Joe Barbera and Bill Hanna.

the music cues and sound effects that we felt worked best."

The finished edited albums ran an average of thirty-five minutes. For the Hanna-Barbera Cartoon Series 45 rpm singles, the stories were condensed to roughly twelve minutes. Except for the *Top Cat/Robin Hood* single, which was edited from the final cut, all the singles were cut from the dialogue first with the music and sound effects added afterward, which is why they vary slightly from the album versions. The songs from each album were sold separately on an EP 45 rpm disc.

HBR's highly prized album cover art was created in-house by its top talents, including Jerry Eisenberg, Harvard Pennington, Ron Dias, and Willie Ito. Meticulous hand lettering was custom-made for most of the covers by Robert Schaefer, whose magnificent title work enhanced countless Hanna-Barbera films and other materials. As a rule, print production takes longer than recording and disc pressing. The art and copy are often required before all the final audio is available. Contracts, schedules, revisions, and many other matters can take place between script and final mix. Because they were released first and the sys-

tem was still being created, the initial six LP covers bear the fewest credits and some turned out to be incorrect. The magnificent cover art does not always accurately describe what happens on the record, for any number of reasons, chief among them speed.

"We didn't have the records to listen to ahead of time," explained Willie Ito, art director for most of the early records. "We did them based on basic information—characters, titles, things like that. Most of the time we figured it out on our own. It was a lot of fun."

▲▼▲▼▲▼

The enigmatic Charles Shows, whose H-B TV career dated back to *Ruff and Reddy* and *The Huckleberry Hound Show*, wrote and directed every story album as well as song lyrics. Mentioning the name of Texas-born "Charlie" Shows sometimes was met by a smile, a chuckle, or a comment to the effect of "He was quite a character!" by his associates. He had a remarkable career, from space documentaries and animal comedy shorts to cartoons and early television programs. Shows tells out-of-this-world stories in one of the early autobiographies about the era, *Walt: Backstage*

Adventures with Walt Disney, a colorful collection of anecdotes and reminiscences.

In live-action, Shows's biggest claim to fame was the action series *Racket Squad* starring Reed Hadley (of radio's *Red Ryder* and TV's *Public Defender*). He contributed to the *Mickey Mouse Club* series and several other Disney projects. Between 1959 and 1964, Shows wrote over two hundred cartoon stories for Belvision's *Adventures of Tintin* and Larry Harmon's *Bozo the Clown*. Prolific and quick witted, Shows was a skilled raconteur with a keen ability to put together comic monologues, spirited dialogue, and vivid action scenes. All of this served him well in writing the HBR Cartoon Series album scripts. Like many writers, Shows's work evinces an efficient mental file filled with connections to situations, gags, and references that gave the series a true sense of style. There are certain Shows "trademarks," especially wordplay using rhymes and running phrases.

The skills of Charles Shows were made to order for the Hanna-Barbera Cartoon Series records. He had vast experience, if only by sheer number, in both comic and adventure-based animation storytelling. His writing was flexible enough to provide an album-length story, divide the LP into two separate tales, or come up with two situations per disc side within one story. Segments were divided as needed to allow for songs, which were slotted in like commercials rather than seamlessly blended into the narrative.

▲▼▲▼

Hanna-Barbera Records' staff studied the current children's album and single market to find out what was selling best, what could be improved upon, and how they could differentiate themselves. For the most part, mainstream children's records of the early sixties were not as "hip" as pop records, not in a "naughty" sense, but in a sharp, witty "Bullwinkle" or "Looney Tunes" way. Stan Freberg's fairy tale spoofs, such as "St. George and the Dragonet," with Daws Butler and June Foray, were mass-audience comedy records (and massive hits) but not specifically

made for kids, though they loved them. This does not suggest that there was a shortage of excellent records for children produced during this era, indeed it was the opposite. There was abundant variety in the selections of music and stories by outstanding talent. Many of them are true masterpieces, but the comedy is generally amusing rather than satirical.

There were a few humorous exceptions, like Paul Frees's hilarious *Professor Ludwig Von Drake* LP and Sterling Holloway's droll *Absent-Minded Professor* disc, both on the Disneyland label. Golden Records released *Morey Amsterdam's Mixed-Up Stories for Sharp Kids*, a festival of one-liners. But few skated very close to the satirical edge of what kids were seeing on TV, as when *The Flintstones* saw Dino join the "Sassie" show, or when *The Alvin Show* took viewers to "Crash-cupland." Records for kids seldom took the "sketch comedy" approach that thrived in the vinyl heyday of *Sesame Street*, *The Electric Company*, and *The Muppets* and began with the Hanna-Barbera Cartoon Series.

In addition to relatively faithful adaptations of well-known tales, Shows wrote several irreverent spoofs in addition to serious dramatic adventures and new comedy stories featuring new and established characters. When it came to the send-ups, Shows brought the recognizable "voice" familiar from his cartoon work with dashes of Stan Freberg, Sid Caesar, and the Marx Brothers. Fairy tales in particular are like extended versions of Jay Ward's *Fractured Fairy Tales*.[1]

▲▼▲▼

Another element virtually absent from other records made for children in the early sixties was contemporary rock-and-roll music. The musical form made brief appearances on children's discs, usually as an extension of the jazz already being presented. Besides pop records and the increasing number of teen dance shows, the three appearances of The Beatles on *The Ed Sullivan Show* in February 1964 had a dramatic effect on inching rock and roll into America's comfort zone. The Beatles' sound, influenced by Chuck Berry, Little

The HBR logo was an eye-catching soundwave appearing with teal labels for retail releases and magenta for promotional copies.

Richard, and Elvis Presley, soon became a favorite of young kids and the records followed suit.

The most celebrated early rock-and-roll record for kids was Ross Bagdasarian's Grammy-winning *The Chipmunks Sing the Beatles Hits* in 1964 (at Bohanan's previous record label). In 1965, the year Hanna-Barbera Records began, Liberty also released a collection of chart-topping hits on the LP, *Chipmunks a' Go-Go*, capturing the variety of musical styles still heard together on AM stations. (In 1959, the Chipmunks also recorded a gentle rock-and-roll take on "Whistle While You Work," on the 1959 LP *Let's All Sing with the Chipmunks*.)

Beatles spoofs and knockoffs were plentiful. A small British label released a children's album called *Once Upon a Beetle*, a fairy tale based on "The Princess Who Could Not Laugh." In this comic version (which sounds like it could have also been a stage play), four mop-top "Beetles" arrive on a kite string (a la Mary Poppins) to sing groovy, funny songs for the royal court. Golden Records chimed in with *Sing and Play Mother Goose with a Beatle Beat*. Pioneering TV musical director and composer Milton DeLugg (*The Tonight Show*, *The Paul Winchell and Jerry Mahoney Show*, *The Gong Show*) cowrote, arranged, and conducted the album, with familiar rhymes and modern lyrics (with a quartet and musical style most anticipating the future sound of Hanna-Barbera Cartoon Series records). However, the record contains several dance beats, only some of which are truly rock and roll, like "The Frug" and "Bo Diddley." Only a handful of artists brought a rock-and-roll sound to children

before 1966–1967, when The Monkees brought the sound into America's living rooms every week in a more familiar, comfy sitcom way.

Bill Hanna wanted the most up-to-date, mainstream label possible as well as records starring H-B characters. By both necessity and design, HBRs artists and production procedures intertwined, resulting in children's records with a sixties pop sensibility. Hanna-Barbera's Cartoon Series was the first full children's records line dominated by an early sixties sound of rock and roll, surf music, folk, and just a touch of soul, in addition to the stories and songs.

▲▼▲▼▲▼

Children's records, especially those connected to brands like Disney, tended to wait and see when it came to trends. One reason was long-term sales potential. Children's records were regularly repackaged in updated covers or back catalog songs were reconfigured in new ways. The more dated the material, the less likely it could stay on the shelves. Disney's best example of this process was the way they repackaged identical *Mickey Mouse Club* TV cast albums from the fifties as "general" records (*Happy Birthday and Songs for Every Holiday*, *Walt Disney's Most Beloved Songs*, *Fun with Music*), that sold from the sixties to the eighties. Disney's emerging pop/rock material, such as albums by Annette Funicello and R&B singer Billy Storm (who recorded later for HBR), was generally classified as teen music on their all-purpose Buena Vista label. There was also some caution. In the early sixties, rock and roll was still a hot button for some parents; even entertainment industry insiders still believed it was a temporary trend.[2] Hanna-Barbera Records was many months ahead of the curve as far as children's records were concerned. For the most part, HBR Cartoon Series songs offered kids a "tough little garage band" attitude in place of the cozy, comfy sound of decades prior.

However in assessing A&R director Larry Goldberg's approach, Kliph Nesteroff wrote, "Goldberg wasn't exactly the hippest guy in town. While every-

HANNA BARBERA RECORDS

The formation of Hanna-Barbera Records is the natural outgrowth of the highly successful character merchandising operation established by Hanna-Barbera Productions. With fifteen half hour cartoon shows on the air weekly, the established characters—such as, THE FLINTSTONES, YOGI BEAR, HUCKLEBERRY HOUND, QUICK DRAW McGRAW, TOP CAT, THE JETSONS, JONNY QUEST, TOUCHE TURTLE, etc.—are viewed more than 300 million times a week by the children of the United States. Hanna-Barbera Records will utilize the names, the likenesses and the original voices of these same characters in all lines of record production and will reach the same tremendous pre-sold market of TV viewing audience.

The new Hanna-Barbera studios in Hollywood have the finest facilities available for all recording forms, from 1/4" tape to 35mm full-coat magnetic triple track recording. The quality of the record pressings will be of the highest, using the finest vinyl materials available.

Specially designed and constructed racks for point-of-sale merchandising will be used to display the record albums conveniently. The albums will feature the various cartoon characters in four-color printing and will be skin-packed to maintain their original appeal. These racks, strategically located, in high traffic areas, will enjoy optimum point-of-purchase appeal.

The pre-sold characters and the production facilities of the Hanna-Barbera studios and the vast distributing organization of NATD will provide the most profitable record sales and distribution operation ever created.

Each year millions of new viewers will be added to the established audience, and with the constant creation of new characters and new shows we have an ever expanding market.

The original sales brochure proclaimed the arrival of the HBR label to distributors, retailers, and other business partners.

one else was shifting to the music of the drug culture, Goldberg's vision was to turn Hanna-Barbera into an island of surf music. The genre was a huge craze in the early 1960s with Dick Dale, The Ventures, The Beach Boys, and several others, but by 1965 surf music was out of fashion. Goldberg didn't care."

For those who first heard these discs, the musical style was one of the many fresh surprises. Some were very pleasing, while others took some getting used to and would require HBR to make adjustments with each new wave of Cartoon Series albums.

▲▼▲▼

Like Colpix, Hanna-Barbera Records did not have the budgets to license the most famous theme songs when their first six records arrived in stores. Golden Records had licensed themes from Screen Gems

Music, but soundtrack themes were still decades away. Hanna-Barbera Records, being an in-house label, had wide access to the accumulated music cues with hints of the theme melodies, which make "guest appearances" on some discs. In place of a theme song, a peppy new tune, presented in a pop style, was provided for almost every major character heard on the Cartoon Series albums: Yogi Bear, Huckleberry Hound, the Jetsons, Touché Turtle, and Top Cat. Characters without themes were also provided with songs, like Fibber Fox, Super Snooper, Snagglepuss, Pebbles, Augie Doggie, and Doggie Daddy. *The Flintstones*, Hanna-Barbera's current crown jewel, inspired two songs.

Larry Goldberg was described by colleagues as more of a dealmaker than a music expert, but he had industry connections. His producer friend Kim Fowley brought twenty-two-year-old Danny Hutton

Just a few years before he became part of Three Dog Night, Danny Hutton (right) was hired to help bring the sound of contemporary youth to Hanna-Barbera Records.

in for an interview. Hutton was a songwriter and musician who within a few years would be a member of the hit-making band, Three Dog Night ("Joy to the World," "One").

"I came in when they just started," said Hutton. "They wanted to get, quote, 'hip,' so they wanted a young musician that hung out on the strip and kind of knew what was going on, what the new trends were going to be and all that stuff." Goldberg also enlisted singer, songwriter, and former disc jockey Lynn Bryson, and promoted both performers as new talents behind the scenes at Hanna-Barbera Records.

"I went and there was this guy, Charles Shows," continued Hutton. "He gave me lyrics. I didn't know who 'Hippity Hoppity Kangaroo' was. So I went into the other room and not fifteen minutes later I came back and played him the song." Presumably, the character was Hoppy the Hopperoo of *The Flintstones*, but Hutton is not sure so many years later.

I don't remember what I wrote, I don't even remember what it was on. Once I got there, I was so naïve, I mean business-wise I was terrible. I think they had my publishing rights. I would write a song for whatever reason they wanted. I'd write the song and I would sing. I would sing the lead in all three-part harmony, you know, like Three Dog Night, and play. If I needed drums, I would use a leather chair for the snare. If I had the guitar part to do, I might slow the tape down and then play the part, if it was a little lead part, then put it back up to regular speed and all of that crazy stuff.

(Hutton's "chair drumming" accounts for the very unusual percussion on the first few HBR album songs.)

"I was like the handyman," said Hutton. "When somebody couldn't do it, I could sing a pretty good harmony, all the harmony parts on anything, I could sing a lead or do a falsetto. With the kid's songs, you didn't have to be the greatest singer."

Danny Hutton is the first voice heard on the initial entry in Hanna-Barbera's Cartoon Series record catalog. *Monster Shindig* stars Super Snooper, Blabber Mouse, the Gruesomes, plus the uncredited Hutton and Bryson, singing the three songs, "Monster Shindig," "Super Snooper," and "Monster Jerk."

The freewheeling story features two of animation's greatest voice actors. But they were playing characters usually voiced by others. Thus began an issue often discussed among enthusiasts: were these the right voices for the wrong characters, or the other way around?

Chapter 11

THE GRUESOMES HAVE A MONSTER PARTY

~~~~~~

**What am I gonna tell Lily? She's been counting on a raise
and if she finds out I've been fired she might get mad at
me. And stamp on the floor. And say mean things to me.
And shake her finger at me. She might even break my
Huckleberry Hound records!**

—HERMAN MUNSTER (FRED GWYNNE), "HERMAN'S RAISE" (1965)

The use of "cover voices," as discussed earlier, can occur for any number of reasons, including budget, time, contracts, and location. Time and schedule were always a challenge at the studio. Hanna-Barbera recorded dialogue radio-style with all the actors present whenever possible (exceptions were made in special cases, as with Tony Curtis).

If Bill Hanna and Joe Barbera were involved in these decisions, perhaps it was part of an established entertainment mindset, affected not only by interchangeable theatrical cartoon voices but also by readily accessible movie stars for radio. Several extremely popular radio shows in the early and mid-twentieth century—including *Lux Radio Theater* and *Screen Directors Playhouse*—presented weekly adaptations of new and classic feature films. *Lux* might get Jimmy Stewart and Donna Reed to reenact *It's a Wonderful Life*. Audiences were delighted, but they were also accustomed to hearing, for example, *Casablanca* starring Alan Ladd and Ann Sheridan instead of Humphrey Bogart and Ingrid Bergman. In one instance, Burt Lancaster was late to a live Lux broadcast and a little-known radio actor named Ira Gossel filled in until he arrived. No one noticed. Ira Gossel later became a movie star by the name of Jeff Chandler, an unmistakable visual inspiration for Race Bannon.

▲▾▲▾

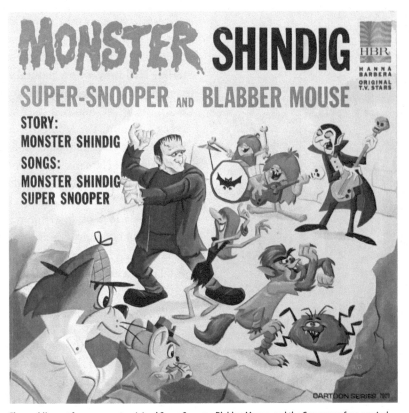

The world's most famous monsters joined Super Snooper, Blabber Mouse, and the Gruesomes for a musical fright fest.

The first six albums in the Hanna-Barbera Cartoon Series are the most extreme examples of the label's approach to recasting. While it remains disconcerting, it is also fascinating and entertaining (if only in an "alternative universe" way).

Monster Shindig might be described as a comedy inspired by Bobby "Boris" Pickett's 1962 novelty hit, "Monster Mash." The idea of multiple monsters having a celebration is a sure way to please both classic monster fans and kids—and the mid-sixties were a time when monsters, both scary and comedic, reached a pop culture peak. Snooper and Blabber begin their adventure with a phone call from a neighbor of the Gruesomes, complaining of the noise. Three masterful sets of sound-effect mashups follow, soon to be a highlight of several HBR releases.

The Gruesomes are listed on the cover as part of their recurring role in *The Flintstones* series, but they are historically linked to Snooper and Blabber cartoons, as Earl Kress chronicled in the sixth season *Flintstones* DVD bonus feature, "The Gruesomes' Road to Bedrock." Early versions of the characters took the forms of Mr. and Mrs. J. Evil Scientist and made their way to comic books. Joe Barbera long wished to sell a funny monster series to TV in the sixties and was galled by the final season defeat of *The Flintstones* on ABC by *The Munsters* on CBS. (Hanna-Barbera finally got an *Addams Family* animated series on NBC Saturday mornings in 1973.)

As in the 1969 Rankin/Bass feature *Mad Monster Party*, the ghoulish group gathers to celebrate a scientist's latest creation. Creepella and Weirdly Gruesome play host to dancing and mingling to their records of "Monster Shindig" and "The Monster Jerk." Along the way, we get lots of goofy Charles Shows puns and always-delightful HB library music. This album

Voice acting magician Paul Frees appeared on screen with Humphrey Bogart in 1954's *Suddenly* (*pictured*), and Bette Davis in 1952's *The Star*.

begins as an inside joke for collectors of the HBR Cartoon Series. "Monster Shindig" and "The Monster Jerk" are usually heard briefly whenever a character turns on a radio or TV on subsequent albums. On this record, we also hear an ersatz funny reference to Magilla Gorilla, because mentioning other characters is another running HBR gag.

Paul Frees provides Snooper's voice in place of Daws Butler. He also substitutes for Howard Morris as Weirdly Gruesome, using a Peter Lorre impression for which he received some renown. When he did the voice for Spike Jones on the record "My Old Flame," even the real Peter Lorre was impressed. For the *Monster Shindig* LP, Frees tones down Weirdly, making him less bloodthirsty than on the Jones version. The album does not focus on Snooper and Blabber so much as the rest of the characters (perhaps diverting attention from the fact that they are not played by their original voices). Don Messick makes a cameo by proxy through a vocal effect of a dog whimper. Vocal effects may have skirted some residuals, (e.g. Howard Morris's "Dyah-dyah-deeeya-duh!" from *The Jetsons* episode, "Jane's Driving Lesson," is sometimes heard in other cartoons).

Great actors may create similar-sounding voices, but they do not always play them exactly the same way for every character. One of the best examples is Sterling Holloway, whose natural voice is not too different from his Disney characters of Winnie the Pooh, the Cheshire Cat, and Kaa the Snake, yet the acting is very different. For *Monster Shindig*, June Foray's Creepella Gruesome (in place of Naomi Lewis in the TV version) is Natasha-like in tone but completely different in personality. Foray adds joie de vivre (or is it "joie la mort?") to Creepella that is not in the script. She exudes a love of entertaining and fondness for her kooky old friends. Casting issues aside, the performances of Frees and Foray are spectacular, doing a total of thirteen voices. What a fitting number for the Gruesomes!

Monster Shindig established Charles Shows's dual story-line scripting system for many of these albums. It was very similar to Disney features from the mid-fifties to the late seventies. They were designed to break cleanly into roughly fifty-minute segments for later use on the weekly anthology TV series. Other multipart TV broadcasts were edited into features for overseas release. It was very obvious in some features because their fifty-minute breakpoint had a noticeable fade out and the next section had an entirely new story line. Shows used a similar process for almost all the Hanna-Barbera records. In the case of *Monster Shindig*, side one was about the party with each guest arriving for a few moments of friendly conversation. On side two, the guests settled in for the night and the professor's creation became the focus.

One of Shows's topical gags in the series ends *Monster Shindig*. (Warning: spoiler alert!) The professor's new creature is so tall, that Snooper calls the Los Angeles Lakers basketball team to suggest him as a star player.

▲▼▲▼▲

HBR gave *The Flintstones* the royal treatment on their premiere album in the series, *Flip Fables*. Alan Reed

Alan Reed and Mel Blanc, with Jean Vander Pyl as Pebbles, are heard on one of the best albums in the Cartoon Series.

stars as Fred and Mel Blanc as Barney. It's one of two albums in the first six with original cast leads.

Hanna-Barbera characters telling fairy tales in their own way was a regular Hanna-Barbera TV story device. In the 1963 episode, "Groom Gloom," Fred Flintstone told Pebbles the story of Goldi-Rocks and the Three Dinosaurs. This story is different on this record, Wilma is away so Fred and Barney can't go bowling unless Pebbles is asleep. (Leaving her alone is questionable. Would Dino watch over her?) Jean Vander Pyl is at home, however, as Pebbles. This would be Alan Reed's only full HBR LP as Fred, though he would be heard in brief sections of two other albums. For *Flip Fables*, Reed delivers a tour de force here for "Goldi-Rocks and the Three Bearosauruses." Shows makes full use of Reed's availability for the album. Rather than narrating, Shows wrote one of his best comic monologues, allowing Reed to play all the characters. Again, though Reed cannot quite lose himself in the voices as Mel Blanc does on side two, his seasoned acting brings Goldi, the three bears, and even Goldi's mother (with one line) to life.

Several Cartoon Series albums in this wave took a few existing music cues that fit nicely together to create a primary "underscore." Two Jetson cues were used under Goldi-Rocks. The cue heard as Goldi explores the home of the bearosauruses was given lyrics in 1970 when it became the theme song of *Josie and the Pussycats*.

Side two presents Mel Blanc as all the voices in Barney's "Three Little Pigosaurs," making a few changes along the way within some voices, probably due to the speed of the session. Little pig Chubby is a cousin to Looney Tunes' Porky Pig and the most consistent of the three. Stubby seems to be whatever Blanc needs him to be at the time. And Tubby starts

Versatile actor/impressionist Allan Melvin appeared in many of TV's greatest series and worked for almost every animation studio in Hollywood.

song. Lynn Bryson sings the lead melody as Danny Hutton does a "Yabba-Dabba" falsetto in the manner of singer Lou Christie ("Lightning Strikes"). Hutton also provides percussion on the aforementioned leather chair "snare drum."

Surely *Flip Fables* provided HBR's sales team with a strong sample of the label's quality to distribute among retailers and potential partners.

▲▼▲▼

The other original cast disc in the first wave in the Cartoon Series LPs is *Magilla Gorilla Tells Ogee the Story of Alice in Wonderland*. Within a few years of its release, humorist Steve Allen had a daytime TV talk show during which he often went into the studio audience to share fun and laughs. After one such amusing exchange, he awarded this album to an elderly lady as a prize: saying something to the effect of, "I'm sure you'll get a lot of enjoyment from this." The woman could not be reached for comment. However, the album builds up to being one of HBR's funniest. If any of Allen's staff members missed hearing it (a safe bet), they missed out on a comic gem, especially if they heard the entirety of side two.

The premise of the LP, harkening back to such cartoons as "Come Blow Your Dough" and "Prince Charming," is framed by a typical Magilla cartoon plotline. Ogee (Janet Waldo instead of Jean Vander Pyl, despite the jacket notes) buys Magilla for the price of—depending on its location in Shows's script—75 or 98 cents. Ogee's dyspeptic parents complain about Magilla's arrival until her father's boss calls to offer them two tickets to *My Fair Lady* (presumably the hit 1964 movie). Dad (Sam Edwards, who was voicing supporting roles for *Jonny Quest*) and Mom (also Waldo) and Shows's script convey a most contentious household. Dad is superficially pleasant to his boss on the phone and changes his tone with his family after he ends the call. Both are stressed by suburban social-climbing pressure, all conveyed in a very short scene, easily sensed by any young listener (including the author in his youth).

out sounding like Foghorn Leghorn and turns into Charlie the Dog. By the time all three pigs make it into the house of bricks, they have somehow gone from Atlanta to Brooklyn, all probably due to Blanc's getting only a few takes on the session. None of this is a major concern, since this is the one and only Mel Blanc, giving every line a special brilliance.

There is no doubt that Shows was seldom, if ever, told "They won't get this joke," or "I don't get this joke," after he wrote these scripts. Instead, it was typical for the HBR discs to include gags like the one in which the Three Little Pigs were visited by the Big Bad Wolf disguised as a representative for Neilsen TV ratings. When he asks the pigs what they're watching, one of them replies, "What else? *The Flintstones.*"

"Three Little Pigosaurs" weaves the songs into the narrative to a greater degree than on any other HBR disc. The pitched-up "Three Little Pigs" ditty has a similar melody to the catchy "F-L-I-N-T-S-T-O-N-E-S"

Because this is a cartoon record about a talking gorilla, Magilla sings, dances, and does tricks, which convinces the parents to leave their child with a complete stranger (without calling Mr. Peebles for a reference). He also brings some fun to a rather tense atmosphere. Once again, Shows uses the premise of a lead character telling a story to a younger insomniac. Allan Melvin does all the voices in *Alice in Wonderland* while narrating as the Magilla character. A gifted impressionist, Melvin gives Magilla's voice a touch of Red Skelton's Clem Kadiddlehopper. For the "polka-dot-blue caterpillar," Melvin chose to imitate classic movie actor Victor Moore. Almost every voice he uses on the disc has its own separate quality. The versatile Melvin is one of the most undercelebrated actors in the history of animation and television comedy.

"Few usually consider that Allan Melvin had recurring roles on some of TV's greatest shows," said writer Mark Evanier. "*The Dick Van Dyke Show*, *All in the Family*, *The Brady Bunch*, *Gomer Pyle*, as well as hundreds of cartoons and commercials. He is rarely if ever brought up when discussing legends of TV or cartoons, but he was as talented as all the others."

Magilla's vinyl version of *Alice* has a one-year jump on Hanna-Barbera's first network special, *Alice in Wonderland or What's a Nice Kid Like You Doing in a Place Like This?* Both the special and the Magilla album share the plot device of Alice following her little dog to Wonderland instead of the White Rabbit. By his recollection, Shows worked on the script for the TV special, which was in production at the same time as this album. If he was involved at some point, perhaps the runaway doggie may have been one of his contributions.

This is one of the few HBR Cartoon Series albums with no songs. However, it overflows with sound effects, especially on side two. The artistry of Hanna-Barbera's editors, so vital to the development of what evolved as television cartoons, is even more impactful on records like this one. When Magilla suggests a soothing TV show to relax Ogee, the sounds combine all manner of excruciating violence—a little swat at the state of television. Wonderland (called "The Land of Limbo" in Magilla's story) is crazy with noises and funny musical cues. Curtin's off-key "William Tell Overture" is used for chases; organ music punctuates a melodramatic courtroom moment. Beautifully timed effects pop after each piece of action in a scene in which Alice runs to the brook, makes a cup out of a leaf, and fills it with water. After we hear the "Royal Dogcatcher" gulp the water (with a shrinking pill in it), a little "symphony" of sounds accompanies his transformation. The grand finale is the Queen of Hearts calling out to the armed forces to rescue her from a mouse. A barrage of battle sounds ensues.

Two of Hoyt Curtin's most memorable cues are used near the end of the story. A royal party is accented with Mendelsohn's "Song without Words Op. 67 No. 4 (Spinning Song)," a popular piano lesson piece, the same cue was used when Fred Flintstone was "Mister Blblblblblblblah." Ogee sleeps to Curtin's lilting lullaby, a cue set to strings that may have been recorded during the *Top Cat* sessions when violinists were available. Some music is, appropriately, from *The Magilla Gorilla Show*, perhaps attributable in part to Jack de Mello. One is a chase cue that was later revived for director Tex Avery's "Dino and Cavemouse" cartoons.

As Willie Ito previously explained, the artists did not hear the records first, so the sight of Magilla on the front cover participating in the mad tea party does not match the story on the record, but both stand delightfully on their own.

▲▼▲▼▲▼

In addition to *Monster Shindig*, the remaining three LPs in the first six Cartoon Series releases are not voiced by the original actors. *Pixie and Dixie with Mr. Jinks Tell the Story of Cinderella* may be most easily forgiven. The absence of Daws Butler and Don Messick naturally makes one wonder what it might have been, but with Paul Frees and June Foray (plus an assist from Dick Beals), this album comes closest to combining Hanna-Barbera with Jay Ward and Stan Freberg. There is a one-liner every few seconds

Lovely Lady June: the great June Foray appeared on the 1952 radio program *Smilin' Ed's Gang,* while she was also recording for Capitol Records, often with Daws Butler and Stan Freberg.

("They'd turn on television and they'd all sit around watchin' like, ya know? But the only thing they'd let Cindy watch was the commercials! Talk about cruelty!"). But because of the talent involved, the album becomes more than a string of jokes. Frees's Jinks is a tribute to his colleague. He is believable whether the narration requires Jinksy's usual cool beatnik detachment or some empathy for Cinderella's plight.

June Foray is in top form as Cinderella, the Stepfamily, and the Fairy Godmother (beloved Foray voices all, including a bit of her "Marjorie Main" and "Witch Hazel"). Very few recordings offer such a wide cross-section of Frees and Foray. Also on the recording is the voice of Dick Beals as Pixie. An actor of wide dramatic range who specialized in child and teen voices, Beals was heard in classic radio programs as well as cartoons and commercials, including the long-running Speedy Alka Seltzer spots.

Keith Scott, the author of *The Moose That Roared,* the definitive history of Jay Ward Productions, remarked about Frees, "I suspect he loved the Jinks voice that Daws did . . . not only was it Daws's own favorite of his characters but at that time a lot of the industry folk loved it."

The music editor transformed two Hoyt Curtin solo piano music beds from Golden Records' *Songs of the Flintstones* album ("Dum Tot Song" and "I Flipped") into an underscore. Heard with Frees's seriocomic performance, the same music acts as a sympathetic theme for Cinderella. This album is also wildly, willfully groovy. Of all the Hanna-Barbera Cartoon Series albums, this one most unabashedly celebrates the height of the mod mid-sixties, from the Fabian crooner era to the British and American rock invasion's progressive journey into shades and shadows.

Writer Shows also seems to be either a car buff or he studied an issue of *Hot Rod Magazine* because he puts a lot of emphasis on such auto details as fuel injection engines, flatty mills, and dummy spots, some of which would resurface on HBR's *Hot Rod Granny* album. He also adds a clarifying statement about blended families that was unusual for its day, especially in adaptations of *Cinderella.* Dixie asks, "Lucky, most stepmothers and stepsisters aren't like that, huh, Jinks?" "To be sure," he replies. "I was just talkin' about this *partica-lar* stepmother."

This album contains a side reference that now might be called an "Easter egg." When Cinderella and the Prince dance the Jerk, one of Hanna-Barbera's first pop records begins to play. It's an instrumental by the Bompers called "Early Bird," the "B" side of "Do the Bomp," on the second single in their catalog.

"I was one of The Bompers and The Bats," said Danny Hutton. "I didn't really think about credits until I was recording under my own name." "Early Bird" and "Do the Bomp" were written by Roger Christian ("Don't Worry Baby," "Beach Party," "Little Old Lady from Pasadena") and future Oscar-winner Carol Connors (*Rocky, The Rescuers*).

The pensive, moody closing ballad of "Cinderella" is one of the most elegant in the Cartoon Series. It's a contrast to the relentless spoofery of the rest of the album, but it makes sense with Jinks's transition. The electric guitar accompanying Lynn Bryson sounds like Fred Flintstone playing the kerosene guitar on HBR's *Songs from Mary Poppins* album and may also be the same one heard in several Flintstone episodes.

▲▼▲▼▲▼

A lot of things are mixed up on HBR's *Yogi Bear and Boo-Boo Tell the Stories of Little Red Riding Hood and Jack and the Beanstalk*, from the album cover and the casting to the actual vinyl record itself. The cover depicts Red Riding Hood and Jack switching roles. That's an idea with lots of potential, but it does not happen on the record.[1] Still, the album spoofs both tales with a witty, snappy script and marvelous performances as well as inspired editing of music and sound effects. Even the songs are fun and unpretentious.

Allan Melvin and June Foray are marvelous in every role. They do their best as Yogi and Boo-Boo, and their best is great if not by accuracy but by skillful comic timing. Still, one cannot avoid wondering how the album might have been if Daws Butler were telling these stories as Yogi, Don Messick was playing Boo-Boo, with both in supporting roles plus June Foray as Red Riding Hood and the Giant's wife. The album has some prime H-B music cues in its favor, several that do not surface on any other HBR discs. One is a lovely piece from *The Flintstones* that plays when Jack first explores the Giant's kingdom. Another is an instrumental of the *Loopy DeLoop* theme.

Once again, Charles Shows proves he was not one for letting a premise gather dust. This time "Boo-Boo Foray" cannot fall asleep and go into hibernation. "Yogi Melvin" offers two freewheeling fairy tales with almost as much punch as Mr. Jinks's *Cinderella*.

"Little Red Riding Hood" takes an even more satirical approach. Red, up to date on the latest hits, plays "The Monster Jerk" twice during her story. She takes a shortcut off the freeway to Grandma's house and, driving 99 miles an hour, Red is stopped by a policeman. (Technically this album comes before *Cin-*

derella in the HBR catalog so this is the gag's first appearance.)

The policeman is really the Big Bad Wolf. He accuses her of being astronaut Gus Grissom, making an interplanetary bust. This rather strange reference must have been an inside joke, as Charles Shows could have been friends with Grissom through his work on space documentaries. (The gag became dated, inadvertently and tragically, two years later when Grissom died along with fellow astronauts Ed White and Roger Chaffee from smoke inhalation from a fire aboard an Apollo 1 Command Module.)

▲▼▲▼▲▼

The only other HBR album to recast a classic Daws Butler character starred Huckleberry Hound as played by Paul Frees. Frees's career with Hanna-Barbera took place primarily in the mid-sixties. He was cast in lead voices (Squiddly Diddly, Fluid Man of *The Impossibles*, Thing of *The Fantastic Four*) and countless supporting roles, including several in *The Man Called Flintstone* feature. Billed as "the most heard man in the world," Frees was ubiquitous in narrations, trailers, cartoons, and theme parks, most famously as the Ghost Host in the Haunted Mansion.

In search of tales that might work for Huckleberry Hound to tell, Hanna-Barbera Records looked at what other best-selling children's records were doing at the time. Homes and retailers throughout the US were stocked with *Uncle Remus* records; schools and libraries offered the books in their children's sections. The *Uncle Remus* stories are a source of continual controversy, discomfort, and conflict. They are the creations of African Americans collected by journalist Joel Chandler Harris. The books and stories, usually told in an interpreted dialect, were retold in countless print editions and other media.

The stories and characters of *Uncle Remus* were popular throughout most of the twentieth century. The reasons are too numerous and complex for such a discourse as this, but briefly, a piece of popular culture has a way of inserting itself into the ether of the mainstream, and once there, it seems normal and "okay," even if the material is questionable. The voices objecting to Harris and the way the stories' terminology, and dialect in the stories were at issue took a long time to be heard in the face of such popular adaptations of the tales, and they became part of many a childhood. Only with the increase in communications and transportation have people been able to engage in thoughtful discourse.

But back in 1965, *Uncle Remus* and *Brer Rabbit* stories were readily available on store shelves near numerous adaptations of such titles as *Pinocchio* and *Cinderella*. Almost every major label recorded a version or two of the tales, often in dialect form. The best selling of these records were the plentiful discs based on the 1946 film *Song of the South*. Nearly every store with children's records in the sixties offered releases adapted from this film and/or the stories.

Huckleberry Hound Tells Stories of Uncle Remus begins with a short monologue in which Huck talks a little about himself. The first music cue used here is another version of a *Jetsons* piece that became the *Josie and the Pussycats* theme. This monologue was previously written (presumably by Shows) for occasions in which Daws Butler was asked to speak in character during personal appearances. Butler also recorded his own revised, longer version of this monologue. One of Huck's lines is an old gag also spoken by Fred on *The Flintstones*: "But that's enough of talking about me, let's talk about you. Now, what did you think about my latest TV cartoon?"

This Huckleberry Hound LP is unique among most adaptations of the stories. Paul Frees tells the stories in the voice of the cartoon character, with a southern accent but not an "Uncle Remus" dialect. He is a cartoon dog with a southern accent. Nevertheless, these are still stories at the center of much controversy, including the one in which Brer Rabbit becomes stuck, which uses an unacceptable term. None of the song lyrics uses the term. The remaining story on the album is a twist on "Brer Rabbit and the Briar Patch," adding a modern touch with Brer Fox's wanting to try out a recipe for "Welsh Rabbit."

Unless Daws Butler and Don Messick were tied to other recording contracts or some such conflicts, then it may have been a financial decision to use other actors. Another theory is that time was saved by booking whatever actors were available since the recording budgets were so limited. But if fees were in question, why were Alan Reed and Mel Blanc asked to voice Fred and Barney for *Flip Fables*? One theory could be based on what entertainment companies today call "current initiatives." *The Flintstones* was Hanna-Barbera's biggest initiative at the time and was most worthy of the extra expense on one of the record division's first releases. The series was doing well in prime time, generating massive revenue in merchandise and there was a feature film in the works. The earlier characters were popular but not as current and not in prime time. Even Golden Records used the original cast of *The Flintstones* when they replaced voices for other H-B characters.

Hanna-Barbera, and the industry itself, could not have anticipated the unprecedented place their characters—and their voices—were taking among the public growing attached to them. These were "everyday folks-next-door" characters, like best friends one saw all the time. Others were like dear faraway friends and relatives who visited on special occasions. Voices, music, and sounds were vital to this new kind of media closeness.

It was one thing for Golden Records to use outside actors. But Hanna-Barbera Records was an in-house label from the people who made the cartoons. Hanna-Barbera album covers promised "original TV stars" on the cover and the "actual TV voices" on the back cover, with a photo of Hanna, Barbera, and Yogi in their "ultra-modern office building." While the cover copy is basically true, it could be seen as misleading because of the casting. Indeed, these were the "original TV stars," in the sense that they were cartoon stars of the studio. Yes, they were being performed by "actual TV voices," the top-of-the-industry, multitalented people associated with Hanna-Barbera cartoons, like June Foray, Mel Blanc, Paul Frees, Daws Butler, Don Messick, Alan Reed, Jean Vander Pyl,

▴▾▴▾▴

Janet Waldo, Allan Melvin, Dick Beals, Henry Corden, and John Stephenson.

Chas Butler recalls his father's lawyer visiting the studio for a confrontation about the records, insisting that "Daws Butler helped build this studio!" The studio likely received some letters wondering why this was happening. Things did change. From the very start, Hanna-Barbera Records was different, surprising, and often startling. But for all three to be considered a good thing, some retooling needed to take place.

"Thank heavens we did have him in the formative years of Hanna-Barbera," said Bill Hanna in 1987. "If we hadn't had Daws, I don't know, there may not have *been* a Hanna-Barbera." Butler did indeed make his debut on Hanna-Barbera Records in grand style with the very next album in the Cartoon Series. More iconic voice actors joined in on the grooves as well.

Chapter 12

PEBBLES AND BAMM-BAMM GO TO HOLLYROCK

〰〰〰〰〰〰〰〰〰〰〰〰〰〰

I might just mention in passin' that these here new Cartoon Series albums—you know, the ones with the swingin' versions of all the great classic stories? Well, they're a big smash all over the country, and in the cities, too! These new LPs feature such TV favorites as The Flintstones, Yogi Bear, Magilla Gorilla, and Huckleberry Hound—whoops, there I go name-droppin'.
—HUCKLEBERRY HOUND (DAWS BUTLER), FROM THE LP *DROP-INS, VOL. 1*

After the first six Hanna-Barbera Cartoon Series albums were released, Daws Butler recorded the above for *Drop-Ins, Vol. 1*, a promotional album sent to disc jockeys, broadcasters, and anyone else who might be able to promote the new Hanna-Barbera Cartoon Series records. (There were no further *Drop-In* volumes.)

Huck's short message is followed by comedy "drop-ins" from various Cartoon Series LPs. These comic "punctuations" were often used by disc jockeys to pop within their broadcasts. Every Hanna-Barbera Cartoon Series story album is a treasure trove of drop-ins. Side two presents the first collection of sound effects released, which must have been solid gold to DJs. This may have been the first time an animation studio made some of its sound effects library available beyond its own productions, except for Disney's 1964 retail release, *Chilling, Thrilling Sounds of the Haunted House*, another handy radio station album. Hanna-Barbera's effects had become so recognizable that giving them to broadcasters was shrewd marketing. If a listener hears the familiar effects, they might think of H-B cartoons.

▵▴▵▾

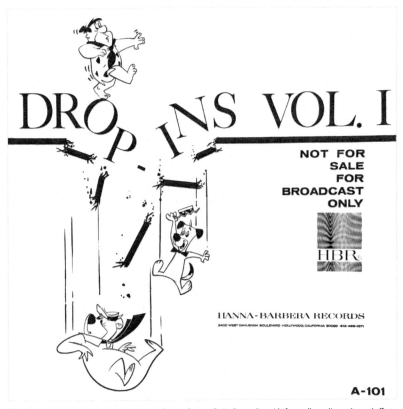

This album was sent to broadcasters to promote the new Cartoon Series line and provide funny album clips and sound effects.

Huck mentions that these are a new style of records, the "swingin'" versions of all the great classic stories. Butler did not appear on the first wave of records represented on *Drop-Ins*, but that changed immediately. The next wave of Cartoon Series albums would see advancements and changes in casting, songs, and even lettering. The art director credited is studio background artist Harvard Pennington, along with many of the greatest names in Hanna-Barbera history creating the designs, sketches, and paint work. The art was even more lush, with illustrations that were dense with artwork that "bled" to the edges. Hand-lettering was used instead of block type. It was this artistry that eventually gained Hanna-Barbera Records a following for its cover art.

The album art for *Snagglepuss Tells the Story of "The Wizard of Oz"* by Willie Ito and Ron Dias is a sparkling example of classic '60s Hanna-Barbera. A serpentine, weightless Yellow Brick Road weaving through the sky suggests the "Unwinding Road" seen in H-B's upcoming *Alice in Wonderland* TV special. The gleaming Emerald City seems straight out of *The Jetsons*. Also on the cover, Snagglepuss is seen in the role of the Cowardly Lion even though he does not play him on the record because, as mentioned earlier, scripts and/or recordings were not always ready for the artists when the art was due, as printing takes longer than recording.

Snagglepuss Tells the Story of "The Wizard of Oz" makes a spectacular debut for Daws Butler on Hanna-Barbera Records. The adaptation balances the tone of the narrative with the personality of the Snagglepuss character and is one of the most faithful audio dramatizations of L. Frank Baum's book ever produced. Details from the book most often left off most audio adaptations are two adventures in which Cowardly

Heavens to Margaret Hamilton! One of the most faithful adaptations of the L. Frank Baum book on vinyl with Daws Butler and Janet Waldo as the entire cast. It also marked the debut of Ron Hicklin, Al Capps, Stan Farber, and others as "The Hanna-Barbera Singers."

Lion, Tin Woodman, and Scarecrow demonstrate that they really have brains, courage, and heart. Without diverting the message with symbolism, the dialogue directly states the key point that Dorothy's friends already had what they believed they were lacking. Listeners may not "laugh until they ache," as the album's title song suggests, but the script moves seamlessly between the funny and the dramatic. In the cartoons, we never really saw how good an actor Snagglepuss could be, given the chance. Here he often conveys a sincere sense of gravitas for the tense, uncertain moments in the story in addition to the comedy.

Shows and Butler were old friends, having worked together in radio as well as animation. (One of the shows was called *That's Rich* starring Stan Freberg.) Tailor-made gags, asides, and wordplay pop up throughout the script, making one wonder whether Butler contributed more than a few of them to Charles Shows's script. Butler and Shows's love of wordplay and offbeat pronunciation is a highlight of several Hanna-Barbera albums, including the word "ree-zul-lize." Snagglepuss favorites include "cas-till" and "whis-tull."[1]

Janet Waldo costars as Dorothy and Aunt Em, but her standout performance is the Wicked Witch of the West. She grew to enjoy voice acting so much, every opportunity to stretch was a joy. As the Witch, Waldo gets a rare opportunity to chew the scenery—and must have had a blast. In the '80s she would voice a cousin to this witch on *Smurfs*, the outrageously vain Hogatha. The H-B stock background music was selected to fine effect, especially with a *Jetsons* cue familiar from the episode, "Astro's Top Secret," as a Yellow Brick Road theme.

▲▼▲▼▲▼

The *Snagglepuss Oz* album also introduces new sounds to the Cartoon Series. Danny Hutton, while perhaps providing occasional backup, had moved up to A&R (Artists and Repertoire) at HBR. Lynn Bryson continued to write and sing, but a new group of studio vocalists was gradually joining the discs who would be part of Hanna-Barbera animation for at least the next two decades, including second tenor Ron Hicklin, first tenor Stan Farber, bass Al Capps, baritone Bob Zwirn, and bass Bob Rolla.

These five, in various combinations, began singing together when they were kids in Washington State. As The Eligibles, they moved to LA and enjoyed success in clubs, on TV, and on Mercury and Imperial Records. Each continued to work together or separately even as the group itself was no longer necessary.

"I loved working behind the scenes, much more than on stage," said second tenor Ron Hicklin, who can be heard in a solo section of the dreamlike "The Land of Oz" song (which introduced a string section to the Cartoon Series). "I became a vocal arranger and contracted singers for records, movies, and TV."

Al Capps is credited as an arranger for several HBR titles. As an ensemble, they would be heard constantly on Hanna-Barbera's TV cartoons as well as its records. Their album debut is in HBR's answer to "Ding! Dong! The Witch Is Dead," the catchy "Wicked Witch" song. It has a Kingston Trio style with a guitar opening that is similar to Bacharach and David's theme to "The Blob."[2]

▲▼▲▼▲▼

To hear Jean Vander Pyl's beautiful, sensitive telling of a classic children's story, one only wishes she had recorded more of them. When *Wilma Flintstone Tells the Story of Bambi*, there are moments of charm and fun, but no kidding around. This is an album that takes its subject seriously and with a great deal of heart.

Charles Shows's script frames a *Flintstones* situation around the "Bambi" story: Fred brings home a pet for Pebbles—a dinosaur named Dino. In a previ-

ous chapter, the Colpix *Flintstones* soundtrack album contains the very 1961 episode that contradicts Dino's origin from season one ("The Snorkasaurus Hunter"), but then canon and origin are not necessarily sacrosanct when it comes to Hanna-Barbera. Wilma's maiden name was "Pebble" in two early *Flintstones* episodes and Wilma's mother was never called by either first or last name while Verna Felton performed her voice. It was not until late in season four that Betty called the character "Mrs. Slaghoople" and Janet Waldo assumed the role late in the episode, "Fred el Terrifico."

In a scenario that is out of character but serves the album's premise, Pebbles and Bamm-Bamm innocently hurt Dino. Wilma decides to teach them about compassion for animals and nature by telling the *Bambi* story. Fred, who is exceptionally ebullient during his few moments on this record, expresses delight in Wilma's selection.

From that point, it is a Jean Vander Pyl-Tacular and its very existence is a treasure. Shows's adaptation pulls no punches. Bambi's mother's death is followed by an introspective song called "Alone," reminiscent of Shelley Fabares's "Johnny Angel," followed by Bambi's mourning and recovery. While it is not on the level with the award-winning way that *Sesame Street* handled the passing of Mr. Hooper, the delicate, compassionate way that this so-called kiddie record examines death from a young person's perspective is notable.

Dick Beals, who voices Bambi, was providing various *Flintstones* voices during the time of this album's production. He would soon voice Buzz Conroy on one of Hanna-Barbera's most fondly recalled series, *Frankenstein Jr*. As Bambi, Beals conveys a gradual change from cute, innocent childhood to maturity, when his Bambi asserts grim conviction. He also voices Bamm-Bamm opposite Vander Pyl's Pebbles.

The only things that might take a listener "out" of the life-or-death gravitas of Bambi's adversity are the music cues. The more familiar one is with H-B cartoon music, the less impact the cue might have on the drama. This is simply all the library had and Bambi

Jean Vander Pyl's warm, compassionate performance graces this touching version of the Felix Salten book.

was out of the ordinary for Hanna-Barbera. "Bambi" opens with a gentle "Meet George Jetson" melody. A rarely used violin solo that follows Mrs. Deer's demise recalls the "Sassie" spoof on *The Flintstones*. H-B's most dramatic cues were from Jonny Quest and they were obvious. When "Man" is chasing the helpless deer, to H-B fans it might as well be Doctor Zin.

The melody from one of the songs, titled "Why," later appeared as a go-go dance single by "The Pop-Ups" on Hanna-Barbera's pop label. Two of the songs have a "Pebbles and Bamm-Bamm"–like sound, with slightly sped-up vocals. One of them, entitled "Love Is for All," contains the lyric, "Open up your heart . . ." which would turn up again when Pebbles and Bamm-Bamm launched their musical career on TV.

▲▼▲▼▲▼

Now that Daws Butler had "arrived" at the label, he was there to stay. And with the departure of Doug Young from the L.A. area, Butler played both leads on the album, *Doggie Daddy Tells Augie Doggie the Story of Pinocchio*. This Carlo Collodi tale (originally written as a series of magazine cliffhangers) was tailor-made for the "dear ol' dad" and "his son, his son." There are two Hanna-Barbera guest characters as well: Fibber Fox and, in the guise of Conniver the cat, Butler's Mr. Jinks voice.

Charles Shows adheres more to the 1940 Disney film than Collodi, including making the cricket a conscience without giving him the name "Jiminy." And while the overall approach is not '60s satire, there are some "mod nods," as when Drip the Dropout (in place of Lampwick) tells Pinocchio how "Dropoutland" is "crazy, wild, real gear." The album sends worthwhile messages to kids while keeping the production entertaining rather than didactic. "Drip the Dropout" is also a song, to make the message catchy. The subject of prejudice is addressed by name when the other kids make fun of Pinocchio for being different. Dick Beals plays Pinocchio and the other puppets and children. When the puppet becomes a real boy, Beals changes the voice. Janet Waldo has a small but graceful role as the Blue Fairy.

Butler handles the story with the same blend of comedy and drama as *The Wizard of Oz*, which comes even more naturally to a Jimmy Durante–like voice like Doggie Daddy, who wants to impress these lessons upon his son. Butler deftly conveys Daddy's disdain when he "ain't too pleased" about Pinocchio's mistakes, as well as his joy in having Augie as a loving son.

The voice of Touché Turtle, Bill Thompson was responsible for many of radio and animation's most memorable voice-acting performances.

▲▼▲▼

Disney did not bring Bill Thompson back to record for its label. All of the materials with his voice were from soundtracks. By the mid-sixties, Thompson was not doing as much voice work, but Hanna-Barbera Records—which could have hired Don Messick to fill in, as he had for Droopy—scored a coup by getting Bill Thompson to do several voices on *The Reluctant Dragon Starring Touché Turtle and Dum-Dum.*

In addition, this was the first HBR LP to offer a classic that was not as often retold on other labels. A 1958 album presented an adaptation read by Boris Karloff on Caedmon Records, a boutique educational label available in limited locations. Golden Records reissued its 1954 version of the theme from the 1941 Disney *Reluctant Dragon* film on a *Puff the Magic Dragon* compilation. Disneyland Records did not release the song on its own label until 1966.

Hanna-Barbera was among the first to create a dramatization of *The Reluctant Dragon* for records, albeit a funny and timely one, taking special aim at media frenzy. This time the artists must have been given some information about the story; the cover art depicts the climactic but phony televised battle between Touché and the dragon (the camera bears the insignia, "HBR TV").

The record brought back the veteran voice actor Bill Thompson (who was cast by Disney as the White Rabbit in *Alice in Wonderland*, Smee in *Peter Pan*, Ranger Woodlore, and the first film voice of Scrooge McDuck, as well as radio's Wallace Wimple) to voice Touché for the first time since 1962 when he recorded sixty-five cartoons. HBR's recasting process takes the form of Daws Butler replacing Alan Reed as Dum-Dum, playing him less in Reed's childlike way and more in a deep, dull tone.

Touché gets a call from the mayor of a small town, asking him to investigate some noise coming from a cave. Once inside the cave, he and Dum-Dum discover that the dragon is a lovable, pleasant person. Butler's voice for Smokey the Dragon is a delightful audio creation. He takes Shows's amusing lines and builds an engaging personality around them. This is a friendly, kooky fellow who enjoys his peaceful life. He sometimes gets lonely, even though he has two heads.[3] Touché tries to tell the mayor about

Smokey but just the idea of a dragon makes him start the hysteria. Soon Touché confronts a mob, one of whom is also played by Thompson in his Irish "Butch the Bulldog" voice. He says, "We don't allow dragons in our town" and "The only good dragon is a dead dragon."

> TOUCHÉ: They're coming after you, Smokey!
> SMOKEY: What on earth for? I haven't done anything wrong.
> TOUCHÉ: They're after you just because you're a dragon.
> SMOKEY: It's against the law to be a dragon? You gotta get a permit to be a dragon?
> TOUCHÉ: It's a long, long story, Smokey. You wouldn't understand.

They hatch a plan to stage a make-believe duel and on the big day, a young man and his grandpa tune in for "the fight of the century," but only after a few seconds of "Monster Shindig." On the field of battle, people are having picnics, kids are climbing trees to see better, and vendors are selling snacks and programs. After the first round, the announcer pauses for a commercial for "Mother McCree's Little Liver Pills for People with Little Livers."

The Reluctant Dragon was always a tale of a village in fear of something they didn't understand and a make-believe "show" to convince them of a truth that was already true. The Hanna-Barbera version puts a modern-day spin on the fable, not unlike a science-fiction "B" movie, which was also an allegory for a civilization seeking to destroy rather than understand. In this sense, Touché Turtle was starring in *The Day the Earth Stood Still*. Even with these layers, it's still a fun-filled Touché Turtle cartoon record filled with action and laughs for kids, who will get the message of treating others with respect. It's also one of the few children's records that takes satirical aim at the media circus phenomenon.

Like the HBR *Cinderella* album, it combines the sharper edges of Stan Freberg and the savvy of Jay Ward in a mix of characters, music, and format that makes it play in a way unique unto itself. One thing is for sure, there were no other records in any genre like the Hanna-Barbera Cartoon Series.

▲▼▲▼

20,000 *Leagues Under the Sea starring Jonny Quest* is the first album in which one of the characters has been reading the actual book and then participates in an experience resembling it. Jonny opens the story by reading Jules Verne's book, later commenting that their adventure is just like it. This served as a helpful device in cartoons; Warner Bros.' *Windblown Hare* (1949) finds both the Three Little Pigs and the Big Bad Wolf by reading their source material. In Hanna-Barbera's 1966 *Alice in Wonderland* TV special, Alice must study the book for homework and later finds herself in Wonderland, encountering references such as a signed message from Lewis Carroll reading, "This place is okay in my book."

On the *Quest* album, Jonny and the Professor explore the ocean, going down not quite 20,000 leagues, inside a diving bell, and things go terribly wrong. Race, who had been monitoring the controls, disappears, and Jonny and Dr. Quest start losing oxygen. By side two, we learn that Race had been battling a giant squid, or as they more often call it, "That . . . That Thing!"

Action stories can be difficult to pull off in pure audio because of exposition in the absence of visuals. The dialogue must describe without it seeming forced. The script manages this skillfully for the most part until the denouement when Jonny and Dr. Quest's lines ping-pong: "What might work, Dad?" "What do you mean, Dad?" etc.

In addition to the proliferation of exciting music cues, some unique to this LP, 20,000 *Leagues* is the only Hanna-Barbera Cartoon Series story release with an instrumental and the first to feature a genuine TV theme song. The label decided to give one of Hoyt Curtin's most iconic compositions double duty, as it had the potential to become a hit beyond the use on this album as it was the equivalent of the best-selling

Tim Matheson, John Stephenson, and Mike Road star in this suspenseful adventure featuring a Bond-like rendition of the theme by Shorty Rogers.

James Bond or *Peter Gunn* themes. While Curtin and Ted Nichols did not participate in the 20,000 *Leagues* album, there are plenty of exclusive musical passages to represent them. Shorty Rogers and His Giants, no strangers to animation thanks to their work in the renowned 1957 Friz Freleng–Stan Freberg short *Three Little Bops*, recorded a single version of the theme for HBR's pop label. Rogers's arrangement is a slower, hard-driving tempo á la the James Bond theme. It was probably recorded in stereo but HBR had not yet made the transition on the children's line and the singles were also still in mono.

Hadji, a popular character and Jonny's best friend, is sorely missing from the album. It is difficult to work too many characters into an audio adventure without it becoming too "busy." There have to be sufficient sequences to keep them balanced for the listeners' ears to keep track of them. Even in a classic radio program like *Lux Radio Theater* that might have a large cast, rarely are there numerous voices within a single scene. From a budget standpoint, adding Danny Bravo as Hadji would have increased the budget as well. Bandit is on the album but limited to a few canned barks. It is quite wonderful, though, that John Stephenson was able to return to his original role as Dr. Quest especially for the album.

▲▼▲▼▲

The *Robin Hood Starring Top Cat* album boasts one of HBR's tightest scripts, neatly building to a thrilling conclusion, flawlessly performed and edited. Top Cat is bemoaning the gang's usual low funds when he spots Choo-Choo reading *The Adventures of Robin Hood*, which inspired T. C. to "borrow" from the rich and give to the "poorrrr," namely himself and his friends. Yogi attempted the same on TV and in his feature film. Officer Dibble puts a stop to it, but building bows and arrows and practicing their use sets up the adventure on side two.

Like the *Top Cat* episode "Naked Town" (the title nodding to the TV series *Naked City*), two bank robbers stage a heist under the guise of making a movie, a plotline common to both cartoons and live-action.[4]

When this album was in production, Top Cat's TV cartoon voice, Arnold Stang, joined the cast of the TV sitcom *Broadside*, so Daws Butler does a variation of his Phil Silvers/Hokey Wolf voice, again striking a deft balance between the comic and the desperate, as in this scene:

> BRAIN: What are they gonna do with Dibble, T. C.?
> T. C.: They're gonna use him as a hostage, Brain!
>   A hostage!
> BRAIN: Isn't that against the law, T.C.?

It's always good to note that a seasoned performer may create a similar voice but not a mere duplication; Butler's TC is neither Arnold nor Hokey, the former having a higher register and less cynical tone and the latter tinged with more edge and sarcasm.

The *Robin Hood* album reunites three original Top Cat cast members: Marvin Kaplan as Choo-Choo, Leo DeLyon as Brain, and Allen Jenkins as Dibble. The presence of other cats is implied in a tongue-in-cheek manner. When T. C. calls the roll and the missing alley cats don't answer, he says, "All those absent, please raise your right hand. . . . Well, I see we're all here." A few grooves later, T. C. asks Fancy-Fancy to "borry him an apple." To this day, it still seems unclear and contradictory. There was not enough budget for John Stephenson and Maurice Gosfield, but Leo DeLyon was in the cast and could have played Spook. It was also a matter of, again, too many characters to juggle in an audio script. In addition to providing several voices (but not Spook for some reason), it sounds as if Leo DeLyon is singing a few songs, which would make him the only voice actor on an HBR record (besides those on cast albums like *The New Alice in Wonderland*

and *Jack and the Beanstalk*) heard on the songs as well as the story segments.

The songs offer an expanded range of rock and rhythm-and-blues styles, moving even further from the tone and manner of the spoken portions. Pop sounds were being featured occasionally on Hanna-Barbera TV cartoons as well, but they were presented within a performance or media context. On the records, one had to guess why they happened and where they originated. It became part of the unique, somewhat odd Hanna-Barbera Records experience. This album includes a "Robin Hood" ballad and a comical paean to "Dibble" sung in mock tribute with lyrics like, "Man's best friend is not his dog / Man's best friend is Dibble," closing with hilariously mawkish harmony, "Diiiiblllle." When it ends, Top Cat says, "Hold it, fellas, hold it!" The intent was to convey that they were all singing "Dibble," but the tone and performance bear so little resemblance, Top Cat's line seems out of place. Another song is called "M-O-N-E-Y." Taken at face value, it describes the age-old pursuit of wealth. However, taken as an ironic diatribe on greed, the bitter lyrics and sardonic performance can be seen as social commentary. Whether a child would understand such social underpinnings depends on the child, but its presence is an example of how Hanna-Barbera's Cartoon Series story records never talked down to kids, even if they had to ponder the words and phrases a bit longer than usual. Even for years.

▲▼▲▼▲▼

The Cartoon Series line was broadened to a category making it essentially the HBR children's line, so the occasional non-animation title would be produced for a family-friendly audience. The label launched a series-within-a-series with the "Hanna-Barbera 'Real-Life' Documentary" concept. Only one LP resulted, combining the recent NASA space missions dramatically.

The *Gemini IV: Walk in Space* and *Gemini V: Eight Days in Space* LP is one of a subgenre of space mission record albums released throughout the 1960s as excitement grew for the moon mission. While the moon landing was a major historic moment, each of the individual missions that made the landing possible was celebrated one by one through the new medium of television. However, because TV did not have the capabilities to capture all the actual visuals, the coverage still consisted mostly of audio, often tinny telephone-like messages between correspondents, astronauts, and NASA. This made the missions perfect for audio.

Some of the space-related children's records were whimsical fantasies (Bil and Cora Baird's *Man in the Moon, Bobby and Betty Go to the Moon*), and others were fact-based (Golden's *A Child's Introduction to Outer Space*). Hanna-Barbera's album was indicated as "real-life" in quotes because it was a serious dramatization of actual transcriptions and true events. Based on Charles Shows's experience with space-related programming in the early days of live TV and the Disney anecdotes in his autobiography, he had been enthusiastic about the subject for years. His fervor and detail are very much in evidence on the record and throughout the album package.

The gatefold is loaded with details about the missions and the astronauts. Mission radio transmissions were adapted faithfully. The "mission-speak" on the album between the NASA techs and the astronauts is fairly realistic, save for the tendency for the actors to get a little stentorian. All the speaking roles are uncredited. There seems to have been an attempt to avoid the more recognizable Jonny Quest cues but some of the marches especially give it away. The voices do not sound like H-B regulars; perhaps they were Shows himself and various associates.

Striving for as much authenticity as possible has the consequence of making the album less of an entertainment experience and more of a stolid school lesson, reminiscent of 16mm Coronet and Encyclopedia Britannica Films. Because they're intended to be "real" people, they aren't directed to emote very much. Only astronaut Ed White becomes a little lively as he starts to enjoy walking in space, if for only a moment.

Nineteen sixties TV viewers seeing hours of mission coverage saw a lot of interviews with scientists, techno-chatter between mission control and the astronauts, and "NASA Animation," which seemed little more than still pictures of spacecraft moving slowly along the TV screen. This album, while admirably well researched, is very much like that coverage. Nevertheless, it's a "capsule" of the events and presentation style of the space program in the US.

▲▼▲▼▲▼

One of the Hanna-Barbera Records initiatives was working records into programming to encourage sales. *The Flintstones* opened ABC's 1965 prime-time fall season with "No Biz Like Show Biz," an episode in which Fred dreams that Pebbles and Bamm-Bamm become pop music stars. Hanna-Barbera Records had been in operation all year and this was a promising cross-promotion of Pebbles and Bamm-Bamm and other HBR artists as well.

At the beginning of the episode, Fred flips the TV channels. Not by chance, two of these channels are playing Hanna-Barbera Records. The first, accompanied by a visual of teens dancing on a beach, is HBR's very first single, "Dance in the Sand" by The Creations IV. The second is a caricature of Danny Hutton himself, playing one of HBR's charting hits, "Roses and Rainbows," a song he performed in live-action on teen shows and included on a Three Dog Night compilation album. Hutton didn't pose for the caricature, it just happened.

"I remember watching it on TV," Hutton said. "I thought it was great. They gave me one of those animation cels of my picture, but somebody stole it."

▲▼▲▼▲▼

"Open Up Your Heart (and Let the Sun Shine In)" is an inspirational tune written by "singing cowboy" Stuart Hamblen, whose many successful tunes include Rosemary Clooney's "This Ole House." "Open Up Your Heart" was recorded many times before

Hanna-Barbera Records circulated this advertising flyer announcing two Christmas LP releases, in addition to Pebbles and Bamm-Bamm's single, "Open Up Your Heart."

Hanna-Barbera obtained ownership of the song for *The Flintstones*. The 1954 Little Golden Records version by western movie stars Roy Rogers and Dale Evans was available on Golden LPs through the '70s.

The original singing voices of Pebbles and Bamm-Bamm were the speeded-up voices of mother-and-daughter vocalists Ricky and Rebecca Page. HBR promoted the song with flyers and ads, releasing it on a 45 rpm single with a picture disc resembling the scene on the episode with Pebbles and Bamm-Bamm on stage, an image that would repeat for several end title sequences in the series. While never a

huge hit, it became the most well-known version of the song.

Hanna-Barbera never released "Open Up Your Heart" on an LP. Instead, Pebbles and Bamm-Bamm recorded two albums of other music. In addition to the Pages (who also performed as The Bermudas and The Majorettes), other singers reportedly sang for Pebbles and Bamm-Bamm, including Jessica Brown and Dominic Whitaker (presumably for the Flintstones feature) and versatile nightclub performer and studio singer Jean King. Ron Hicklin recalled King singing for Pebbles and Bamm-Bamm (perhaps using doubled vocals), and her distinctive voice sounds discernable as do the Pages on numerous albums featuring "The Hanna-Barbera Singers." Another possible P&BB could have been Sally Stevens, one of Hollywood's most prolific studio singers and contractors, whose career included The Randy Van Horne Singers and countless Hanna-Barbera vocal groups.

On the Good Ship Lollipop Starring Pebbles and Bamm-Bamm, originally titled *Shirley Temple Songs*, combines tunes from the child star's classic films and some originals. It's the first album in the Cartoon Series without a story since the two leads didn't speak beyond baby talk (yet). The *Lollipop* album is skewed very young. What is interesting is that they are still orchestrated with the basic combo from the other album sessions with some woodwinds, still a departure from the standard "kiddie" sound of the early days but not as far. The standout, style-wise, is "At the Codfish Ball" with a tribute to the sound of the roaring '20s that segues into a pop rhythm with special lyrics about groovy '60s dances. The striking album cover art by layout artist Homer Jonas and background artist Fernando Montealegre is the brightest and most colorful of all the Cartoon Series LPs.

Pebbles and Bamm-Bamm Singing Songs of Christmas (1965), or as listed on the vinyl label, *We Wish You a Merry Christmas*, includes some very inventive arrangements with modern "hooks" and fine vocal backing. Traditional carols and a few popular songs like "Frosty the Snowman" are among the tracks, plus a haunting original piece called "Snow Flake" with no lyrics other than those two and a lead guitar melody. As of this writing, *Songs of Christmas* is the only Hanna-Barbera Cartoon Series album ever reissued on CD in its entirety. New Line Records carefully restored the album cover, including all the notes on the back, and created some nice color treatments of the label design on the inside. Two a cappella carols, "Silent Night" and "God Rest Ye Merry Gentlemen," were restored in stereo, adding to the possibility that more material was recorded in two channels because the master tape lists contain unreleased stereo editions of most titles in the catalog.

The previous year, ABC aired an episode called "Christmas Flintstone" in which Fred, as a department store Santa, sings two songs by John McCarthy. There was every reason to expect HBR to release "Christmas Is My Favorite Time of Year" and "Dino the Dinosaur" on an LP or a single, but it was not to be. In 1965 Hanna-Barbera Records released the LP, *Merry Christmas*. On the cover, Fred plays a stone-age organ with Barney on tambourine, Yogi on cymbals, Magilla and Bamm-Bamm on triangles, Snagglepuss with a bass fiddle, and Top Cat on drums, with Wilma conducting using a candy cane as a baton. None of these characters are heard on the record. The cover plainly states, "Featuring The Hanna-Barbera Organs and Chimes," but with all the characters on the cover, some kids might have felt let down. To others who had grown to love the HBR label and were ready to expect anything, it was a cool cover with music that was traditional and a little weird, too. The unique pre-Moog computer version of "Jingle Bells" sounds as if robots Rosie and Mac were playing it. "Twelve Days of Christmas" is also mercifully short, cut in half. The musician misses a few notes here and there, likely due to a short session with little time for retakes.

A proliferation of organ-and-chime holiday albums was available in the mid-twentieth century. The music on this album is played on a Thomas organ, conveniently advertised on the back cover no doubt as promotional consideration. When the organ and chimes play "It Came Upon a Midnight Clear," it still suggests the moment when Fred Flintstone received his high school diploma. Maybe this fine Thomas product also accompanied him on his special day.

"We Three Kings" shows up on this album, the Pebbles and Bamm-Bamm LP, and years later on *Hanna-Barbera's Christmas Sing-Along* video. Was it a favorite of Bill and/or Joe?

▲▼▲▼▲▼

Through most of 1965 and well into 1966, pop singles generated by Hanna-Barbera Records were being marketed and plugged to encourage radio play and

▲▼▲▼▲▼

sales. In those days, regional sales were key to a song's success and a record could be a hit in several cities or states before it hit nationally (if ever). The regional market was where HBR was finding the most traction, as they were a small concern, angling for space and airplay with the very big, established record companies. The Cartoon Series was also being marketed by Hanna-Barbera Records, so while the albums were plentiful in Southern California, not all parts of the country were getting them in large quantities, though that was changing.

The 45 rpm extended-play records with either edited versions of Cartoon Series stories or songs from the albums were only 49 cents or less and were a popular impulse item in stores, also sold in toy departments with other children's records. A few of the smaller records combined a story with a few songs.

HBR also signed a deal with Pye Records, Ltd., to create an exchange of materials between the labels in Britain and the US. Soon albums and compilations of HBR singles were appearing on the EMI-Drum label, a division of Pye. At this point, another significant group of characters was about to make their debut on Hanna-Barbera Records—the stars of the first cartoon shows the studio produced especially for Saturday morning television.

Chapter 13

MARY POPPINS AND JAMES BOND

~~~~~~

**It's simple, Fred. Remember last week, we went to the
drive-in movie . . . and we saw *Mary Poppins*?**
—BARNEY RUBBLE (DAWS BUTLER)

Fred Flintstone and Barney Rubble in Songs from "Mary Poppins" must have inspired
more double-takes than any other LP covering the Oscar-winning Sherman Brothers score. Dozens of major recording artists and economy labels throughout the
world released songs or the entire score on records, making *Mary Poppins* one of
the most successful original scores ever created specifically for a film.

Poppins's huge box-office success inspired a myriad of pop culture references,
from Neil Simon's *The Odd Couple* to Sherwood Schwartz's *Gilligan's Island*. Surprisingly, *Poppins* was not spoofed on Hanna-Barbera TV shows. On the HBR LP,
the film's story is not told at all, as both the book and film details were likely copyrighted. Instead, the premise is similar to the second season *Flintstones* episode,
"The Hit Songwriters." Fred convinces Barney that they should quit their jobs and
become instant successes by writing surefire hits. Barney brings Fred a kerosene
guitar to help him write songs. Fred spends the rest of the album calling Barney to
hear his latest sure-fire hit. Barney recognizes every song and eventually reminds
him that they are from *Mary Poppins* (if jazz and rock and roll can be current in the
Stone Age, why not Walt Disney movies and Sherman Brothers songs?). Using this
frame story, Charles Shows came up with a clever way to sell an album starring
their own characters using songs licensed from another property.[1]

The album is respectful and in no way satirical regarding *Mary Poppins*, positioning the film and its songs as major hits on records, radio, and television. Barney
is finally able to convince Fred that these songs already exist, once "Chim Chim
Cheree" is performed on *The Ed Sullivan Show* (allowing Daws Butler to do one of
his funniest impressions, as he also does on the Snagglepuss *Wizard of Oz* LP).
The fact that the songs are produced so separately from the story material works

Great Sherman Brothers music meets Hanna-Barbera hijinks in this unique album.

in the album's favor because one of the unique qualities of the HBR Cartoon Series is the disconnected feeling of the songs and how they seem to "break into" the stories like commercials. This time they are designed that way. The arrangements have the cheeriness of the Pebbles and Bamm-Bamm albums with woodwinds and tambourines added to the band. (Note to *Poppins* score collectors: the song, "Jolly Holiday," includes the "raspberry ice" verse, which was not included on most recordings of the score in the sixties, including the soundtrack album.)

This album marks the world premiere of Henry Corden as the voice of Fred Flintstone. He must have impressed Barbera with his range of voices in *Jonny Quest* as he was becoming increasingly busy in supporting voices as the decade continued. The studio was in the process of producing two films requiring a singer who understood music and pitch. Alan Reed

handled the earlier "Christmas Is My Favorite Time of Year" and "Dino the Dinosaur" with warmth and charm, but Corden sounded even more like Alan Reed when he was singing than when speaking for Fred. He was chosen to sing for Fred in the upcoming *Alice in Wonderland* and *The Man Called Flintstone* and any other songs that required heightened singing skills.

The casting of Corden was also financial. According to Mel Blanc's studio engineer and biographer Chuck McKibbon, Reed's status as the star-billed voice of *The Flintstones* made his salary considerably higher than that of the other cast members, including Blanc. Whatever arrangement Reed made for the three HBR albums (one full side and a few lines on side two of *Flip Fables*; cameos on two other LPs), Corden was able to speak as Fred on three complete albums most likely for a budget-friendly fee.[2]

Henry Corden's film and TV career spanned decades, from *The Ten Commandments* and *The Asphalt Jungle* to *The Brady Bunch* and *The Monkees*.

Alan Reed's Fred Flintstone is uniquely his own. No one understood that more than Henry Corden. He incorporated Reed's Fred into the characters as best as he could at first but eventually eased his own personality into the voice. Anyone seeing him in his most famous character roles can easily hear the same tones, especially on *The Monkees* and *The Brady Bunch*. Corden's Fred began to use phrases like "Haah?" and call Barney "Pally."

Daws Butler, of course, had already voiced Barney for the TV series when Mel Blanc had his accident. He lampooned Art Carney's Ed Norton for Stan Freberg and Warner Bros., so it was not a far stretch, yet his Barney is not all Blanc, Carney, or Yogi. Like Corden, it's another actor's interpretation with respect to the original. Fred and Barney work (for some "boss" instead of Mr. Slate) in the same rock pile in this story. This conceit, convenient for the story, was not

current to the '60s series but became more or less the premise in the '70s and later revivals.

▲▼▲▼▲▼

The Flintstones: Hansel and Gretel is the only other HBR story LP with Alan Reed and Mel Blanc as Fred and Barney. It is a sequel of sorts to the *Flip Fables* album (though it's also possible that both albums were recorded together). It really should have been called *Barney Rubble Tells the Story of Hansel and Gretel* since Fred has only a few lines, just as he did on the *Bambi* album. Once again, Fred and Barney are trying unsuccessfully to get Pebbles (Jean Vander Pyl) to sleep. Barney offers to tell the tale while Fred (Alan Reed) makes occasional comments. Blanc does all the voices in *Hansel and Gretel*, giving Hansel a street-smart, Bugs Bunny–like attitude (but unlike Bugs's classic *Bewitched Bunny*, no one asks, "Hansel? Hansel!?"). (If Gretel had a heavy southern accent, she sounds like she could have asked Hansel to borrow "a nickel for the juke-box machine" in the Warner Bros. Bugs Bunny cartoon *Hillbilly Hare*.)

Blanc creates a particularly bloodcurdling step-mother in "Fang," a carping, abusive creature who browbeats the passive woodcarver. Fang first deceives the children by sending them on a "snipe hunt," an old dupe used on the naïve and trusting. When that doesn't work, she suggests a fishing trip and suc-ceeds in getting them lost in the woods. The two try to start a fire but are stopped and chastised by none other than Smokey the Bear. Once lost in the forest, Hansel and Gretel are lured by Blanc's "Lionel Barry-more"–type witch, by way of "Burma Shave" signs (a series of advertising signs that used to line highways in the mid-twentieth century) to "Grandma Grizzly's Goodyland." Barney explains that the two found the candy cottage "a bit Rococo" but they continue to have "lunch on the house" until the witch appears.[3] The kids eventually triumph in the same manner as other Hansels and Gretels, but the twist is that they become celebrities, appearing on TV shows like *Huckleberry Hound, Yogi Bear*—and *The Flintstones*!

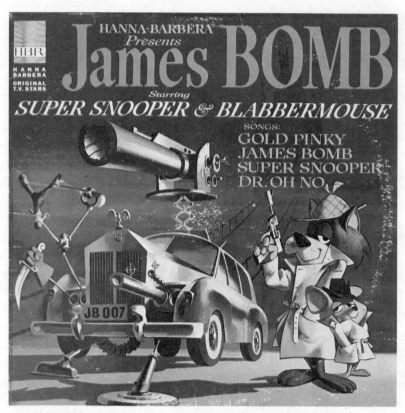

Hanna-Barbera Records salutes the Bond craze with this wild story about Snooper being mistaken for 007.

They turn Goodyland into an amusement park, the sign of sixties success to kids and aspiring animation companies.

In addition to the third appearance of "Bedrock Rock," this album contains two of the peppiest songs yet included on a Cartoon Series album, "Pebbles" and "Candy Cane Lane," both rendered in a more traditional "kiddie record" idiom than in the sixties pop style that was evident on future HBR discs (except the 1966 line of Cartoon Series 45s and the last two LP volumes of *Golden Cartoons in Song*, to be discussed in a later chapter).

▲▼▲▼

With the release of the *James Bomb Starring Super Snooper and Blabber Mouse* disc, Daws Butler returned effortlessly into both lead roles with old colleague

Don Messick making his HBR debut as Gold Pinky and James Bomb. While James Bond would battle SPECTRE (Special Executive for Counter-intelligence, Terrorism, Revenge, and Extortion), this record pits Super Snooper, Blabbermouse, and James Bomb against SQUISH (Society of Uncouth and Quarrelsome Idiots and Secret Horrors).

Nothing James Bond has done in the last several decades compares to the character's influence on worldwide culture during the 1960s cold war era. Bond mania was at such a fever pitch that it was reflected in almost every aspect of popular culture, merchandise, and fashion. Dozens of cartoons were already hopping into their versions of Bond's Aston Martin and several series would follow. On Saturday morning TV, Hanna-Barbera was just introducing Secret Squirrel, Rankin/Bass would include *Tom of T.H.U.M.B.* in 1966's *King Kong Show*, and King Features premiered Cool McCool in 1967. Super and Blabber were already private eyes, so it wasn't as much of a stretch to fit them into a spy caper as it was for TV's Mister Ed and Wilbur (yes, they did episodes in which the talking horse took on international spies).

James Bomb is the first story in the Cartoon Series that is not based on a classic fairy tale or legend, though it is of course inspired by the Ian Fleming novels. Like the *Top Cat/Robin Hood* LP, the blend of comedy and adventure plays to Charles Shows's writing strengths, using the art of listening to its full advantage, keeping the dialogue lively, and building to a genuinely exciting finish. For example, Dr. Oh No's exposition of his evil plans is kept from lagging by Gold Pinky's nagging, "What about the gold?" It also offers Gold Pinky some amusing character-based humor.

Butler and Messick are at their multitalented best. Butler turns in an especially nuanced, chilling performance as Dr. Oh No, a complete psychopath with touches of George Sanders (and of course, Joseph Wiseman, who played Dr. No in the first Bond film). The "good doctor" speaks with a tense, measured calm teetering on the edge of madness. For instance, when hitman "Killer" protests taking Snoop and Blab out of the shark pool, Dr. Oh No says, quietly, "I said . . . bring them here." The tone and pause intimidate Killer. He knows the consequences of disobeying Oh No.

The album divides seamlessly into two parts by devoting almost all of side one to Super and Blabber's encounter with Doctor Oh No and Gold Pinky. Side two introduces James Bomb and his luxurious, flying Rolls-Royce—after all, Ian Fleming also wrote *Chitty Chitty Bang Bang*. In the spectacular denouement, Snoop and Blab help 007 (or is it "Uh-Oh Seven?") in aerial pursuit of the villains, throwing the car's absurdly opulent accessories overboard to gain altitude.[4]

▲▼▲▼▲▼

The Jetsons in First Family on the Moon is an original adventure/comedy for records featuring Penny Singleton as Jane, Janet Waldo as Judy, and Daws Butler as Elroy. However, Don Messick is the voice of George

in place of George O'Hanlon, whose absence can be speculated as due to availability or budget.

Like the veteran actors on the early HBR albums, Don Messick is an interesting but different George Jetson. He's a nervous George, more in the nervous Dick York "Bewitched" vein, with a script that calls for George to be especially anxious. George is the only one against a trip to the moon, for fear of his life and that of his family. In one scene, NASA official Colonel Culpepper is in contact with George on the Moonbeam One rocket:

COLONEL: Jetson, what is your position right now?
GEORGE: My position? Well if you must know, I'm kneeling!

The story begins with Elroy entering a government-sponsored "free trip to the moon" contest, to which George asks, "What's the government got to do with a trip to the moon?" (and this was in 1965!). Hanna-Barbera cartoons made occasional in-jokes about life in Southern California, and so did the records. Twice on the album, George is reminded that rocket travel in his futuristic world is just as safe as driving on the freeway, which adds to his terror.

Astro is represented in one scene when he greets George. Daws Butler voices Astro instead of Don Messick, who is already speaking as George. This may have been done to save recording time since Messick would have had to be double-tracked to play Astro, and the doggie only makes a cameo in the story. In the absence of Mel Blanc, Butler plays Mr. Spacely, using the voice of Spacely's rival, Cogswell. More HBR voice-casting antics!

One of the highlights of the story is that surefire "the controls are broken so we need someone to land this thing" story situation. George has to operate the rocket himself, amid another mini symphony of Hanna-Barbera sound effects, timed beautifully by editor Milton Krear. Shows includes references to a fictional children's space TV show called *Commander Cosmic*. This is a nod to the live, daily regional NBC 1953 TV series *Commander Comet*, starring Larry

When the Jetsons win a free trip to the moon, everyone is thrilled except George, who is far from calmed when told that "space travel is as safe as driving on the freeway."

Harmon (before he bought the rights to *Bozo the Clown*) and a cast of puppets.

According to historian Don Yowp, Shows was hired for his stint in the initial phase of the Disney space TV project because of *Commander Comet*. The series featured educational segments and guests like Chuck Yeager. *First Family on the Moon* offers elements of education, somewhat at the expense of Elroy's usually advanced intelligence. Elroy asks a few obvious questions and opens a hatch door into the vacuum of space (we assume while wearing his helmet, as there was a reference to space suits earlier in the story), but then none of the Jetsons receive any training, instructions, or human accompaniment on this journey—at least not any the listener is allowed to hear.

The album's songs (introducing a fuzz guitar to the Cartoon Series) seem to share George's ambivalent view of space travel. While the LP's story tells of a family sent to the moon by the government, three of the songs question the wisdom of the program when there are other issues at hand back on Earth. The fact that this recording examines the issue from several sides exemplifies the highly unusual approach of HBR Cartoon Series records in the mid-sixties. Just after the Jetsons blast off, the song "Space Crazy" follows with lyrics like: "If man is looking for the way to happiness afar / He'd better learn this very day to live right where we are."

After the story closes and the final gag finishes with a familiar H-B music library sting, one of the most bizarre songs completes the album, a short pre–David Bowie "Major Tom" soliloquy with Ron Hicklin as a clueless, "Jeeves"-like astronaut who would rather be in "Bedrock-land" but has been given a one-way ticket. He thinks something went wrong and as he hollers,

Tim Matheson returns to the HBR Cartoon Series, along with Mel Blanc and animation artist/cartoonist Warren Tufts, for a modern-day voyage to *Treasure Island*.

"Hel-puh! Hel-puh!" the music descends into a cymbal crash. Even "The Jetsons" song that opens the album has a tinge of regret in the final lyric: "A futuristic life they lead with ultramodern ways / But what the Jetsons wouldn't give for the good old days." The song also says that the Jetsons "spend weekends on Mars," even though the story premise depicts a moon voyage as a pioneering venture.

Like the songs, the cover art differs from the story. *The First Family on the Moon* cover art by Don Shepard and Harvard Pennington is filled with inventively designed moon creatures surprising the Jetsons at every turn. Along with the volcanic hand-lettering by Robert Schaefer, one could spend hours marveling at this art as if in a gallery.

Perhaps the best philosophy for enjoying HBR records is to think of them as varied elements of a creative whole, even if the lush artwork and pop songs are not always in sync with the story content. That's how they got them done and thus created the highly unusual HBR effect.

▲▼▲▼▼

With Tim Matheson playing another of several Hanna-Barbera lead characters, *Treasure Island Starring Sinbad, Jr.* is like a companion album to *20,000 Leagues Under the Sea Starring Johnny Quest*. Sinbad, Jr. is a young mariner who finds adventures at sea with his sidekick Salty the parrot (Mel Blanc). Ted Cassidy, iconic for numerous on-screen and voice-acting roles (most famous as the original "Lurch" in *The Addams Family* TV series) makes a rare appearance on records as Red Beard the pirate. Mel Blanc reprises his TV voice role as Salty the parrot. The background music varies from most HBR LPs, with some nautical themes that would be utilized into the seventies. The songs are bouncy sea shanties and rhythmic calypsos.

Story/layout artist and cartoonist Warren Tufts was the only person who lent his talents to the sound of Hanna-Barbera Records as well as their cover art. For the *Sinbad, Jr.* album, he provides the opening narration and is credited as Pegleg. Tufts dabbled in acting on and off camera. He can be heard in many of Cambria's *New Three Stooges* cartoons and in the lead role of TV's *Captain Fathom*. (Tufts's voice, a cross between Hal Smith and Mike Road, sounds as if it might also be uncredited on HBR's *Gemini* and *Tell-Tale Heart* albums.) The *Sinbad, Jr.* cover art (created by Tufts with Harvard Pennington) adds depth to the look of Sinbad and Salty and takes a few steps away from the typical H-B house style for Pegleg and Red Beard.

The LP story has little at all to do with Robert Louis Stevenson's *Treasure Island* except that Pegleg is a Ben Gunn–like character. There are pirates and an island with treasure. Red Beard replaces Long John Silver and the setting is called Skull Island. Sinbad has not been reading a book like Jonny Quest or Choo-Choo. For Salty the sea parrot, Mel Blanc crafted a blend of Porky and Bugs. He makes comments and reminds Sinbad to use his belt. Tim Matheson would voice a few more Hanna-Barbera heroes, before moving into older roles (*Yours, Mine and Ours, Animal House, 1941*). Transitioning into a highly prolific career, he looks with fondness upon his work at Hanna-Barbera, working with great actors, and returned to voice "the President" in the 2015 direct-to-video feature *Tom and Jerry: Spy Quest*, which teams the cat and mouse with Jonny Quest (played by Reece C. Hartwig).

This is the only Cartoon Series album without a Hanna-Barbera copyright. Instead, American International Pictures is listed. *Sinbad, Jr.* was one of several animated projects from AIP, the independent film and TV company, specializing in beach party/horror flicks. The company ventured into animation with series like 1966's Miami-dubbed *Prince Planet* (which boasted a theme song by Annette Funicello song-

writers Guy Hemric and Gary Styner) and the 1964 Japanese feature *Alakazam the Great* dubbed with Frankie Avalon and Sterling Holloway. American International first produced *Sinbad, Jr.* for syndication with Sam Singer Productions, as a spinoff from the Singer series, *Bucky and Pepito*. Hanna-Barbera produced its own *Sinbad, Jr.* cartoons, recasting the voices, scoring them with studio library music, and adding a brassy new theme.

American International's association with Hanna-Barbera took some interesting twists and turns. Joe Barbera, whose dream of being a playwright never left him, had penned a stage comedy called *The Maid and the Martian*. Barbera was delighted to see his play produced on the Southern California stage successfully in 1952, directed by Gordon Hunt, who would become head of voice direction for many years at the studio. In 1964, American International released *Pajama Party*, a comedy with the same premise starring Annette and Tommy Kirk. Barbera's play was not credited, but the premise was the same, and Annette's Buena Vista soundtrack album also included a song that was not actually used in *Pajama Party* called "The Maid and the Martian." It suggests that negotiations of some sort occurred between Barbera and AIP.

In the early seventies, H-B and AIP announced a series of family-friendly theatrical features to compete with Disney's hit comedies, resulting in just one, *C.H.O.M.P.S.*, about an electronic surveillance dog.

▲▼▲▼▲▼

Fall 1965 brought the premiere of Hanna-Barbera's first Saturday morning TV series, *The Atom Ant/Secret Squirrel Show*. On September 12, NBC presented Hanna-Barbera's first prime-time network special, *The World of Atom Ant and Secret Squirrel*. For many viewers, this hour of live-action and animated sequences was the major debut of Bill Hanna and Joe Barbera on television. (The 1964 *Here Comes a Star* film promoting Magilla Gorilla was not as widely circulated.) They arrived by helicopter at their modern-looking Cahuenga studio to introduce the first new

Hanna-Barbera cartoons created for Saturday morning TV.

Hanna-Barbera Productions, NBC, and their partners had enormous confidence in the benefits possible through these six new Hanna-Barbera cartoons. So did Hanna-Barbera's record company, which came up with a very ambitious plan unlike anything done before for records based on cartoon characters.

Chapter 14

ATOM ANT, SECRET SQUIRREL, AND THE WAY-OUTS

We went all the way to New York, spent six weeks listening to everyone from Barbra Streisand to The Beatles, and we still didn't find the new sound we're looking for!
—DARRRYL MOGUL (HENRY CORDEN),
THE HILLBILLY BEARS IN HILLBILLY SHINDIG (1965)

The Atom Ant/Secret Squirrel Show was precedent-setting in several ways. As the world's largest animation studio, this was Hanna-Barbera's venture into Saturday mornings with new programming. Other companies had previously introduced new series on Saturday morning (Total TeleVision's *Tennessee Tuxedo* and *Underdog*) and new versions of classic cartoons (Harvey's *New Casper Cartoon Show*), but after Hanna-Barbera's prime-time reruns had proven to have such strength and appeal in this relatively new animation frontier, the industry was watching the new series closely.

This also marked the first time an entire record album line was produced featuring every lead cartoon character in a new series, right out of the gate. Each of the six new albums was designed for instant recognition from television. The title cards of the broadcast cartoons resembled the album covers, using the sketches and layouts. The album art was painted and finished with additional detail.

To be effective, LP album covers had to stand out from the other records in retail stores. They must catch the eye quickly, usually making the top third carry a lot of the "headline" information. Parents were the primary buyers, so the covers had to convince them to make the purchase as much as children, which is why there was so much text on the early albums and so much technical sound information on the HBR covers. Astute children's record album art directors also know that children sometimes like to look at the covers as they listen, as well as yearn for more records in the catalog. The Hanna-Barbera records delivered lush artwork and tantalizing photos of other albums to look for in the store.

The six albums based on *The Atom Ant/Secret Squirrel Show* began to credit "The Hanna-Barbera Singers" on the front covers. This was a wise move to assure that listeners understood that the characters would not be singing the songs. What few realized was that these singers were actually a part of the TV cartoons, too. Members of Ron Hicklin's male vocal assemblages picked up where The Randy Van Horne Singers left off.

As early as 1964, they could be heard singing the themes for *Magilla Gorilla*, *Peter Potamus*, and *Sinbad, Jr.* They are the voices behind the *Flintstones* rock-and-roll group called The Way Outs in "Masquerade Party," a sixth-season episode inspired by a 1933 radio Martian invasion hoax by actor/director Orson Welles. The Way Outs are four mop-topped Liverpudlian lads (designed to detach their modular bodies while singing) who are part of a similar radio publicity hoax. Singers who were regularly contracted by Ron Hicklin were heard on vinyl as The Hanna-Barbera Singers, though he recalled that Stan Farber handled the contracting for the label. For the six albums that tied into *The Atom Ant/Secret Squirrel Show*, three of the songs in this group of LPs were also cover and/or soundtrack versions of tunes heard on the TV version of the new series.

▴▾▴▾▴

The first two-thirds of *Atom Ant* in *Muscle Magic* are among the most well-executed twenty-one minutes in all the HBR Cartoon Series. At the very least, it's a chief example of why this series of records is still remembered and revered by so many of its devotees.

Taking a page out of histrionic 1950s sci-fi movies, a small rural town is terrorized by giant ants from outer space. How this plays out in audio is superb, between the voice acting, the H-B library music (mostly from *Jonny Quest*), sound effects, and editing—making the mental picture more spectacular than a visual could (especially in limited animation). Don Messick, who plays Atom Ant, does his classic "creepy alien gibberish" voice for the ants, a vocal

Bill and Joe, seen here making big plans with giant office supplies, appeared in an NBC prime-time special to introduce their first series created for Saturday morning TV, *The Atom Ant/Secret Squirrel Show.*

effect that Hanna-Barbera could use equally well in action or comedy cartoons. Add to that a little 1965 political satire (complete with HBR's favorite comedy foil, Lyndon Baines Johnson), and this is primo stuff for the label.[1]

The album does not sustain this level of comedy and "B"-movie excitement all the way through. A few minutes into side two, the story is abruptly resolved. This could have been the end of the album, and with the four songs, could have been accepted as a children's LP with a short running time. Some records, even though they were LPs, ran fifteen to twenty minutes. But instead, more material is included that could be seen as padding or as a way to offer a comparable value to other HBR LPs. In that last section, a reporter (Daws Butler) interviews Atom Ant about fitness and nutrition. Some of Atom Ant's responses

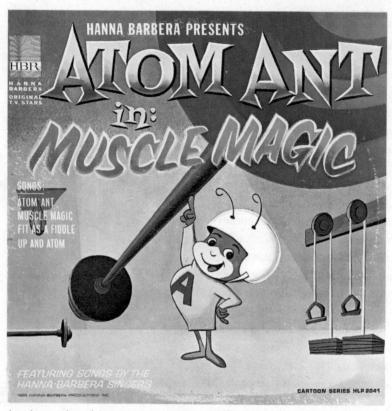

Atom Ant saves the earth from giant monster ants on this album celebrating the tradition of outrageous sci-fi movies.

are common sense: get plenty of exercise and eat right. Some show their mid-twentieth-century age: eat lots of red meat. Another technique is not exactly easy to access. Atom tells of the Greek myth about Milo, who became strong from running around with a calf that grew into a bull. NOTE: Ask your doctor before beginning any excessive red meat diet or bovine exercise program.

Writer Frederick Wiegand described the *Atom Ant* album for the Animation Spin feature on cartoon research.com:

This album is a true tour-de-force. I love Janet Waldo's reaction to the giant ants. It sounds like a 50's sci-fi movie. And the gentle political humor is rich and holds up even today. What's missing is where the giant ants came from—no explanation is given—and Atom Ant's "thinking like an ant,"

which he promises but does not deliver. Instead, he beats the ants through super strength and no particular strategy.

I do feel that after the big buildup to Atom Ant, more could and should have been done with the character once he is introduced. The menace is dispatched almost too quickly and easily. Even in the cartoons, Atom had to use strategy to solve some of the challenges. The latter part of the story could have been beefed up, thus rendering the interview less necessary to fill time.

The rendition of the *Atom Ant* theme song makes a nice change for this series, instead of replacing it with a "new" song for the character. It's also nice to hear the lyrics sung instead of spoken [in the TV version, actor Ted Cassidy— Lurch of *The Addams Family* and voice of many H-B villains—talks/sings the theme].

Wiegand is correct in that only these two LPs included actual H-B vocal themes, with Shorty Rogers's instrumental of *Jonny Quest* being the only other theme on the album series. There is one more piece of music from the TV cartoons that made its way to Hanna-Barbera records: "Do the Bear."

▲▼▲▼▲▼

The Hillbilly Bears in "Hillbilly Shindig" is an expanded version of story artist Tony Benedict's TV episode, "Do the Bear," including the song from the soundtrack. In the TV version, "Do the Bear" also makes Paw Rugg a pop superstar with a new sound. Screaming fans chase him until he returns home, only to find that dopey Claude Hopper is going to woo Floral Rugg with "Do the Bear." Paw angrily goes after Claude for the familiar H-B "chase-to-fade" ending.

Floral Rugg is not part of the album story. Jean Vander Pyl could have provided the voice of both Maw and Floral, but this is another instance of keeping the audio simpler with fewer characters, regardless of the economic situation.

The TV version of "Do the Bear" did not air until October of the following year, so the record gave listeners a special advantage. Benedict's story was expanded beautifully for the album, using side one to introduce typical Hollywood big-shot Darrryl ("with three r's") Mogul (played with Warner Bros. '30s aplomb by Henry Corden) and his smarmy publicist, Flack Fletcher (Daws Butler at his Phil Silvers-iest). Looking for "a new sound," they meet Maw and Paw Rugg and cultures lightly clash.

Paw's mumble is easily Henry Corden's greatest original vocal creation. Using the voice within a pop music context is a natural for comedy. He is "discovered" and by the end of side one, he's singing the soundtrack of "Do the Bear." While it may not be a theme song, "Do the Bear" is indeed the version that is also heard in the cartoon. By the time the record is flipped, Paw's been marketed into a sensation and booked for *The Ed Sullivan Show* (starring Daws Butler).

After Paw disappears, he is found back home enjoying his favorite dish, possum gizzards and hominy grits. The TV crew decides to produce the show in the Big Smokies (by sheer chance a similar solution was reached in the 1963 movie, *Hootenanny Hoot* starring Peter Breck and Ruta Lee). It's a "r-r-r-rreally big" success.

The album presents the "Do the Bear" soundtrack version once on each side, plus an additional version by The Hanna-Barbera Singers, in addition to other original songs. *Hillbilly Shindig* also contains the wildest edited "suite" of Hanna-Barbera sound effects to appear on any record album, HBR or otherwise. It occurs when Darrryl and Flack's car is filled with moonshine instead of gasoline. The ignition initiates a Milch masterpiece, over thirty-five seconds including Gazoo's snap, the El Kabong-er, a cash register, a music box, a baseball bat, a telephone, and dozens more in rapid succession. Near the end, it sounds like an outtake was inserted of Jean Vander Pyl sighing between takes!

The Hillbilly Bears cartoon was the third segment of *The Atom Ant Show*, which NBC originally combined into an hour with *The Secret Squirrel Show*. The second cartoon starred a sweet little old lady and her dog, a crafty canine whose signature laugh was a Messick magnum opus.

▲▼▲▼▲▼

Precious Pupp cartoons were consistently the funniest of all six segments in *The Atom Ant/Secret Squirrel Show*. It harkened back to theatrical cartoons in which the main character had to go on an errand, leaving a mischievous pet or child at home to wreak havoc. Precious Pupp's usual motivation was to protect the unaware Granny Sweet, making him a lovable rogue. His cute/ugly design instantly "reads" a comically sly character, and Don Messick's trademark mocking, hissing laugh fits perfectly. The hissing, laughing Messick dog goes back to early Hanna-Barbera cartoons, though Muttley and Mumbly eventually became the most internationally famous

The Eligibles, later as members of The Ron Hicklin Singers, sang on Hanna-Barbera Records, TV cartoons, and features into the 1980s.

incarnations. Granny was the epitome of the sixties "hip little old lady" who as the album says, "digs The Beatles, does a little surfing, dances a groovy Watusi, and drives a hopped-up little jalopy that isn't far from being a hot rod." Granny Sweet is one of Hanna-Barbera's most contemporary females, a lady who makes her own choices and lives an active life, far from a stereotypical fuddy-duddy.

Side one of *Precious Pupp and Granny Sweet in "Hot Rod Granny"*[2] concerns her efforts to win a big drag race to pay off her mortgage. It shares two elements of a TV episode called "Queen of the Road," with the album story of Granny being in a race, and an opponent named Leadfoot. But in the cartoon, Leadfoot seems to be a prototype of who would become Dick Dastardly three years later on *Wacky Races*, creating elaborate cheating schemes that fail. The script treats the race in a gag-free, straightforward manner with

Allan Melvin and Don Messick as track announcers. Leadfoot is mentioned only by name as the last of several competitors, with a last name of "Bohanan." It's an inside joke referring to the president of Hanna-Barbera Records, Don Bohanan. Perhaps his driving skills were the talk of the water cooler. After Granny wins the race, she and Precious return home and she turns on the TV so Precious can watch *Yogi Bear*. Instead, The Hanna-Barbera Singers perform "Queen of the Drag," followed by a news report about killer bank robbers on the loose. Precious makes it clear that he will carry out Granny's request to keep her money "from those crooked crooks."

Side two switches the focus to Precious and the robbers, Muscles and Slapsy. They read about Granny's race winnings and, disguised as old ladies, decide to have tea with Granny and search her house. Little do they realize that Granny has a "secret weapon."

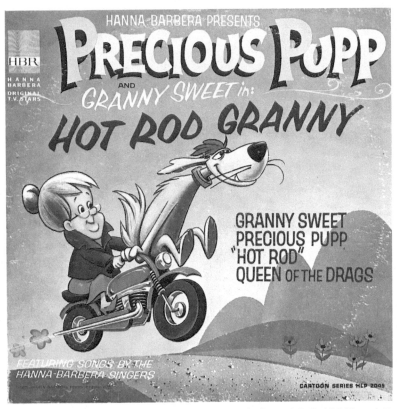

Granny Sweet becomes a car racing champion and Precious Pupp protects her from crooks in this delightful comedy LP.

Precious manages to be everywhere they search, snapping at them like a live mouse trap. The story builds to a wild chase with Granny and Precious in the hot rod pursuing the crooks, bringing all the characters together neatly. The album truly captures the spirit of the cartoon.

Even the groovy songs work. Sometimes the HBR songs are conspicuous by their stylistic distance from the narrative, but in the case of *Hot Rod Granny*, the surf sound of the same people who sang for The Way Outs is ideal. It's just what Granny would be listening to on her portable plastic fold-down stereo.

▲▼▲▼▲▼

The Cartoon Series had set its own kind of standard by the time *Secret Squirrel and Morocco Mole* in *Super Spy* was released. Super Snooper's *James Bomb* LP

established a high level of comedy and adventure, and Precious Pupp's disc successfully brought what was essentially a visual gag cartoon to audio. It turns out that "Super Spy," while a competent album with fun moments, falls short of its vast potential. So vividly can audio depict fantastic things in one's imagination, there is reason to expect Secret Squirrel's vinyl adventures to be as inventive as many of the earlier HBR LPs. Instead, the entire record is about a cow. Instead of brilliant symphonies of crazy gadgets in sound effects, the same "moo" effect punctuates most of the punch lines.

The album begins with promise. Secret demonstrates his "sub-copter-plane-car," offering the opportunity to imagine the wild contraption through sound. Next, Secret and Morocco are assigned to rescue a sacred cow and return it to the Kingdom of Moo. On side one, they don a cow disguise to infil-

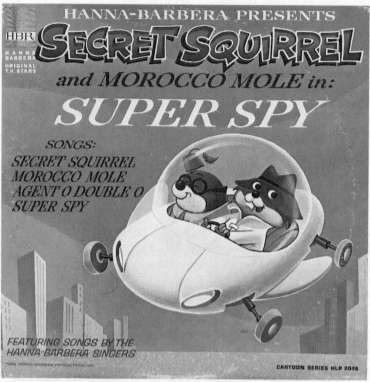

Secret and Morocco outwit Yellow Pinky in Palm Springs, where writer/director Charles Shows has a star on the Palm Springs Walk of Fame.

trate a band of rustlers at an Arizona ranch run by Yellow Pinky, a villain from the TV series. On side B, the two of them check into a hotel in Palm Springs with the rescued cow. Yellow Pinky also pursues them throughout side two.

The best aspects are, of course, Mel Blanc as Secret Squirrel, and Daws Butler as Morocco Mole. Paul Frees, the TV voice of Morocco, must have been booked elsewhere. Yellow Pinky's voice is not credited but sounds like Don Doolittle, an actor rarely credited who is heard on the *Gemini* LP and some later discs.

Like the *Atom Ant: in Muscle Magic* album, this album begins with the theme song instead of a song "about" the character. Even though the album version of the Secret Squirrel theme is not the soundtrack, it is sung by much the same vocalists heard on the TV version. Another plus is the hotel sequence. A fancy hotel is usually a great place for comedy, so sneaking in a cow and ordering room service for it is wonderfully absurd.

The Palm Springs setting on this album has several behind-the-scenes connections. Joe Barbera was fond of spending time sunning and mingling among the Palm Springs glitterati. Charles Shows was an active part of the community. Thirty-two years after this Secret Squirrel album was produced, Shows was awarded a star on the Palm Springs Walk of Fame on March 15, 1997. It is located at 139 South Palm Canyon Road.

▲▼▲▼▲▼

The six albums based on *The Atom Ant/Secret Squirrel Show* were given such generic story titles, it left no clue as to what the premises were, or if they had stories at all. One of them did not. At first glance, *Squiddly Diddly's Surfin' Surfari* might suggest a story in which Squiddly escapes from Bubbleland aquarium, heads for a beach party and ends up on a surfing adventure. Instead, as the subtitle states, this is a collection of "Squiddly's favorite surfing songs." Squiddly himself makes no appearance on the disc except on the cover and through his mention on the first track.

The "Squiddly" song, a strangely minor-key tune for such a whimsical character, has the same melody as "The Jetsons" song and a similar arrangement as "Space Crazy" from *First Family on the Moon*. The remaining songs are original surfing-related tunes, all sounding as if this could be yet another release from those "creatures from way, way out," The Way-Outs.

Maybe there was a need to balance the budget for this wave of albums by producing something quick and inexpensive. A song LP involves only the music element with no scriptwriting, no voice recording, music and effects editing, and the blending of the songs with the story. It's possible that "The Hanna-Barbera Singers" could record all twelve songs for a fraction of the cost and time involved with producing a Cartoon Series story album.

As a retro item, *Surfin' Surfari* is worthwhile, especially from an aesthetic aspect. As a listening experience, it's a kick for those who enjoy fun, foamy, carefree beach party music. It might have done its subject more justice had there been more lyric material created that related directly to the cartoon. But maybe the whole idea was to depart from the obvious and instead give kids almost a whole platter of surf pop. Such seemed to be in keeping with the loose, experimental nature of Hanna-Barbera Records.

▲▼▲▼▲▼

In the third segment of *The Secret Squirrel Show*, Hanna-Barbera introduced Winsome Witch, TV's first animated female lead character, as well as the first human lead character in H-B short cartoons. *Winsome Witch in It's Magic* is, like Wilma Flintstone's *Bambi* LP, a wondrous showcase for Jean Vander Pyl in the title role. True to her name, Winnie and her cartoons are among the most pleasant and easygoing of the era. Winnie uses her magic to make things more fun and make bad guys change or take a hike. She can turn the world on with her wand.

Once again, the title has nothing to do with the story, which combines elements of two 1965 TV episodes, "Winnie the Sheriff" and "School Teacher Winnie" from 1966. Winnie moves to an old western town to teach in a schoolroom filled with kids voiced by Dick Beals. As in the cartoon version, she makes learning fun with magic. When Killer Miller (Daws Butler) and his gang arrive in town, Winnie is appointed sheriff and changes the crooks into all kinds of silly things. The various magical transformations work beautifully in this instance because the action is balanced with the exposition, which generally avoids being too obvious. In essence, the Winsome Witch album reached a level that the Secret Squirrel LP did not quite achieve, including a generous mix of effects and music cues, some fresh from the new Ted Nichols batch created for the NBC series.

Winnie's magic is accompanied by one of Hanna-Barbera's most renowned sound/music effects. It's known as "Jet Screamer" because it originated in the second *Jetsons* episode for the dynamic entrances of Judy Jetson's favorite pop star. However, it is notable that Winnie does not use her magic words from the TV version: "Ippity-Pippity-Pow!" The songs make reference to the phrases *abrakadabra* and *va-va-va-vroom*, which might have been under discussion earlier in the cartoon's development. This album must have been put together before "Ippity-Pippity-Pow!" was made official.

The songs are stylistically unique among the other Cartoon Series records, with a casual, cool jazz vibe, perhaps in keeping with the easygoing style of the Winsome Witch cartoons.

If all six albums were played in the order of the original *Atom Ant/Secret Squirrel* cartoon shows, *It's Magic* is a warmhearted and funny way to close out the 1965 line of Cartoon Series record albums. Things were off to an extraordinary start. Now it was getting even more ambitious, with the label taking a key role in Hanna-Barbera's first animated network special and second theatrical feature film.

Chapter 15

FRED, BARNEY, SAMMY, AND ALICE IN WONDERLAND

~~~~~~

What's a nice kid like you doing in a place like this?
—THE CHESHIRE CAT (SAMMY DAVIS JR./SCATMAN CROTHERS),
HANNA-BARBERA'S *ALICE IN WONDERLAND* (1966)

After its first year, Hanna-Barbera Records boasted a substantial line of Cartoon Series children's records in selected stores nationwide, as well as in the UK through Pye Records. HBR pop singles and albums were already in circulation, to be marketed regionally and nationally, and a few planned to tie in with H-B television. There were fewer Cartoon Series releases in the second year, but they were more eclectic than ever. Hanna-Barbera would also increase its number of teen and adult interest albums.

When it came to singles, the label took a new approach to tie with *The Atom Ant/Secret Squirrel Show*. No more would HBR edit down the narratives from story records for 45 rpm records. So there were no condensed versions of *Hot Rod Granny*, *Hillbilly Shindig*, *Muscle Magic*, and *It's Magic* on 45s nor were there EPs of songs from these albums. Instead, over a dozen two-song singles with picture sleeves offered tried-and-true public domain Mother Goose and nursery songs. The musical style was skewed younger, more akin to the Pebbles and Bamm-Bamm *Good Ship Lollipop* LP of the previous year.

On the picture sleeves, children's tunes like "London Bridge" and "The Alphabet Song" were seen as "presented" by Atom Ant, Precious Pupp, the Hillbilly Bears, Secret Squirrel, Squiddly Diddly, or Winsome Witch. The picture sleeves clearly stated the artists as The Hanna-Barbera Singers. HBR was simply following Disneyland Records' lead. Many Disneyland "Little Gem" singles featured Mickey Mouse, Donald Duck, and friends on record sleeves for children's songs upon which they did not sing. The marketing and merchandising mindset here was not unlike using a character on a can of orange juice or a box of breakfast cereal. The characters were depicted in scenes suggesting the songs, e.g., Atom Ant carrying a big cake for

134

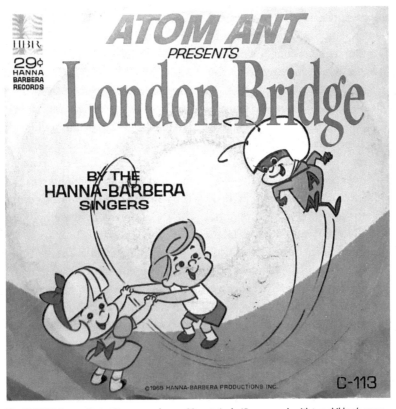

The 1966 HBR Cartoon Series 45 rpm records were 29-cent single 45 rpm records with two children's songs rather than the 1965 49-cent EP with H-B stories and/or character-related songs.

"Happy Birthday," etc. The most emotionally affecting art was, perhaps surprisingly, for the two Precious Pupp singles. For "Brahms Lullaby," Precious is contentedly resting with his beloved Granny Sweet. "The Lord's Prayer" art finds them praying at the bedside.

This 1935 musicalized version of "The Lord's Prayer," recorded by hundreds of artists from Barbra Streisand to The Beach Boys, was composed by Albert Hay Malotte (1895–1964), who also scored many classic Mickey Mouse and Silly Symphony cartoons including *Lonesome Ghosts*, *Brave Little Tailor*, and *The Ugly Duckling*. Both "Brahms Lullaby" and "The Lord's Prayer" are given moving performances by Jean King, who had run the gamut of HBR moods, from a Shirley Bassey belt for "Gold Pinky" to Shirley Temple cuteness for "Candy Cane Lane."

Side two of each of these records presented a pick-up from an earlier Pebbles and Bamm-Bamm

release or more often an original song built over an existing Cartoon Series music bed. For example, the "Top Cat" song with new lyrics became "I've Got a Pony," and "Doggie Daddy" was converted into "Hide and Seek."

At 29 cents each, these "Presented By" song records were sold at lower price points than the earlier line of HBR 45s, which were 49 cents, competitively priced alongside Disneyland, Golden, Peter Pan, Pickwick, and the children's lines of major labels like RCA and Columbia.

▴▾▴▾▴

Four LP albums called *Golden Cartoons in Song* were released in conjunction with these singles and earlier releases. On the singles, Hanna-Barbera characters appeared in scenes representing the songs. On the albums, the characters were seen in close-ups next to the large song title text, emphasizing the fact that the music featured not the characters but The Hanna-Barbera Singers. It was still confusing because of the "Golden Cartoons in Song" title.

The answer was clearest when it came to volume one in the *Golden Cartoons in Song* LP series. This was a collection of fourteen character-related tracks that spanned the Cartoon Series all the way back to *Monster Shindig*'s "Super Snooper." Pete Rugolo's *Jonny Quest* theme was included. One song, "Quick Draw McGraw," had not appeared on a previous release. Volume two collected twelve story-related songs from the same albums, like "Three Little Pigs," "Cinderella," and "The Wicked Witch." Volumes one and two offer the listener a sense of creative cohesion because the songs themselves were fairly consistent as to the performers and productions. The effect might have been better presented as a novel idea to set the discs apart from their competition—two children's albums of cartoon and storybook songs in pop style. Volumes four and five of *Golden Cartoons in Song* consist of songs for young children, starting with "Happy Birthday." For many years, the ownership of the birthday tune was thought to be the property of Mildred and Patty Hill, though that has been disproved. When this album was recorded, to avoid payment, the music bed of "Dibble" from the *Top Cat/Robin Hood* album was given birthday lyrics. However, on the "Atom Ant Presents" single version, the actual "Happy Birthday" is sung along with "For He's a Jolly Good Fellow."

▵▾▵▾▵

One reasonable question might be: What did Bill Hanna and Joe Barbera think of the records bearing their name? Surely they listened to some, but probably not all of them, any more than they are likely to have read every Hanna-Barbera comic and storybook. Each of them had stereo systems in their offices.[1] Walt Disney was familiar with some of the records made by his in-house label but unaware of others.

Some of them are still neatly filed in his private office as he left it in 1966.

One thing is for sure, *The Flintstones* in "S.A.S.F. A.T.P.O.G.O.B.S.Q.A.L.T." was made with barbershop singer Bill Hanna in mind. The initials stand for "Stone-Age Society for Aiding the Preservation of Good Old Barber Shop Quartets and Like That." This is a parody of the acronym, "S.P.E.B.S.Q.S.A.," the Society for the Preservation and Encouragement of Barber Shop Quartet Singing in America. The album's title became so confusing for HBR that the titles on the inside vinyl disc cover and inside label don't match.

The album reworks *The Flintstones* season four episode "The Flintstone Canaries," which would resurface on *The Pebbles and Bamm-Bamm Show* in 1971 as "The Golden Voice." Henry Corden and Daws Butler are back, playing Fred, Barney, and all the other characters. In the TV episode, Barney could only sing in the bathtub; this time, Fred has to be in the shower.

Fred and Barney realize this after arriving in Hollyrock, where Fred spots his old pal Stony Curtis on Hollyrock and Vine and is ignored (did Stony forget Fred that quickly?). Fred and Barney are set to appear on *The Ed Sullivan Show* with the quartet when suddenly Fred can't sing, but Barney has a last-minute idea . . .

Even Ed himself gets into the act, courtesy of Daws Butler when he joins the quartet. It may be the only time Ed Sullivan is presented as singing "in character." Butler goes above and beyond on this LP, sometimes playing three roles at once.

The background score contains a few Flintstone cues that were not heard on earlier albums. Instead of The Hanna-Barbera Singers, the songs are provided by a real quartet who are credited on the jacket: Fred Dregne, Chuck Killen, Red Burroughs, and Steve Clark. It is possible that these were friends of Hanna, as he was a longtime S.P.E.B.S.Q.S.A. member and loved to sing barbershop style.

It is also likely that the mustached character on the front cover sitting in the chair between Fred and Barney is a cartoon version of Hanna. Also of note

One of Bill Hanna's favorite pastimes, barbershop quartet singing, is showcased on this LP. Is that Bill behind the mustache?

is that this was one of a few HBR albums that was printed with a lenticular cover for a 3-D effect. The results were far too expensive to make a profit, so the idea was abandoned, but the spirit of experimentation was evident just the same.

▲▼▲▼▲

Hanna-Barbera's first animated prime-time network special was *Alice in Wonderland*, an original musical with five Broadway-caliber songs, including a potential breakout hit that was added to the title: "What's a Nice Kid Like You Doing in a Place Like This?"

It's a twist on the Lewis Carroll story, gently satirical and delightfully bizarre, that all happens inside a TV. Any ordinary television is like a doorway or a window anyway, so it was brilliant in 1966 to depict the idea of falling through it into a flashing, pre-

TRON portal to another world. The artists made it especially fantastic by making Alice's TV a very ordinary portable set, sitting on a stand, not even flush against a wall.

Network animated specials were still relatively new in 1966. *Alice in Wonderland* boasted more celebrity voices than any preceding specials and most features. Only Jim Backus was featured in the opening titles of *Mister Magoo's Christmas Carol* (1962), leaving Jack Cassidy, Morey Amsterdam, and Jane Kean for the end. The same was true of Burl Ives in *Rudolph, the Red-Nosed Reindeer* (1964), and Boris Karloff in *How the Grinch Stole Christmas* (1966).

Walt Disney did not usually promote star voices extensively except for Peggy Lee in *Lady and the Tramp* (1955) and the radio and singing stars in the "package features" of the forties. Disney's version of *Alice in Wonderland* touted its multiple rosters of

Rexall presented commercials featuring the *Alice in Wonderland* characters and offered exclusive premiums in their drugstores.

celebrity names in 1951 and would not repeat the process until 1967 with *The Jungle Book*. Only the 1966 Rankin/Bass feature *The Daydreamer* prominently mentioned its all-star voice cast, but the film was never in a wide release or prime-time major network broadcast.

Joe Barbera mentions Zsa Zsa Gabor as a longtime friend in his autobiography, so he may have influenced her casting as the Queen of Hearts. According to his biography, when he needed a celebrity to add some glitter to a business meeting, Zsa Zsa delighted in surprising an out-of-town guest by "being Zsa Zsa."

The biggest star in the voice cast was Sammy Davis Jr. as the Cheshire Cat. Davis's casting was a favor to composer Charles Strouse, who, with lyricist Lee Adams, had written the score to the hit musical *Bye Bye Birdie*, the film of which connected Hanna, Barbera, George Sidney, and Columbia Pictures. Davis

was making a high-profile Broadway debut in the musical *Golden Boy*.

Davis later told Strouse that he agreed to voice the Cheshire Cat because Strouse had accompanied him to the Selma rally with Martin Luther King Jr., where they also met with Leonard Bernstein.

"I asked Sammy to do the voice, but I certainly didn't go to Selma just because of Sammy, as he later remarked," wrote Strouse in his biography. "Sammy just assumed that."

Sammy Davis Jr.'s role made Hanna-Barbera's *Alice* the first network prime-time made-for-television cartoon with an African American voice actor, and the first time an animated Cheshire Cat was voiced by a person of color.

Actor-writer Bill Dana, who had just starred in his own NBC sitcom over the previous two years, was a creative catalyst behind the *Alice* project. In addition

The *Alice in Wonderland* album featured the largest voice cast ever assembled for one Hanna-Barbera album.

to the TV script, he provided the voice of the White Knight. A few years after this special aired, Dana wrote the famous Sammy Davis Jr. episode of the sitcom *All in the Family*, for which Strouse and Adams wrote the theme song.

Harvey Korman's career was on the rise during the few years he voiced characters for *The Flintstones* (most memorably the Great Gazoo), *Alice in Wonderland* (the Mad Hatter), and *The Man Called Flintstone* (Chief Boulder). He made frequent appearances on sitcoms like *The Munsters* and *I'm Dickens, He's Fenster* but was gaining recognition for his versatile sketch comedy skills on *The Danny Kaye Show*, which captured awards and critical acclaim. One year after *Alice*, he would join *The Carol Burnett Show* on the road to immense success.

Howard Morris was also featured as one of the stars. Already an H-B veteran, he was well known

to audiences as Ernest T. Bass on *The Andy Griffith Show* and a member of the classic *Your Show of Shows* comedy troupe.

Hollywood newspaper columnist Hedda Hopper voiced "Hedda Hatter," reciting a Carrollesque verse about hats. Sadly, she passed away just before the special aired.

Janet Waldo was delighted, grateful, and a bit surprised to be selected for the lead role of Alice over a "big name." Her voice has a distinctive lilt that gives this special its "Hanna-Barbera" identity, in the finest sense of the term.

Alan Reed and Mel Blanc "guest star" as Fred and Barney, a two-headed caterpillar showbiz duo; Allan Melvin as "Humphrey" Dumpty; Don Messick as Fluff and the Dormouse; Daws Butler as the King of Hearts (based on W. C. Fields) and the March Hare (inspired by Frank "Crazy Guggenheim" Fontaine) and other characters by members of the cast. Disney planned a "Guggenheim" rhino sequence for *The Jungle Book* that was reportedly deleted for time. This special did air while that film was in production.

The primary sponsors of the hour were Rexall and Coca-Cola. The drugstore chain launched an "Alice in Rexall-Land" campaign with print ads to match the commercials that Hanna-Barbera had animated for the broadcast. It was unusual to create merchandise for a TV special, but Rexall built excitement for the event with small comic book adaptations of the story available with any purchase, Alice-themed cosmetics, and a glass change tray at the checkouts to remind patrons to mark their calendars.

▲▼▲▼▲▼

Hanna-Barbera Records had proven capable of cross-promotion within the filmed entertainment division, with Pebbles and Bamm-Bamm's "Open Up Your Heart." The pop records seemed to be gaining momentum as new artists were signed. For the first time, the studio did not have to depend on an outside label when it launched new projects, like *The Atom Ant/Secret Squirrel Show*, which was completely handled in-house.

The album version of *The New Alice in Wonderland, or What's a Nice Kid Like You Doing in a Place Like This?* (only the LP added the word "new") represents the label at its zenith. With double the usual number of cast members and specially recorded music, it had the highest budget of any title in the Cartoon Series.

Janet Waldo, Mel Blanc, Daws Butler, and Allan Melvin were assembled to reprise their roles. Waldo provided an excellent impression of Zsa Zsa Gabor as the Queen of Hearts, with Butler filling in for Korman as the Mad Hatter, Don Messick for Howard Morris as the White Rabbit, and Scatman Crothers for Sammy Davis, Jr. as the Cheshire Cat. Henry Corden replaced Alan Reed for Fred Flintstone's speaking voice: he had already done Fred's singing.

Sammy Davis Jr. had a recording contract with Reprise Records. Even if his appearance on the album

could have been negotiated, it would have made the budget prohibitive for a $1.98 retail children's disc. Presumably, everyone in the cast was paid scale and needed to be present when the session was scheduled.

Scatman Crothers was such a unique vocalist in his own right, he was able to do justice to Davis's Cheshire Cat and create his own version at the same time. Crothers has the distinction of being the first African American voice actor in TV animation, in the 1962 episode, "Wild Man of Wildsville" on *Beany and Cecil* in 1962. His performance as the Cheshire Cat album so impressed the Hanna-Barbera staff, it led to memorable character voices including Meadowlark on the Harlem *Globetrotters* series and in the title role of *Hong Kong Phooey*.

"Howie had recorded the White Rabbit voice for the TV special, but he was directing an episode of *Hogan's Heroes* during the time the record was scheduled," explained Mark Evanier, a longtime friend of Morris. "Joe Barbera assured him that the studio

Scatman Crothers (*left*) made his Hanna-Barbera debut on the album version (*right*) of the studio's first fully animated prime-time special.

would send for him to make the record. Someone at the studio scheduled the album session anyway, so when Howie was back to do another cartoon voice and asked about the White Rabbit, he was told it was already done by Don Messick."

Terribly upset, Morris sought out Barbera and unleashed his anger, telling Barbera, in a manner of speaking, to do something unprintable to himself. Morris did not work for the studio for about a dozen years (Messick handled his roles as Mr. Peebles and Atom Ant). When he did return, Barbera expressed no rancor, but in fact made a joke about the graphic suggestion Morris angrily made back in the sixties. This is one of numerous accounts of people leaving Hanna-Barbera and encountering little or no animosity if they returned. "They wanted and needed people to work there," said Tony Benedict.

Another returning cast member was Doris Drew, credited in the film as "Doris Drew Allen." A highly regarded Hollywood studio soloist of the '50s and '60s, Drew was also a popular West Coast jazz artist. She sang in clubs and on TV for several years and recorded for Mercury, Mode, and Tops Records, the latter also featuring young composer/conductor John Williams, when he went by the name of "Johnny."

A few portions of the album were excerpted from the soundtrack. Bill Dana's performance as the White Knight is completely picked up from the film, as is Janet Waldo's dialogue with him, though she adds some descriptive lines for the record. Doris Drew's soundtrack singing is also used in this sequence. When Henry Corden and Mel Blanc are speaking, it was created for the album, but their singing is from the film track.

None of the songs have the instrumental backing heard in the TV special but were re-created with a smaller orchestra, including strings. This was still rather expensive and time-consuming. Al Capps, an HBR singer who often arranged many of the Cartoon Series songs, adapted Marty Paich's TV arrangements for a smaller group of musicians.

All of Hoyt Curtin's background score from the TV special is used on the album. These *Alice in Wonder-*

land cues came in handy for H-B cartoons for the remainder of the sixties and well into the seventies.

HBR made only one exception to the soundtrack song issue. Scatman Crothers's "What's a Nice Kid Like You Doing in a Place Like This?" was released in two versions. His vocal for the album is accompanied by Al Capps's adapted arrangement. He did a different vocal for the single version, which was fully orchestrated with the same soundtrack backing Marty Paich created for the special.

▲▾▲▾▲▾

There was also an *Alice in Wonderland* promotional LP released on a limited basis and not for commercial sale. It was issued by the E. H. Morris music publishing company and manufactured by Capitol Custom Records. It contains all five songs (plus the main title) from the TV special soundtrack with the original cast.

Promotional albums and singles were made for private use for sponsors, clients, publicity, business partners, production participants, and other needs (before it was possible to send coded digital discs or files privately). Sometimes a promotional record was sent to potential investors and record companies in hopes that a commercial recording would result. Because the necessary business for commercial sale had not yet been handled, these were not legal to be sold or used for audio broadcasts.

The sparse, two-color cover art for this one-sided disc is identical to the design on the sheet music from the same publisher. There is no mention of Hanna-Barbera. The reverse sides of both the record and the cover are blank.

Songwriters Adams and Strouse were on the rise, having hit big with *Bye Bye Birdie*. Their assignment to *Alice* may have been due once again to *Birdie* film director and H-B partner George Sidney. Alice was also the final Hanna-Barbera project with a Screen Gems logo at the end.

Hanna-Barbera was hoping to create a series of perennial specials that would run indefinitely. ABC had given them a very hot spot on the schedule,

For the album version of H-B's second feature film, musical director Ted Nichols created special arrangements for the score, much as Henry Mancini did for his movie scores on records.

Wednesday, March 30, in place of the new *Batman* series, which had premiered in January usually followed by *The Patty Duke Show*. The competition was very strong for family audiences on those Wednesdays. Once *Batman* ended, kids often switched to CBS to watch the last half hour of *Lost in Space*. Sometimes NBC's *The Virginian* would win the hour. This particular evening, the *Lost in Space* episode featured Mercedes McCambridge in "The Space Croppers," an episode about space hillbillies that CBS reran in the summer, an indication of initial high ratings.

Alice in Wonderland received an Emmy Award nomination—for Marty Paich and his delightful arrangements. The special was rerun the following year, but *TV Guide* misprinted the schedule in some of their magazines, listing a Debbie Reynolds special in the time slot instead. In 1977, *Alice* was edited and shown in local syndication, and its subsequent intermittent

runs on the Boomerang network were devoid of any promotion or sufficient advance notice.

"This special was one of the reasons I wanted to become an animator," wrote longtime Hanna-Barbera director and animator Scott Jeralds. "I was five at the time . . . poured over and drew the characters from the *TV Guide* article forever . . . still have it . . . and the record . . . and the comic . . . and the Rexall merchandise.

"While working at Hanna-Barbera, I even found a copy of the special with all the Rexall commercials in it. Love this special . . . it had a major impact on me . . . one of the best things H-B ever produced!"

▲▼▲▼

The Flintstones series had a few months left in prime time and was still in reruns on Saturday morning when Hanna-Barbera's second feature arrived in theaters.

The studio had every intention of becoming known for animated movies as well as television. *Hey There, It's Yogi Bear* had done respectable business. *The Flintstones*, their biggest property yet, seemed a natural and popular subject to open a wide market for family films.

The spy premise of *The Man Called Flintstone* allowed the setting to take theatergoers beyond Bedrock for something they couldn't see on TV. This was the thinking behind several concurrent movies based on hit sitcoms, including *The Munsters* and *McHale's Navy*. The idea was to take the characters away from their TV "homes" to expand the horizon for the screen. It also offered many families a chance to see their favorites in color if they had not yet taken the plunge into buying a new TV set.

Hanna-Barbera's layout and background artists put exquisite effort into more detailed scenic and elaborate action scenes, just as had been done with the Yogi Bear feature. According to the movie poster, the six new songs are "sung by Fred, Barney, Wilma, and Betty," but Fred and Barney sing just one song while Wilma and Betty tilt their heads to and fro.

The Man Called Flintstone songs were written separately by tunesmiths with almost opposite styles. The songs by John McCarthy, who also wrote "Bingo Ringo" and tunes for the "Christmas Flintstone" episode, are contemporary to the era. Those by Doug Goodwin, later a composer for DePatie-Freleng, are more classic and timeless. No reflection on their quality.

Renowned bandleader Louis Prima—whose animation career would be better known a year after *The Man Called Flintstone* when he voiced King Louie in Walt Disney's *The Jungle Book*—sings a lovely ballad called "Pensate Amore." The singer most surprised to snag a track in the film was Leo DeLyon (who would also be heard in *The Jungle Book*'s King Louie sequence).

"I went to audition for a song in the movie that was supposed to take place in France," he recalled on the internet program, *Stu's Show*. "When I got to the call, I saw Robert Clary there and immediately figured I didn't stand a chance."

Clary was an internationally renowned French cabaret singer as well as LeBeau on the sitcom *Hogan's Heroes*. DeLyon gave the audition his best, thought little about it, then was stunned to get the job.

"When I asked Joe why I was chosen, he said that he didn't want it to be the kind of exaggerated 'huh-huh-huh' French, but just an elegant, simple delivery, which is what I gave him," added DeLyon. "Maybe because I was relaxed and figured Clary got it anyway, I gave Joe what he was looking for."

▲▼▲▼▲▼

DeLyon's vocal film track is included on *The Man Called Flintstone* record album, but not Marty Paich's orchestral backing. As was the case with *Alice in Wonderland*, HBR was not licensed to use the music heard under the vocals from *The Man Called Flintstone* film soundtrack for records.

Even though the front cover promises "Music from the original motion picture soundtrack," the actual soundtrack material on the disc consists of five vocals: Fred and Barney in "Team Mates," the chorus in "The Man Called Flintstone," Leo DeLyon in "The Sounds of Paree," and the children in "(Someday) When I Am Grown Up" and "Tickle Toddle." Louis Prima's film vocal of "Pensate Amore" is replaced by an uncredited singer.

Ted Nichols, who was now the musical director for the studio, created arrangements and orchestrations for the existing vocals. Unlike Al Capps's adaptations of Paich's *Alice* songs, Nichols's arrangements are his own. There is no string section and there is a stronger emphasis on brass. Nichols captures the less elaborate but no less delightful H-B house sound developed by Hoyt Curtin.

Nichols wrote all the background music for the feature, with Paich handling only the songs (just as Curtin and Paich divided the duties for *Alice in Wonderland*). For the album, Nichols created special arrangements of the background music cuts so that they would play as individual selections. This was similar to Henry Mancini's process for his film and TV scores; he preferred to create special studio versions designed for home listeners instead of using soundtracks.

Like the *Alice* cues, *The Man Called Flintstone*'s background melodies became familiar in numerous H-B TV cartoons. There is one scene in particular in which Fred is looking for Agent Triple X and keeps mistaking other people for him. When he meets a little old lady, Nichols interpolates the nineteenth-century song, "Silver Threads Among the Gold." The underscore of this scene is post-scored to match the action exactly, yet it was later used countless times out of context.

Ted Nichols did wonders with the album arrangements, adding delightful flourishes that compensate beautifully for the smaller ensemble. The HBR release was only sold in mono, even though by this time Hanna-Barbera was producing and releasing stereophonic recordings. A full stereo master recording does exist.

▲▼▲▼▲▼

Alice in Wonderland was unable to fulfill the goal of long-running perennial animated specials, though H-B produced plenty of successful specials in the '70s and '80s that ran once or twice. *The Man Called Flintstone* did not lead to becoming more feature focused. But Hanna-Barbera Productions was still on a roll and busier than ever. Multiple hit TV series were underway, while others were in reruns worldwide. Merchandise was also popular all over the world. The characters did endorsements and personal appearances just like movie stars.

The two features, a TV special, and an up-and-coming record company as well as the current and "classic" cartoons were steps toward positioning Hanna-Barbera as a full-service entertainment company.

Hanna-Barbera Records was poised to become a major independent record label catering to all ages and musical tastes. The reality was more like Fred Flintstone's gravelberry pie business.

Chapter 16

LAUREL AND HARDY AND THE THREE STOOGES

We're not Batman and Robin, Sweetie.

—CLEOPATRA (JANET WALDO, WITH DAWS BUTLER AS MARC ANTONY)

Films like *Sunset Boulevard* and *All About Eve* still ring true because of an unfortunate tendency for society to forget those of a certain age. Yet often the newest technology rescues, resurfaces, and refreshes vintage material. Creative works with merit and appeal of some kind somehow survive. Some comedians of the early twentieth century were fortunate enough to enjoy second looks by new generations. They did so in large part because of television's need for programming. Long-dismissed and somewhat unappreciated films of The Three Stooges, Laurel and Hardy, Abbott and Costello, and other teams were run for children at the whims of local TV channels. According to marketing studies, the truth is that young people don't check dates or critical reviews. Absent of the sway of peers or marketing campaigns, kids have proven capable of choosing what to enjoy for themselves.[1]

For some of these entertainers, who had never been properly compensated for their early work, comebacks earned much-needed income. One of the subsets of children's entertainment in the late fifties and early sixties was classic comedy and comedians for kids. Shrewd entrepreneurs snapped up the rights to the films. The King brothers built their empire (including *The Oprah Winfrey Show*) by syndicating *The Little Rascals*. Producer/actor Larry Harmon bought the rights to the characters of Laurel and Hardy. Harmon did not own the films that Laurel and Hardy starred in for Hal Roach, MGM, or 20th Century Fox, but he gained control of their images, enabling him to use their likenesses for commercials and merchandise. They were depicted in caricature or cartoon form as "Larry Harmon's Laurel and Hardy." In the early 1960s, he announced a Laurel and Hardy cartoon, publicizing the approval of Hardy's widow, Lucille.

The familiar "March of the Cuckoos" was reworked into another tune called "One Together Is Two," sung exclusively on this Little Golden Record.

Harmon also did not own the Marvin Hatley tune, "March of the Cuckoos," so closely associated with Laurel and Hardy. Songwriters Leonard Adelson (*The Incredible Mr. Limpet*) and Jerry Livingston ("Que Sera Sera," "This Is It," "Mister Ed") were hired to write what is sometimes called a "sideways" song. An example of this is the way Cole Porter, when asked to come up with something like "Make 'Em Laugh," wrote, "Be a Clown." The structure is similar, but it's not the same piece of music, per se.[2]

"One Together Is Two" was the resulting Laurel and Hardy song written for Harmon. It was released as a 45 and 78 rpm single by Golden Records in 1963. Side one contains an instrumental, with some repartee between the two fellows, and then the complete vocal.

▲▼▲▼▲▼

The same year, Larry Harmon also produced an album released by Peter Pan Records called *Laurel and Hardy: This Is Your Laff*. It uses the then-familiar format of TV's *This Is Your Life* (which in 1954 hosted the real-life Laurel and Hardy) to "flashback" to six comical misadventures from their fictional 1930s past. One of the stories is a nod to the classic short, *The Music Box*, in which Stan and Ollie make match sticks from a piano as they try to move it up hundreds of steps.

Harmon himself voiced Laurel on these records. He also became the voice of Bozo the Clown on the TV cartoons and subsequent TV tie-in recordings after purchasing the rights to Bozo the Clown from Capitol Records, for which the character was created by Alan W. Livingston and voiced by Pinto Colvig. Hardy is played by Henry Calvin, who costarred on Broadway in "Kismet" and played Sgt. Garcia on

Disney's *Zorro* series. Calvin impersonated Oliver Hardy in a *Dick Van Dyke Show* episode called "The Sam Pomerantz Scandals" and played a Hardy-like character in Disney's *Babes in Toyland*.

This Is Your Laff has the high audio production quality of a fine TV cartoon. Paul Frees, a regular in Harmon's Bozo cartoons, is part of the album cast, along with another actor playing a wealthy dowager. Bozo cartoon writer Charles Shows was likely also the *Laurel and Hardy* LP scribe. The music resembles the Hanna-Barbera "house style," even though the studio was not yet involved with the project. It might be assumed that it was composed by Don Ralke (*Snoopy Come Home*, William Shatner's *Transformed Man* LP) since he is credited on the L&H Golden Record.

Harmon made his Laurel and Hardy cartoon plans very public at this time, so these two records could have also been demos for prospective producers, backers, and sponsors, as well as to help sell other L&H merchandise. When Harmon finally was able to get an animated Laurel and Hardy on the air it was produced by Hanna-Barbera. Documentary film producer David L. Wolper was also involved in bringing 156 five-minute Harmon/Hanna-Barbera *Laurel and Hardy* cartoons into syndication. The animated Oliver Hardy was voiced by Jim MacGeorge, who actually resembled Stan Laurel and often portrayed him on camera, including in Anco windshield wiper ads with the aforementioned Chuck McCann as Ollie. Harmon and MacGeorge returned to voice Stan and Ollie for an episode of *The New Scooby-Doo Movies* in 1972.

In 1967, Hanna-Barbera produced another 156 syndicated cartoons, this time starring animated versions of Abbott and Costello cartoons in conjunction with RKO Pictures and Jomar Productions. These featured the voice of Bud Abbott and were reportedly a welcome source of revenue at this stage in his life. Character actor, *Tonight Show* producer, and Sahara Hotel entertainment director Stan Irwin voiced Costello. Besides being similar in story and scope to the five-minute 1962 Hanna-Barbera syndicated cartoons like *Lippy the Lion*, these two series were the first to make extensive use of Hoyt Curtin's music from *Alice in Wonderland, or What's a Nice Kid Like You Doing in a Place Like This?*

When the 1966 Harmon/Hanna-Barbera Laurel and Hardy cartoons were returned to TV syndication in 1977, Peter Pan reissued *This Is Your Laff* simply as "Laurel and Hardy." A seven-inch 33 1/3 rpm record of a story from the LP ("Chiller Diller Thriller") was also released.

▲▼▲▼▲▼

Almost every animation studio had tried creating shows around popular comedians. Hanna-Barbera and Filmation each tried to sell Marx Brothers cartoons. Both Bob Clampett and Rankin/Bass pitched Edgar Bergen series. Filmation sold a short-lived Jerry Lewis show to ABC.

The Three Stooges enjoyed one of the greatest renaissances among juvenile audiences. Their films were running in tandem with cartoons on local kid's shows, gaining millions of young fans. In 1956, Moe Howard added Curly Joe DeRita to the trio, and with Larry Fine, they began a lucrative return to fame. The trio experienced success through a series of feature films, starting with *Have Rocket, Will Travel* in 1959, guest gigs on national TV and local TV shows, personal appearances, new merchandise, and a recording career on Coral, Golden, and other labels.

The New Three Stooges premiered in 1965 with 156 episodes. This syndicated five-minute cartoon show featured color live-action comedy wraparounds starring the trio. It was produced by Cambria Studios (*Clutch Cargo*), but the cartoon likenesses found their way to the album and single cover art from Peter Pan Records.

Hanna-Barbera Records released the final record featuring The Three Stooges, costarring one of the studio's biggest cartoon stars. Joan Howard Maurer (Moe's daughter), Jeff Lenburg, and Greg Lenburg, coauthors of *The Three Stooges Scrapbook*, consider *Yogi Bear and The Three Stooges Meet the Mad, Mad, Mad, Dr. No-No* to be the team's best venture on vinyl.

Daws Butler joins Moe Howard, Larry Fine, and Joe DeRita for a comedy/suspense/sci-fi spoof, the last Three Stooges recording ever produced.

"The record has all the sure-fire material that became Hanna-Barbera's trademark, like the corny but funny ending, typical in all their cartoon shows," they wrote. "As a result, the Stooges are funnier— since they thrive on old puns and jokes—and come across more visual than in any other recording. Their stock-in-trade material lent itself to a visual presentation that didn't need graphics to explain the story. It is too bad, however, that the producers didn't consider making this into an hour *Yogi Bear* television special." The authors were on to something. The album plays as if it may have been pitched as a possible special. Either way, Joe Barbera was proud of his artists' work and even if the projects didn't sell in one pitch, they might be presented again or find their way into future cartoons.

A series of specials, or a weekly series, in which Hanna-Barbera superstar characters meet famous personalities was a natural, if not obvious, concept. In 1972, *The New Scooby-Doo Movies* employed the idea to great success with caricatured real-life performers and fictional characters, including The Three Stooges. As he made his way around the H-B studio, Charles Shows could have had some access to storyboards and scripts for perfectly good ideas that were shelved for good or until someone found a way to repurpose them for another project.

That could be why, on the record album, Jellystone Park found itself amid another round of problems with pesky Yogi Bear, so much so that a meeting of park rangers decided to bring three "specialists" to supervise him. Yogi already knows Moe, Larry, and Curly (much better than the rangers) and immediately fools them with a disguise to escape. Unfortunately, a heavy storm breaks out all over side one and Yogi seeks shelter in a creepy old castle, where the Stooges find him on side two. Therein begins the ultimate "B" movie comedy. "I can't think of another record album that brings so many of these great elements together in one story," said actor/songwriter Will Ryan. "For a fan of Saturday matinees, cartoons, comedies, horror movies, science fiction—it's all there, blended so beautifully!" He continues:

> Here is Yogi Bear at his best, breaking rules and sneaking out of the park. The Three Stooges completely mess up their jobs right away, then get mixed up with a mad scientist, which is the classic two-reeler premise. The mad doctor changes Moe into a gorilla, so now you've got a gorilla! With super-strength! What more could you want? The only other thing I can think of to compare this album to is a 1935 Gene Autry serial called *The Phantom Empire*. Gene's a singing cowboy on this ranch with two lovable kids, and he's got a radio show, but they're kidnapped and taken to a fantastic underground civilization right under his ranch! It's got science fiction, cowboys, singing, radio, and comedy. Somehow it works great!

Daws Butler plays every character on the album that isn't a Stooge. There are no new songs except the 1965 "Yogi Bear" tune sung by Danny Hutton and Lynn Bryson, pitched slightly up this time for no apparent reason.

In addition to *The New Scooby-Doo Movies*, The Three Stooges made further appearances in Hanna-Barbera productions, through the aforementioned *Scooby-Doo* appearance and *The Robonic Stooges* series. Moe's son-in-law Norman Maurer, who also worked on their feature films and *The New Three Stooges* cartoon, was a writer for many a hit H-B series.

"The *Yogi* LP," continue *The Three Stooges Scrapbook* authors, "wins on its own merit as a cartoon story with plenty of action and situations that complemented the Stooges' patented brand of humor and allowed them to wind up their recording careers with a well-deserved success."

▴▾▴▾▴▾

The versatile Bill Dana scripted classic TV like Sammy Davis Jr.'s visit to *All in the Family*, and helped launch the careers of Don Knotts and Don Adams.

Bill Dana returned to HBR to star on another album that could have been part of that "celebrity series." In *The Flintstones and José Jiminez in the Time Machine*, José launches himself into time travel aboard a secret experimental high-speed rocket ship. His first stop is the Stone Age, where he meets Dino, Fred, and Barney. A similar premise fueled a one-season 1966 CBS sitcom called *It's About Time*, also sending two astronauts into the Stone Age, then to boost ratings, sent the cave people to the present day. *Flintstones* fans will also recall that Fred, Wilma, Betty, and Barney traveled through time when they visited the World's Fair in the episode "Time Machine."

In the tradition of Charles Shows's HBR scripts, there is much topical humor. In this case, the year 1966 is mentioned specifically. There are references to TV commercial slogans like "Put a Tiger in Your Tank," the 1962 movie, *Cleopatra* (slyly imitated by

Fred, Barney, and José tumble through time and space on this album starring Bill Dana, Henry Corden, Daws Butler, Janet Waldo, and Don Doolittle.

Janet Waldo with just two lines of dialogue), and LBJ, who is mentioned on more HBR discs than Yogi Bear. On the record, the rocket takes José, Fred, and Barney from Bedrock to ancient China (home of "USC—the University of Southern China"), Nero's Rome, and Revolutionary Philadelphia. Almost everyone is voiced by Daws Butler and Henry Corden. Butler plays a confused Columbus, who, historically and incorrectly, argues that he is in India, and José later lets listeners know that Leif Erickson got to the continent first. Actor Don Doolittle voices Confucius. Doolittle's opening album narration betrays his uncredited work on other HBR LPs (*Gemini* and *G.I. Joe*). His voice is recognizable in the ultra-low-budget 1962 sci-fi feature *Creation of the Humanoids*.

José Jiminez (sometimes elsewhere spelled Jimenez) is also locked in the world of 1966. Writer Mark Evanier commented that José "may have been something of a stereotype but it was a sweet, non-threatening funny one which even some folks concerned with the image of Latinos gave a pass." José became popular in TV appearances in a variety of occupations, one of the most popular featuring him as an astronaut. This led to a hit comedy single, *The Astronaut*, and an LP, *José Jiminez in Orbit*, followed by a series of albums. By 1963, José was the lead character on *The Bill Dana Show*, a sitcom that ran for two years on NBC. Dana appeared as the character on ABC's mega-hit series, *Batman*, the same year HBR released *The Time Machine* LP.

In the cover art by Tony Sgroi and Fernando Arce, depicting José, Fred, and Barney whirling through time and space, Bill Dana's caricature resembles his appearance as the White Knight in 1966's *Alice in Wonderland* special. The White Knight was not referred to as "José."

The only cartoon to feature the character by name is a theatrical short produced by Paramount's Famous Studio, also in 1966. "It was co-written by Dana and cartoonist Howard Post, who was running the studio at the time," said animation historian Jerry Beck about 1966's *That's My Mummy*. "Post started production on the film but he was abruptly replaced by veteran animator Shamus Culhane."

Bill Dana was one of TV's finest comedy writers, as well as a good friend to many comedy greats. For example, he brought a young Don Knotts to *The Steve Allen Show* when Knotts believed his career would be over after he finished appearing in "No Time for Sergeants." Dana was known to be generous with his talent, sometimes to a fault. The rapid-fire one-liners on *The Time Machine* album suggest Bill Dana might have added a few gags to the script. Either way, Fred, Barney, and José make a fine comic trio:

In 1970, Bill Dana officially retired his José Jiminez character. Dana clarified the situation in a 2011 interview with comedy historian Kliph Nesteroff:

Nesteroff: It was around this same time that you chose to stop performing as Jose Jimenez and retire the character. In retrospect, you have said that was a mistake . . . I am curious if there was a level of protest from the Hispanic community about the depiction that led you to that decision . . .

DANA: It was as much about my desire for my own identity. My biggest fans were in the Latino community . . . anybody that was part of the [civil rights] movement knew that I was part of the movement . . . I got the very first award [from] The National Hispanic Media Coalition; their first Image Award. So, it was mainly a public relations problem that I wasn't more aggressive in [letting my activism be known] . . . [The late sixties backlash] was kind of a shocking thing for not only me but Ricardo Montalbán . . . they had him pegged as a Latin lover [stereotype]. He was denigrated as much as I was. But people like Anthony Quinn and Vikki Carr loved

Jose and identified him as a unique character and not as a "We don't need no stinkin' badges" kind of thing; a negative thing.

▴▾▴▾▴

Scary Halloween records were another small corner of the record business. The golden age of radio often scheduled especially scary programs in late October, the most famous being the aforementioned Orson Welles's *War of the Worlds* "Martian Invasion" (which inspired The Way-Outs) broadcast. Popular radio programs like *Lights Out* and *Inner Sanctum* took great advantage of the mind's ability to embellish mere sound effects, footsteps, and groans. Many of these shows were preserved on records through transcriptions, and as full productions based on the original radio plays, such as the classic "Sorry, Wrong Number" from CBS's *Suspense* program starring Agnes Moorehead on the Decca label. In 1963, Disneyland Records struck perennial gold with *Chilling, Thrilling Sounds of the Haunted House*, a collection of scary effects collected by sound effects whiz Jimmy Macdonald and narrated by Laura Olsher.

In this context, Hanna-Barbera Records' dramatization of *Edgar Allan Poe's "The Tell-Tale Heart"* was not alone among fall records that "went bump in the night." Self-proclaimed "The Most Frightening Album Ever Made," the recording starred the flamboyant horror movie producer/director William Castle, an unabashed showman who found his niche in chintzy horror movies with goofball gimmicks attached to them. For example, a skeleton was flown over the theater patrons as they watched *The House on Haunted Hill*. Mild electric shocks in theater seats made audiences scream, thinking *The Tingler* was in their seats. Presiding over these delightfully silly antics was camera-friendly Castle, a Wal-Mart Hitchcock who chomped on cigars and offered insurance policies in case someone was stricken during his "horror fests."

Castle is first heard as himself at the beginning of Hanna-Barbera's *The Tell-Tale Heart* album, giving a nod to his insurance gimmick and puffing up the

"Please do not panic! But scream! Scream for your lives! William Castle has recorded the scariest record ever made! The cover says so!"

scariness of the story and the "dangers" of listening to it. Like Arch Oboler's famous suggestion on the radio horror show, "Light's Out," Castle asks listeners to play the record in a darkened room. He then very comfortably settles into his broad performance as the "narrator" of Poe's grisly short story. A born performer, Castle sinks his teeth with zeal into the histrionic role and keeps on chewing/acting as if he were on an airplane seeing a monster on the wing. Writer/director Charles Shows preserves the tone of Poe's work, allowing for the use of sound effects from the Hanna-Barbera library.

It's one thing to read or even watch something scary, it's quite another to set your mind free to picture an audio dramatization and let it loose. It's harder to "turn off" the mind's eye. So when Castle speaks of dismembering the dead body and very realistic sounds accompany the grisly description,

suddenly the claim of "most frightening ever made" is certainly applicable to sensitive ears and minds. While some of the effects are from the H-B library, for these special scenes, foley work seems to have been done. Effects sound as if they were created in the studio to accompany Castle's narration. Editors Tony Milch and Hal Geer avoided the most recognizable music cues as much as possible.

Hal Geer was later known for his extensive work for Warner Brothers cartoons, as an editor and eventual producer of movies and specials with new and archived animation. He worked briefly for Hanna-Barbera, just long enough for this album, and the enthusiasm he shared with Milch is evident in truly "sound-designed" production.

Visually, the album connects directly with UPA's Oscar-winning 1953 theatrical short version of *The Tell-Tale Heart*, narrated by James Mason. It was very much Paul Julian's film, the designer and color artist. As a background artist at H-B, he painted several album covers. His cover art for *The Tell-Tale Heart* LP could have served as UPA concept art. Certain details and colors are different, but the lettering is similar and the overall pallor is striking. On the cover, the narrator is shown; he does not appear in the film.

When this album was recorded, Castle was in discussions with Hanna and Barbera about joint ventures. The only result of their collaboration, to my knowledge, was a low-budget sci-fi feature called "Project X" starring Christopher George, Monte Markham, and good ol' Whit Bissell. In an attempt to overcome the threadbare finances, Hanna-Barbera created "Special Sequences" for *Project X*, to affect dream sequences and foggy memories without building sets, shooting on expensive locations, or employing more sophisticated effects. There is some rotoscoped animation and some truly impressive artistry in the sequences. The film was not done on a blockbuster budget so the result still could not help having a television look, but it was an earnest attempt at getting Hanna-Barbera into special areas of filmmaking outside their usual output.

▲▼▲▼▲▼

The Hasbro toy company introduced the popular G.I. Joe and a vast selection of accessories. The term "action figure" was coined in 1964, to open up a parallel market to boys comparable to the industry that built an empire for Mattel with Barbie and her collection of clothes, friends, and fashions. There were several versions of G.I. Joe sold to represent branches of the military. G.I. Joe had been a generic nickname for soldiers, but it became a household name for the popular Hasbro toy line in the mid-sixties. Hanna-Barbera may have been in the process of developing a cartoon series because their record label released the first G.I. Joe album. H-B would not produce such a series nor any further albums, though there would be more G.I. Joe records on other labels as the product changed with the times and general public perceptions.

The title of the record album, *G.I. Joe Stories of Patriotic Americans: The Story of the Green Beret*, suggests that additional records about heroes might have followed (but did not). It is not a direct adventure starring the toy characters, but instead a curious tribute to the Special Forces division, known as the Green Berets.

The LP opens with a cover version of the somber, reverential "The Ballad of the Green Berets" sung by Bob Johnson. This album was completely up to date in 1966 as far as music charts were concerned because Sgt. Barry Sadler's song, which he cowrote with Robin Moore, was a four-week number-one hit, again reflecting a very different balance of public opinion. That this opinion was teetering on the edge is much clearer in hindsight.

The voices are uncredited, as they were on HBR's *Gemini* space album. The story follows a Special Forces officer, presumably played by Warren Tufts, who welcomes two boys to the training facility. One, voiced by Dick Beals, is a highly knowledgeable adolescent and the other is much younger, perhaps played by Chris Allen or a double-tracked Beals. Special Forces is a catch-all for numerous areas of the military, including the Navy Seals. The two boys are awestruck as they learn the history of the Forces and get a tour of the training. The words "G.I. Joe" are interspersed into the dialogue, but not in the context of the toy, perhaps so the story could stand on its own and not sound too much like a commercial. Once the subject turns to real-life Medal of Honor–decorated captain Roger Donlon and the 1964 Battle of Nam Dong, G.I. Joe is not mentioned again. The dramatization takes on a grim, "war movie" tone, with incidental Viet Cong voices and deaths. Hal Geer, coeditor of the *Tell-Tale Heart* LP, turns in a frightening production but this time not in a "trick-or-treat" fiction way. Nevertheless, it seemed "gee-whiz wow" in the context of mainstream entertainment, as reflected in the reactions of the "kids" on the record.[4]

However, things changed dramatically. Antiwar protests perceived as unacceptable one year could be reevaluated the next as facts and perceptions continued to unfold. G.I. Joe was eventually rebranded as a hero of the environment and battled fictional, fantastical foes, eventually creating distance from the 1964 origins. G.I. Joe would go on to inspire numerous toy and accessory lines, TV series, and records in the realm of make-believe fantasy action. They avoided the consequences of tying into real occurrences and addressed positive social issues while still selling the same "gee-whiz wow."

▲▼▲▼

The year 1966 also brought to television Hanna-Barbera's landmark Space Ghost superhero series which premiered on CBS on Saturday mornings. Fea-turing the melodramatic gravitas of Gary Owens (two years before Rowan and Martin's Laugh-In), Disney Legend Ginny Tyler as Jan, Tim Matheson as Jace, and Don Messick as Blip, it was a smashing success. Space Ghost would prove to be a Hanna-Barbera influence that would alter the course of television in two separate decades.

Along with Filmation's first series, *The New Adventures of Superman*, a new superhero wave was ushered into Saturday mornings, while *Batman* was affecting the look and style of prime time. Also, this year brought a high-gloss prime-time series from England that combined all of the above along with a dry sense of humor, a flair for the surreal, and the weekly clink of two martini glasses.

Chapter 17

THE AVENGERS, ELVIS, AND THE BEANSTALK

~~~~~~

Now that's a cue if ever I heard one.
—RACE BANNON (MICHAEL ROAD)

In just two years, a total of thirty-eight Cartoon Series albums were produced and released by Hanna-Barbera Records. Twenty-six of these LPs contain stories starring Hanna-Barbera characters. Twelve of them feature the original TV voices; seven feature members of the casts with some replacements; and seven are completely recast with different (though highly renowned) voice actors. Three HBR LPs tell stories with no Hanna-Barbera characters and the other nine Cartoon Series records are song and/or instrumental albums.

In addition to that catalog, Hanna-Barbera was amassing a library of "mainstream" material for albums and singles. Rock and roll, country, folk, soul, blues, big band, and even some psychedelic pop. One of these was a release from England that made its US debut on Hanna-Barbera Records: the theme from *The Avengers*.

▲▼▲▼▲▼

Two years before the Marvel heroes of the same name were assembled in comic books, there was already a British television series called *The Avengers*. Starting in January 1961, it aired only in the UK as a gritty, crime drama starring Ian Hendry as a doctor entangled in crime and intrigue, and Patrick Macnee as a mysterious partner named John Steed. In the second season, Hendry left the series, and Macnee became the star and was paired with Honor Blackman as Cathy Gale. Her character was the first "cat-suited," self-assured female heroine on television. After two years, Blackman left to appear in films like *Goldfinger*. It was her successor who would have the greatest worldwide impact when *The Avengers* began broadcasting on prime-time American TV in 1965.

Hanna-Barbera Records imported the first recording of *The Avengers* theme to the US from England's Pye Records.

Dame Diana Rigg (*On Her Majesty's Secret Service*, *Game of Thrones*) helped turn *The Avengers* into a sensation as Mrs. Emma Peel. The concept of the "action female," a prototype of subsequent characters in popular culture, Mrs. Peel was empowered but empathetic, cool-headed and compassionate, fierce and fun-loving. Diana Rigg's unshakably independent performance, her chemistry with Patrick Macnee, and the quirky nature of the series were breakthrough TV in America. As *The Avengers* progressed, stories increased in imaginative eccentricity. Everything about the series was carefully stylized, including composer Laurie Johnson's evocative music, perfectly capturing the action, humor, and fashion sense. America's ABC Network had decided to run the series concurrently in the US and Britain, sharing the bumped-up budget with the British

producers. *The Avengers* episodes were now capable of approaching movie quality.

Composer John Dankworth composed the pre-US *Avengers* theme. According to historian Jeff Missinne, Laurie Johnson's replacement theme melody began as an instrumental called "The Shake." It appeared amid a collection of familiar instrumentals and several Johnson originals on a 1965 Pye Records album called *The Big New Sound Strikes Again*. "The Shake" was reorchestrated and augmented. Adding a dramatic brass and percussion fanfare and an equally bold close in place of the original fade, it was transformed into the "Theme from *The Avengers*."

Hanna-Barbera Records released *The Big New Sound Strikes Again in 1966* in the US with significant alterations. The earlier version of "The Shake" was removed, the tracks were rearranged, and Johnson's freshly minted "Theme from *The Avengers*" was added. Hanna-Barbera released the LP in mono and stereo with the revised title *The Avengers: The Laurie Johnson Orchestra*. In this way, Hanna-Barbera Records released the first "official" version of "Theme from *The Avengers*." From that point, Pye and other labels reissued the revised LP in the UK and other countries.

HBR also released "Theme from *The Avengers*" as a single in 1996, while Pye released it in the UK. This was part of the exchange deal between the two companies. Many of the Cartoon Series albums were pressed and packaged by Pye for the UK. In addition, Hanna-Barbera was the first label to release Laurie Johnson's original *The Avengers* theme on an album and a single in the US, and it was also the first to reissue *The Big New Sound Strikes Again* as an *Avengers* LP with the modified version of "The Shake." Pye's modified reissue LP was released in 1967.

HBR's 45 rpm single was sold as a picture sleeve with black-and-white photos of Diana Rigg and Patrick Macnee, tinted with bright orange and magenta in four squares like an Andy Warhol painting. This modern art sensibility extended even further for HBR's LP version. The gatefold cover contains no photos of Rigg and Macnee but instead a list of the songs and the title hand-lettered by Robert Schaefer in a particular tense, dramatic way. The image at the bottom of the front cover depicts a surreal, contorted body surrounded by web-like strands. A closer glance reveals that this art was created (and signed) in 1964 by H-B background artist Fernando Montealegre. The desired effect seems to have been sophistication, fine art, and elegant music. The album is not a collection of cues from the television series but an eclectic gathering of tracks, most of the easy-listening variety, some more classical, and a few modern. There is another Laurie Johnson theme, from a 1963 movie about beauty contests called *Beauty Jungle*, which also starred Ian Hendry.

Johnson is renowned for live-action film scores like *Tiger Bay* (Hayley Mills's movie debut) and *Dr. Strangelove*. In cartoons, Johnson is a latter-day Raymond Scott, composer of several instrumentals often used in classic animation, especially Warner Bros. shorts. Johnson's catchy library cues, such as "Happy Go Lively," were often used to sprightly comic effect in comedy sketches and cartoons like *SpongeBob Squarepants*.

▲▼▲▼▲▼

The Avengers was the only Hanna-Barbera LP imported from Pye Records, but the label did release a handful of Pye singles. "*Blue Turns to Grey* by The Epics was a lovely little 45 featuring Bill Legend on drums," wrote entertainment specialist Kliph Nesteroff in his detailed essay, *Wall of Sound to Huckleberry Hound: The Weird History of Hanna-Barbera Records*. "Shortly after HBR folded, Bill Legend became the drummer for T-Rex. The Riot Squad featuring Joe Meek had some great, upbeat tracks distributed by HBR. Meek was well regarded for his instrumental hit *Telstar* and less regarded for his belief that an Ampex tape machine, when played backward, could communicate with the dead."

The "Wall of Sound" refers to a highly imitated form of arranging, conducting, and reverb recording that when done well, yields a record approaching but not exceeding overproduction. The idea was to create a hit that would sound "big" on the smallest, cheapest, tiniest transistor or car radio of the sixties. The "Wall of Sound" is most widely heard today at holiday time by music greats including Darlene Love ("Christmas [Baby Please Come Home]," "Marshmallow World") and The Ronettes ("Santa Claus Is Coming to Town," "Sleigh Ride") from the LP, *A Christmas Gift for You from Phil Spector*.

"Some of the best HBR tracks were inspired by Phil Spector," Nesteroff explained. "Tom Ayres produced *Nobody's Boy* by Porter Jordan, a noisy, full-bodied Wall of Sound, arranged by future Nilsson collaborator Perry Botkin." Other Spector take-offs included *Please Don't Mention Her Name* by Billy Storm, which was a pseudo-Righteous Brothers number, and a solo LP from Jean King, a member of Phil Spector's vocal group The Blossoms. The Blossoms had provided

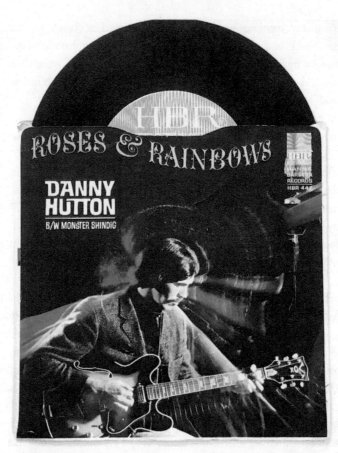

Danny Hutton's biggest hit for Hanna-Barbera was "Roses and Rainbows," the song Fred Flintstone heard on his TV set.

backup for Shelley Fabares on "Johnny Angel" and "Johnny Loves Me" for Colpix back when that label was also producing Hanna-Barbera albums. HBR artist Billy Storm was the first R&B artist on Disney's Buena Vista label. He also recorded a Sherman Brothers song called "Puppy Love Is Here to Stay," from the 1962 stop-motion featurette *A Symposium on Popular Songs*. The song appeared on the 1965 Buena Vista LP, *Tinpanorama*, a collection of original Sherman songs in the style of various eras of popular music. The last cut on the album, a Beatles spoof called "You Bug Me Ann-Arlene," is sung by Ron Hicklin, Al Capps, and Bob Zwirn, the same year they were The Hanna-Barbera Singers and The Way-Outs.

▲▼▲▼

Danny Hutton recorded several singles for HBR but no solo albums, as he was still an emerging young talent mostly working behind the scenes. "Bohanan and Ayres ran things, but there was no office culture at all," he said. "I'd either be in a studio, writing, or I'd be out at night looking for groups."

He was not thrilled to see "Monster Shindig" on the "B" side of "Roses and Rainbows." It wasn't because he didn't like the song; indeed, it was included in compilations for years. But as a young pop artist, each of the two songs was for different markets. When Hutton recorded for the Cartoon Series, it was as a "Hanna-Barbera Singer," not as himself. Not only does the entertainment business have a way of pigeon-holing performers, but he felt that a top 40 type song did not belong with a children's Halloween tune. That was the reason artists performed under various names for records, depending on their purpose. "Roses and Rainbows" was reissued with "Big Bright Eyes."

"Roses and Rainbows" became a substantial hit. Hutton made TV appearances, now performing the tune on camera rather than as an off-camera *Flintstones* caricature. The success of the song led to some contention. Songwriter/producer Kim Fowley, who had brought Hutton to HBR, was paid a small fee for publishing rights but the song belonged to Anihanbar Music. Eventually, both Fowley and Hutton moved on, Hutton for a deal with Frank Zappa and MGM Records.

▲▼▲▼▲▼

In his essay, "Hanna-Barbera Records: The Other Side of Bedrock," historian Chuck Miller explains how Hanna-Barbera acquired a garage-rock trio called The Guilloteens, who had "already proved their mettle as one of Memphis' top rock bands (with no less than Elvis Presley calling them his favorite band)."

Kliph Nesteroff confirms the Elvis connection. "Elvis Presley caught their act and brought them to Hollywood," he explained. "Phil Spector caught their act and said he'd like to record them the following week. But the manager of The Guilloteens was so eager to get a deal, that he signed the boys to HBR before Spector had the chance. Guitarist Louis Paul complained, 'We went from Wall of Sound to Huckleberry Hound.'"

Spector wanted to give their song, "I Don't Believe" the Wall of Sound treatment. The band arrived and began to work on a highly elaborate track. However, as Louis Paul recalled, "Phil spent more time in the studio with The Righteous Brothers, and we were next on the list—but during that period, our manager sold us to Hanna-Barbera."

The scaled-down HBR-sized production of "I Don't Believe" was still a hit in Memphis and several other regions. More HBR singles followed. "Hanna-Barbera did spend some money on us," Paul told Miller. "They

bought two pages in *Billboard*, one page was us, one page was Danny Hutton," Miller reported that The Guilloteens later did some records for Columbia and Paul did some voice work for Hanna-Barbera.

▲▼▲▼▲▼

To bring potential hits into wider distribution and develop the catalog, HBR acquired the licenses to recordings that were already produced. Some of the singles were given picture sleeves with art direction by the studio.

A few of the artists and songs included R&B singer Art Grayson, soul group the Four Gents, pianist Larry Butler, and Irish vocal group The Abbey Tavern Singers. Numerous garage bands on the label include LA's The Chocolate Watchband, a hard rock group licensed on HBR under the name of The Hogs. Many such regional recordings were released under license, including songs by The Dimensions (Seattle); Unrelated Subjects (Detroit), and even radio music director Jimmy Rabbitt under the name of Positively 13 O'Clock. Some bands were licensed by Detroit's SVR Records, including The Tidal Waves.

Moving into "the big time" was a thrill to fifteen-year-old Tidal Waves drummer Bill Long. "I would have hoped for Capitol Records, but we were more into making the music than worrying about the label. When I saw our first 45 with HBR, it was pretty cool looking, compared to the SVR label, which was pretty plain."

One of the rarest HBR singles is thought to be "You're Gonna Miss Me" by Texas group Thirteenth Floor Elevators because of a contractual dispute. Voice actor Paul Frees also recorded some bizarre novelty singles under his name and as "Peter Harcourt and the Subjects."

Danny Hutton was the HBR performer/staff member who went on to the greatest fame as a founding member of Three Dog Night. Originally called The Redwoods, the rock band was formed in 1967 by Hutton with Chuck Negron and Cory Wells. Three Dog Night recorded three top-ten hits by the end of the sixties ("One," "Eli's Coming," "Easy to Be Hard"); and three number-one hits by 1972 ("Joy to the World," "Mama Told Me," "Black and White"); as well as earning nineteen gold and two platinum records. In 1969, MGM Records released a compilation called *Danny Hutton: Pre-Dog Night* that included his two Hanna-Barbera label hits, "Roses and Rainbows" and "Big Bright Eyes" plus "Monster Shindig, Part 2" (the version with crowd sounds). In 1993, MCA released a two-disc set called *Celebrate: The Three Dog Night Story, 1965–1975.* The first song on the collection is the original recording of "Roses and Rainbows."

There were other Hanna-Barbera recording artists who gained substantial renown. HBR's Rainy Day People evolved into Bread (with *Hey There, It's Yogi Bear* theme composer David Gates), and the lead singer for The New Breed became the bass player for the Eagles. HBR experienced its greatest pop success with The Five Americans of Dallas/Fort Worth. "I See the Light" was an HBR hit single. The cover of their HBR album, also called "I See the Light," showed band members bouncing on trampolines. This was photographed on the Hanna-Barbera studio lot. Unfortunately, the band that gave HBR its biggest hit left the label right before striking number one with their next hit single.

"John Abdnor took his Abnak Records label to the national level," wrote Chuck Miller. Ironically, the very week HBR announced they were ceasing independent distribution, The Five Americans' song "Western Union" was finishing its run atop the Top 10. Decades later, HBR's 1966 "I See the Light" LP had developed a strong following and was reissued by Sundazed Records, first on CD, then on vinyl.

▲▼▲▼▲▼

Hanna-Barbera Records released over three dozen pop singles and thirteen pop/general interest albums. These were not part of the "Cartoon Series" and did not have those words printed along the bottom of the physical record label. All Hanna-Barbera Records bore the striking "HBR" design—a close-up pattern taken from an oscilloscope, tinted teal for consumer products, or magenta for promo copies.

A sense of deluxe treatment was given to the first set of pop album releases, packaged with gatefold covers adorned with photos and original H-B studio-created art, all with the involvement of H-B studio artists. Robert Schaefer did virtually all the original hand lettering, just as he did for the cartoon titles.

The first HBR soundtrack album unrelated to a Hanna-Barbera property is also the first pop LP in the catalog—and the first recording to feature the singing of Raquel Welch, in her first major movie role. *A Swingin' Summer* is one of many teen-oriented, low-budget musical romantic comedies produced in the wake of the Annette Funicello–Frankie Avalon Beach Party films. Carol Connors sings the peppy title song for the album (Jody Miller sings it over the film titles). Ten years later with Bill Conti and Ayn Robbins, she won the Oscar for "Gonna Fly Now" from *Rocky* and was nominated with Robbins and Sammy Fain for "Someone's Waiting for You" from *The Rescuers.* Also featured on the album are Rip Chords, Donnie Brooks, and The Righteous Brothers. Gary Lewis and the Playboys appeared in the film but were signed to another label and are not on the LP.

Gloria A-Glo is a lilting, unmistakably sixties instrumental album that could easily stand alongside those of Herb Alpert or Henry Mancini. Harpist Gloria Tracy made national tours and TV appearances with a jazz/dance band rather than a chamber orchestra. Ubiquitous 1950s and 1960s TV host Art Linkletter wrote the liner notes for *Gloria A-Glo* and featured her on his popular daytime talk/variety show, *House Party.* LP selections include Ms. Tracy's signature tune, "A Walk in the Black Forest," "The Sweetheart Tree" (from *The Great Race*), and *Peanuts* composer Vince Guaraldi's "Cast Your Fate to the Wind."

Versatile singer Jean King made her long-awaited solo album debut after singing with The Blossoms alongside Darlene Love and Fanita James. The trio had their own hit, "He's a Rebel" and backed up such hits as "Monster Mash," "Johnny Angel," and "You've Lost That Lovin' Feeling." Recorded live, *Jean King*

Jean King of The Blossoms ("He's a Rebel," "Johnny Angel") and many HBR Cartoon Series songs recorded this album live.

Sings for the In Crowd including "My World Is Empty without You," "A Hard Day's Night," and Petula Clark's "My Love." This album is a particular treat for those familiar with her work in the pop music field as well as her eclectic vocals (like "Gold Pinky," "Brahms' Lullaby," and "The Lord's Prayer") on so many Cartoon Series albums.

Hanna-Barbera Records even featured The Rolling Stones, sort of. "HBR got on the bandwagon of a short-lived record industry fad—Baroque albums," explained Nesteroff. "This brief genre took popular, contemporary songs and released them with harpsichord sounds evoking the Renaissance era. The liner notes to the HBR release *Baroque 'n Stones by the Renaissance Society* said the album was 'not the outgrowth of someone's warped sense of humor.'" During the CD "boom" of the late twentieth century, this would be repeated with discs filled with TV themes in the style of Mozart and so forth.

▲▾▲▾▲▾

Several HBR albums were licensed from regional labels just as some singles were, to fill out its potentially growing catalog. This is not unusual for record companies, particularly smaller ones. *The Dynatones: The Fife Piper* came from St. Clair Records in West Virginia. The title tune, played by a combo with the novelty of a flute as the lead, was released as a single and did fairly well.

Another album found "on the road" has the rough sound of a demo. "Ayres met with disc jockey Huey P. Meaux at Tribe Records where Meaux produced Texas soul artists, Barbara Lynn and Joe Medwick," writes Nesteroff. "Ayres licensed a collection of gritty Medwick tracks and released them as a full-length LP—*Barefootin'*—under the pseudonym 'TV and the Tribesman.'"

Soul artist Earl Gaines sang lead on 1955's "It's Love Baby (24 Hours a Day)," by Louis Brooks and His Hi-Toppers. "His first single [and album] for HBR, *The Best of Luck to You*, was a strong soul hit in the autumn of 1966 (albeit credited to 'Earl Gains')," wrote Chuck Miller.

New Orleans–born bandleader Louis Prima may not have been on the HBR album version of *The Man Called Flintstone* singing "Pensate Amore," but the label's *The Golden Hits of Louis Prima* collects his most popular songs. Most were rerecorded in stereo, though at this time record companies were still giving consumers the option of buying albums in mono as there were record players that could not play stereo records without damaging them. He is accompanied by his band, Sam Butera and the Witnesses, and his wife, Gia Maione. This album was reissued on CD by Prima's company with the same cover graphics.

▲▼▲▼

The very last album released by Hanna-Barbera Records in 1967 was the soundtrack of the studio's most prestigious productions up to that time: *Jack and the Beanstalk*, narrated by its star and producer, Gene Kelly.

Originally broadcast Sunday night, February 26, 1967, on NBC, *Jack and the Beanstalk* was television's first live-action/animated TV special. Because the animation and live-action sequence took up the bulk of the fifty-two-minute program, few if any previous feature films could match the sustained length using the same technique. The special was highly rated and well regarded, but somewhat troubled behind the scenes as Kelly was not used to the rushed world of television and the shortcuts necessitated by budgets at only a fraction of those for the sequences in *Anchors Aweigh* or *Invitation to the Dance*. Despite his misgivings, Kelly promoted it personally on network

TV the night before. When Kelly hosted a celebration for Jackie Gleason, then one of CBS's top stars, Gleason specifically mentioned *Jack and the Beanstalk*. It was a rare concession afforded only the most influential entertainers, as *Jack* aired on rival network NBC.

In the Hanna-Barbera tradition of powerful audio, no expense was spared on the soundtrack to mount the outstanding score by Sammy Cahn and James Van Heusen ("Swinging on a Star," "All the Way," and other hits for Frank Sinatra and more). The musical direction by Kelly's longtime MGM collaborator Lennie Hayton is just as lavish as any big-screen Hollywood musical of the golden days. Another positive note is that writers Larry Markes and Michael Morris (*The Andy Griffith Show*, *Bewitched*, *The Flying Nun*) nicely fleshed out the simple fairy tale with a romantic twist as well as an army of mice, which made for a high-kicking chorus line.

According to voice actor Dick Beals, Hanna and Barbera had planned to use Bobby Riha's voice for the songs. Dissatisfied with the results, Beals was asked to loop the singing after the filming. With H-B's permission, Beals announced his performance in a *Variety* ad. Mrs. Riha was livid, as she wanted to market her son as an all-around talent. The following year, Bobby Riha's actual voice was heard in Disney's *The One and Only, Genuine, Original Family Band*, though essentially talking or group singing. Janet Waldo voiced Serena, the princess-turned-enchanted-harp. Cahn and Van Heusen wrote a stirring love song for Serena and Kelly's character, Jeremy Keen, called "One Starry Moment," a soaring tune every bit the caliber of MGM's golden days. Had Kelly been singing and dancing with Cyd Charisse, the studio soloist for Charisse might have been India Adams. In the case of Janet Waldo, it was Hollywood legend Marni Nixon, who sang on the earliest Hanna-Barbera themes as part of The Randy Van Horne Singers.[1]

"I had some fun playing with the stereo sound," recalled Tony Milch about editing this album. To "widen" the mono orchestra track and make it sound fuller, Milch slightly doubled two identical mono tracks and separated them a little to the right and

Hanna-Barbera Records' grand finale as a record label was the soundtrack to the studio's Emmy-winning special, narrated by Gene Kelly.

left channels, then added the vocals at the center or on either side.

One of the album's (and the special's) highlights is "The Woggle-Bird Song," sung by Leo DeLyon and Cliff Norton with Kelly. The sequence was staged like Kelly's "chain dance" with the palace guards in *Invitation to the Dance*. The album version contains a groovy "yeah, yeah, yeah" section that was replaced in the film with a flamenco, perhaps to make it more timeless. Cahn and Van Heusen wrote the song originally for Filmation's theatrical feature, *Journey Back to Oz*, which began production in 1962. There was to be a sequence with a "Woggle-Bug" from the L. Frank Baum book. That was discarded, so the songwriters put the tune "in the trunk" and used it for *Jack and the Beanstalk*.

▲▼▲▼▲▼

Hanna-Barbera's most ambitious television project made a fitting if unintentional finale to its catalog of the HBR in-studio label. As of May 1967, Hanna-Barbera–related recordings would thereafter be sold, distributed, and promoted by outside companies,

both independent firms and large corporations. Some would still be produced by Hanna-Barbera Productions, like Golden's 1961 *Songs of the Flintstones* LP, while some would be licensed and produced externally, like Golden's *Jetsons* album.

Danny Hutton and Lynn Bryson were promoted in trade advertising together as young talent, but while they worked together on a number of HBR songs, Kliph Nesteroff reports that he perceived that their careers were not handled equitably.

"Lynn Bryson felt that Danny Hutton had marginalized his efforts at HBR," wrote Nesteroff. "Hutton implemented his vision on several recordings while Bryson resented being stuck writing songs for cartoon animals . . . Embittered by his time with HBR, Bryson railed against the record industry, and claimed John Lennon was conspiring to overthrow the government." Among the bands that rankled Bryson were Rush and KISS. He was likely displeased years later when NBC broadcast Hanna-Barbera's 1978 live-action TV movie *KISS Meets the Phantom of the Park*, costarring Anthony Zerbe, when Fred Flintstone appeared in KISS-like makeup on a 1979 NBC Saturday morning episode of *The New Fred and*

Barney Show, and when an animated KISS solved a mystery with Scooby-Doo in a made-for-video movie.

If Bryson could have realized how many listeners he had over the decades, it would not have resulted in fame, cash, or sufficient solace, but perhaps just allowed some reflection on why each artist is born to create. NOTE: The author has told many an "anonymous" entertainer that they will never know how many millions of lives they have brightened, but they have done so just the same. To quote the arachnid writer, Charlotte, "That in itself is a tremendous thing."

▲▼▲▼▲▼

Thanks to rare record stores, collector's shows, and online auctions, the original Hanna-Barbera Records made between 1965 and 1967 have kept spinning on the worldwide turntables of those who still cherish them or continue to discover them. Cartoon Series albums and singles are prized by collectors as popular audio and visual art. HBR's brief, prolific enterprise lived up to the appraisal that several insiders gave it: "experimental." Even HBR children's records teetered on the cutting edge and continue to astonish with flashes of brilliance, mountains of talent, and more than a little unmitigated nerve.

There were still well over a hundred new records ahead in the decades to come, as well as hundreds of Hanna-Barbera characters and hours of animation. The end of HBR was only one issue amid significant changes taking place at Hanna-Barbera.

Chapter 18

BANANA SPLITS AND CATTANOOGA CATS

~~~~~~

I used to sing in a band . . . before I married you.

—FRED FLINTSTONE (ALAN REED) TO WILMA, A LITTLE TOO OFTEN

Things were getting serious at Hanna-Barbera, behind the scenes, and in the cartoons themselves. Hanna-Barbera's classic Alex Toth–designed *Space Ghost* superhero series debuted to tremendous ratings on CBS on Saturday mornings, as did Filmation's first venture into the competition with *The New Adventures of Superman*. Fiercely ambitious CBS executive Fred Silverman was a new kind of programming executive, who basked in the limelight and eagerly engaged in the creative work.

The first of H-B's Saturday morning superhero series, *Space Ghost* centered on a mysterious, mighty fellow who fought evil in outer space with two teens (Ginny Tyler and Tim Matheson). Two *Space Ghost* adventures bookended another cartoon *Dino Boy*, about a lad (John H. Carson, not the talk-show host) lost in a land of prehistoric creatures. These were rollicking throwbacks to the early movie serials and pulp novels of both Hanna and Barbera's youth, dressed up for sixties sci-fi and action—just as blockbuster films continued to mine the conventions of vintage westerns, war movies, and *Flash Gordon* matinees with more elaborate effects and current sensibilities.

Space Ghost began a long Hanna-Barbera association with Gary Owens. One of Los Angeles's most popular radio personalities, he was known for his comedic shows on KWFB. His super-sounding voice had already graced Pantomime Pictures' syndicated 1965 cartoon, *Roger Ramjet and the American Eagles*, a tongue-in-cheek spoof in the Jay Ward vein. *Space Ghost* was Owens's first animated network series. His career with H-B continued while he became a star as the announcer on *Rowan and Martin's Laugh-In*, a pop-art, rapid-fire TV comedy gag fest. So popular was *Laugh-In*, it soon influenced the look, humor, and pace of Saturday morning shows. Catchphrases, quick gags, and skits made their way into cartoons and live-action.

The versatile performers soon became staples of TV and film cartoon voice casts as well.

The Herculoids became another H-B hit in 1967, featuring a loyal, brave family that was more "Tarzan and Jane" than "Fred and Wilma." They also were nothing like George and Jane, but flew around in spaceships and used advanced technology when needed. Dad Zandor was voiced by Mike Road, the voice of Race Bannon. By 1967, Hanna-Barbera's newest cartoons were action oriented: *Moby Dick and Mighty Mightor*; *Birdman and the Galaxy Trio*; and *Fantastic Four*, H-B's first Marvel comics adaptation and the first animated version of the characters.

Joe Barbera commented that a *Herculoids* cartoon was created in the classic mold of a Tom and Jerry short. In a *Herculoids* cartoon, a situation would occur, a stranger would need help, a character might be lost or captured, or most often, an outside force would challenge them. The story would be set up quickly, followed by a series of action attacks and counterattacks in place of gags, then a resolution, sometimes followed by a threat of later conflict.

▲▼▲▼▲▼

The employees at Hanna-Barbera Productions found themselves metaphorically in a "Herculoids situation" in the mid-sixties. Was another force descending on their studio, and if so, how dramatically would things change? Creatively, the cartoons were leaning toward action/adventure and away from comedy, at least in the foreseeable future. Some artists were looking elsewhere as this was not their preferred forte. Others were learning new techniques and getting used to adjustments as they came along.

In his autobiography, Bill Hanna carefully and candidly explained the decision to sell the company. His first point was to dispel rumors that it was due to a rift between them; it was quite the opposite. "The offer from Taft Broadcasting to purchase Hanna-Barbera was actually a tremendous validation to us," he wrote. "The Taft executives were not kidding themselves. They were investors, not producers ..."

The contract allowed the duo to continue running the studio without dealing with issues like "taxes, insurance, and other responsibilities attendant of ownership."

Like so many creatives who became administrators, they wanted to get back to what they loved to do best. Taft was not the only potential parent company courting them. Columbia Pictures and Screen Gems were excellent distribution partners as well as guiding forces. Charles (Chuck) Fries, a familiar name to those who read the credits of seventies TV, became a major producer after years with Screen Gems as vice president in charge of production. Fries and longtime H-B supporter John Mitchell were in favor of the purchase. Decades later, in a video interview with the Television Academy, he is still visibly frustrated at the short-sighted thinking when Screen Gems allowed Hanna-Barbera to slip away by such a small and easily recouped amount.

And who should know better than *us* how much the company's worth? Because we've been distributing all this, right? We know how much money is being generated by the various series. (sighs) And we had a guy in New York who was pretty good with a pencil ... And he'd get everybody's ear, and not to put him down, but he was doing a lot of pencil work on this, and he finally convinced everybody, twelve million, that's it. Not another penny.

So, Taft Broadcasting came along and paid fourteen, and the guys took it, and we lost it. That was the end of it. It was over. Now John [Mitchell] always maintained a good relationship with Joe [Barbera]. I did too. But we never could pull that back together again. John had me running all over ... Scheimer and Prescott [of Filmation] ... I was trying to make deals with everybody to buy an animation company ... Friz Freleng ... but never could duplicate that ... we just cut it too close and just lost an unbelievably valuable asset.

"Thereafter, the two men were employees—well-paid, powerful employees but still employees," wrote Mark

Evanier on his blog, newsfromme.com. "When I was there, it sometimes felt like the agents and merchandising people were running the place . . . with the approval (usually) of Bill and Joe. At times though, it seemed more like acceptance than approval."

The Hanna-Barbera in-house record division may have not worked out, but there was little rancor or retribution, as several staffers continued doing business with H-B either on staff or contract. HBR A&R director Tom Ayres stayed with Hanna-Barbera for a while in the animation area, supervising the songs for *The Impossibles*, and continuing his relationships with Pye Records and other contacts. Ayres then moved to RCA Records, where he spotted a young artist with potential.

"A year after HBR folded, Joe Meek recorded a cover of the Velvet Underground's *I'm Waiting for My Man* and the track featured an unknown David Bowie doing guitar and vocals," wrote Kliph Nesteroff. "Smitten with his ability, Ayres brought Bowie over to RCA and got him a record deal." ("David Bowie" changed his name from his original "David Jones" because of Davy Jones of The Monkees.)

▲▼▲▼▲▼

Premiering in the fall of 1966 on CBS, *Frankenstein Jr. and The Impossibles* show was a three-segment half hour. The middle segment concerned young genius Buzz Conroy (Dick Beals), his giant super robot, and their adventures in futuristic Civic City. Along with Total TeleVision's *The Beagles*, *The Impossibles* was among TV's first original animated rock bands, debuting the same fall as *The Monkees* on NBC, a year after the animated Beatles on ABC—and two years before *The Archies* on CBS. Veteran TV writer Jack Mendelsohn (*Rowan and Martin's Laugh-In*, *The Carol Burnett Show*) was invited to Hanna-Barbera to work on *The Impossibles* (as well as *Frankenstein Jr.*) because he wrote King Features' *Beatles* cartoon, a number-one hit for ABC.

Visually, The Impossibles were superheroes with individual powers: Coil Man (Hal Smith); Fluid Man (Paul Frees); and Multi-Man (Don Messick). The trio appeared in two cartoons per show, each featuring one of their pop songs. The Impossibles sounded like The Way-Outs and most of The Hanna-Barbera Singers because they were the same busy studio vocalists, including Ron Hicklin, Al Capps, and Stan Farber.[1]

With Tom Ayres in charge of *The Impossibles* music, there was every intention of releasing a soundtrack album of pop songs, giving Hanna-Barbera a year's jump on *The Archies*, but their record company began shutting down before that could be possible.

▲▼▲▼▲▼

Former Hanna-Barbera Records president Don Bohanan did what he could to keep the existing HBR recordings alive as well as initiate the start of new albums at his previous label. "Don Bohanan was quite down about the folding of the label," said John Chekaway, president of the Detroit label SVR Records to interviewer Chuck Miller. "He made an effort to transition all the licensed product wherever he could, and they immediately connected us with Liberty Records for distribution."

Hanna-Barbera Productions announced to the record industry trades that they were staying active in the record business, this time in partnership with Liberty Records. Hanna-Barbera's titles appeared on Liberty's Sunset label, the equivalent of the RCA Camden or Columbia Harmony labels, a "catch-all" division for children's records, reissues, and budget albums to be sold as impulse items in grocery and variety stores.

Liberty established Sunset Records in 1965 and had already transitioned LPs by Alvin and the Chipmunks into the line. Stickers covered the Liberty logos on older LP covers, though consumers who bought them might still find a leftover Liberty-labeled disc inside the jacket.[2] The previous Hanna-Barbera Cartoon Series LP covers were never given new pressings by Liberty/Sunset. Each cover had its shrink-wrap removed, a black Sunset sticker was affixed over the HBR logo, and it was rewrapped. The records inside did not change.

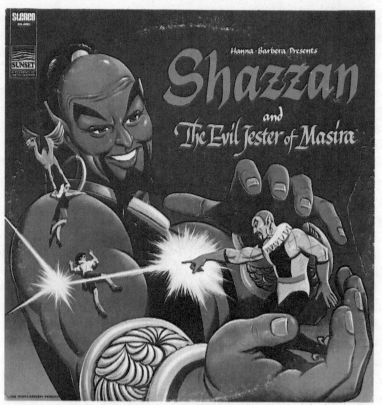

One of the two musical adventure albums Hanna-Barbera produced in partnership with Liberty Records, this features the TV cast plus Thurl Ravenscroft singing for Shazzan.

Two brand-new Hanna-Barbera record albums were produced and released on Sunset Records. Replacing Charles Shows as director was H-B studio staffer Paul DeKorte, overseeing the projects, and John McCarthy, writing the stories and songs. DeKorte would have a long, distinguished career as music supervisor at Hanna-Barbera on virtually all the studio's work, along with, as a singer himself, special attention to vocal sessions with Ron Hicklin and the studio singers. McCarthy was now a *Flintstones* veteran, having written songs for the TV series and the feature film. His Sunset Hanna-Barbera songs would be worked into the stories to a greater degree than in the Cartoon Series records. Another difference was scope. The Sunset albums presented new musical scores in addition to the songs. Instead of picking up cue music from the studio library, the background music for the two new albums was composed, arranged, and conducted especially for the records by Ted Nichols.

▲▼▲▼▲

The first album was based on one of Hanna-Barbera's newest hit shows. *Shazzan and the Evil Jester of Masira* (1968) offers an idea of what Hanna-Barbera-produced albums might have been like had they continued in the quantities of the original HBR Cartoon Series. The album follows the Cartoon Series format in that there are original songs about the characters in addition to the narrative. Also, like the HBR discs, the songs don't quite match the tone of the story portions, arguably part of the HBR charm and strangeness.

The Sunset/Hanna-Barbera albums were promising from a visual aspect. The same meticulous artwork, painting, backgrounds, and lettering were again lavished on these covers by the H-B studio artists. Like the HBR album covers based on *The Atom Ant/Secret Squirrel Show*, the *Shazzan* cover reworks the title card art seen in the series, a major recognition advantage that fans were thrilled to see.

Shazzan was an animated action-fantasy series about two young teens who find a magic ring. Transported to an ancient Arabian Nights land of adventures, they meet their genie, Shazzan, who can do almost every kind of magic but send them home, setting up the premise. A flying camel named Kaboobie flew them from one fantastic land to another. The premises of Saturday morning programs in the late twentieth century were designed to accommodate the circular nature of programming. Since daytime budgets were much smaller than prime time, networks ordered an average of sixteen episodes of an animated or live-action series compared to twenty-six to thirty yearly prime-time series episodes. If a Saturday morning show was successful, it only meant about eight more episodes would be added the following year. One episode could run six times over two years, so it was deemed necessary to stay away from concluding episodes, to keep the stories in constant flow.

Hanna-Barbera used the theme song to pull audiences in, as good theme sequences did during their heyday. A lot of special time and effort is evident in the "sixty-second sell" of H-B themes, often containing bits of fluid animation, rapid-fire editing, and always catchy music. They are the equivalent of today's "sizzle piece" in promotional terms.

A series like *Shazzan* had an especially complex premise, so an additional set-up segment followed the theme to explain the premise. Each of the two segments also began with "tease" clips before the title cards, usually a dictum from the networks. In the case of *Shazzan*, the efforts paid off because it was yet another hit in CBS's highly touted "Cartooniverse."

The *Shazzan* album features all the major original cast members: Barney Phillips, a character actor whose credits include four *Twilight Zone* episodes;

Jerry Dexter, in his one and only Hanna-Barbera vinyl appearance (soon to voice Alan for *Josie and the Pussycats*); and Janet Waldo, who speaks and sings as Nancy. *The Evil Jester of Masira* is adapted directly from a TV episode with some additional dialogue, adjustments, and slight recasting. Playing the gentleman needing help is prolific actor Jay Novello, who starred on CBS radio's *Life with Luigi* sitcom with Alan Reed for five years. Hal Smith, longtime Hanna-Barbera "utility player" best known as Otis Campbell on *The Andy Griffith Show*, also makes his Hanna-Barbera vinyl debut with this item in several roles.

One especially interesting difference between the album and TV versions, and an example of the dynamism of audio storytelling, is a scene in which Nancy (Waldo) appears to be asking Chuck (Dexter) to throw her a magic book. When he does, Nancy is revealed to be the Evil Jester in disguise. In the cartoon, Waldo voiced Nancy normally, and then visually Nancy transformed into the Jester. However, on the record, it was done with sound: Waldo says Nancy's lines in a strange, suspicious way, then when Chuck throws the book, her vengeful laughter is edited in mid-giggle to the Jester's evil laughter. It is just as dramatic and memorable, if not more so.

While Janet Waldo sings, it is not clear whether Dexter is singing. It may be DeKorte or another top Hollywood studio singer, Jerry Whitman. When Shazzan sings the ballad, "The Land Where Genies Live" to close the LP, it is not Barney Phillips but another newcomer to Hanna-Barbera recordings, Thurl Ravenscroft. One of the renowned Mellomen quartet of *The Jack Benny Program* and *Lady and the Tramp*, Ravenscroft's beloved bass graces The Haunted Mansion at various Disney theme parks and the song, "You're a Mean One, Mr. Grinch."

▲▼▲▼▲▼

The most spectacular Hanna-Barbera record produced in the sixties is *The Flintstones Meet the Orchestra Family*, a children's music appreciation record in the tradition of the beloved classic, *Tubby the Tuba*. On side

The most elaborate Hanna-Barbera production created specifically for records starred *The Flintstones* cast with superb original songs.

one, conductor Mister Orchestra (Don Messick) and his family move to Bedrock. Fred (Alan Reed), Barney (Mel Blanc), Pebbles (Jean Vander Pyl), and Bamm-Bamm (Messick) meet each section of the orchestra in each "section" of the house. (To indicate walking from room to room, the sound of clattering shoes is used even though bare feet are a Flintstone tradition.)

Like 1965's exceptional *The Flintstones Flip Fables*, a flagship album for the HBR Cartoon Series with the original cast, *The Flintstones Meet the Orchestra Family* shows every indication of being the showcase title for what would have been a continuing series. In this case, the budget had to be even higher considering the huge orchestra and top-dollar cast. The music may have been recorded in Europe to reduce costs—as it still is sometimes today—but for a $1.98 children's record, this sort of original recording, drawing

from no source material, like a soundtrack or a stock library, is downright opulent.

Aimed more directly at kids, this album does not offer the snappy, multilevel Charles Shows writing heard in the HBR Cartoon Series. Alan Reed's Fred is at his most jovial and Mel Blanc's Barney refrains from saying anything that would make Fred cast aspersions on his intelligence, as he did on the HBR LP, *Flip Fables* ("So who goes bowling at dawn, rockhead?"). They do remain true to character, especially Barney, who still gets his share of amusing lines, even amid the panic when he remarks that the pterodactyls are "zooming around very zoomy!" Barney is in a panic as is Fred, because Pebbles and Bamm-Bamm have become helplessly aloft on giant balloons. With the help of the Orchestra Family—particularly the harp—Fred and Barney are able to save them, while moving from one stereo channel to the next, singing all the way.

Their safe return is celebrated with a big production number, oddly recalled in flashback. Even though the listener was "there" when Fred and Barney rescued the children, they tell Mister Orchestra that the kids thought it was all a game. The Hanna-Barbera "Jetson Jazz" sound kicks into gear in all its glory as the singing Pebbles and Bamm-Bamm, along with Henry Corden (again singing for Fred) and Mel Blanc, perform the eleven o'clock number. Ted Nichols's bold, brassy arrangement puts John McCarthy's "If You Could Fly" in the mold of Hoyt Curtin showstoppers like Jet Screamers "Epp-Opp-Ork" and Hoagy Carmichaels "Yabba Dabba Doo."

The simple melody repeated throughout side one of *The Flintstones Meet the Orchestra Family* is like the theme in the classic children's recording, *Tubby the Tuba* melody. It showcases each instrument to teach musical appreciation. The melody has no printed title, though it is played in response to the words, "Good morning, Mr. Flintstone."

Side one concludes with the melody played as a Hanna-Barbera mini-symphony of sorts. Nichols ends it with the same distinctive sting and reverb as the theme music to Hanna-Barbera's most ambitious TV series since *The Flintstones*.

▲▼▲▼▲▼

The New Adventures of Huckleberry Finn was the first television show to combine live-action and animation every week. The critical success and high ratings of *Jack and the Beanstalk* helped sell it to NBC. In the fall of 1968, it was placed against Disney's long-running anthology series, just as *The Jetsons* was in 1962.

The series owed its premise more to *Shazzan* than to Mark Twain. Each episode found Huck, Tom Sawyer, and Becky Thatcher in a different land of adventure, fantasy, or even science fiction. The boisterous theme tune is heard over picturesque scenes of the trio aboard a live-action riverboat, followed by either a one- or two-minute prologue (the same way Shaz-

Lu Ann Haslam as Becky Thatcher greets a cartoon friend in this composite photo promoting TV's first animation/live-action series, *The New Adventures of Huckleberry Finn*.

zan did it) explaining the premise of the trio running through a cave that gradually becomes more like animation as they get lost inside it. Some episodes conclude with a friend helping them on a "sure way" to return home, but the opening of each episode resets the premise by showing them lost in a storm or other such event to take them off course again.

Like *Loopy DeLoop, The Magilla Gorilla Show, Alice in Wonderland*, and a few other Hanna-Barbera productions seldom recognized for their place in history—particularly in the music department—*The New Adventures of Huckleberry Finn* had a lasting effect on background music long after the series left the airwaves. The generous budget for *Huck Finn* allowed Ted Nichols something Hoyt Curtin seldom if ever experienced until years later at Hanna-Barbera—the chance to post-score TV episodes in addition to creating music cues. In the past, the composers were made very aware of what was needed and provided with both specific and general story information, but nothing was scored to picture.

Marty Paich created pre- and post-score material for *Hey There, It's Yogi Bear*, and Ted Nichols did the same for *The Man Called Flintstone*, but *Huck Finn* was the first TV series to get such special treatment. It was the first Hanna-Barbera TV series in which there were selected episodes with post-scored music that fit the action precisely. Those familiar with H-B cartoons of the seventies and their most repeated music cues can watch an episode like "Mission of Captain Mordecai" and see the events that initially inspired the scoring and interpolations.

Because of its cost, *The New Adventures of Huckleberry Finn* could have only succeeded if it was a major hit. Disney was still holding strong despite almost two years since the loss of host Walt Disney, but once again the high cost of new Huck Finn episodes needed to show tremendous strength to justify its competition against the ever-popular *Lassie* and Irwin Allen's *Land of the Giants*, the advertising revenue would have justified the expense. Instead, the three programs split the choices among family audiences and age groups. NBC's replacement, the low-cost documentary-style *Mutual of Omaha's Wild Kingdom*, offered a higher profit margin than either *Lassie* or *Land of the Giants*.

The New Adventures of Huckleberry Finn would become one of Hanna-Barbera's most fondly remembered works. Its musical score lived on for years through its cues, heard in countless episodes of *Scooby-Doo*, *Josie and the Pussycats*, and other H-B series. In addition to the considerable publicity it attracted when it premiered, the series had a long cable run and especially in syndication when it was packaged with another 1968 Hanna-Barbera series: *The Banana Splits Adventure Hour*.

▲▼▲▼

"Action! Adventure! Suspense! Laughs!" opened the sixty-minute grab bag that was *The Banana Splits Adventure Hour*. It did not blend animation and live-action together but was instead comprised of separate live-action segments and adventure cartoons (*The Three Musketeers*, *Arabian Knights*,[3] *Micro Venture*); and a live-action serial (*Danger Island*, directed by Richard Donner); wrapped in a psychedelic flower-power package framed by slapstick sketches and music videos by a live-action band in character costumes designed by Hanna-Barbera artists.

Critics like *TV Guide*'s Cleveland Amory didn't know what to make of the series except to express head-shaking derision. The show didn't seek their approval, it seemed not to care. *The Banana Splits* was sugar-frosted kiddie counterculture served courtesy of specially marked boxes of Kellogg's cereals. The hour was actually a clever concept, designed to appeal to the childhoods of several generations. The *Danger Island* segment is a direct throwback to *Tarzan*, *Sheena, Queen of the Jungle*, and other Saturday morning serials of the thirties and forties, this time in color with groovy music and lots of trendy zooms and "hip talk." The cartoon segments have elements of comedy but are more in the spirit of epic Errol Flynn and Stewart Granger movies. *The Banana Splits* filmed comedy segments could have been clipped from the silliest and most "family-friendly" segments of *Rowan and Martin's Laugh-In* (also on NBC). By no coincidence, the Banana Splits were guest stars on *Laugh-In*.

Sid and Marty Krofft, internationally renowned for either staging or providing puppets, elaborate character costumes, and sets for live shows, events, and theme parks, were selected by Hanna-Barbera to transpose their studio artists' designs into character costumes. H-B, NBC, and Kellogg's needed the costumes to work visually as walkarounds for live appearances, but most importantly to look good on television from various angles, close-ups, and long shots, the same way that Jim Henson's Muppets were designed in this specific manner. NBC was so impressed with the work of the Kroffts and their

One in a series of paintings by Joseph Csatari depicting Taft Broadcasting Activities

A scrapbook day.

It was a happy day. A family day that brought everyone closer together. Tomorrow's memories, to be relived and enjoyed together.

Family entertainment. It's part of our business and our philosophy. Even though our name is Taft Broadcasting, our themed amusement parks host over 5½ million people a year. We consider the support of basic family values as our most important job. And we're proud of it.

In addition to our themed amusement parks, our radio and television stations serve seven major markets; and Hanna-Barbera, our television and motion picture arm, counts its audience in the hundreds of millions all around the world.

TAFT Broadcasting Company Informing and entertaining the American family.

This ad for *Broadcasting Magazine* combines the Kings Island theme park with Hanna-Barbera characters, positioning Taft as a full-service entertainment company with Hanna-Barbera as its "television and motion picture arm."

talented staff that they encouraged the brothers to produce the first in a line of hit TV series, the beloved *H. R. Pufnstuf*. The Kroffts had a successful partnership with Six Flags Over Texas, where they produced one of their puppet extravaganzas.[4] It was no accident that the season one opening titles of *The Banana Splits Adventure Hour*, as well as various musical romps, were filmed at Six Flags. The opening to the 1971 Krofft live-action series *Lidsville* was also filmed at the park.

The four Banana Splits, Fleagle (with the voice of Paul Winchell), Bingo (Daws Butler), Drooper (Allan Melvin), and Snorky (who just honked), were later seen in "their own" park. Under the ownership of Taft, Hanna-Barbera characters would be populating their parks, including Coney Island in Cincinnati, a filming location for Banana Splits songs. Relocated and renamed Kings Island in 1971, it was the setting for a 1972 *ABC Saturday Superstar Movie* called "The Banana Splits in Hocus Pocus Park" featuring both live-action and animated versions of the Splits.

Musically the Banana Splits "group" style was all over the map. Among those involved behind the scenes were Barry White, Gene Pitney, Joey

Levine, and Al Kooper. The Banana Splits might have appeared to be four funny animals playing in a whimsical band, but there was no singular performing style for them, unlike The Archies, which also debuted that year and maintained a certain consistency with lead singer Ron Dante.

The music was formatted and marketed on records in two different ways. Since Hanna-Barbera no longer had a record company, the insignia "H-B Premium Division" appeared on a set of two 4-song stereo 45 rpm EP records called *The Banana Splits Sing 'n Play "The Tra-La-La Song"* and *The Banana Splits Sing 'n Play "Doin' the Banana Split."* They were available only by mail order by saving Kellogg's box tops, filling out a form, and sending it all with just fifty cents for both discs.

Producer David Mook sought out some of the best talents in pop music to write and perform the songs, many already with substantial credits, some on their way to other things. One of the most prominent vocalists was Ricky Lancelotti, a studio singer and aspiring voice actor of substantial range who was billed under the name Rick Lancelot. "Doin' the Banana Split" best exemplifies his heavy James Brown–like soul singing capabilities, but the jubilant "It's a Good Day for a Parade" shows a merrier mood.

The two Kellogg's records range from uncharacteristic romantic ballads ("That's the Pretty Part of You"), songs of despair ("Let Me Remember You Smiling," "The Very First Kid on the Block"), or the far-out "I Enjoy Being a Boy" with lyrics like, "I live in a purple plum mansion / In the mist of a strawberry stream / And mellifluous bells ring out softly / From a hill of vanilla fudge cream."

One song on each disc captures the Hanna-Barbera signature sound. "The Tra-La-La Song," released as a single in an alternate version, is credited to Mark Barkan and Ritchie Adams (who would write the *Scooby-Doo, Where Are You?* theme and several Archies songs). However, it was also reported to be the work of the aforementioned Burnett agency writer H. B. Winkless. "The Tra-La-La Song" became one of the most popular Hanna-Barbera themes. Hoyt Curtin himself collaborated with Winkless for the inventive tongue-twister "The Beautiful Calliopa." Bearing a classic "house style" arrangement by Curtin, it refers to a mammoth contraption called a "Calliopasaxavia-trumparimbaclarabasatrombophone." Like "Supercalifragilisticexpialidocious," it's fun to learn and had the potential to become a children's standard.

The 1968 LP *We're The Banana Splits* was the first Hanna-Barbera album on the Decca label. It was just as eclectic as the Kellogg's EP set but seems aimed at a slightly older listening audience as it featured a greater number of rock, soul, and R&B songs. It is worth noting that, for all its apparent frolicsome frippery, The Banana Splits offered the changing America of 1968 some "entry-level" soul music for many kids whose parents might otherwise not have felt they were ready for the "grownup" versions. Of course, few if any mainstream heavy '60s pop albums mentioned Yogi Bear in the lyrics or put a peppy ragtime instrumental like "Toy Piano Melody" between two soul songs.

The Hanna-Barbera studio didn't commission the music people carelessly; they brought in the best. Ricky Lancelotti could later be heard on several Frank Zappa records including "Zomby Woof," and he appeared with Zappa at the Hollywood Palladium. Al Kooper's accomplishments were putting together the band, Blood, Sweat and Tears, and composing numerous movie scores. Gene Pitney is now considered a legendary pop singer, with such hits as "Town without Pity" and compositions like "Hello, Mary Lou." Barry White, of course, became a big recording star with a signature sultry, romantic murmur over his music.

The Banana Splits enjoyed new life in the late seventies when it became the umbrella series combining several earlier H-B shows. Because of the daily syndicated *Banana Splits and Friends*, many more remember *The Adventures of Gulliver*, *The Atom Ant Show*, *The New Adventures of Huckleberry Finn*, and *The Secret Squirrel Show* from the seventies rather than from the sixties.

▲▼▲▼

Music legend Barry White wrote "Doin' the Banana Split" for *The Banana Splits Adventure Hour*.

Cattanooga Cats was a one-hour 1969 ABC "package series" like *The Banana Splits* with no live-action and more comedy. The hour featured the band in cartoons, short segments, and song sequences, plus three other cartoons: "Around the World in 79 Days," "Motormouse and Autocat," and the most memorable one, "It's the Wolf"—changing the Hanna-Barbera staple of cats and mice to a wolf and sheep, each delightfully voiced by Daws Butler and Paul Lynde, respectively. The success of *The Monkees* and especially *The Archies* (since it was animated) ignited a wave of cartoon rock bands on Saturday morning TV, from *The Hardy Boys* to *The Brady Kids*. The art style of *Cattanooga Cats* was as steeped in sixties pop art as their neighboring "groovy band" shows. Their sound was somewhat unique among H-B cartoon pop, keeping the band simple without too much production and a new touch of country.

H-B turned to influential music entrepreneur Mike Curb, who among other things, led a vocal group, The Mike Curb Congregation, that performed independently ("Burning Bridges," "Sweet Gingerbread Man") and as backup for singing stars like Sammy Davis Jr. ("The Candy Man"). He also presided over MGM Records, later going into politics and becoming lieutenant governor of California. Curb hired composer/producer/singer Michael Lloyd, whom he had made VP of Artists and Repertoire at MGM Records. Lloyd had a vast musical resume for film, TV, and records before and after *Cattanooga Cats*, and contributed to Saturday morning music through the Krofft series *Far Out Space Nuts* and *The Lost Saucer*.

Lloyd provided the vocals along with Peggy Clinger, who was one of the perky Clinger Sisters a few years earlier, often showcased on CBS's *Danny Kaye Show*. Peggy continued writing and singing, con-

Late '60s designs and music directed by Mike Curb brought new styles to Hanna-Barbera cartoons.

tributing several songs to *The Partridge Family*, including "Rock Me Baby" with husband Johnny Cymbal. Lloyd and Clinger modified the style of H-B TV cartoon pop, favoring a simpler, "small club" band style. Almost every arrangement on the album starts with a swift drumbeat and continues in a pulsing rhythm, which can be helpful elements in animation timing and production efficiency. Some songs are inspired by children's games and playtime activities, like "Mother May I?" and "Country Carnival."

A curious tune called "My Birthday Suit" managed to get on the cartoon show as well as the album. In this peppy dance tune, Clinger sings, "How do you like me in my birthday suit? Am I cute in my birthday suit?" In the animated visualization, the cat characters are seen as cute little kittens, dressed in diapers at a birthday party. "My Birthday Suit" was one of a handful of songs that was not written for *Cattanooga*

Cats, but created earlier for a 1968 independent film for nonfamily audiences called *Jennie: Wife/Child*. Other songs reused in *Cattanooga Cats* include "My Girlfriend Is a Witch" and "I Wish I Was a Fire," from a 1968 Michael Lloyd–produced album by the group October Country; and "Cold Wisconsin Night (Sittin' by the Fireside)" recorded by The American Revolution. The latter two, in their *Cattanooga Cats* versions, were not released on records.

The final song on the LP, "Merry Go 'Round," stands out among the playtime pop in both theme and treatment. The orchestration is richer, including strings, brass, woodwinds, and a slightly more Hanna-Barbera "house" sound. The plaintive harmony, presumably Clinger double-tracked, adds to the mood of this melancholy song about growing up and the wistful longing for the past. The bouncy rhythm is offset by tense trombones, building up to a "Time in a Bottle" dramatic punch in a high register: "Children go downtown / And forget merry-go-round / Soon enough will come December / And then you shall remember / Better go-round, let it go round, merry go round." It's not the first song to deal with the passing of time, but it handles the subject in a novel and touching way. For the animated version of "Merry Go 'Round," Hanna-Barbera used some interesting designs. It can even be surmised that the visuals do indeed support the moody lyrics. Viewers may note that, while there's an overall emphasis on the usual frolic, there are virtually no shots of the Cats during the darker lyrics. Instead, there are obscuring clouds, then a full moon, and a close-up of a horse's eye. Maybe that's overanalyzing. It's not an Ingmar Bergman film. Still, any number of images could have been chosen over these. Specific discussions must have taken place about the visual treatment of these songs, as opposed to, say, "Alle Alle Oxen Free," which consists of little more than graphics and color patterns.

▲▼▲▼▲▼

Joe Barbera kept hardbound books filled with brilliant, outlandish concepts for TV shows and films that he and his creative staff had conceived for various projects. Somewhere in the "almost" files is a cartoon pop series called "Captain Groovy and His Bubblegum Army." It was one of several proposed projects Hanna-Barbera concocted with Jerry Kasanetz and Jeff Katz, founders of Super K Productions, originators of the term "bubblegum music," and creators of the Ohio Express, 1910 Fruitgum Company, and The Music Explosion. The proposed concept never became a cartoon, but Captain Groovy and His Bubblegum Army did release an eponymous single on Super K Records, which hit #127 on the charts—an accomplishment that was, according to music historian Bill Pitzonka, "actually faring better than many other cartoon outfits which never cracked the chart in any capacity."

Hanna-Barbera Productions would never launch an animated pop group to equal The Archies phenomenon. The studio would, however, break significant ground in its further attempts and, at the same time, launch one of the biggest and most popular successes in animation history.

Chapter 19

SCOOBY-DOO, WHERE ARE YOUR RECORDS?

I hope we're not too late for our recording session!
—DAPHNE BLAKE (HEATHER NORTH), "SCOOBY-DOO AND THE DIABOLI-
CAL DISC DEMON"

Hanna-Barbera sustained its lead in TV animation, even as tastes and trends were rapidly changing. Keeping up with what appealed to viewers was only one challenge. Now there was a parent corporation, increasing input from network personnel, and pressure to tone down violence from various groups. *Space Ghost* and *Herculoids* had been in dispute; cartoon rock and roll seemed to assuage some concerns. Within a few years, each program would have to convey "pro-social" messages and there would have to be clear breaks between show segments and commercials.

The appeal of The Beatles, The Archies, The Monkees, and other teen-oriented pop culture to children was not lost on the networks. The 1970s ushered in the age of research, and many a study observed that each age group aspired to see themselves a few years older than their actual age. This is one reason for the continued success of *The Brady Bunch*, which had the age differences built into the premise of six children.

Hanna-Barbera was in the thick of teen-oriented cartoon show development. Two of their key writers were Joe Ruby and Ken Spears, who worked their way up at H-B from editors to the story department, gaining the favor of both Joe Barbera and network brass like Fred Silverman. The four of them bounced a concept around with elements of the classic CBS sitcom *Dobie Gillis*. One of the characters in the mix included a goateed beatnik that resembled the Bob Denver "Maynard G. Krebs" character. However, further examination of the *Dobie Gillis* TV concept reveals it also to be inspired character-for-character by Archie Comics. The original Max Shulman *The Many Loves of Dobie Gillis* short stories focused on Dobie in a different phase of life. Only Thalia Menninger appeared in the text, and only in one story. The other characters were added for the sitcom and can be matched to Archie icons: Dobie/Archie, Maynard/Jughead, Thalia/Veronica, Zelda/Betty, and Milton/Chatsworth/Reggie. Even Archie owes its inspiration to both the MGM Andy Hardy films and radio's Henry Aldrich.

The key to the success of what became *Scooby-Doo, Where Are You?* in 1969 was the decades-old childhood fascination with being scared, but not too scared. Giving the show the chicken-hearted, ever-hungry Great Dane and partnering him with a human counterpart was as appealing to kids as *Abbott and Costello Meet Frankenstein*. Blending terror with laughter is a potent combination as old as campfire ghost stories and seriocomic films like *The Cat and the Canary*.

On the surface, the repetitive formula of *Scooby-Doo* cartoons appears to defy every logical notion of longevity, yet its unparalleled success makes perfect sense. There is a comfort in the repetition, especially for kids. The repetition can also be inverted and satirized. The more the characters and stories repeated themselves over the decades, the more fun audiences had either laughing along with the silliness or at the occasional spoofs that drew attention to the endless utterances of "And I would have gotten away with it, if it weren't for you meddling kids!" Few things in contemporary culture are so completely shared by millions, whether they love or loathe them. Either way, have fun with it, just watch and be entertained.

▲▼▲▼▲▼

Scooby-Doo, Where Are You? enabled Ted Nichols to create another influential Hanna-Barbera background score. Perhaps due to the special attention that *Scooby-Doo, Where Are You?* project was getting with Silverman and other participants, the first episode to air, "What a Night for a Knight," was budgeted for post-scoring, a rare instance for a Saturday morning cartoon episode. The cues Nichols composed for "What a Night for a Knight" are familiar to longtime viewers of the first several seasons, as well as other Hanna-Barbera shows of the era. It can be a revelation

for these viewers to return to episode one and see the cues as they were originally matched to the action.[1]

The vocal theme song by Mark Barkan and Ritchie Adams ("Scooby, Dooby Doo, where are you / We've got some work to do now . . .") may not have been the original theme, as it is not heard during the actual episodes of the first two seasons as much as Ted Nichols constant "mystery theme" music, which is also played under each episode's title graphic. CBS broadcast a fast-paced version of this instrumental as the main title theme at least once in the original series run. Like "Meet the Flintstones" replacing "Rise and Shine," this might be another case of a vocal being a better way to explain the series at the top of every show (H-B's "sixty-second sell").

Groovy as Scooby and the gang were, they were not part of a pop record marketing plan with "The Scoobys" or some such band. There were also no *Scooby-Doo*-related record albums released in the US for the first eight years of the show's run in its various formats. Season two of *Scooby-Doo, Where Are You?* introduced a musical "romp" with vocals by four-time Grammy-nominated singer/songwriter Austin Roberts, whose hits include Helen Reddy's "Keep on Singin'" and the Oscar-nominated "Over You" from the Robert Duvall film, *Tender Mercies*. His collaborator on the latter was Bobby Hart, cowriter of "Last Train to Clarksville" and the theme for *The Monkees* TV series. In the H-B Saturday morning tradition of "why ask, just go with it," there was no reason for the off-screen band, except that it was cool and funny.

It would be over twenty years before these songs, including the familiar "Recipe for My Love" and "I Can Make You Happy" (also recorded by Davy Jones for *The New Scooby-Doo Movies*), would be released commercially. The only exception notable at this writing is the 45 rpm record accompanying the Kenner Talking Show Projector in 1971. This was a hybrid of two best-selling Kenner toys: the Close 'n Play phonograph, which played 45s when the lid was closed; and the Give-A-Show projector, a lighted device that threw still images on walls or screens from long pasteboard slide cards. One of the Talking Show refill

Future Oscar nominee Austin Roberts wrote and sang "chase songs" for the second season of *Scooby-Doo, Where Are You?*

packages included an adaptation of the Scooby-Doo episode, "That's Snow Ghost," with Norma Macmillan (Casper, the Friendly Ghost; *Underdog*'s Sweet Polly Purebred) voicing both Daphne and Fred. Other recordings connected to toys would be the small record inside the Talking View-Master, also based on "That's Snow Ghost." Special lines of Hanna-Barbera educational materials, like filmstrip presentations, were not available to the general public. These are fascinating, vast subjects unto themselves, as is the world of foreign language recordings.

▲▼▲▼▲▼

The first Scooby-Doo LP record album ever released was British. Produced in England by MFP (Music for Pleasure) Records, Ltd., 1973's *Scooby-Doo and the Snowmen Mystery* is an example of how a valiant, competent creative work can be limited by scant

information and result in "off-model" audio results. The UK cast sports American accents as the five leads with a glib "Goofy"-sounding Scooby, a conceited "Maxwell Smart"–like Fred, and a southern-drawling Shaggy.

Perhaps to come up with enough dialogue to fill the fifty-six-minute album and with no further information available, the script takes the characters' personalities outside the confines of the series description, something the writer must have felt necessary given the sparse guidelines. The story also does not have an "unmasking," but rather a science fiction "mad scientist" reveal. This kind of theme was explored in later Scooby-Doo feature-length films, but in 1973, the now-famous format was being set.

Many licensees may not have been aware of this without seeing multiple episodes, however, depending on how much support material was sent to them for their merchandise. A studio merchandise license guide, *The Happy Land of Hanna-Barbera*, covering shows from 1965 to 1971, describes *Scooby-Doo, Where Are You?* and the characters in general terms and does not mention that almost every show ends with the unmasking of a phony monster "scaring people away" from something they coveted.

While the resources seem to have been limited, the level of talent was not. The producer of this album is Barry Ainsworth, who engineered "Bohemian Rhapsody" for Queen. Ainsworth's career extends back to Liverpool's The Cavern, where he was one of those involved with The Beatles' success, as well as that of Otis Redding, Rush, Petula Clark, and The Kinks. Vocal arranger Mike Sammes sings for the evil Professor Zero. Sammes was one of the world's greatest vocal directors of the sixties and seventies, with too many credits in records, TV, and advertising to count. The Mike Sammes Singers performed on records, and occasionally on camera, with The Beatles, Tom Jones, Frank Sinatra, Barbra Streisand, and many more. They also performed for Disney and Rankin/Bass productions. The other voices on the album could be members of Sammes's vocal ensemble or another prolific group, such as The Rita Williams Singers. Their

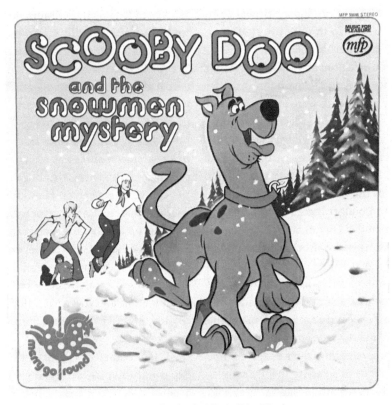

The first *Scooby-Doo* record album was produced and sold in the United Kingdom.

skills are clear, but their direction is far from the way the characters should sound, even an approximation.

As is often the case with limited budget records, music rights were an issue, so the Barkan/Adams "Scooby-Doo, Where Are You?" theme is not included. Instead, the phrase was reversed and one of the original songs is called "Where Are You, Scooby-Doo?"; there are four original early seventies pop-style songs, including "Where Are You?" and "Mystery Incorporated," sung by the cast, which was also released on a single record. The songs by Mike McNaught and Ken Martyne have a bright, late sixties/early seventies pop sound in the manner of Burt Bacharach, Donovan, Harry Nilsson, and Herb Alpert.

The duo wrote twenty more original songs for another 1973 British children's album called *Spin a Magic Tune: 20 Fantastic Tunes About Your Favorite Cartoon Characters* on Tempo Records. Like most of the HBR records, there are no theme songs. Some of these pop-infused songs convey the characters more accurately than others. There are songs about Warner Bros. characters, Noddy and Rupert the Bear, but Hanna-Barbera characters dominate the selections, most with no other presence on records (of their day) other than this album, including Space Kidettes, Dastardly and Muttley, Yankee Doodle Pigeon, Penelope Pitstop, *It's the Wolf!*, Motormouse and Autocat.

▲▼▲▼▲▼

The New Scooby-Doo Movies (1972) was network TV's first weekly one-hour, continuing character cartoon with a single story instead of multiple interior segments. When CBS let the contract lapse, Barbera took Scooby-Doo to ABC, where new cartoons were formatted as either half- or quarter-hour segments

(11 or 22 minutes minus ads and interstitials) combined in various 60- to 120-minute programming blocks with "show" or "hour" in the titles.

Peter Pan Records produced and released the first Scooby-Doo Records in the US, starting in 1977, the second year Scooby and friends were on ABC. One of the oldest children's labels in the industry and among the few privately owned children's label in existence, Peter Pan was founded in a New Jersey complex that also functioned as the Synthetic Plastics Company. Peter Pan was one of the most competitive and successful children's and budget record companies. Its subsidiary labels included Diplomat, Parade, Promenade, Caroleer, Ambassador, Rocking Horse, and Tinkerbell Records. Peter Pan's Power label released action and some horror titles for older kids and teens, though some of those spilled over into the Peter Pan line, like Kojak and Star Trek. During the disco era, Peter Pan led the industry with the Irwin the Disco Duck series, releasing over a dozen albums filled with cover versions of hit songs to huge sales—years ahead of the bigger, boutique labels. They sold so many book-and-record sets during their heyday that they were the equivalent of a best-selling book publisher in terms of printing and distribution.

Peter Pan exists today under several of its labels and as Symphonic Distribution, releasing thousands of children's, classical, pop, and spoken word titles. They outlasted their chief rival, Golden Records, which by 1977 had changed to Wonderland Records having lost the Golden name to Western Publishing. Legal entanglements sent the Golden Records catalog through a series of ownerships and its Hanna-Barbera material was never reissued on CD or digital.

Children's record veteran Ralph Stein was the first to bring the original Scooby-Doo voices to records. Stein was a producer, writer, and art director at Peter Pan, Golden, Pickwick, Happy Time, and Cricket. Stein met Don Messick several years earlier, and the two collaborated on a 1967 Golden LP called Jim's Fairy Tales. Messick may have been helpful to Stein in accessing the rest of the TV cast. Heather North, the voice of Daphne from almost the beginning of the series (following Stefanianna Christopherson), makes a welcome addition to records in the Janet Waldo tradition. Pat Stevens, the voice of Velma after the characters moved to ABC, replaced Nicole Jaffe, who had become a talent agent. Stevens can be seen in endless reruns of fifteen classic M*A*S*H episodes, including "Margaret's Marriage." Frank Welker has been the voice of Fred from the beginning, speaking in an extension of his natural voice. Joining the cast of Scooby-Doo, Where Are You? completely changed the course of his career. He went from success as a young impressionist and actor to becoming one of the all-time top voice actors and creators of vocal effects. If the box-office receipts of every one of Welker's film credits were tabulated, he would be considered one of Hollywood's top-grossing box-office performers in animation and live-action films like Aladdin, Poltergeist, Mars Attacks!, and Star Trek III: The Search for Spock.

"When I started, I noticed that the other, more experienced voice actors were chiming in to do other voices in the script," he said in an interview. "These were some of the biggest names in the voice acting business so at first, I was a little intimidated, but after a while I would start in with some [makes weird sound] and a voice and I've been doing this ever since." Welker is one of a handful of actors who have voiced hundreds of lead and incidental Hanna-Barbera characters.

The only original cast member that was unavailable for Peter Pan's first Scooby-Doo records was Casey Kasem as Shaggy. So in the "cover voice" tradition, an actor named Duncan Robertson was cast to approximate the voice of Shaggy, giving him the high, nasal dashes of Don Knotts.

▴▵▴▵▴

Four Scooby-Doo stories adapted for Peter Pan Records also appeared in children's storybooks published in Canada by Ottenheimer and in the US by Wonder Books. The recorded adaptations are unique among most read-along sets. They are printed and

Two songs from the British LP *Scooby Doo and the Snowmen Mystery* were released on a single 7" disc.

performed entirely through dialogue with no narration. In adapting the book to audio, all the narrative text was removed and the action was worked into expository dialogue. The text accompanying the records is similar to a play script, but they do not indicate who is speaking with a name and colon before each line.[2] In the tradition of '70s Hanna-Barbera cartoons, the stories end with a "laughing fade," in which the characters chuckle at some mildly amusing thing, and the music comes in. The "Ha-Ha's" in the book are jumbled about the last page "in tribute."

There were four books and recording sets. *Scooby-Doo and the Mystery of the Strange Paw Prints* predates *Jurassic Park* but is certainly not the first time cartoon or comic book characters discovered that the dinosaurs they encountered were created for paying guests. In *Scooby-Doo and the Mystery of the Sticky Money*, the team enters a seemingly abandoned house and subdues counterfeiters with forty pancakes they cooked up with materials that happened to be there. *Scooby-Doo and the Ghost in the Doghouse* is a change-of-pace story in which the gang builds Scooby a doghouse but something inside frightens him. And *Scooby-Doo and the Rider Without a Head* is most akin to a TV adventure, with a rodeo being terrorized by a headless creature. *The Rider Without a Head* was only released as a read-along set with either a 45 rpm record or a cassette. The first three were combined on an LP called *Scooby-Doo: Three Stories*, later released as a picture disc. The first two were combined on an LP with an album-sized read-along book entitled *Adventures of Scooby-Doo*. Only the LPs were in stereo.

The production values are humble, with some library music and electronic cues, and the pace is gentle. For Scooby fans and young children in particular, after all the years of waiting it was nice to have

This portfolio of Hanna-Barbera model sheets was sent to merchandise companies to license the studio's output from 1965 to 1971. Each series is given a brief description and some character profiles.

some of the original cast on records to play anytime at home.

Peter Pan was able to bring in Casey Kasem to complete the cast for two more Scooby-Doo albums later that year, each with two noticeably stronger stories and tighter presentations than that of the first album and read-along sets. *Scooby-Doo: Two All-New Adventures!* features all four original cast members in their TV roles, this time foiling bank robbers and helping to clear an impoverished boy of stealing. *Exciting Christmas Stories with Scooby-Doo and Friends* tells a similar heartwarming tale of an orphanage Santa accused of theft plus a dream story with Scooby meeting the gang at the North Pole to solve a mystery for the real Santa. Low-tech carols by a few singers and an organ were accessed from earlier Bozo the Clown and Romper Room albums on Little World Records.

Among the qualities that challenged the creators of cover versions, matching the general energy of Hanna-Barbera cartoons was difficult, if rarely attempted. By the seventies, there was a decided rhythm to H-B shows that set them apart. If it was, even audio-wise, a formulaic sameness, it was built and polished over time and buffeted by the elements (budget, time, partnerships, pressure groups) coming from all sides. The same might be said about classical composers who had to answer to benefactors and collaborators.

Joe Barbera was keenly aware of snapping sharks, what usually made his productions work, and how to draw back into those MGM years if necessary. In a *60 Minutes* profile, he is seen discussing increasing sound effects and music levels with the editor. It was no accident that Hanna-Barbera cartoons, especially on Saturday mornings in the late sixties and

▲▼▲▼

Peter Pan Records released several Scooby-Doo LP records and read-alongs with 45 rpm records or cassettes, but to date, this is the only Scooby-related LP record with a full-sized read-along book.

throughout the seventies, maintained a consistent level of almost nonstop dialogue, music, and sound effects, especially in action and gag cartoons. It was less apparent in story-driven cartoons, but it was still there.

Network executives and sponsors did not want viewers to change channels, so the so-called energy level had to be maintained. This "level" can be arbitrary, but it is nonetheless still an issue today and that is why audiences, sound effects, and other auditory and visual elements are at play throughout every program. These are rhythmic patterns that Barbera and Hanna both learned and developed with each Tom and Jerry cartoon. One can hear the form through Scott Bradley's deliberate interaction with sounds and vocal effects. These sound techniques served the cartoons well, especially in the more gag-related comedy and action shows. They were modified as the

capabilities of television sound changed through the decades by Hanna, Barbera, their staff, and those influenced by them.

"Disney made animated stories," said former NBC executive Sam Ewing. "Hanna-Barbera made situation comedies. They set up interesting characters and let them go. That's why you wanted to keep on watching."

One might also say the same for "situation adventures," another form of animation Hanna-Barbera brought to television. In the late '60s and early '70s, almost everybody was singing something on Saturday morning. What they sang was often by some of the best talents in music, whether it was for TV's first animated female pop group or one of the world's most renowned basketball teams.

Chapter 20

MAKING TRACKS WITH JOSIE AND THE PUSSYCATS

~~~~~~

Each week, we all get to save the world from the bad guys!
Yeah, yeah, yeah! We get time to do our numbers, too.
—JOSIE, IN THE 1970 CBS SATURDAY MORNING PRINT AD

Josie and the Pussycats crossed situation comedy with action-adventure the way *The Flintstones* series did occasionally and its feature film did completely. This series took characters from the Archie comic book series and placed them in *Jonny Quest*–like science fiction exotic locations, with villains just as stern and grim. The lead teenage characters were given idiosyncrasies—some more than others—to provide the comedy. For the first time, a female pop group arrived on Saturday morning TV.

One of The Archies' limitations as a pop group was the inability to tour since they existed only in animation. Lead singer Ron Dante was not permitted to reveal his identity at the time. At one point he had both "Sugar, Sugar" and The Cuff Links' "Tracy" at the top of the charts but the public at the time was unaware Dante was the singer. When The Archies were "guests" on *The Ed Sullivan Show*, CBS simply ran a clip from the Filmation cartoon, laugh track and all.[1]

Filmation tried to create its own live band with animated counterparts twice. *The Hardy Boys* (1969) was an animated mystery show with a live-action band that was also seen during musical sections within the show. *Groovie Goolies* (1970) was an animated series that attempted to launch a live band in monster costumes, complete with a fan club. Both series were successful, especially *Groovie Goolies*, but little came of the live bands. For the *Josie and the Pussycats* group, four singing performers were chosen from the dozens who auditioned. It was intended that the band tour in person. Both singing and speaking voices were selected for each of the four lead characters. Cathy Dougher, who sang as Josie, was a classically trained opera and musical theater vocalist.

The original speaking voice of Josie James (later changed to McCoy) was Judy Waite. She recorded several episodes before being replaced by Janet Waldo because of Waite's difficulty in voicing a concurrent program hosted by the *Josie and the Pussycats* characters, the CBS News program, *In the Know*.[2] It consisted of a series of short, interstitial segments placed between CBS Saturday morning shows, the way *Schoolhouse Rock* premiered on ABC in 1973. They were among TV's earliest kid-friendly news reports, covering anything from making watches or the issues of strip mining to riverboats or a visit to Mount St. Michel. *In the Know* scripts demanded longer, more complex dialogue reads within a more restricted running time than Josie's lines.

"They found that she couldn't handle the scripts for *In the Know* and I was really hired because of that," Waldo explained on a *Josie and the Pussycats* reunion for the online *Stu's Show*. "I re-recorded the Josie dialogue for the shows she had already done."

Drummer Melody Valentine's singing voice was Cherie Moore, shortened from Cheryl Jean Stoppelmoor. According to the liner notes on the Capitol album *Josie and the Pussycats: Songs from the Hanna-Barbera TV Show*, Cherie was "an accomplished actress and dancer" who as a singer "appeared as the 'warm-up act' for Jack Benny at the Corn Palace in Mitchell, South Dakota." That was in 1970. In a few years, Moore would become an international star as Cheryl Ladd, after Farrah Fawcett left *Charlie's Angels*. She launched her singing career based on the higher profile that was afforded by being an "Angel," but her frequent vocals on the Josie songs were her first opportunity to be heard by a wide audience.

Melody's inimitable speaking voice was recognizable to many prime-time viewers of the day as beloved actor/writer Jackie Joseph. She gained cult status as the original Audrey (not the plant) of 1960's *Little Shop of Horrors* and was a highlight of such sitcoms as *The Dick Van Dyke, Bob Newhart*, and *Doris Day* shows. Joseph also appeared with magician Mark Wilson on *The Magical Land of Allakazam*, a long-running network and syndicated children's variety show which

Josie and the Pussycats: Cathy Dougher, Patrice Holloway, and Cherie Moore, later known as Cheryl Ladd.

featured rebroadcasts of favorite Hanna-Barbera cartoons. Peter Pan Records released an album based on *The Magical Land of Allakazam* introduced by Wilson with no references to H-B cartoons or Ms. Joseph.

The singer who gives the trio its striking female soul sound is Patrice Holloway. She was already highly regarded within the industry, many of whom believed she deserved greater fame. At Motown Records, she cowrote the classic "You've Made Me So Very Happy" with her sister Brenda, Berry Gordy, and producer Frank Wilson. Brenda recorded it two years before the hit version by Blood, Sweat and Tears.

In the series, Patrice Holloway is the singing counterpart to Barbara Pariot as the two voices of Valerie Smith (later named Brown). In an internet episode of *Stu's Show* reuniting Pariot with members of the cast, she remarked that, while she was unaware of the history she was making at the time, she was proud of her work and enjoyed her experience on the series.

In addition to bringing the first female African American animated regular TV character to television, *Josie and the Pussycats* is the first animated series in which the voice was also played by an African American, or to be more precise, both the speaking and singing voice. (A year earlier, Filmation introduced Pete Jones on *The Hardy Boys*, the first regular African American cartoon character on Saturday morning TV, by way of his onscreen visage and singing voice, but not by his speaking voice.)

Also in the *Josie* cast were Jerry Dexter as herotype Alan M. Mayberry; Casey Kasem as Alexander Cabot III, group manager and chief chicken heart (major shades of Shaggy); Don Messick as Sebastian, a feline Muttley; and villain stalwarts like John Stephenson and Vic Perrin.

The most irrepressible character of the *Josie* gang is Alexandra, rich in wealth and personality flaws, with pride that went before every fall. She gave the show its bite and its best lines. Sherry Alberoni was already a young veteran of television, having been a Mouseketeer and frequent guest star on the aforementioned *Monkees* and scores of other baby-boomer favorites. "Alexandra was one of my very favorite characters because she was 'spunky with attitude,'" she recalled. "It was such an enjoyable show to do because of the warm and wonderful camaraderie of the cast—so much laughter and a true love between us all."

▲▼▲▼▲▼

Danny Janssen was the seasoned producer of the live group, already well versed in bubblegum/franchise pop with Bobby Sherman and *The Partridge Family*. These songs were not created as mere afterthoughts. They stand as well-crafted songs with tight backing from top musicians. One of the arrangers was Al Capps, formerly of the HBR label. Also singing backup is vocal arranger/songwriter Sue Steward Sheridan, who recalled the process:

It was high energy and under really strong deadlines. I remember us writing on a Wednesday, rehearsing [Cheryl, Patrice, and Cathy] towards the end of the week, and then going in, either on the weekend, or on Monday, and recording the tracks. Danny would be doing the tracks separately from the vocals. [We mixed the vocals and

music tracks] on Tuesday, and then we'd start the process again with a new song on Wednesday. We showed them to Hanna-Barbera and they picked the ones they wanted for that episode.

To produce the songs for *Josie and the Pussycats* and season two of *Scooby-Doo, Where Are You?* Janssen established La La Productions, named for his Bobby Sherman hit "La La La (If I Had You)." His business partner was Karl Engelmann, VP of A&R at Capitol Records and brother of Bob Engelmann, a member of the vocal group The Lettermen.[3] Moore, Holloway, and Dougher were chosen by Janssen from sixty-eight vocalists selected for consideration by Susie Frank of Capitol. He had not seen the key artwork, including the storyboards, that had been approved depicting three young Caucasian women in the group.[4]

"They were very nice about it," Janssen said of the people at Hanna-Barbera. "But nobody had ever done a Black [female character in an] animated cartoon series before. Times were different in those days." Janssen said that he had picked the best singers and could not bring himself to go back and tell these things to Holloway. He amiably passed on the project, hoping to do the next one. Three weeks later, he was delighted to learn that Patrice and the other two Pussycats had been hired. All of this had to have transpired at least a year before the series' 1970 premiere, because of Valerie's December 1969 comic book introduction, as this necessitated modifications to style guides and promotions. These and countless other details required approvals. Janssen had initiated a discussion that Hanna-Barbera took to CBS, Kellogg's, and Archie for a positive agreement.

"Of course, I was really happy," he said. "They had to go back and re-do all the storyboards. They went through a lot of trouble to do that, and I was thankful that they did."

When Janssen arrived at Independent Recorders for the first Josie and the Pussycats session, he was surprised and a little concerned. A who's-who of session musicians had been assembled for a project that had already turned out to be very costly by Saturday

Kellogg's cereals and two singles intended for radio and retail; six songs from the series were never released on records.

morning cartoon standards because of the top producers, singers, and songwriters he had added to the budget. There were more premium musicians in the room than he was expecting.

"They were doing it for Patrice," Janssen recalled. "There were only four or five guys who were working [for a fee] on the session, the rest were working for nothing. Working with those girls and the whole experience of everybody comin' in and helping us because Patrice was there made it one of the most memorable times of my life."

▲▼▲▼▲▼

The music from *Josie and the Pussycats* was divided and marketed in the same manner as *The Banana Splits*. Kellogg's sold four 45 rpm single records with two songs each through the mail for a small

fee and box tops. Most of the songs came from the soundtrack, including the theme, which was simply titled "Josie." The "Josie" theme song is actually a background tune from *The Jetsons* with added lyrics, just as "Meet the Flintstones" came from a previous music cue. Hoyt Curtin was credited for "Josie," along with Denby Williams and Joseph Roland, pseudonyms for Bill Hanna and Joe Barbera using their middle names. Perhaps there was some bookkeeping reason for this, but these names also turn up in the credits of a Hanna-Barbera musical made-for-TV animated feature called *Oliver and the Artful Dodger*, which aired on the *ABC Saturday Superstar Movie* weekly anthology.

Capitol Records released all the Josie records, including the Kellogg's singles, which appeared in their "Creative Products" line. The Capitol LP was, again like the Splits, a little more sophisticated in

The record album notes promote the band as a live group in addition to the animated series.

sound and appearance. Most of the tracks were given richer orchestrations than heard on the show. In addition to some songs from the series, the trio also offered their musical take on some popular tunes of the early seventies, including Bread's "It Don't Matter to Me," another Hanna-Barbera–David Gates connection; and Janssen's "With Every Beat of My Heart," one of those "should have been a top ten hit" previously recorded by an artist named Shawn; and the aforementioned "La La La (If I Had You)." Capitol released two Josie singles from the LP for retail and radio play. Some tracks appeared only on the LP and some only on Kellogg's discs, but few overlapped. The theme does not appear on the album, nor does one of the most played songs on the series, "Inside, Outside, Upside-Down." Six songs were also never released officially, even on the 2001 Rhino Handmade CD compilation.

Good as the *Josie* songs are, the cartoon pop music success of The Archies remained unequaled. One reason could be hesitance in the music and radio business to promote another animated group. It's worth speculating whether some of these records might have found greater success if they were marketed as a "serious group" rather than "just a cartoon." There was resistance even in the early days when *The Archies'* records were circulated to stations—it was the public rather than the broadcasting and music industry that truly embraced them. Music impresario Don Kirshner's marketing machine was also a powerful factor in The Archies' success, but it was not always a sure thing with every talent he promoted. As for the possibility of a live touring Josie and the Pussycats, Danny Janssen believed that Capitol Records had become too complacent with The Beatles' success and did not follow through on tours and publicity. "They could have gone out as a group or Capitol could have broken them up individually and done it that way," he said. "Capitol didn't know how . . . they'd forgotten how to use the talent."

There was also quite a bit of competition from other TV groups vying for their piece of the bubble-gum pie, the most successful being *The Partridge Family*, which was comparable in size, scope, and success to The Monkees. As it turned out, Janssen, Roberts, Hart, and most of Ron Hicklin's singers went to work for Wes Farrell, the driven, charismatic songwriter/producer in charge of *The Partridge Family* pop songs. Hanna-Barbera musical regulars Ron Hicklin, Jackie Ward, John Bahler, and Tom Bahler provided the off-screen vocals for four of the on-screen Partridges, to supplement lead vocals by David Cassidy and backup singing by Shirley Jones.

▲▼▲▼▲▼

The first sixteen *Josie and the Pussycats* episodes ran for two years successfully enough for CBS, Hanna-Barbera, and Archie comics that, rather than adding on additional episodes, a different format was created. In the days of Saturday morning television, when an existing series was successful enough to warrant new episodes, the network would ask for roughly half as many in the second season. However, additional episodes are not as marketable as a new series or premise. Giving a popular show a new premise can be risky but if successful, it can justify marketing and promotions. Most importantly it can interest a sponsor in a full order of new episodes. That was one reason the Archie and Scooby-Doo programs continued to change their formats or add companion cartoons to form new "umbrella" series. Thus, *Josie and the Pussycats in Outer Space* premiered in 1972. But this time around, the songs were not released on records. The ten new songs were also given less prominence in most of the episodes, sometimes heard only for a few seconds.

Neither of Hanna-Barbera's comedy-adventure and outer space "universes" of *Josie and the Pussycats* ever appeared in comic book form in the way that

Filmation's Archie and Sabrina stories did on a few occasions. There must have been agreements established about the distinctions between the premises of the *Josie* characters in Hanna-Barbera TV shows and within the Archie comic books. H-B never depicted the characters in the suburban home setting of the comics; Archie never published a Josie comic with a story resembling that of either TV series. Even when the Josie characters guest-starred on a *New Scooby-Doo Movies* episode in 1972, it was within the premise of their first series.

While there were no story-related *Josie* albums, the aforementioned Kenner Talking Show Projector refill with Scooby-Doo in "That's Snow Ghost" also included an adaptation of "The Nemo's a No-No Affair" from the TV series. Janet Waldo told the story for the 45 rpm EP record, which contained a total of four short stories. The other two were Lassie in "To the Rescue" with Ginny Tyler, and Superman in "Merlin's Magic Marbles" with Gary Owens, Mel Blanc, and John Erwin.

▲▼▲▼▲▼

Television networks, producers, and record companies were still eager to nurture new properties combining television and music. A year after CBS and Hanna-Barbera introduced *Josie and the Pussycats*, they brought *The Harlem Globetrotters* to TV in 1971 as a coproduction with CBS. Like *Josie and the Pussycats*, each episode features a song. This time, H-B went directly to the music supervisor behind The Archies, Don Kirshner.

The real-life performing basketball team was established in 1926 in Chicago, displaying astonishing athletic skills as well as comedic timing and magician-like skills. Transcending demographics, the Globetrotters continue to inspire young people, delight even those with little basketball knowledge, and engage in humanitarian work. One of their fans, Pope John Paul II, was made an honorary Globetrotter.

Even though no amount of animation or special effects can match the real Globetrotters in action,

Meadowlark Lemon sang backup with a "who's-who" of rock and R&B vocalists for the songs used on the animated series.

Hanna-Barbera came up with a Scooby-Doo–like formula in which the team would visit a new location each week and solve a problem using basketball. Like many a convoluted H-B premise, it makes more sense if one watches it or Joe Barbera presents it.

Scatman Crothers was given his first animated lead role as Meadowlark Lemon. Like *Josie and the Pussycats*' Barbara Pariot, he was an African American actor providing the off-screen voice for an on-screen African American animated TV character. In 1974, Crothers also became the first African American to voice a lead animated TV "animal character" when H-B cast him as canine *Hong Kong Phooey*, with a feline sidekick named Spot, who resembled H-B's 1966 Cheshire Cat. The other animated Globetrotters were also voiced by professional voice actors: Stu Gilliam (Curly); Johnny Williams (Geese); Richard Elkins (Gip); Robert DoQui as Pablo; and Los Angeles disc jockey Eddie Anderson as the forgetful Bobby Joe.[5]

The real life Meadowlark Lemon was involved in the singing as a backup. "They had some great professional studio singers and musicians there to put that thing together, and they—not the team—sang it," he told music historian Rick Simmons.

Simmons wrote: "The vocalists standing in for the group were: Sammy Turner, who had charted with 'Lavender Blue' in 1959; J. R. Bailey, formerly a vocalist with the Cadillacs of 'Speedo' fame; and a songwriter later nominated for a Grammy for co-writing the Main Ingredient's 'Everybody Plays the Fool'; Robert Spencer, lead vocalist on Crazy Elephant's 'Gimme Gimme Good Lovin''); and Rudy Clark (singer and writer of such hits as Betty Everett's 'The Shoop-Shoop Song,' The Rascals' 'Good Lovin',' 'Got My Mind Set on You'—the song George

Harrison would cover and take to #1—and who was also later nominated for a Grammy for co-writing the Main Ingredient's 'Everybody Plays the Fool,' among others."

Hopes were high for the group's remake of the Neil Sedaka/Howard Greenfield tune, "Rainy Day Bells," sung by J. R. Bailey. "It had an infectious melody," Lemon told Simmons. "It's one of those songs that when you hear it, over and over and over, you begin to like it even more."

The album, entitled *The Globetrotters* ("Harlem" may have been removed for trademark reasons), and singles were a joy for enthusiasts but not on the charts. However, Simmons found that "Rainy Day Bells" lived on. "Oddly enough though, in the ensuing years, the song became popular on the Carolina beach music circuit, where it has been one of the genre's most popular tunes for more than four decades," he wrote. "Lemon found that the most surprising thing of all about the song."

"It's amazing to me that it's still so big in the Carolinas," said Lemon. "Even though Neil Sedaka did the song before we did, his version didn't catch on like ours. Now why, I have no idea. But I realize that our version is still a hit, up and down the East Coast. People talk to me about it all the time. It's unbelievable."

Jeff Barry, who cowrote and produced the number-one song of 1969, The Archies' "Sugar, Sugar," also produced the Globetrotters with some of the same personnel. This would take Hanna-Barbera full circle in a way. Kirshner was in charge of the music for Screen Gems in the early sixties when his cubicle-bound songwriters were toiling away at songs for TV and movie stars like Shelley Fabares while H-B was making *The Flintstones*, *Top Cat*, and *The Jetsons*.

▲▼▲▼▲▼

The lead voice of The Archies himself, Ron Dante, wrote for the Globetrotters. Along with Jeff Barry, Dante cowrote one of the most familiar tunes, "Cheer Me Up," and soon found himself singing and writing for another H-B cartoon with songs.

Archies lead singer Ron Dante wrote and sang for H-B's *The Amazing Chan and the Chan Clan* and still tours with classic performers, including Danny Hutton. Photo by Louise Palanker. (CC-BY-SA 2.0, Wikimedia Commons.)

"Hanna-Barbera asked me to work on songs for a series called *The Amazing Chan and the Chan Clan*," he said. "It was a fun project and I was pleased with the songs I wrote for the show. One of the songs that was supposed to be the theme ended up used only in an episode." In the Hanna-Barbera tradition, the lyrics mention all the characters. Unlike the other songs played under action in the series, this one is not shown with the band playing, but rather with the characters of Henry and Stanley searching for clues at a circus.

One of the musicians/singer/songwriters who worked with Dante on the Chan Clan pop group was a struggling young talent named Barry Manilow, well regarded within the music and advertising industry, but not yet known to the general public. Manilow had written some of Madison Avenue's most salable jingles and worked with some of the greatest names in music. He was just on the brink of hitting the big time himself when he was working on the Chan Clan tracks with Ron Dante and Melissa Mancester. Within three years, Manilow became an international star after his first hit, "Mandy." Ron Dante was the producer of Manilow's first nine albums.

The instrumental theme that ended up being used for the main title of *The Amazing Chan* was the work of the returning Hoyt Curtin. Ted Nichols enjoyed his work for Hanna-Barbera but decided to go into writing inspirational music, for which he enjoyed success with such works as his operatic adaptation of *Pilgrim's Progress*. Curtin renegotiated his composing agreement with the studio and resumed his role as musical director with Paul DeKorte continuing as music supervisor. Curtin also resumed writing theme songs with Hanna and Barbera. One of the first he wrote on his return was a new main title for *The New Scooby-Doo Movies*, which would replace the "Where Are You" theme.

▲▼▲▼▲▼

The cartoon band trend took quite a while to completely fade away into the seventies. The final Hanna-Barbera animated pop group to generate any commercial recordings was part of a 1973 NBC series called *Butch Cassidy*. The series was another teen mystery-comedy about a pop band named The Sundance Kids with a lead singer named Butch Cassidy. The premise has nothing else to do with the infamous bandits, but the names leveraged the popularity of the 1969 Paul Newman–Robert Redford movie.

Micky Dolenz of The Monkees was among the voice cast of *Butch Cassidy*, as well as Hanna-Barbera's *The Funky Phantom*, *Devlin*, and in various guest roles.

It is yet to be determined whether he did any singing, but his voice may be discernable within the songs. Two single records were released with two songs each on an MGM subsidiary label called Romer Records but received little distribution or airplay. A "forthcoming album" was mentioned on the labels of the singles, but it never came to pass.

Even The Partridge Family made it to the Hanna-Barbera studio by way of a planned *Jetsons* revival series pitched as a teenaged version of Judy and Elroy. However, CBS wanted a series to compete with ABC and Filmation's popular *Brady Kids* animated series, so H-B and Columbia partnered again to combine the concepts into *Partridge Family, 2200 A.D.* H-B also adapted Columbia's *I Dream of Jeannie* into an animated teen Jeannie with Julie Dees and a young Mark Hamill. The *Partridge Family, 2200 A.D.* cartoon songs were not released as an album, but one of the songs heard on the animated version, "Take Good Care of Her," was recorded by David Cassidy and The Partridge Family for the "Notebook" album on Bell Records.

By the time Hanna-Barbera took a pop band under the sea with 1977's *Jabberjaw*—with a zany shark on drums—the studio had all but abandoned the cross-promotion of songs from the show on records. Those who remember each series, however, often can sing a few bars of the songs.

The traditional animated musical feature, in which the score and songs advanced the story and deepened the emotional impact, seemed to be at a low ebb during the seventies. Yet one such feature film from this decade proved to be especially enduring, coming from what some might think an unlikely studio and featuring unlikely lead characters: a sympathetic spider and a terrific, radiant, humble pig.

Chapter 21

CHARLOTTE, WILBUR, BILL, JOE, BOB, AND DICK

~~~~~~

This film remains one of my personal favorites as a showcase of the best of what our people were creating, an endeavor of stunning excellenoo.

—BILL HANNA, TWENTY-THREE YEARS AFTER
THE PREMIERE OF *CHARLOTTE'S WEB*

Domestic animation was becoming prohibitively expensive in the 1970s, amid a recession and an energy crisis. Outsourcing work was a reluctant but impending option. Filmation, Hanna-Barbera's main competitor on Saturday mornings, fought for years to avoid it. Bill Hanna and Joe Barbera, having never shaken the pangs of unemployment in their early careers, could not have liked facing the grim realities of the decade. If seams showed in the cartoons, it was not for a lack of effort to produce good work under often impossible circumstances. The studio needed to keep its operation productive. The work had to be good but it also had to be consistent, efficient, and on a competitive budget. Balancing demands for sudden workloads and the people needed to get these done was an ongoing challenge. Barbera's presentational skills and Hanna's need for more shows to sustain the workforce could result in so much material to produce that Hanna would somehow bend the laws of time and space to produce something entertaining by the airdates.

"At one time I asked Bill Hanna why they couldn't say no to at least one new series so they wouldn't have to sometimes spread things so thin," Mark Evanier recalled. "He looked at me and said, 'Mark, see those people working over there? Tell me which ones I should fire. If I can keep them working, it's worth it to take on as much as we possibly can.'"

Despite this frantic activity, Hanna-Barbera managed to transform a "magnum opus" of literature into their third feature-length animated film. E. B. White's 1952 allegorical children's fantasy *Charlotte's Web* was, like *Mary Poppins*, an elusive property held tightly and very personally. It is a book about the power of words (White is also the coauthor of the revered *Elements of Style*) and an evergreen satire on fleeting fame, the fickle public, media frenzy, and the perceptions of the writer's role. Most of all it is about loyalty and friendship.

Charlotte's Web is a film of extraordinary depth and beauty that could only have come from the people who ultimately brought it to the screen. It fell into their hands through a series of circumstances that had a great deal to do with what the author did NOT want to see done to his book. Many creative artists get so close to their material that releasing it into the world makes them sensitive and vulnerable to its treatment and reception. White had turned down Walt Disney. He did not want a Disney-style film, nor did he want to see animals in a chorus line singing bright tunes.

White himself read the complete book with no music on a four-LP set for Pathways of Sound Records in 1952; it remains available digitally today. One might expect that he envisioned Garth Williams's drawings moving about on the movie screen. While possible, it still required modifications in design.

Charlotte's transition from page to screen was as dramatic and emotional as the one behind *Mary Poppins*. Oscar-winning animators John and Faith Hubley were attached to the project—as far from Disney as it could be since they had worked for UPA, the "un-Disneyest" studio of its era. Another Oscar winner, Gene Deitch, creator of the animated series *Tom Terrific*, chronicled the long and painful ordeal of the attempt at an earlier version on his now-defunct website. Deitch had become very close to the project and developed an elaborate adaptation, but when Edgar Bronfman Jr., of the Seagrams company, became interested in the movie business, the production executive saw Deitch's treatment as too dark. It was an unfortunate situation that devastated Deitch, especially after Bronfman did not want White to see any of his developmental artwork. According to Deitch, Bronfman gave the project to Hanna-Barbera as part of a three-film deal with his Sagittarius Productions.

According to Joe Barbera's autobiography, the book was not simply handed to his studio. Barbera was required to personally convince E. B. White to allow Hanna-Barbera to adapt the book. In his book, Barbera describes enduring a circuitous series of flights and connections to access White's remote rural home to present sketches and storyboards. He was made most welcome by the great author and his wife. After the presentation and a country dinner, White gave his approval for Hanna-Barbera to make *Charlotte's Web* into a movie.

▲▼▲▼▲▼

Charlotte's Web had already deeply touched countless lives, including those who were selected to be part of the film. Few screenwriters were better suited to adapt the book than Earl Hamner, whose classic family drama series *The Waltons* had recently premiered on CBS. Hamner's work also included *Twilight Zone* episodes, such as "The Hunt" in which a man decides certain angels are genuine because they allow his beloved dog into Heaven with him.

"My agent called and he said, 'You've been offered this job,' and I said, 'Yes! I'd do it for nothing!'" Hamner told Stu Shostak at stusshow.com. "He said, 'You will not!'"

Debbie Reynolds's agent must have said the same thing. The musical star, who became a star at Hanna and Barbera's former studio, MGM, also would gladly have signed on for free. "I loved playing Charlotte and I loved working in animation," she said on *The Larry King Show*. "I decided to make her sound warm, maternal, and caring." When a caller said that he no longer was able to kill household spiders because of the 1973 film, she was touched. "When I do personal appearances, one of the items I am most asked to sign are *Charlotte's Web* record albums."

One of the reasons the film still captures successive generations regardless of technological filmmaking developments is that Charlotte is a perceptive, no-nonsense female character. "I live by my wits," she tells Wilbur. Charlotte has a firm sense of who she is. As a sedentary spider, she must watch the world go by, but not without drinking in all she can about what she sees, hears, and feels. She may not veer far from the barn, but she knows how to deal with the world around her and ultimately impact it. Charlotte demonstrates that being loving and caring can go hand in hand with being assertive and sometimes a bit tough. "Wilbur, I forbid you to faint!" because she "can't stand hysterics" and she knows better than he about the time crunch.

Charlotte's firm attitude toward responsibility is demonstrated in a scene Hamner created for the film. After Templeton the rat skips a crucial meeting to save Wilbur, Charlotte tricks him into treading close to a hungry cat to drive her message home.

"That wasn't nice, Charlotte!" says Templeton in the unforgettable voice of Paul Lynde.

"In the future, Templeton," she replies, "when I call a meeting, I expect you to attend."

Charlotte knows how to overcome her limits and restrictions. Her strength comes from character, compassion, and hope, not from aggression and bitterness. The film adaptation does not force Templeton through a preposterous personality arc to see "the error of his ways." In an emotional scene when Wilbur begs for help with Charlotte's eggs, Templeton does not offer to help. A true rat, he seizes the opportunity to complain of perceived ingratitude, striking out at the grief-stricken pig. He uses Wilbur's desperation and generosity for his own self-interest.

Not only is Charlotte's beauty, grace, and strength conveyed in Reynolds's performance, but it is also seen through her design by Iwao Takamoto, who codirected the film with Charles A. Nichols. Charlotte is a minimalist creation, with enough detail for sufficient close-up and expressions, but not too much to make her too literal as a spider. Her legs are as much a part of her personality as her face, animated with a great deal of elegance and fluidity. Her webs are treated with delicacy and grace, like fine linen tapestries and wispy gossamer.

▲▼▲▼▲▼

Movie legend Debbie Reynolds and *The Waltons* creator Earl Hamner were delighted to work on *Charlotte's Web* with Hanna-Barbera. Photo by Allan Warren. (CC-BY-SA-3.0, Wikimedia Commons.)

Paul Lynde's vocal performance as Templeton the rat is considered one of the best cast in animation, yet it almost did not happen. Lynde nearly missed out on a side career in cartoon voice acting.[1] Janet Waldo, who worked with Lynde on 1969's *The Perils of Penelope Pitstop*, recalled that the actor also struggled to convey his persona through voice alone. Joe Barbera was able to coach Lynde on how to do his own voice accurately. Lynde picked it up so well that he became a favorite Hanna-Barbera cast member—as Mildew Wolf in the "It's the Wolf" segments of *Cattanooga Cats* and as cranky neighbor Pertwee on H-B's 1970 CBS primetime summer replacement sitcom, *Where's Huddles?*

Barbera originally cast Tony Randall, Felix Unger of TV's *The Odd Couple*, as Templeton but decided that his interpretation was too sophisticated and his singing too operatic for the character. Lynde was pure animation voice gold, making such lines as "It says 'crun-chee,'" and "it's worse than caramel cann-dy!" unforgettable. A few months later Randall

Paul Lynde, who made an indelible impression as the voice of Templeton, played Uncle Arthur on TV's *Bewitched*, costarring *Flintstones* guest star Elizabeth Montgomery and *Charlotte's Web* castmate Agnes Moorehead.

was introducing Barbera at an event, and using his well-known mock seriousness, he presented him as "The only man who ever fired me." Barbera took the stage and replied, "Tony, I just thought you were too classy to play a rat!"

As in many earlier Hanna-Barbera voice sessions, Joe Barbera directed while most of the actors were together at the same session, a practice that is popular in TV animation but rare in theatricals. In attendance were veterans like John Stephenson, Bob Holt, and Joan Gerber and great actors from radio and film like Martha Scott as Mrs. Arable and Agnes Moorehead, who makes an indelible mark as the Goose. Together they sing one of the film's signature numbers, "A Veritable Smorgasbord." Gary Winick, director of the 2006 live-action/CG remake of *Charlotte's Web*, said in the DVD commentary that

his fairground scenes with Templeton in his film had to be extended because test audiences kept asking why the "Smorgasbord song" was missing.

Dave Madden, a regular player on *Rowan and Martin's Laugh-In* and Reuben Kincaid of *The Partridge Family*, considered his nuanced performance as the Old Sheep to be among his favorite roles. He was appearing on *The Partridge Family* when he was cast for *Charlotte's Web*, along with *Partridge* castmate and friend Danny Bonaduce, who voiced Fern's brother Avery as well as "Danny" for Hanna-Barbera's *Partridge Family, 2200 A.D.* cartoon. A new character, Jeffrey the newly hatched gosling, was created for the film, voiced by one of Hanna-Barbera's original star actors, Don Messick. Young and naïve, Jeffrey puts Wilbur in a grownup role as a friend to mentor.

Pamelyn Ferdin was one of the most popular child actors of the sixties and seventies, with roles including Lucy Van Pelt in *Peanuts* specials and the first feature film, *A Boy Named Charlie Brown*; the H-B series *The Roman Holidays* and *Sealab 2020*; and the musical TV movie *Oliver and the Artful Dodger*. *Charlotte's Web* stands out as a personal highlight of her career.

"The line that moved me most was when Fern says to her father, 'Would you have killed me if I were born small?'" she recalled. "That line just tore me up. I wept when I recorded it—you can hear it."

▲▼▲▼▲▼

Earl Hamner took special care with Fern's character in the fair sequence, making a significant change. In the film, when Wilbur has lost the first prize, Fern is upset as the audience might expect. In the book, she asks her mother for money for the midway; she wants to spend time with her young friend Henry Fussy. Her mother tells her to stay put and she tears up. While Fern shares the excitement of Wilbur's special award, she looks at the Ferris wheel in the distance. Reading this within the book makes sense, but Hamner may have thought that in a film it could have seemed out of character. Hamner's script is so faithful to the book, one can usually read portions along with the film. The only major deletion was a chapter in which Fern's mother visits the family doctor after Fern tells her family about the goings-on with Wilbur and friends at the barn. Hamner never forgot when he wrote Charlotte's farewell scene. "When I was working on the script, the phone rang and someone said, 'Earl, you sound all choked up. What's wrong?' And I said, 'A spider just died.' So I was that involved with the script emotionally."

He also included some of White's most famous narration, given a homespun texture by Rex Allen, a Hollywood singing cowboy, Purina Dog Chow TV commercial spokesman, and Disney animal film narrator. Though Allen's presence was an auditory tie to Disney, Allen had never done narration for Disney animation. It is Allen who speaks White's famous closing line from the book, "It is not often that someone comes along who is a true friend and a good writer. Charlotte was both."

▲▼▲▼▲▼

The greatest musicals are defined by songs that advance the narrative and provide a depth of feeling impossible through words alone. Richard M. Sherman and Robert B. Sherman, who had won two Oscars for 1964's *Mary Poppins*, were experiencing changes at the Disney studio in the wake of Walt's passing. They scored three more excellent post-Walt musicals, but it became clear that their position was no longer the same at the studio they had called home. The brothers, as well as their friend and musical director Irwin Kostal, found the reception at Hanna-Barbera to be reminiscent of the Walt days in terms of the H-B staff's shared enthusiasm for the project. They were actively involved in the story, music, and production processes. *Charlotte's Web* came along during an emotionally charged period in the brothers' lives. The intensity made its way into the movie.

One of Robert Sherman's sons, Robert (Robbie) J. Sherman, remembered when *Charlotte's Web* was in production. "You have to remember that in 1971–72, my uncle and my dad were still feeling the loss of

Walt Disney in 1966. The studio had changed, they were not making films the same way. The people at Hanna-Barbera were very welcoming to the Sherman Brothers."

"I was also at the recording sessions and I will never forget being part of seeing that music come together. It really is one of their best," said Laurie Sherman, daughter of Robert. "Of course, I love the other music my father and uncle did for Disney and others—I feel very close to them, too, but there isn't anything like *Charlotte's Web*."

When the Sherman Brothers' 1968 big-screen musical fantasy *Chitty Chitty Bang Bang* became a stage hit on London's West End in 2002, two of their sons, Jeffrey and Gregg, struck up a friendship. It resulted in *The Boys*, an acclaimed 2009 feature documentary about Richard M. Sherman and Robert B. Sherman. *Charlotte's Web* became the first Hanna-Barbera production to appear within a Walt Disney Pictures feature because it was included in *The Boys*. Writer/composer Jeffrey Sherman, son of Robert, told the author:

It was difficult just to get that clip in there. Between getting the Disney and Paramount people to come to an agreement, and dealing with the music rights. But we had to have a clip of "Mother Earth and Father Time" in our film. It was, to my family, one of the most important songs in their career.

Very few people could understand how much of themselves my dad and uncle put into the songs for *Charlotte's Web*. The story is about life, death, friendship—partnership. There is a lot of context woven into the songs, some that the public didn't even need to know about—the emotions were appropriate to what was happening at the time.

One of the things *The Boys* documented was the complicated relationship between my father and uncle. Even we kids didn't completely understand it. They were total opposites. Yet because of that, the music and lyrics created something special that only those two could create.

"There Must Be Something More" is all about the mysterious "thing" that makes a relationship work. When two people get together, it creates another kind of being, in a way. This isn't just a little girl singing to a pig. That's why this movie has never dated and people keep on loving it.

How could a spider and a pig be friends? They each need something from the other that they are lacking. That was my dad and my uncle. My dad was quiet and introspective. My uncle was gregarious and impulsive. Each drove the other crazy.

When the animals sing, "We've Got Lots in Common Where it Really Counts," that's all of us as people singing about our relative similarities and differences, but deep down it's again my father and uncle, after all the arguments, coming up with great scores and making their collaborations work.

The score of *Charlotte's Web* was a favorite of Al Sherman, the songwriting father of Robert B. Sherman and Richard M. Sherman; it was among the most personal works of their careers. Photo by Howard352 at English Wikipedia. (CC-BY-SA-3.0, Wikimedia Commons.)

When the Sherman Brothers were honored with a "window on Main Street, U.S.A." at Disneyland, the Entertainment division presented a living version of the mother and father from the Carousel of Progress, one of many Disney attractions featuring Sherman songs. The characters played and sang their Disney songs, but both "Mother Earth and Father Time" and "Zuckerman's Famous Pig" were briefly slipped into the sketch.

"My father insisted that 'Mother Earth' be included even though it was not a Disney song," said Robbie Sherman. "*Charlotte's Web* was the favorite score of his father, Al Sherman, who was one of the great songwriters of the early twentieth century, and our grandmother was very ill when my dad and uncle were working on the *Charlotte* score."

One of the songs in *Charlotte's Web* dates back to 1959. "Long before the song 'Chin Up' was (re)written for use in the 1973 movie, *Charlotte's Web*, it existed in a very different form, written to be an up-tempo pop song," Robbie Sherman explained. "The original version was never recorded and would remain in the Sherman Brothers' 'trunk' for about a decade

when they would eventually dust it off and massively recast it to espouse 'Charlotte's' philosophy of life . . . the rhythms are completely different, as are the lyrics and point of view of the singer. Still, a lot of the ideas that went into the song, including the title and sketches of the lyrics do remain. . . . One of the most personal lyrics my father worked into the score is the short 'Deep in the Dark' verse sung by Charlotte right before the chorus sings the title song. It's inspired by E. B. White's words but modified to 'Sleep my love, sleep my only, deep in the dark. . . .' This is my father writing about his mother, lying at home with his father at her side, holding her hand."

Pamelyn Ferdin vividly remembers the session for "There Must Be Something More." "The day I recorded my song, Debbie Reynolds went before me and recorded 'Mother Earth and Father Time,'" she said. "She sang it so tenderly, there wasn't a dry eye in the studio. Then I, the 12-year-old kid, had to follow that. Reynolds stayed to watch me, which just made me even more nervous. But she was very encouraging. She and I listened to the playback together and she told me how good I was and that I was going to be a big star. That meant a lot to me."

▲▼▲▼

Debbie Reynolds stated that the *Charlotte's Web* soundtrack album was one of the most frequently requested items she was asked to autograph.

Paramount Records gave *Charlotte's Web* the grandest treatment ever awarded a Hanna-Barbera feature soundtrack album, with a gatefold pop-up Zuckerman barnyard playset complete with punch-out characters. H-B staff music supervisor Paul DeKorte oversaw the album's production. The LP was reissued a few years later by MCA as a picture disc. Debbie Reynolds herself recorded an additional 45 rpm single with a pop contemporary rendition of "Charlotte's Web" on Paramount Records. The soundtrack version of "Mother Earth and Father Time" is on the other side.

Columbia Records released *Ray Conniff: Charlotte's Web*, which opened with a new cover version of the title song. By this time, Ron Hicklin was contracting singers for Conniff, so essentially this was "The Hanna-Barbera Singers" version. The remaining tracks on the album were previously released, family-friendly tunes by the Ray Conniff Singers from the sixties.

Paramount Pictures celebrated *Charlotte's Web* with a major premiere at Radio City Music Hall in New York. Later, at a theater in the Westwood area of Los Angeles, the six TV "siblings" of *The Brady Bunch* appeared at a screening of the film to promote their new single combining the theme from *Charlotte's Web* and "Zuckerman's Famous Pig," which was also the first track on their new LP, *The Brady Bunch Phonographic Album*. It was the third Brady Kids album for Paramount Records, the first two containing soundtrack songs for Filmation's Saturday Morning cartoon series.

They did their own singing on the records, sometimes augmented by the same studio singers who sang for the Partridges, most all from Hicklin's group. When *Brady Bunch* star Barry Williams guest-starred

The Brady Bunch kids recorded two songs from *Charlotte's Web* for their fourth album and appeared at a premiere event for the feature.

on ABC's *The Dating Game*, the new single was promoted by host Jim Lange as Williams entered the stage. Later, Williams pondered which "bachelorette" to select as his "family" version of "Charlotte's Web" played into the fade to commercials.

Paul Lynde also promoted his role in the film. On the fondly remembered children's program *Wonderama*, host Bob McAllister interviewed Lynde and welcomed a barbershop quartet to sing "Zuckerman's Famous Pig." It cannot be an accident that one of Bill Hanna's favorite pastimes was worked into one of his favorite studio projects.

The film is imbued with compassion without a trace of patronization. Genuinely moved by witnessing the on-screen death of a creature that they might otherwise have squished themselves in real life, both adults and children came out of movie theaters teary-eyed after they first saw *Charlotte's*

Web. Many critics were impressed, including John Huddy of the *Miami Herald*, who gave it a rave review. Some were lukewarm, others were stuck on the need for Disney-level fluidity and meticulous, exhaustive detail. Yet what White wanted, to begin with, was, in a way, what Hanna-Barbera gave him. Despite his issue with what he and his wife felt were bright, happy Sherman songs (which is only partially true), this is not a Disney film.

▲▼▲▼▲

Just as *Mary Poppins* was the culmination of Walt Disney's career achievements in 1964, *Charlotte's Web* was emblematic of the kind of work Hanna-Barbera could put together by 1973, no matter what the obstacles and restrictions, employing some of the century's best talent. It is the story of an unlikely friendship made by two completely different animation partners with songs by two opposite personalities.

While *Charlotte's Web* made money for Paramount, it was not the hit that Disney's *Robin Hood* was the same year, nor did its production enjoy the luxury of time, meticulous detail, or budget. There were hundreds of feet of animation film to get out the door and many hundreds more animators to keep employed. *Charlotte's Web* made some industry people smile, but some frowned a bit at what they saw as inferior quality, not worth considering what lies deeper than technical polish. On Wilbur in particular, almost every human paintbrush on stroke is visible, like living cells. This is a series of hand-painted drawings laid against background paintings and they all look like it with no embellishments. It is a cartoon in the purest, most honest sense. It's humble in its flaws and terrific in its gentle power.

"I don't think I would have liked to see *Charlotte's Web* animated any other way," said Laurie Sherman. "It's not perfect, but that is part of its charm. That's what the story is about. It isn't fancy and doesn't try to be. But how many movies touch you as deeply? I wouldn't change a thing."

However some may differ about various details, most will agree that the soundtrack of *Charlotte's Web* is its most magnificent foundation. Like Charlotte, it is in a class by itself. Like so much of Hanna-Barbera's work, what one hears is a powerful part of what one sees.

Charlotte's Web was also only the second animated feature in which every song was a Sherman creation. In *The Aristocats* and *The Jungle Book*, other songwriters also participated. "What Bob and Dick Sherman had accomplished was appreciated at Hanna-Barbera," said Robbie. "Their input was invited and implemented. Back at the Disney studio in the late sixties and early seventies, that wasn't quite the case anymore."

▲▼▲▼▲▼

These Are the Days was a well-received animated turn-of-the-twentieth-century family drama some considered an ABC answer to the hit CBS series, *The Waltons*. The casting of Pamelyn Ferdin as one of the lead characters, as well as the extra care and detail, makes this series feel like an affectionate follow-up to *Charlotte's Web*. The impressive voice cast, including June Lockhart, Henry Jones, Frank Cady, Jackie Earle Haley, and Andrew Parks, grounded their performance in a natural reality. The animated domestic "dramedy" *These Are the Days* was one of several H-B series that, like *Devlin* and *Sealab 2020*, proved H-B was capable of delivering a variety of programming that pleased critics and those who watched the shows, but there weren't enough of them to compete for ratings. The bright "Main Street"–style theme to *These Are the Days* first appeared in 1965 on Hoyt Curtin's aforementioned *Hollywood Directory* album. Curtin's wife, Liz, is credited with the tune, originally titled "On the Pier at Ocean Park."

Charlotte's Web gained considerable momentum through network television broadcasts. Proving to be infinitely rewatchable, it was one of the few animated features given repeat prime-time broadcasts. Most cable channels ran it as well, including the Disney Channel, which also enjoyed tremendous viewer success with *The Man Called Flintstone*. Accessibility that formed strong audience attachments continued to be a Hanna-Barbera asset. *Charlotte's Web* was one of the earliest animated features to be released on home video. The Walt Disney Studios initially kept their classic features away from television or video, leaving the field clear. *Charlotte's Web*, like 1971's *Willy Wonka and the Chocolate Factory*, became more cherished by each new generation. It was one of the highest-selling home video releases of 1994, over twenty years after its release.

E. B. White and his wife were not happy with the final film. Mrs. White wished the film had been scored with the music of Mozart. They were unaware of the intense, heartfelt feelings that the scenarist, songwriters, cast, and other participants also brought to this classic work. Hanna-Barbera's version of *Char-*

lotte's Web digs very deep for an animated family film and most live-action films, if not on the surface, certainly in allegory.

"It's the most profound thing I ever did and the work of which I'm most proud," Pamelyn Ferdin reflected. "I'm thrilled that it continues to reach new generations almost a half-century after it was made and will do so long after I'm gone."

Chapter 22

THE FUNTASTIC, RADIANT, HUMBLE SEVENTIES

~~~~~~

Wonder Twin powers, activate!

—JAYNA (LIBERTY WILLIAMS) AND ZAN (MICHAEL BELL)
OF *SUPER FRIENDS*

One of the major impacts of Taft's ownership of Hanna-Barbera was the larger company's ability to get the characters into bigger venues, especially theme parks. Taft had already begun to purchase and retheme Coney Island Park in Cincinnati, Ohio. Instead, Taft opened Kings Island in 1972, a year after the second "Magic Kingdom-style" park opened at *Walt Disney World* Resort in Florida.

"Some think they 'moved' Coney to create Kings Island, but KI and Coney were—and still are—two separate, independent parks," explained author/historian Barry Hill. "Coney didn't reopen as KI, but was an entirely new thing."

Kings Island expanded from 155 acres to over 1,600, featuring an Eiffel Tower as its "icon." Among its attractions were two signatures: a roller coaster called the Racer and, one of the most expensive attractions of its time, the Enchanted Voyage in The Happy Land of Hanna-Barbera section, where costumed characters cavorted among themed rides and live shows. The Enchanted Voyage ride took park guests through a gigantic TV set—shades of 1966's *Alice in Wonderland*—into a dark ride filled with elaborate scenes with dimensionally rendered characters moving to the beat of various musical styles of a single theme. The song, by Bill Hanna, Paul DeKorte, and Kings Island's Dennis Spiegel was heard with different lyrics in the syndicated half-hour special, *The Thanksgiving That Almost Wasn't*.

Kings Island was the setting for "special episodes" on two of the most iconic youth-oriented seventies sitcoms of the decade: *The Partridge Family* and *The Brady Bunch*, each with a tissue-thin story designed to propel the families around the park and see a few characters. The longevity of these series has created a "side identity" for the park and characters for those completely unaware of their actual origins. The Banana Splits, The Hair Bear Bunch, and *It's the Wolf*'s Lambsy and

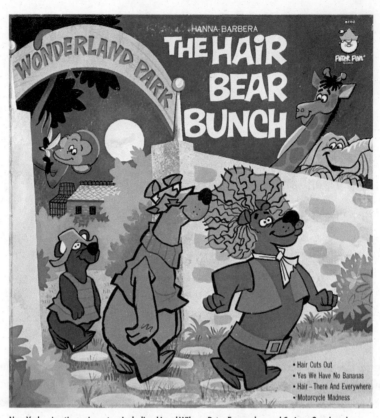

New York animation voice actors including Lionel Wilson, Peter Fernandez, and Corinne Orr played characters in Peter Pan Records' versions of *The Hair Bear Bunch*, *The Funky Phantom*, and *The Flintstones*.

Bristlehound danced with The Partridge Family to the song, "Together We're Better," from their 1972 *Notebook* album.

Disney continued to keep their costumed character appearances generally exclusive to theme parks, "Disney on Parade" shows, and community relations events, but Hanna-Barbera characters were more accessible than ever around the world (both companies were generous with children's hospital visits). The Yogi Bear Campground Resort franchise started in 1969 when Doug Haag and Robert Borkovetz licensed the name and characters from both Screen Gems and H-B, which shared the rights at the time. Yogi, Boo-Boo, Cindy, and Ranger Smith still make appearances at the campgrounds, now numbering over seventy-five nationwide.

Live regional entertainment is a staple of any resort, fair, or theme park, and often the performers offer their privately pressed albums or CDs for sale. It may be impossible to account for every soloist or group that played at a park or resort that sold an album, but there are at least two LPs that showcase the Yogi Bear locations. An Orlando singer released a disc called *Sing Along or Listen while "PAT" Sings Your Favorite Song*; a group called "The Brand 'L's'" made a live album; and singer Johnny Selph released his *Yogi Bear Record*, a 45 rpm single with a picture sleeve adorned with the Campground logo, including Yogi himself.

▲▼▲▼

Television was seeing a resurgence in classic material as the syndication boom was creating new audiences and "cults" for shows that were popular in their day as well as underappreciated or "ahead of their time" shows that might gain a following. The studio started developing revivals of classic cartoons in addition to developing new series and feature films.

In 1971's *Pebbles and Bamm-Bamm Show* the youngest Flintstone was suddenly teen-aged. She was given the voice of Sally Struthers, who was just on the brink of stardom as Gloria Stivic on *All in the Family*. Struthers proved adept at voice acting and later played memorable roles in such shows as *TaleSpin* and *Jim Henson's Dinosaurs*. Jay North of Screen Gems' *Dennis the Menace* sitcom was the voice of Bamm-Bamm. A background cue from the Pebbles series was later used with lyrics as the theme for *Partridge Family, 2200 A.D.* When the series was folded into *The Flintstone Comedy Hour* the following year, Pebbles and her friends suddenly had a pop group called the Bedrock Rockers, actually The Ron Hicklin Singers, most of whom were singing not only the Pebbles theme but the main titles for all the H-B shows. Most of them were Hanna-Barbera record and film veterans like Stan Farber, Jackie Ward, Sally Stevens, Sue Allen, and the Bahler brothers, all under the supervision of Paul DeKorte.

Yogi's Ark Lark was an hour pilot on the ABC Saturday Superstar Movie that became the *Yogi's Gang* series. This was the first of many series and specials in which the classic characters would appear together, with Daws Butler doing well over a dozen voices at once and Don Messick doing nearly as many.

The largest assemblage of Hanna-Barbera characters, or perhaps any characters up to that time, were teamed in *All-Star Laff-A-Lympics*, a wildly successful satire of sportscasting using the clever, audacious pretense of being "live" as characters competed in events around the world. The *Laff-A-Lympics* main title melody was derived from a cue that originated on the *Jonny Quest* episode "Arctic Splashdown." Special guest characters also appeared, such as Fred Flintstone, to comment on the competition of the day. Alan Reed's work for *Laff-A-Lympics* was one of his last performances as Fred. In the seventies, the loss of Reed came as a blow to millions of fans. Losing iconic actors of Alan Reed's generation and stature was a relatively new occurrence at the time.

On records, classic and newly minted H-B characters were still starring in musical and narrative productions, in addition to generating thousands of merchandise items.

Kenner, a toymaking forerunner of kids' home video, was always coming up with new ways to project or view characters on film. With the Play 'n Show record player/slide projector, Kenner found a way to attach the slides to the record itself. A seven-inch record was anchored by a metal grommet to a ten-inch plastic disc with picture slides along its perimeter. The slides changed as the record played. Kenner released several of these "shows" with fairy tales and legends starring original cast voices of *The Flintstones* and *Yogi Bear* as well as UPA's Mister Magoo.

Peter Pan Records produced and released more new titles with Hanna-Barbera characters than any other label in the seventies. While the Scooby-Doo titles were recorded in Los Angeles with original cast members, all of Peter Pan's other H-B products were not done in that manner.

Like Golden Records, producer of many Hanna-Barbera character records in the late '50s and early '60s, Peter Pan was an East coast company usually producing on paltry children's record budgets that were expected to stretch over several titles. Peter Pan approached the H-B properties in a decidedly different style and manner than Golden, but it also cast experienced New York stage, TV, and commercial voice talents. Like Hanna-Barbera Records' penchant for casting outstanding voice actors in their colleagues' roles, Peter Pan cast some New Yorkers known for very famous characters, but not the ones they were doing for these particular records. The upside was twofold. Sometimes Peter Pan would release an album based on a cartoon that was otherwise never represented on records. And like some of the Golden records, even if the results are far from accurate to the originals, there are appealing aspects of the productions that have a certain charm. It is as if a touring company or a capable regional theater were performing their versions of *The Hair Bear Bunch*, *The Funky Phantom*, or *The Flintstones*.

▲▼▲▼▲▼

Help! It's the Hair Bear Bunch was a throwback to the classic Hanna-Barbera cartoons, tie-dyed to match the 1970s. Instead of a five- or seven-minute cartoon about zoo or park animals who outwitted authority figures, this used the half-hour sitcom format to tell stories about three bears with hidden high-tech cave facilities who ran rings around their clueless keepers. Because this was the '70s, the bears were furnished with groovy clothes and hairstyles. Daws Butler voiced lead character Hair Bear in what historian Earl Kress called Butler's "Jack Oakie" voice, not so much based on Phil Silvers but another character actor from early stage and screen. Paul Winchell channeled double-talking comedian Cliff Nazarro as Bubi Bear and Bill Callaway, who would become a prolific H-B actor for *Smurfs* and many other shows, as country bear Square Bear. Comedian Joe E. Ross (*Car 54, Where Are You?*) did the first of several H-B voices using his "Ooh! Ooh!" catchphrase.

Popular TV and film actor Joe Flynn (*McHale's Navy, The Computer Wore Tennis Shoes*) was cast as zookeeper Peevly. However, he had difficulty duplicating the expressiveness of his renowned persona broadly enough for animation, a problem Barbera and vocal directors Alan Dinehart and Gordon Hunt had encountered before. Ultimately, Flynn was paid but replaced with John Stephenson doing an impersonation. The same thing had happened at DePatie-Freleng with their *Ant and the Aardvark* cartoons. Comedian Jackie Mason could not replicate his voice into the microphone as well as impressionist John Byner, so Mason suggested that Byner replace him as long as he received his fee.

▲▼▲▼▲

Help! It's the Hair Bear Bunch was a special treat for fans of Hanna-Barbera background music, as the series used more classic cues than most of its contemporary H-B series, including selections from *Alice in Wonderland, The Flintstones, Loopy DeLoop, Magilla Gorilla, The Jetsons, Jonny Quest,* and the more recent *Huckleberry Finn, Pebbles and Bamm-Bamm,*

and *Scooby-Doo* cartoons. There were other nods to Hanna-Barbera's history, some intended, others perhaps not. The pilot included Yogi Bear's line, "Lookit the bears! Lookit the bears!" In another episode, the "bunch" formed a band "Three Bear Night," a nod to Three Dog Night, a group including former Hanna-Barbera Records staff member Danny Hutton.

In 1972, Peter Pan Records could not access the actors, scripts, or music cues for their *Hair Bear Bunch, Funky Phantom,* or *Flintstones* albums. Only the theme songs were licensed, and they were sung by the "Peter Pan Players," a catch-all phrase for uncredited performers. Children's records referred to their actors in this way over decades, renaming the "stock company" as needed. In this case, the three albums were produced and directed by the husband-and-wife musical team of Herb Davidson and Charlotte Sanders, who worked on dozens of Peter Pan titles in the late sixties and early seventies. They were stage entertainers as well as instructors and theater writer/directors. All of their Peter Pan recordings bear their signature arrangements and orchestrations.

Like so many producers, Sanders and Davidson often called upon a handful of trusted talents. One actor who appears on almost all their records is Lionel Wilson, an extremely versatile actor who did every voice on the acclaimed Terrytoons series *Tom Terrific* (for CBS's *Captain Kangaroo* series) and every voice on the 1969 animated revival of *Winky Dink and You.* Wilson voices Barney Rubble, Bubi Bear, Mr. Peevly, and Muddsy (*The Funky Phantom*). *Speed Racer* enthusiasts will recognize the voice of Speed, Peter Fernandez, and Trixie, Corinne Orr. Fernandez voices the Speed-like Skip voice, and Orr is April on *The Funky Phantom* LP.

The Funky Phantom was a cartoon series of the Scooby-Doo variety, featuring three teens who free a chicken-hearted ghost—Daws Butler doing a Snagglepuss-like voice—from an old clock and solve mysteries together. It was the first series Hanna-Barbera produced in Australia, at a studio called Australia's Air Programs International (API), which animated literary adaptations for Kenner TV specials and comedic cartoons like *Arthur and the Square Knights of the Round Table* and *Around the World in 80 Days*.

Davidson and Sanders formatted the albums into four stories each. They come fairly close to the spirit of the shows, though they sound nothing like them. However, in the absence of the H-B music cues, they created a small library of their own—a series of little themes that play under the scenes and repeat often, much like the cartoon cues. It is a technique that Disneyland read-along records would use five years later when musical backgrounds were added for the first time.

▲▼▲▼▲▼

In 1975, Peter Pan released their second and final *Flintstones* album, an LP with two stories entitled *Ghost Chasers* and *Fred Flintstone Meets Weevil Primeval* (named "Even Steven" on the actual recording and label). The producer for this disc is Broadway arranger/orchestrator Cornel Tanassy, whose specialty at Peter Pan was the "Power" series featuring Superman and other action/adventure heroes. In these particular Flintstone adventures, Fred, Wilma, Barney, and Betty are not particularly true to their established characters, though it is interesting to hear the East Coast legends voicing Fred and Barney this time around. Longtime Little Caesar's pizza spokesman Jackson Beck voices Fred. Beck was the voice of Bluto in countless Popeye cartoons and the narrator of Superman for radio, the Fleischer cartoons, and the Filmation cartoons. Barney is voiced by Broadway and TV actor Allen Swift, well known for his voices on Total TeleVision cartoons like *Underdog* (as Simon Barsinister and many others) and Rankin/Bass (as most of the *Mad Monster Party* characters).

Jack Shaindlin is credited with the music, but it was not scored specifically for the album. The cues were selected from his long-standing stock library, which was also a source of cues that Hanna-Barbera used before Hoyt Curtin started the studio music cue library with his Loopy DeLoop material. One of Shaindlin's cues, "Grotesque No. 2," included on a

Peter Pan read-along book and recording set called *Fred and Barney: Best Friends*, was also used in early Hanna-Barbera cartoons. The library music of Shaindlin and other stock composers was often licensed for children's records.

▲▼▲▼▲▼

Best Friends was one of eight Random House Hanna-Barbera storybooks that Peter Pan Records converted to audio between 1976 and 1978, in addition to the Scooby-Doo titles. Created by Ottenheimer Publishers, all of them were written by Horace J. Elias. The storybook art has merit but not the artistry of earlier Whitman and Golden books by Hanna-Barbera staff. The line drawings inside some of the paperbacks look like they were done with Flair pens.

Peter Pan modified the book titles, starting with the first group in 1974. For example, *Fred Flintstone and the Snallygaster Show* became *Fred Flintstone the Magician*; *The Flintstones at the Prehistoric Zoo* was changed to *The Flintstones Zoo Adventure*; and *Huckleberry Hound Puts the Fire Out* was renamed *Huckleberry Hound at the Firehouse*. Other Peter Pan 1974 titles are *Yogi Bear and His Jellystone Friends* and *Fred and Barney: Circus Fun*.

In 1976, Ralph Stein produced three more records: *Fred Flintstone and Good, Old, Unreliable Dino (Dino Gets a Job)*; *Fred and Barney: Best Friends*; *Pebbles and Bamm-Bamm and the Friendly Witch*. Stein was able to budget for the Scooby-Doo cast on the 1977 albums, but that was not possible for the other H-B characters in these modest 45 rpm/cassette read-alongs. Instead, he recruited several "regulars" from his many years at Peter Pan, Golden, and Pickwick, including narrator Tom Cipolla and Laine Roberts, who plays Wilma. Fred is voiced by prolific advertising and recording actor James Dukas, who was the first Count Chocula.

Across the Atlantic, a stage musical featuring Hanna-Barbera characters opened in 1973. On the cast album, UK actors do their best to replicate the voices. In Canada, a French-language album appeared on the CBS label entitled *Nos Amis del al Télé (Our*

Pierre Douglas sings about Hong Kong Phooey, Mightor, Captain Caveman, the Great Grape Ape, and Scooby-Doo on this French Canadian album.

Friends of the TV). Entertainer Pierre Douglas performs songs about Hong Kong Phooey, Mightor, Captain Caveman, the Great Grape Ape, and Scooby-Doo.

Hanna-Barbera's educational division continued to produce filmstrip sets, sometimes juggling actors for the companion audio cassettes. On the cassette called *Barney Borrows a Book*, Sally Struthers plays teen Pebbles (as in the 1971 revival), but John Stephenson voices Barney. In the next cassette, *Barney Returns a Book*, Mel Blanc is Barney, but Janet Waldo voices teen Pebbles (as she once did in the original series). Alan Reed is Fred on both cassettes.

In a sea of recast voice records, one of the most fascinating examples is *The Hanna-Barbera Record of Safety*. Released in 1973 as a TV mail-order offer from Baker-Rhodes Marketing, the album contained coloring activities and a poster, but questionably rendered artwork lifted from model sheets without much regard to relative size or layout. The album is graced with an abundance of Hanna-Barbera cartoon music cues and sixteen different tracks featuring H-B characters. All the tracks run exactly the same length, suggesting that they were actually radio public service announcements that were repurposed by Baker-Rhodes for this promotion.

Jean Vander Pyl is heard on several tracks as Wilma. Daws Butler does all the other voices, including his own Yogi Bear, Huckleberry Hound, Quick Draw McGraw, Snagglepuss, Super Snooper, Elroy Jetson, Peter Potamus, Lippy the Lion, Augie Doggie, Wally Gator, and Dixie. He also does voices usually done by others: Boo-Boo, Magilla Gorilla, Ricochet Rabbit, So-So, Yakky Doodle, and Touché Turtle. He also reprises his versions of Top Cat, Dum-Dum, and

Barney Rubble. In addition, Butler makes his sole commercial recording appearance as Fred Flintstone, a role he originally played in the series pilot film.

▲▾▲▾▲▾

"The Funtastic World of Hanna-Barbera" first became a familiar phrase in the late '70s as the studio created a new tag for its shows and a logo for new merchandise and publications. The best result of this era for comic book collectors was that Marvel had signed with H-B for a new series of titles produced at a higher quality level than most of the Charlton Comics published earlier in the decade. Mark Evanier, Earl Kress, and other well-versed writers scripted most of the new series with top H-B artists. Each Marvel comic book included a history page with the "The Funtastic World" logo as the header, as the studio began to celebrate itself.

For the studio's twentieth anniversary, CBS ran a two-hour prime-time retrospective called *Yabba-Dabba-Doo! The Happy World of Hanna-Barbera*. Hosted by longtime friend Gene Kelly and coproduced by Emmy-winning documentarian Marshall Flaum (*Hollywood: The Selznick Years*, *The Undersea World of Jacques Cousteau*), each segment covered a specific aspect of the Hanna-Barbera story featuring a different presenter: Cloris Leachman, Jonathan Winters, and Lorne Greene, who was seen in recording sessions for what would become the feature, *Heidi's Song*. High ratings convinced CBS to air a follow-up hour called *Yabba-Dabba-Doo II*, hosted by Bill Bixby.

These were only two of many show business retrospectives produced in the wake of the surprise theatrical hit, *That's Entertainment!* Intended to draw a curtain over Hollywood's golden era, it instead was so profitable it was followed by three sequels. The second was hosted by Fred Astaire and Gene Kelly and included new animation of MGM star caricatures by Hanna-Barbera.

Inside the Marvel comics were ads for 1977 reissues of the 1965–68 Hanna-Barbera Records. At first, these seemed like wishes come true, but on closer inspec-

Dedicated July 21, 1976, this star on Hollywood's Walk of Fame represents the great work of thousands of people as well as Bill and Joe.

tion, the new discs and covers did not compare well to the originals. The painterly artwork and detailed lettering were replaced by tracings of character poses from model sheets alongside very basic drawings and blocks of color. The back covers were emblazoned with the "Funtastic World" logo, with the subhead, "Where Children's Fun Begins." Generic ad copy about the series follows, along with track information picked up from the earlier release. To their credit, Columbia Special Products pressed the new discs on high-quality vinyl and someone also noticed that the *Yogi Bear: Jack and the Beanstalk/Little Red Riding Hood* album sides were flipped, so that was corrected.

The recordings themselves were given very little love and care. The engineering renders them tinny and thin; some "cheat" stereo sound by tossing voices from right to left channels; others have unnecessarily added reverb. None of this was necessary as ten of the titles were never released in stereo. The only album originally released in stereo, *The Flintstones Meet the Orchestra Family*, was unfortunately presented only in mono by Columbia, a waste of a spectacular production. The unfortunate thing is

H-B revived Tom and Jerry for Saturday morning TV in 1975, and two albums of stories based on the cartoons were recorded by Ilse Werner in German.

that these albums seem to have been manufactured in large quantities. They did not appear in as many retail stores as other children's records until they became remainder items. Sadly, these reissues may have left the impression that the original HBR Cartoon Series was also inferior.

Columbia reissued eleven albums from the HBR Cartoon Series and one from Sunset/Liberty. Four of the albums combined three condensed HBR 45 rpm stories.[1] The four-story combo discs, plus volume 1 of *Golden Cartoons in Song* (renamed *Kiddie Klassics*), were sold by mail in a five-disc box set as *Fred Flintstone Presents All-Time Favorite Children's Stories and Songs*. The Columbia Musical Treasury series reissued Hanna-Barbera's first recording, *The King Who Couldn't Dance*, on a two-LP set called *Gene Kelly: Stories and Songs for Children*. At the end of the '70s, Columbia established another label for children's

and archival materials called 51 West, after the corporate address of CBS. In addition to the final original Captain Kangaroo albums, 51 West reissued *The King Who Couldn't Dance* on another Gene Kelly compilation called *The Happiest Birthday in the World*, as well as a mono reissue of Hanna-Barbera's 1967 *Jack and the Beanstalk* soundtrack.

Tom and Jerry returned in 1975 for the first time in a TV series. *The Tom and Jerry/Grape Ape Show* featured new cartoons starring the duo (this time produced completely by Hanna-Barbera without MGM) alternating with shorts featuring a giant purple ape and his little beagle buddy. There were no corresponding records created nor classic reissues to tie into the new series, but in Germany, two volumes of *Tom and Jerry (Original Cartoons)*, narrated by Ilse Werner, were adapted from H-B's 1975–1976 TV episodes for the German-language albums.

▴▾▴▾

Nineteen sixty-six's *Alice in Wonderland* made a network comeback of sorts in a 1978 NBC live-action videotaped special called *The Hanna-Barbera All-Star Comedy Ice Revue* with *Little House on the Prairie* star Michael Landon from Australia. The premise of the ice show replaced Alice with teen Pebbles (still voiced by Janet Waldo) in a Wonderland setting, complete with an onstage Cheshire Cat and the soundtrack voice of Sammy Davis Jr. singing "What's a Nice Kid Like You Doing in a Place Like This?"

H-B favorites returned in several new series and specials. One was a daily syndicated anthology that, like *The Banana Splits and Friends*, featured reruns of earlier H-B series. *Fred Flintstone and Friends* presented a 1977 series that connected Columbia Pictures and Hanna-Barbera, like *Jeannie*; *Partridge Family, 2200 A.D.*; *Goober and the Ghost Chasers* (since the Partridges guest-starred); *The Pebbles and Bamm-Bamm Show*; and *Yogi's Gang*. Each episode was staggered to make the halves act as cliffhangers from day to day. *Fred Flintstone and Friends* depicted Fred in a TV control room and was the first regular series with Henry Corden in the role, followed by *A Flintstone Christmas* in prime time later that year. In 1979 *The New Fred and Barney Show* partnered him with Mel Blanc as Barney for a Saturday morning NBC series that took a more whimsical approach to the story lines. For many HBR Cartoon Series listeners, Corden wasn't Reed but he was the Fred they also knew well since 1965.

Scooby-Doo celebrated his tenth birthday in 1979 with his first prime-time special, the surreal satire *Scooby Goes Hollywood*. This can also be considered the first prime-time musical special with songs by Hanna, Barbera, and Curtin. The songs would not be released commercially for several years. Shaggy, in one of the few instances in which Casey Kasem sings in the role, decides to bombard a Hollywood executive (comedian Rip Taylor) with absurd pilots that imitate hits of the day, including *Happy Days*, *Laverne and Shirley*, *Donny and Marie*, *The Love Boat*, and even *The Sound of Music*, with Scooby whirling atop the mountains á la Julie Andrews.

Superheroes were still big business on Saturday mornings and the various production companies were as aggressive in competing for characters as the heroes were in the comics. Batman and Robin's toned-down but still gung-ho guest appearances on *The New Scooby-Doo Movies* convinced the networks, sponsors, and pressure groups that these heroes could work on Saturday morning if presented to everyone's satisfaction. The result was 1973's *Super Friends*, the longest continuously running comic book hero series on Saturday morning TV (if you count its various format changes). The greatest heroes in DC comics were pitted against a rogue's gallery of villains, but they also took time to tell kids to cross the street at corners and observe traffic signals. Peter Pan Records unleashed its line of Power Records to tie in with Hanna-Barbera, Filmation, and any other adaptation in prime-time TV, as they had licensed both Marvel and DC characters. One of their albums, *Stories and Songs of the Justice League of America*, was released in 1966 on its Tifton label but reissued in 1975 to coincide with ABC's broadcast of *Super Friends*. There is no direct connection audio-wise, but it is the closest thing to a *Super Friends* record kids could have at the time. *Super Friends* powered through the seventies and lasted on network TV until 1985.

The Hanna-Barbera studio continued bursting at the seams with projects based on old and new properties, but there was something else over the horizon waiting to change the face of Saturday morning TV. Something borrowed. Something new. Something blue.

Chapter 23

SMURFS HEARD 'ROUND THE WORLD

~~~~~~

Please pass the poi.

—FRED FLINTSTONE (ALAN REED), "HAWAIIAN ESCAPADE"

In 1957, two young comic novel artists were vacationing with their families on the Belgian Coast. One night at dinner one of them wanted the salt shaker.

"He fumbled for the words and instead asked his friend to pass the 'schtroumpf,'" writes Matt Murray in the book, *The World of Smurfs.*

The salt requestor was Pierre Culliford, known through his art as Peyo. He noted that his colleague and mentor, Andre Franquin, "responded, 'Look, here's the schtroumpf, and when you've finished schtroumpfing, schtroumpf it back to me!' It was so fun to schtroumpf for the few days we spent together, it became a joke for us."

Murray wrote, "It was gibberish, a malapropism, but the two got such a kick out of it that they spent their time finding ways to inject it into their everyday conversations as a noun, a verb, or an adjective."

Schtroumpfs originated in comic stories led by a popular medieval adventurer named Johan, who debuted in 1946, and his even more popular, mischievous sidekick, Perlouit, later known as Peewit. Peyo devised a story line about a magic flute and created a village of elf-like people who had a peculiar way of speaking. They became an international sensation, with marketing tie-ins and merchandise in many countries throughout the '60s and '70s with a presence but not prominence in the US. Like Tintin and Asterix, they were published in graphic novels and beloved by fans but not part of the general zeitgeist.

In 1977, Belvision studios, the same company that produced the *Tintin* cartoons written by Charles Shows,[1] embarked on an ambitious feature based on *The Magic Flute* story with music by multiple Oscar nominee and winner Michel LeGrand (*The Umbrellas of Cherbourg, Yentl, Summer of '42*). The richly evocative score and catchy theme from *La Flûte à six Schtroumpfs* was released on LP by Polydor Records, but not in the US.

As their fame gained momentum, music and records played a significant role in how the name "Smurf" became the best-known way to identify the little blue characters. "The term 'Smurf' was the Dutch translation of 'schtroumpf,'" explained animation historian Hans Perk. "The word 'schtroumpf' had of course been translated several ways depending on the countries, but the name of 'Smurf' stuck after the hit record, 'The Smurf Song.'" It was one of those songs that can drive one mad because it was very silly and played so often."

"The Smurf Song" was recorded by Dutch singer/songwriter Pierre Kartner. As children's entertainer Father Abraham, he had gained hit status with "The Little Café by the Harbour," covered by several singers including Engelbert Humperdinck. *Father Abraham in Smurfland* became a hit in sixteen countries, followed by more best-selling Dutch Smurf albums, all of which were yet to make their big splash in the US.

▲▼▲▼▲▼

"Hanna-Barbera Productions was running at its peak in the late seventies and early eighties," said Tom Sito, USC professor of film at the School of Cinematic Arts. "At one point, they had twelve series running at once, plus commercials in production and a new theatrical feature on the way. While Disney animation had around 175 on staff, Hanna-Barbera kept about 1,400 people working in the business."

Joe Barbera would sell an exhaustive package of projects. *Yogi's First Christmas*, a feature-length TV movie again reuniting the classic characters, was sold to syndication for the 1980 holiday season. Several Curtin-Hanna-Barbera songs from recent specials, like *Casper's First Christmas* (1979), were incorporated into the ninety-eight-minute film (two hours with commercials). One of the new tunes, "Cindy's Mistletoe Song" was a holiday twist on "Like I Like You" from *Hey There, It's Yogi Bear*. The ratings for *Yogi's First Christmas*, a precursor to the direct-to-video

animated feature bonanza of the nineties, enabled Barbera to sell ten more syndicated full-length animated TV features. Three starred Scooby-Doo (Don Messick), three featured Yogi Bear (Daws Butler), one was headlined by Huckleberry Hound (also Butler), and one gave Judy Jetson (Janet Waldo) the lead. Most historic were *The Jetsons Meet the Flintstones* and *Top Cat Meets the Beverly Hills Cats*, which is the only revival with the 1961 series characters involving Bill Hanna and Joe Barbera.

As mentioned earlier, Joe sold the concepts and Bill got them done on time and budget, using the timing and techniques he had developed. Their systems were being passed along to those looking to open their own studios. "We tried to keep our artists up to the best level we could by starting free classes at the studio," said Barbera. "We found out that the competitors were taking the trained artists away from us and we were told to stop the classes."

In 1982, Kings Island in Cincinnati staged a lavish live spectacular for its tenth anniversary called *Celebration*. Part of the show was a salute to the twenty-fifth anniversary of "our friends at Hanna-Barbera in Hollywood." Dancing with the cast were Yogi Bear, Scooby-Doo, Snagglepuss, and other characters in a medley of songs from MGM's *The Wizard of Oz* and Broadway's *The Wiz*. Taft Attractions released a souvenir cast album.[2]

▲▼▲▼▲▼

Hanna-Barbera had been producing live-action films since 1963. By the '70s and '80s, further opportunities opened up in prime-time TV movies and theatrical films.

Until home video took hold, Disney produced a new animated feature only every four years or so, with classic reissues filling in the gaps. Live-action features became a huge Disney profit center. Nineteen sixty-nine's top-grossing comedy-fantasy *The Love Bug* had an even more dramatic and creative effect than 1959's *The Shaggy Dog*—Disney grew dependent on such comedies. Every live-action

A tribute to fifty years of Hanna-Barbera Productions was among the highlights of this stage show (and cast album) commemorating twenty-five years at Kings Island theme park.

Disney feature was modular. The *Davy Crockett* TV segments of the '50s proved popular when edited into features, so successive films were configured into sections running about fifty-one minutes each. A film could be broadcast in segments on US television and released theatrically overseas. The extra box-office potential sometimes allowed a more generous budget, making the Disney TV product outshine many other broadcasts.

Hanna-Barbera partnered with American-International Pictures to release *C.H.O.M.P.S.*, the studio's first live-action theatrical feature. The comedy starred Wesley Eure (*Land of the Lost*) and Valerie Bertinelli (*One Day at a Time*) in a comedy about a cute robotic doggie "Canine HOMe Protection System." In an unusual move, full animation was used to create Iwao Takamoto's "Pink Panther"–like main titles. The studio's first live-action TV movie was a 1973 *ABC Movie of the Week* western titled *Hardcase* starring Clint Walker. It opened with the Hanna-Barbera name, though subsequent TV films listed Joseph Barbera in the credits and only mentioned the H-B copyright and occasional logo at the end.

Hanna-Barbera's most prestigious live-action TV film was 1977's *The Gathering*, an acclaimed holiday drama starring Ed Asner and Maureen Stapleton. The film has its moments of whimsy, including a scene in which a grandchild gives Asner's character a plush Yogi Bear. Some H-B TV movies veered from the kind of "family entertainment" Bill Hanna talked about in the 1964 *Here Comes a Star* promo film. In 1980 *Belle Starr*, a mature western drama, featured a very different Elizabeth Montgomery than the Samantha character who went camping with the Flintstones.

Hanna-Barbera also launched a production company without their name as Disney would later do with Touchstone Pictures, so the industry and public would not have preconceived notions about the content. It was run by and named for executive Herbert F. Solow, who was instrumental in the development of *Star Trek* and other shows for Desilu and Paramount. Solow's biggest hit for Hanna-Barbera was *The Man from Atlantis*, which launched the career of Patrick Duffy before *Dallas* made him a worldwide star.

Hanna-Barbera's overseas production was also not exclusive to animation. In the wake of such prime-time, over-the-top soap operas as *Dallas* and *Dynasty* came Australian television's *Return to Eden*, an opulent and deliberately overwrought miniseries about a glamorous heiress, backstabbing treachery, changed identity, and chomping crocodiles framed against the stunning beauty of the Northern Territory. Although the hit miniseries and subsequent spinoff series were not shown in the US, the epic *Return to Eden* score was released domestically by Varese Sarabande Records. Australian composer Brian May—not the musician from the pop band Queen—has gained a following for his scores for *Mad Max*, *Tales from the Crypt*, and other film and TV series.

▲▼▲▼▲▼

Hanna-Barbera was not alone in turning to their catalog of characters and premises for reboots and sequels to proven successes. This was not always by choice. Barbera would become frustrated when he would try to convince clients to buy fresh ideas and could only sell the same things. Continuing to greenlight the same concepts not only made the studio an easy target for being derivative, but new concepts were vital to sustaining creative equity in the future. By the end of the seventies, several entities became dependent on redoing what had been done without sufficiently cultivating fresh, potentially evergreen material to sustain themselves in the ensuing years.

Disneyland Records very seldom licensed outside properties in its early days, but by the late seventies, a dearth of strong films and TV shows caused the division to go back to its earliest characters, like Mickey

Mouse and his friends, who had not been on records for years, and aggressively license the characters and stories of other companies. This became wildly successful in animation and children's records. Before the age when large media corporations could acquire vast libraries or entire companies and keep their assets, companies like Disney, Hanna-Barbera, and Filmation bought licenses to popular franchises. Almost all of Filmation's output was based on licensed properties like various Superman and Batman shows, the Archie formats, and *The Brady Kids*. Hanna-Barbera countered with *Josie and the Pussycats*, *Super Friends*, and *Partridge Family, 2200 A.D.* It exploded on records in the '80s, when Disney licensed *Peanuts* characters and stories, the *Star Trek* movies, *Star Wars*, *E. T.*, Indiana Jones, Rainbow Brite, Gumby, Garfield, and Rankin/Bass films like *The Hobbit*.

Among the recent and classic characters that resurfaced were Popeye and his friends. Hanna and Barbera, who had each known people from the earliest days of animation—many of whom were still working at their studio—brought Jack Mercer to California to work on the series. Mercer was able to voice Popeye again as well as work in the story department, both of which he did for decades at Fleischer and Paramount's Famous Studios. Marilyn Schreffler (Brenda of *Captain Caveman* and Daisy Mayhem of *Laff-A-Lympics*) voiced Olive Oyl, as Mae Questel was not able to relocate. Allan Melvin played Bluto and Daws Butler gave Wimpy a W. C. Fields sound. Starting with *The All-New Popeye Hour* in 1978, CBS enjoyed strong ratings for five years. The series overlapped with the 1980 big-screen *Popeye* musical starring Robin Williams with songs by Harry Nilsson. Hanna-Barbera supplied the animated Popeye at the film's beginning, as the studio was currently contractred with King Features for the current TV version. It was an interesting twist, since the film was coproduced by Paramount and Disney. Boardwalk Records issued a soundtrack of the Williams/Paramount/Disney feature.

Peter Pan Records reissued two earlier *Popeye* albums, plus a new one to match the format of the

H-B series. Peter Pan's 1980 LP, *Popeye: Four Stories*, featured an uncredited Mercer and Schreffler in stories written and produced by Arthur Korb, who produced one of the earlier LPs for the sailor and countless discs for the label. Two of the stories— one of which finds Popeye touring a movie studio as an indirect nod to the theatrical feature—were also available in an LP book and record set. The closest disc to an H-B Popeye vinyl soundtrack is in Spanish. Mexico's *Popeye—Musica Original de la Serie de T.V. by Superbanda* combines songs with cartoon soundtracks in Spanish, using the actual background cues and sound effects.

Hanna-Barbera also brought Harvey Comics' very popular Richie Rich character to TV for the first time in 1980, combined with Scooby-Doo cartoons. Using a New York studio cast, Korb coproduced a series of *Richie Rich* story albums and read-along book-and-recording sets to tie in with the series. The other producer was "Bugs" Bower, another veteran of budget and children's labels, this one being a short-lived division of Polygram Records called Parachute.

▲▼▲▼▲▼

Former Disneyland Records staffers brought what they had learned to Florida and started Kid Stuff Records, shipping out dozens of low-budget records featuring Strawberry Shortcake, Barbie, Pink Panther, Care Bears, and many more at a lightning pace.

"We don't sell records," said a Kid Stuff sales manager to the author. "We sell album covers." Kid Stuff's strategy was to use bright colors and characters to attract kids and short, promising ad copy to convince parents to purchase. Some of their albums, like the Paddington LPs produced by Golden Records founder Arthur Shimkin and the Care Bear records produced by Howard Kaylan and Mark Volman of the Turtles, fulfilled the promise of the packaging. American Greetings characters Strawberry Shortcake and Care Bears were part of a burgeoning licensing bonanza that started with greeting cards and soon became merchandise, records, and movies (1985's *Care Bears*

Movie surpassed Disney's *The Black Cauldron*). The first half of the eighties saw a lot of scrambling for such lucrative licenses in the absence of other strong new material from the major studios.

Smurfs were among the characters that had been licensed for US merchandising in 1976 but were not the sensation they would become. They could be found on keychains, in plush, and as little PVC figures, which were a phenomenon with international collectors and as popular office decorations. "There was a Smurf for all kinds of personalities, interests, and moods," said publicity and promotions executive Suzanne Henton. "People would put them on their desks for fun and give them as little gifts."

"Fred Silverman bought a Smurf for his daughter as a gift," said Sam Ewing, an NBC programming executive who helped shepherd *Smurfs* onto the air. "Fred thought we should get the rights for TV before someone else did."

Peyo was protective of every aspect of his Smurfs, right down to nomenclature: one must always avoid adding "The" before "Smurfs" whenever possible. He and his creative partner, Yvan Delporte, worked with Hanna-Barbera to adapt his graphic novel stories for television. Considerable efforts were taken to make the characters resemble the Peyo versions. They looked simple but they were difficult to render properly in animation.

The series became so familiar and imitated, it's worth noting that *Smurfs* was revolutionary for Saturday morning. There had never been a hit series with such a low-key, classic storybook style, especially in the wake of action adventure, teen mysteries, and groovy pop. It was as if a holiday-level special was being broadcast every week. Risk can make networks apprehensive. Barbera requested a ninety-minute programming block to fully immerse viewers in this unique setting and with the characters—and strategically to get a major chunk of airtime. NBC had been suffering low ratings and agreed.

Hoyt Curtin provided another risk and breakthrough. He had long been interpolating classical themes into Hanna-Barbera background cues, but

Celebrating Smurf success at the New York City Toy Fair/Licensing Show are translator Jean (John) Novier; Phyllis Tucker-Vinson, VP of NBC Children's Programming; Peyo (aka Pierre Culliford); and Sam Ewing, VP of Development at Hanna-Barbera. Photo courtesy of Sam Ewing.

the Smurf music would be more dependent on Bee-thoven, Prokofieff, Rachmaninoff, Grieg, Mussorg-sky, and other great composers than any network cartoon in the past. NBC tested the *Smurfs* pilot by playing it for test audiences and the response was "off the charts" to the point that the network said they wanted no further changes.

"BUT," said *Smurfs* producer/director Gerard Bald-win in his memoir, *From Mr. Magoo to Papa Smurf*, "I got a phone call . . ." Despite the overwhelming response, NBC's vice president of children's TV refused to approve *Smurfs* unless every bit of classical music was eliminated, insisting that kids did not like classical, only rock and roll. There was no way around the order until fate intervened. The VP was suddenly no longer at the network.

"As NBC searched for a new boss for children's programming, there was a short period of time when the kid department had nobody in charge," Baldwin wrote (until Phyllis Tucker-Vinson came on board). "The studio already had an okay to proceed with pro-

duction, so we recorded the entire musical library for the as yet unwritten episodes and pretty much spent the entire budget allowed for music, all classical."

Smurfs earned NBC a 44 ratings share on Saturday mornings, making it one of the most popular net-work animated series of all time. Unlike *Scooby-Doo*, *Smurfs* ran for multiple continuous seasons with no format changes, except for the occasional addition of characters and the ninth-season time-travel premise. Over four hundred individual eleven- and twenty-two-minute cartoons were produced by Hanna-Barbera for the run. The series won two Emmys and was praised for "very special" episodes about the hearing impaired and other subjects woven skillfully into the stories.

The voice cast of *Smurfs* is a vast roster of distin-guished talents, including familiar names like Jona-than Winters (who was also in the first two feature films), Brenda Vaccaro, Ray Walston, Alan Young, Rene Auberjonois, Arte Johnson, Ruth Buzzi, and Ed Begley Jr., and Hanna-Barbera favorites like Janet

Waldo, June Foray, Paul Winchell, Henry Gibson, and Marvin Kaplan. Two names connected *Smurfs* to the dawn of television animation, Don Messick as Papa Smurf, and Lucille Bliss—the voice of TV's pioneering cartoon character, Crusader Rabbit—who enjoyed newfound fame as Smurfette.

Smurfs gave Hanna-Barbera one more chance to lead another trend and set a quality standard with no additional budgeting. "They made *Smurfs* for the same amount of money as their other cartoons," said Sam Ewing. "Bill Hanna told me that one of the tricks was to give the viewers 'richness.' Try to make the layouts and backgrounds as rich as possible so there is plenty to look at to compensate for the movement. The idea was to always be entertaining, no matter what the limits were."

▲▼▲▼▲▼

The *Smurfs* theme is rooted in the classics. It begins with a hint of Rossini's "William Tell" and is the combined work of Curtin, Barbera, and Hanna. According to Baldwin, it started with a little hum he did for Curtin. Once again, many of Ron Hicklin's contracted singers (in the case of *Smurfs*, slightly sped up) were heard on the soundtrack as they were for most of the studio themes throughout the seventies and eighties under the supervision of Paul DeKorte and his successors. Essentially, there really was such a group as "The Hanna-Barbera Singers" with a history extending back to the HBR days.

In the wake of H-B TV stardom, *The Smurfs and the Magic Flute* feature was released in US theaters and on video even if the album was not. The other Smurf albums were a very different story. Sessions, a company that specialized in the direct marketing of records and cassettes, sold the early *Smurf* albums through TV commercials with 800 numbers and mail-in offers. This helped Disneyland's *Mickey Mouse Disco* album into triple-platinum history because the commercials stimulated retail awareness in addition to direct responses. The Universal Price Code (UPC) was relatively new and the Handleman Company was a retail "rack jobber" (sales floor vendor service) that measured sales every few weeks by sending sales representatives into stores to electronically scan the UPCs. The best-selling albums were placed in the feature racks so shoppers would see them as they entered the music department. In the early eighties, *Smurfing Sing Song* and *The Smurfs All Star Show* were in the bestseller racks along with the top singing stars of the era. One of the songs on the LP is "Little Smurf Boat," adapted from Pierre Kartner's " The Little Café by the Harbour."

Fully orchestrated, the *Smurf* records are not similar in musical style to the TV version. They reflect a variety of popular European music in the seventies tailored for children, from calypso and reggae to rockabilly and big band jazz. The most dominant musical style on the *Smurf* LPs is a pop-march beat that suggests the music of Eurovision, ABBA, and specifically Dutch singer/composer George Baker (Johannes Bouwens), whose 1975 soft pop hit "Paloma Blanca" was an easy listening hit in the US as well. Eventually, over a half dozen Dutch Smurf albums were released by Sessions and Starland Music. Starland and Kid Stuff also released read-along books with records and cassettes based on stories featured in the series, originally from the Peyo books. There was one uncredited narrator and a simple theme.

In 1983, electronic/funk artist Tyrone Brunson recorded his biggest dance hit, "The Smurf." The Smurfs on disc began to parallel Alvin and the Chipmunks' revival career, releasing a new album every so often blending new songs with contemporary covers in their respective voices far into the nineties. Smurf dance and pop discs took a steady climb internationally. Quality Music in Canada issued a compilation of *Smurf* "covers" of contemporary rock, pop, and dance hits called *Smurfin'! 10th Anniversary Commemorative Album*.

The Smurfs theme joined "Meet the Flintstones" and "Scooby-Doo, Where Are You?" as one of Hanna-Barbera's most memorable title songs. The hit 2011 *Smurfs* live-action/animated feature took comical jabs at the theme's catchy "earworm" effect. The TV

Once the Hanna-Barbera TV series sent Smurfmania over the top, the Dutch-produced Smurf music albums flew off US store shelves, especially after they were marketed through mail order on TV.

soundtrack version of the *Smurfs* was brought to records and CDs when Tee Vee Toons launched the *Television's Greatest Hits* album series starting in 1985. These were the first commercial recordings to offer the genuine theme songs from *The Flintstones, Yogi Bear, The Jetsons, Top Cat, Huckleberry Hound, Quick Draw McGraw, Jonny Quest, Smurfs, Dastardly and Muttley, Josie and the Pussycats, Scooby-Doo, Where Are You?, Secret Squirrel, Atom Ant,* and *Wacky Races.*

▲▼▲▼▲▼

Networks and syndicators clamored for another *Smurf* success with lovable little characters in magical lands. Three years later, even Disney entered Saturday morning animation with storybook fantasy series like *Wuzzles* and *Adventures of the Gummi Bears.* Disney's enhanced production methods and quality standards

nudged up network budgets, but they were also not animated domestically. Overseas production helped make the enhanced level possible. Soon the networks insisted on similar procedures for other cartoons, causing more to be sent out of the US. *Smurfs*, which began as a Los Angeles animation project, converted to overseas a few years into its nine-season run.

NBC enjoyed several years of success with another Hanna-Barbera series that was intended as the next best thing to *Smurfs*, only underwater. "*Snorks* was developed with Freddy Monnickendam, who negotiated the rights for the Father Abraham records and merchandised Smurfs in America," said Hans Perk. "He and Peyo had a falling out over the approach to the series and eventually he bought the rights to a comic series called 'Diskies' by Nic Broca."

"We didn't want to make *Snorks* a total duplicate of *Smurfs*," recalled Sam Ewing. "I remember suggesting

Snorks enjoyed considerable success on Saturday morning, though lightning was unlikely to "Smurf" twice; this music album was released only outside the US.

that maybe they should be school-age and have stories about the things kids that age would do."

A *Snorks* music album was available in the United Kingdom and Canada with an almost identical style to the Smurf albums, right down to a lullaby conclusion. While not a *Smurf*-sized phenomenon, *Snorks* enjoyed a respectable four-season run.

Now that Hanna-Barbera had started the "adorable little character" trend, the studio itself was tasked with adapting other licensed characters and formats as programmers scrambled for more potential hits. H-B's adaptation of Hallmark's *Shirt Tales* became a series of record and film strip sets for the Show 'n Tell projector, a device popular since the sixties but eclipsed by VHS. A record was played on the top as corresponding slides were viewed through a TV-like screen. Flintstones and Scooby-Doo titles were also released in the eighties as well as programs

with *Pink Panther and Sons*, a project that reunited Hanna and Barbera with colleague Friz Freleng after Marvel Productions had taken over DePatie-Freleng.

Pink Panther and Sons was one of several properties that Kid Stuff Records produced that were based on properties that H-B developed for animation at the same time, also including *Pac-Man* and *Monchhichis*. Hanna-Barbera's version of Tonka *Pound Puppies* became two 1985 Peter Pan book-and-recording sets featuring characters from the TV series with studio casts. The 1985 *Pound Puppies Sing 'n Bark Jingle Bells* album on Peter Pan's Child World label—a throwback to the "Barking Dogs" holiday hit—used Nashville instrumental backings that had been used six years earlier on *Disney's Christmas Favorites* LP and several other budget label releases. Thus, the same music tracks backing up Mickey Mouse and friends also accompanied characters from a Hanna-Barbera cartoon.

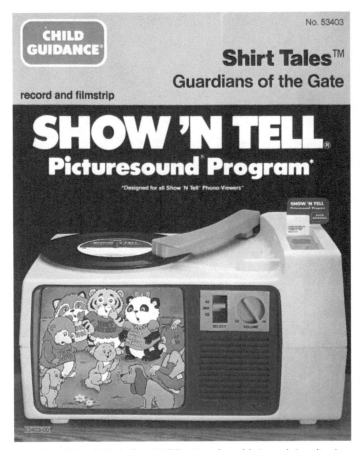

Popular in the '60s and '70s, the Show 'n Tell filmstrip and record device was being eclipsed by home video when several sets were released featuring *Shirt Tales, Scooby-Doo*, and the Flintstones.

The Biskitts read-alongs from Parachute are hybrids, with studio voice casts, but genuine theme music (interpolating Liszt's *Hungarian Rhapsody*) from the soundtrack by Barbera, Hanna, and Curtin, a very rare move for a small children's label. These may be the only commercial recordings that begin with the spoken words: "Hanna-Barbera Presents . . ."

H-B was hiring so many distinguished actors for their cartoons, it would have been preferable if the above records had the budgets for soundtrack dialogue featuring the likes of Robert Morse, Pat Carroll (playing a pre-*Little Mermaid* villain), Frank Nelson, Stanley Ralph Ross, Billie Hayes, and comedian Marty Ingels (whose surprise casting as video game star Pac-Man was a new claim to fame).

Venerable board game maker Parker Brothers took a sojourn into children's records with *Cabbage Patch Kids* albums. These are not connected directly to the Hanna-Barbera animated special, but they are exceptional on their own, with original songs by Tom Chapin and the Sherman Brothers.

The Bible did not require a license for Hanna-Barbera to animate it for television, but it took Joe Barbera over a decade to sell it to the networks. He saw the stories as excellent material for animation and knew the market well enough to realize there was a substantial audience. The arrival of lower-cost, consumer-priced VHS cassette home video created the avenue Barbera needed to produce *Hanna-Barbera's The Greatest Adventure: Stories from the Bible*. The

Even though they do not feature the TV voices, Parachute Records' two *Biskitts* read-alongs include a bit of the soundtrack theme and open with the words, "Hanna-Barbera Presents."

series was cast as if it were a prime-time TV special, with promotable names in each installment including Ed Asner, James Whitmore, Richard Thomas, Roscoe Lee Browne, Dean Jones, Vincent Price, and Helen Hunt, daughter of H-B voice director Gordon Hunt. Barbera spoke about the series on a 1987 syndicated inspirational radio program called "Master Control" saluting the studio that also featured Bill Hanna and Daws Butler. The one-hour show was distributed on a vinyl LP, making it a rare instance in which Hanna and Barbera's voices were heard on records, just as Walt Disney himself only recorded one album for his in-house music company.

With so many characters flying around screens and stores, it was becoming difficult for the average viewer to figure out who created which ones and who owned whom. But to most, the Hanna-Barbera name was still strongly associated with beloved characters like the Flintstones and the Jetsons, and they were a vivid part of this era as well.

Chapter 24

HEIDI SINGS AND THE JETSONS FLY AGAIN

There is nothing wrong with your television set.
—VIC PERRIN AS "THE CONTROL VOICE" ON *THE OUTER LIMITS*
(1963–1965)

"The Control Voice" is one of the most famous off-screen roles in the vast career of Vic Perrin. Perrin became a Hanna-Barbera fixture as the original voice of supervillain Doctor Zin on *Jonny Quest* and subsequent reboots. He rivaled John Stephenson for the number of times he grumbled, "I would have gotten away with it if it weren't for you meddling kids," at *Scooby-Doo* unmaskings as anything from the Snow Ghost to the Phantom Racer. For years, guests at Epcot at Walt Disney World Resort in Florida heard Perrin as the original narrator of the Spaceship Earth icon attraction. Outside the attraction/park icon, Disney's Future World Brass regularly played *The Jetsons* theme, which was included on an album sold at the park called *The Future of Corps*.

Hanna-Barbera selected Perrin to narrate their 1982 *Heidi's Song* soundtrack, available as a regular LP album, an LP picture disc—very popular in the '80s—and a seven-inch read-along storybook and record or cassette. The records were released and marketed by K-Tel, yet another label dabbling in the children's market but ubiquitous for pop compilations advertised heavily on local TV and sold in discount stores.

Heidi's Song was the only production for which the Hanna-Barbera studio's staff produced a story-and-dialogue album and read-along set in-house. It was produced by Hanna-Barbera music department head (and vocalist) Paul DeKorte. He had also coproduced Paramount Records' 1973 soundtrack album for *Charlotte's Web*. The Charlotte album featured songs and instrumentals with some dialogue snippets but not a full story. The decision to go with a story album rather than a song and music soundtrack album may have been to make it more marketable to kids and parents who were familiar with the classic Heidi story. Read-alongs were

K-Tel Records, which usually specialized in pop music compilations, released a *Heidi's Song* story and music album, a picture disc, and a read-along set.

a high-volume business in the eighties as low-cost impulse purchases. Unfortunately, because of limited space on the record, some songs were edited and others were deleted altogether, including Pamelyn Ferdin's "Can You Imagine."

Fortunately for connoisseurs of Hanna-Barbera music, the entire score can be heard in full stereo on the 2012 DVD, restored by Warner Archive. There are dialogue and sound effects of course, but all the songs are intact along with the main and end titles. The expense and work involved in such a task attest to the importance of the film and the result has a notably positive effect on the viewer, especially in appreciating Hoyt Curtin's work on the music. This was Curtin's sole opportunity to score an animated feature, as well as supervise the songs. From the opening titles, especially in stereo, the full range of Curtin's mastery of various genres weaves throughout the film, from

the epic magnificence of "Wunderhorn" to the Jetsons Jazz of "Ode to a Rat."

▲▽▲▽▲▽

Hanna-Barbera hoped from the start that *Heidi's Song* would be "it," a theatrical animated feature done in an expansive, traditional style that the public would embrace as a classic. Much-honored lyricist Sammy Cahn, who had worked on *Jack and the Beanstalk* for the studio, was teamed with Broadway's Burton Lane. Composer of such shows as *Finian's Rainbow* and *On a Clear Day You Can See Forever*, Lane took assignments only on rare occasions. *Heidi's Song* began production in the late seventies—as evidenced by Lorne Greene's appearance at a recording session in the aforementioned 1977 *Happy World of Hanna-Barbera* TV special.

Music-wise, Hanna-Barbera was a decade early before circumstances fell into place for Howard Ashman to help Disney bring the Broadway form to animated features, as well as a return to the traditional "book" musical that harkened back to *Snow White and the Seven Dwarfs*. H-B cast a Broadway star in the lead before it became the trend in theatrical animation. Margery Gray, of such shows as *Anything Goes* and *Tenderloin*, remembered becoming the voice of Heidi. This was her second animated feature, as she played a small role in Richard Williams's 1977 animated feature, *Raggedy Ann & Andy: A Musical Adventure*, as did her spouse, lyricist Sheldon Harnick (*Fiddler on the Roof, Fiorello!*). Gray recalled:

> It was through Burton Lane. He thought that I would be right for it . . . I think Burton recorded [the song demos] in his apartment in New York and sent it to California. They called me and said, "Would you audition?" and I said, "Of course, I'd audition!"
>
> When I went out to California with Sheldon to do the singing for Heidi, they asked me to do the whole thing—the singing and the dialogue.[1] The first time, we did the songs, and all of the music, and the second time we did all of the dialogue.
>
> A lot of it had already been recorded. Lorne Greene and Sammy Davis Jr. were not there, obviously because they had other work to do. When I was speaking as Heidi with Lorne Greene, I heard him in my earphone. I was used to this kind of work because I had done so much radio for so long.
>
> The second time, I brought my son, Matthew, out to California for the rest of the recording. The funny thing is that they needed an owl sound— and being our kid, just for the fun of it, he made an owl sound because he's very good at doing that. They said, "Oh, that's just what we need! Wonderful!"

Pamelyn Ferdin, the voice of Klara, worked in earlier sessions with the rest of the cast, including Janet

Bonanza stars Michael Landon and Lorne Greene each contributed to the Hanna-Barbera legacy: Landon hosted *The Funtastic World of Hanna-Barbera Arena Show* for NBC and Greene voiced the grandfather in the feature *Heidi's Song* and Noah for the video series *The Greatest Adventure: Stories from the Bible*. Photograph by Larry Bessel. *Los Angeles Times* Photographic Collection. Department of Special Collections, UCLA. (CC-BY-4.0.)

Waldo, Joan Gerber, Michael Bell, Virginia Gregg, and Fritz Feld. "I think you lose so much when the parts are recorded separately," recalled Ferdin. "If you weren't speaking in the scene, you sat and watched."

▲▼▲▼

In early 1982, *Millimeter Magazine* ran a cover story on *Heidi's Song*, mentioning how the filmmakers were making major revisions to what would be their most ambitious project. Director Robert Taylor was enlisted to helm the film while it was in progress. One sequence that seems to be added begins when Heidi's grandfather tells her about eerie mythical creatures, followed by an imaginative animated nightmare sequence. A microcosm of the film itself,

Heidi is intermittently frightened and enchanted by the alternately scary and cute creatures. Another sequence brings Sammy Davis Jr. back to Hanna-Barbera animation for the first time since *Alice in Wonderland*. "Ode to a Rat" is a spectacular, fully animated showstopper that allows Hoyt Curtin's big band brass section to cut loose. Curtin's signature discordant closing stabs, so familiar from the end of *Scooby-Doo* and other H-B series) are a treat in full stereo.

Hopes were high for *Heidi's Song*. Paramount Pictures released it in November 1982 for the Thanksgiving holiday. A massive "Heidi's Dream" Thanksgiving Day float appeared on the Macy's parade TV broadcast as the parade hosts promoted the film from their script. Building a big-screen musical around a chipper, optimistic youngster may have seemed out of touch, but Broadway's *Annie* was a megahit in the unlikely midst of the disco seventies. Much was made of the purchase of *Annie*'s screen rights, the director (John Huston), and the cast (Albert Finney and Carol Burnett).

The movie versions of *Annie* and *Heidi's Song* each "underperformed" at the box office. Both films belied their behind-the-scenes challenges to add a little edge in order to attract members of the audience resistant to sunshine-sprinkled buoyancy. Even if that was accomplished, the Star Wars and Indiana Jones era was underway and family films were changing. Soon the animated musical feature would change as well. *The Little Mermaid* would deftly balance the classic with the contemporary, the sweet with the sharp. Mark Evanier theorized that the very strength Hanna-Barbera had in creating entertaining animated episodes for television worked against them in features. "It was difficult to focus on big projects like features," he said. "Hanna-Barbera did features when time allowed between series and other work. It was on-again, off-again, with the available staff. So the changes in staffing would affect how the sequences turned out. Sometimes it showed within the sequences—or a film that seems to change gradually from the beginning to the end."

Taylor's other major project at the studio was the ill-fated but equally ambitious TV feature *Rock Odyssey*, which covers four decades of pop music through the experiences of a young star. This was a case of Hanna-Barbera struggling to reach a wider range of young audiences and attempting creative directions that concerned Taft Broadcasting and ABC. Barbera appeared on Dinah Shore's daytime TV talk show and mentioned *Rock Odyssey* among other projects and showed a clip. As of this writing, it was not broadcast or released in the US except for a Los Angeles animation festival screening in 1987.

"I had a lot of hope for that," said artist Pete Alvarado in a 1990 interview with John Cawley. "I think we did a lot of nice work on that thing, but it just never seemed to get off the ground. I think most of us in the business are so close to these things, we don't really know sometimes when we have something."

▲▼▲▼▲▼

Hanna-Barbera's television and new video business balanced new properties with revivals of established properties. *The Flintstones*, still going strong in daytime syndication, continued to return in new configurations.

The eighties began with *The Flintstones Comedy Show* (later *The Flintstone Funnies* and *Flintstones Frolics*), a mixed bag of half-hours and shorts, among them Tex Avery's *Dino and Cavemouse* (featuring vintage Curtin and de Mello cues); stories with Wilma and Betty as part-time reporters; Fred and Barney as part-time policemen (partnered with the Schmoo from the *L'il Abner* comic strip); Pebbles, Bamm-Bamm, and Dino as a stone-age Mystery Incorporated; and new situations with the Flintstones and their ghoulish neighbors, the Frankenstones. The inspired casting of Charles Nelson Reilly (*Match Game, The Ghost and Mrs. Muir*) as TV repairman Frank Frankenstone as an adversary for Fred (Henry Corden) created fresh antics for Saturday morning. Ruta Lee (*Witness for the Prosecution, The Twilight Zone*) used her signature throaty laugh for Hidea Frankenstone.

"Hanna-Barbera was a company that knew what the hell they were doing," Lee told *TV Confidential* host Ed Robertson. "Whenever you have an opportunity to work off another actor or group of actors in real time, it's always better, so much better, because it's like live theater . . . I just thought it was one of my more wonderful experiences." (Lee noted that, in some episodes, Reilly was not present if he was directing plays at Burt Reynolds's theater in Florida and the difference is noticeable.)

▲▼▲▼▲▼

A revised and short-lived "Electronic" Talking View-Master came along in the 1980s. It was a vast improvement over the original, with enhanced sound quality and authentic recordings. Instead of hard plastic records, this model used thin "flexi-disc" records in a long "blister-pack" card next to the 3-D reel. This time, View-Master obtained several soundtracks in clip form, many never released on commercial records, like Bugs Bunny in *Big Top Bunny* and Scooby-Doo in *That's Snow Ghost*. This was the only instance in which Ted Nichols's "Where Are You?" cues were commercially available in retail audio form. The sound and visuals were excellent but the record and slide card proved flimsy; the slightest "bow" and the record could stick and fail to revolve.

The last time Tom and Jerry appeared on a new vinyl record was in a Peter Pan read-along called *Astrocat and Mouse*. Also released on audio cassette, this original story begins with a page of chasing, which gets them kicked out of the house and leads to Tom learning about his opportunity to go places, including outer space. Along with two Pound Puppies read-alongs, this was a return to H-B character recordings for Peter Pan Records veterans Herb Davidson and Charlotte Sanders.

As the record industry began to move away from vinyl records altogether, children's recordings were in limbo, some only available on cassette before compact discs took a firmer hold. Peter Pan released a handful of Hanna-Barbera read-along books and

cassettes exclusively in that format, two featuring *The Flintstones* and another two starring *The Jetsons*. All were adapted from paperback children's books.

▲▼▲▼▲▼

The Jetson storybooks were part of the merchandising blitz that accompanied the much-heralded revival of the 1962 series. The long-awaited opportunity to add episodes to the original twenty-four was a result of a boom in daytime syndicated animated series, beginning with Filmation's immensely popular *He-Man and the Masters of the Universe*. The daytime children's TV market required a new episode every day for thirteen weeks, totaling sixty-five half hours per season (it was usually sixteen to seventeen episodes on Saturday mornings), throwing the TV animation industry into a frenzy of activity. New companies like DIC were striking gold with series like *Inspector Gadget* and established firms like Rankin/Bass hit big with *ThunderCats*.

The Jetsons seemed like a natural for an extension. Some of the original artists were involved including story artist Tony Benedict. Joe Barbera, Gordon Hunt, and Andrea Romano brought back the original voice cast: Penny Singleton, Janet Waldo, Daws Butler, Jean Vander Pyl, and George O'Hanlon. O'Hanlon was by this time legally blind, but Hunt directed him with a "read-and-repeat" approach.

The background scores for most of the half hours were recorded in stereo. This had become standard for new television programs by 1985, but unusual for classic H-B animation. The Jetsons became the first of the early H-B characters to be heard in stereo in their original series format.

Although all the elements seemed to be in place, Hanna-Barbera simply could not be the same up-and-coming studio it was in 1962, with the "let's put on a show" energy of a smaller, sky's-the-limit company. The production pace was faster and the hierarchy had drastically changed. Several of the original artists and writers were involved, as well as new talents in the industry, so there were some new episodes, several among the fifty-one new episodes, that stood out among the others.

The Jetsons revival did well enough, however, to make the characters become "top of mind" to the youngest generation as well as its original viewers without drastically changing the concept. The business numbers convinced Universal to back a feature film.

▲▼▲▼▲▼

As Saturday morning was beginning to fade, Disney stepped into daytime with Disney Afternoon, a two-hour block of popular shows. This became the cartoon business game grid before cable TV, home video, and streaming.

Hanna-Barbera had no such daily block, but it did establish a Sunday morning two-hour block in major cities. Almost two dozen shows circulated through *The Funtastic World of Hanna-Barbera* over its nine-year run, combining revivals with classic characters like Jonny Quest, Yogi Bear, and his friends, along with new series like *Galtar and the Golden Lance* and *Sky Commanders*. The theme, sung by Scatman Crothers, was a personal favorite of Hollywood film and TV composer Ron Jones (*Star Trek: The Next Generation*, *Family Guy*). Jones told the author:

> We were assigned to add some new sounds to Hanna-Barbera shows, but keep them catchy and fun like they always were. I particularly liked *Funtastic World*. That one really worked great. They used it for *Yogi's Treasure Hunt* when it was a separate show, too.
>
> I learned so much from working for Hoyt Curtin. The way he composed for the studio, and the techniques—I brought all of that with me in my other work. When I went to Disney for *DuckTales*, I did a lot of extra cues and they kept asking me why, but I knew because of my experience at H-B and with Hoyt that they were going to need specific ones for settings they had not written yet. You had to anticipate all that or you got stuck. That came from Hoyt.

Because of the talents he nurtured during this period, the contributions of Daws Butler to the animation and recording industry are incalculable. Every week, Butler would hold workshops at his home for aspiring voice actors. He offered instructive cassettes and advice by mail as well. One of these mail correspondents was Nancy Cartwright, who was one of the students Butler believed was certain of success. Her fame as Bart Simpson would become worldwide after his passing. Acting on the advice of Disney imagineer Les Perkins (who founded the Disney Character Voices Division), Jymn Magon visited his classes to cast Walt Disney Records read-alongs, some of the earliest work for Corey Burton, Linda Gary, Tony Pope, Patty Parris, and other Butler students.

"Daws is an inspiration as a human being as well as a great actor," said Bob Bergen, the voice of Porky Pig, who divides his work schedule with teaching. "I think it's my responsibility to teach the way he did because I know I was fortunate to have known him, to be in this business. It's more than just about getting jobs and getting ahead."

Daws was unable to voice one of his many signature characters for 1988's *New Yogi Bear Show*. One of his students, Greg Burson, reluctantly took his place. It was not easy for Burson, as none of his friends wanted anyone but Daws to do those voices professionally, including themselves. Butler passed away the same year. His influence on voice acting for animation, and his legacy as a human being, is alive and well.

▲▼▲▼▲▼

The Universal Studios Hollywood complex is walking distance from Hanna-Barbera's studio buildings. This made it possible for hundreds of staff members from each company to create a symbolic connection to exciting projects ahead for them. Hand-in-hand, they formed a line that stretched from Hanna-Barbera on 3400 Cahuenga, along the walkway that crosses over Highway 101 to Universal City Plaza on the other side.

▲▼▲▼▲▼

RIDE INTO THE WORLD OF ANIMATION!

Positioned near the front entrance, the Funtastic World of Hanna-Barbera was the first attraction most guests saw as they entered Universal Studios Florida.

One project was a 1990 theme park attraction called The Funtastic World of Hanna-Barbera, a motion-control ride at the Orlando, Florida, version of Universal's theme park. Popular for twelve years, the attraction included a pre-show video featuring Bill and Joe, and an elaborate Hanna-Barbera shop.

Also in 1990, *Jetsons the Movie* became the fourth animated feature for the studio and the first of several coproductions with Universal. A casting controversy shadowed the film for many years. Hanna and Barbera's creative control was limited, as employees of parent company Taft and as partners with Universal—a division of MCA, which boasted a powerful music division. One of MCA's contract singing stars, teen pop queen Tiffany, was signed to sing for Judy Jetson. The music was eighties pop, programmed to sell to kids, tweens, and teens, the same way The Partridge Family did in the seventies and Disney Channel stars would a few years later.

MCA's *Jetsons the Movie* album is designed to play more like an '80s pop album than a traditional movie soundtrack. The format of the cast album and the soundtrack for mainstream pop-oriented features was being replaced by songs of equal programming weight, like a radio station format, with nothing to change the genre level. The songs could vary in tempo, but in the context of a dance album, as if a DJ were playing it at a party. In hindsight, the songs on the *Jetsons the Movie* soundtrack album can now be placed in the "groovy" world where Hanna-Barbera's '60 and '70s cartoons and records also live. They accomplish what they set out to do. It is regrettable, though, that the album does not present John Debney's arrangement of the theme song as it was heard (and cheered) at the start of the film.

It was an MCA decision to cast Tiffany in the speaking voice of Judy in addition to singing. Barbera had no final control over the decision. Janet Waldo's Judy Jetson dialogue (except for a few short phrases) was replaced by Tiffany in the role. Angry fans wrote letters and refused to see the film. Reports differ as to whether speaking for Judy really mattered much

Aimed at teens and young adults, MCA's soundtrack album for *Jetsons the Movie* was formatted completely as a pop disc without background instrumentals.

to the young star or the "bigger picture" of sales and marketing. The subsequent fallout from some fans was targeted at Tiffany, regardless of whether it was really her choice to take the speaking voice. Either way, the misguided decision did no one much good. At an event celebrating Don Messick, Barbera made a point to publicly apologize to a gracious Waldo, who continued to voice Judy and other characters for subsequent H-B projects.

Jetsons the Movie score composer John Debney is another successful Hollywood talent who greatly values what he learned from his early days at Hanna-Barbera with Hoyt Curtin. Debney is greatly responsible for keeping the original Curtin theme song in *Jetsons the Movie*. There was an effort to replace the iconic Jetsons theme from the beginning of the movie with a Tiffany pop song. Debney respectfully but resolutely held his ground, insisting that all audi-

ences will expect to hear "Meet George Jetson" at the beginning. When the film opened in theaters, the audience cheered the moment the first few notes were heard, accompanied by a musical Hanna-Barbera graphic. Applause greeted the entire title sequence. The following year, some decision makers behind the first *Addams Family* movie wanted to leave out Vic Mizzy's unforgettable finger-snapping theme. Test audiences saw *Addams* trailers with and without the theme and common sense prevailed.

▲▼▲▼▲▼

Jetsons the Movie was not the blockbuster that all the fast-food toys, publicity, and hype anticipated, but it was an attempt to try new techniques, make the characters seem more dimensional, and experiment with computer technology, all of which are elements for which Hanna-Barbera is usually not given credit. There was also an environmental message folded in "without preaching," the kind of thing Bill Hanna found detrimental to entertainment if not done with skill and finesse.

"The farewell sequence in the film is bittersweet and always makes me tear up notably for two core reasons," said cinema historian Lee Gambin in his detailed Blu-ray commentary.

> There is a moment shared between Elroy and his dad where Elroy laments having to leave his new friends . . . George agrees with him that having to say goodbye is hard and having to leave is incredibly difficult . . . Also, the film seems to have this sentiment, lingering for a moment with George saying the line and then looking sadly, as if directly at us. It's as if Bill Hanna and Joe Barbera are paying tribute to their wonderful George O'Hanlon and it's as if George Jetson himself is paying tribute to the man who gave him life since the early sixties.

Indeed, the sense of farewell going on behind the scenes had to find its way into the film. George O'Hanlon and Mel Blanc passed away before it was released.

Over the years, Hanna got an exhaustive amount of work out the door with the help of animation professionals in a studio that was lively and energizing. He also was constantly pressured by time and budgets and personalities. Meanwhile, Barbera oversaw story development but spent a lot of time in the field, taking meetings to present ideas, negotiate deals, untangle business issues, and also deal with personalities. *Jetsons the Movie* was the last feature that both partners worked on as a team. Based on their personal assessments, perhaps no other project more sharply exemplifies the dichotomy of who they were, how they perceived things, and how their responsibilities differed.

Bill Hanna looked at *Jetsons the Movie* as the bookend of the partnership. He put it this way:

> It was a joyous and completely hands-on project for us . . . A moviola was set up for us in a room on the second floor of the administration building and the two of us supervised the editing of virtually every foot of film that came in from dailies . . . Joe and I worked as closely together on the film as we had on any of the first shows we produced during the early years of our partnership.

On the other hand, as Barbera recalled:

> The folks putting up the money have a very natural urge to take over everything. When I, at last, had had enough, I walked out on the project. And I can't really say much more about the movie, because I've never had the heart to go see it . . . [it] was not a happy experience.

Yet, like the very different Richard M. and Robert B. Sherman, they had "lots in common where it really counts," making a dynamic team with extraordinary accomplishments.

Chapter 25

THE MAN CALLED SPIELROCK

~~~~~~

Flintstones! Meet the Flintstones!
They're the modern stone-age fam-i-ly!
—JOHN CANDY, LEADING A BUSLOAD OF TRAVELERS (INCLUDING
STEVE MARTIN) IN *PLANES, TRAINS, AND AUTOMOBILES* (1987)

Cartoons became "important" in the late eighties. The work of the Walt Disney Studios, which even detractors admitted raised animation beyond movie theater filler, was rarely the subject of serious historical analysis. Pioneering authors like Leonard Maltin and John Canemaker brought forth landmark newsletters and books extolling the worth of animation and the seldom-recognized people who made it. The combined efforts of people within the industry and the public—generations raised on the art and intimately more cognizant of its worth—saw classic animation being presented in retrospectives, art displayed in galleries, and most dramatically, mainstream movies embracing the characters, studios, and artists if not through honors, then through affectionate emulation.

Who Framed Roger Rabbit? was a turning point. A Steven Spielberg film coproduced by Walt Disney Pictures under its not-necessarily-for-kids Touchstone banner, it offered a cameo appearance to almost every famous theatrical cartoon character ever created. Spielberg became active in animation and Hollywood took notice. When one of the most successful and influential filmmakers in history not only watches cartoons but produces them (*Tiny Toon Adventures, Animaniacs*) and collects memorabilia, the image is forever changed, just as Stanley Kubrick and George Lucas helped change science fiction and the DC and Marvel features elevated comic book heroes to the "A" list. Spielberg also coproduced an animated feature that outperformed Disney at the box office: *An American Tail.* It was directed by Don Bluth, who controversially led a group of artists out of the Disney studio in the middle of a film. Bluth and Spielberg scored again with *The Land before Time*, a charming adventure about young dinosaurs that spawned a multifilm video franchise. Spielberg collected animation cels, which went from being cheap souvenirs to expensive rarities. Cels from actual productions became prized items, as did specially created cels called "limited editions" signed by famous artists, including Bill Hanna and Joe Barbera.

The Flintstones counted Spielberg among its fans, along with *Twilight Zone* creator Rod Serling and movie legend Greta Garbo. Hanna-Barbera's crown jewel had been in discussion for a live-action feature since the late eighties with several sets of actors in consideration and a growing pile of scripts. One writer who asked for a try at revising the script was Brian Levant. The young director had accomplished the impossible before. He created *Still the Beaver*, later *The New Leave It to Beaver*, a revival series with most of the original cast that stayed true to the original and gained a young audience without alienating its enormous fan base. Spielberg was impressed with Levant's enthusiasm for all things Flintstone as well.

▲▼▲▼▲▼

The big-screen vision of Bedrock was getting underway when Hanna and Barbera, now in their eighties, continued their long workdays at the studio they loved. When a struggling Taft Broadcasting sold its company to Great American Broadcasting in the late eighties, the company appointed David Kirchner as chairman of Hanna-Barbera, the first time a specific individual held such a position. (Ruby-Spears had also been purchased by Taft in the late seventies.) Kirchner was a fast-rising writer and artist. Among his credits were the *Rose Petal Place* franchise, a success in animation, toys, and records. The story and characters for *An American Tail* were his creations as well.

Hanna-Barbera's feature film division had completed two more animated theatrical coproductions based on licensed characters (1986's *GoBots: Battle of the Rock Lords* and 1987's *Ultraman: The Adventure Begins*). Joe Barbera had interested Joe Roth at 20th Century-Fox and broadcasting mogul Ted Turner in Tom and Jerry's first theatrical feature. The flamboyant Turner revolutionized television on cable first by transforming a small UHF station into a cable giant TBS, which regularly aired *The Flintstones*, and cre-

Steven Spielberg's love of cartoons led to several major animation-related projects including 1994's *The Flintstones* feature film. Photo by Gage Skidmore. (CC-BY-SA-2.0, Wikimedia Commons.)

ated CNN, the first twenty-four-hour news channel. Kirchner passed on the Tom and Jerry movie project but permitted Barbera to pursue it independently. Film Roman (*The Simpsons*, *Garfield*) coproduced it with Barbera and a German company after Turner left the project as well.

Tom and Jerry: The Movie was, like *Heidi's Song* and *Jetsons the Movie*, filled with many bright spots. Barbera was proud of the fact that its premiere in Europe was followed by weeks of box-office success. Henry Mancini wrote a melodious score with original songs with lyrics by another multiple Oscar winner, Leslie Bricusse (*Doctor Dolittle*, *Willy Wonka and the Chocolate Factory*, *Scrooge*).

The Walt Disney Company was only a few months away from purchasing Miramax Pictures when the latter released *Tom and Jerry: The Movie*. The Disney-MGM Studio Theme Park (now Disney's Hollywood

Multiple Academy Award winners Henry Mancini (*The Pink Panther, Days of Wine and Roses,* "Moon River") and Leslie Bricusse (*Willy Wonka and the Chocolate Factory, Doctor Dolittle, Scrooge*) brought their talents to *Tom and Jerry: The Movie.*

Studios) had opened as the third *Walt Disney World* theme park. Between the MGM and Miramax connections, Disney promoted *Tom and Jerry: The Movie* in the park by creating costumed versions of the famous duo for park guests to meet and greet. Disney Parks and Resorts Marketing Advertising Creative (later called "Yellow Shoes") produced a thirty-second TV commercial featuring the costumed Tom chasing Jerry around the theme park as Mancini's score played.

The same park runs a condensed version of the 1962 MGM short, *Mouse into Space*, every sixty minutes daily at the Sci-Fi Dine-In Theater Restaurant. Directed by Gene Deitch, it gives Hanna and Barbera's characters an ongoing Disney park presence. Near the center of the park for many years, the names of William Hanna and Joseph Barbera were displayed on plaques with other inductees into the Academy of

Television Arts and Sciences Hall of Fame, an honor also commemorated at the Academy's Hollywood location.

▲▼▲▼▲▼

Honors were not awaiting *Tom and Jerry: The Movie* when it arrived in US theaters. The concept of Tom and Jerry talking was an interesting idea, nicely cast with fine, earnest performances by Richard Kind (*Mad about You, Spin City*) and Dana Hill (*National Lampoon's European Vacation, Shoot the Moon*). Hill, who passed away at only thirty-two, was at the top of the voice-acting trade, even playing Jerry's brother on *Tom and Jerry Kids*. Here was a case not unlike the recasting of Yogi Bear or one of his pals for a children's record. But rather than a familiar voice not sounding quite right, this time the voice one might anticipate for a previously mute character might not

Once Upon a Forest was the last feature released solely under the Hanna-Barbera Productions banner.

match. Plus for most of the film, they became friends to help nice characters defeat mean ones. This must have been asking too much for most audiences to accept (except for the European audiences Barbera encountered). The likable score, solid production values by Film Roman, and fine voice work by H-B favorites Henry Gibson and Howard Morris were not enough to make it a cohesive whole.

It was a learning experience, however. Some thought Tom and Jerry were finished in the feature-length format, much less short cartoons, and neither was far from true. If anything, this film was a necessary exercise in getting the characters to work in the feature format, just as *The Flintstones*, *Top Cat*, and *The Jetsons* were steps toward creating effective half-hour cartoons for television.

Henry Mancini's work in animation is rarely discussed, but taken as independent works, both *Tom*

and Jerry: The Movie, released with the songs on MCA Records, and Disney's *The Great Mouse Detective*, which was issued eight years after the film by Varese Sarabande Records, earned their place in his stellar career. Also remarkable is that Mancini's influence affected the jazz sound of TV, which in turn helped make possible Hoyt Curtin's Hanna-Barbera classic sound. Tom and Jerry's first attempt at feature-length films was predicted by some to be their last. Little did they know what chases were ahead.

▲▼▲▼▲

The final theatrical feature made exclusively under the Hanna-Barbera Productions name was 1993's *Once Upon a Forest*, a gentle adventure based on a Welsh tale. It was the story of young creatures called Furlings, resembling Fievel and company from the

American Tail franchise. *Once Upon a Forest* was advertised as being "from the creator of *An American Tail*." It was David Kirchner's film, who put a personal stamp on it as did Hanna, who loved the wilderness and was proud of the finished product, lavishly animated at several global studios.

The mellifluous score by Oscar-winner James Horner (*Titanic*, *Avatar*, *The Rocketeer*) plays a crucial role in driving the emotional shifts from drama to comedy in the film. *Once Upon a Forest* was released on the 20th Century Fox music label, making both the film and the soundtrack album part of the Disney library as of this writing. Michael Crawford proved a natural for expressive animation acting as the wise old badger Cornelius, bringing depth and sincerity to "Please Wake Up," one of the film's few songs. Reportedly, the mere thought of singing to a young person on the verge of death was so sorrowful to Crawford that he was fighting tears during the recording. Except for "Please Wake Up," the film is largely bright and upbeat despite the urgency of the story line and underlying subject. The film is very upbeat, with an effusive gospel number by Ben Vereen and the Andraé Crouch Singers. Several young voice actors were on their way to big careers, including Elisabeth Moss (*Mad Men*) and Will Estes (*Blue Bloods*), who also voiced Jonny Quest in the 1992 direct-to-video feature, *Jonny's Golden Quest*.

With the theatrical movie market saturated with high-profile family films, the low-key *Once Upon a Forest* was crowded out of the running. However, along with *Charlotte's Web*, this feature is not tied to a specific era of popular culture and continues to run for generations, in whatever viewing platform is in vogue.

In addition to *Jetsons the Movie* and *Jonny's Golden Quest*, John Debney composed the score for *I Yabba Dabba Doo!* (1993), a TV movie celebrating the marriage of Pebbles and Bamm-Bamm. Voicing the happy couple were Megan Mulally (*Will and Grace*, *Bob's Burgers*) and Jerry Houser (*Summer of '42*, *The Brady Brides*), both prolific in cartoon voices as well as on-camera acting. Henry Corden and Jean Vander Pyl

were joined by Frank Welker as Barney and B. J. Ward as Betty. (Messrs. Hanna and Barbera also showed up in animated form at the wedding reception.)

▲▼▲▼▲▼

Ted Turner's Turner Broadcasting outbid several major corporations for Hanna-Barbera in 1991—even Disney CEO Michael Eisner considered the purchase. The vast library was key to the 1992 launch of the first twenty-four-hour all-animation cable network. Hanna-Barbera programming dominated Cartoon Network when it was founded by Betty Cohen in 1992.

One of the advantages Spielberg's live-action version of *The Flintstones* enjoyed was the new phenomenon of cable marathons. Enjoying round-the-clock episodes of the original *Flintstones* allowed viewers to look forward to the new film. It was marketing "leverage" that sold the new movies for hours and days at a time.

One of the most powerful elements is the theme song. Longtime Spielberg producer Kathleen Kennedy—unlike those who saw no value in "Meet George Jetson" or the finger-snapping *Addams Family* theme for reboots and revivals—appreciated and encouraged the use of "Meet the Flintstones." Kennedy was not the first Hollywood powerbroker to recognize this fact. As mentioned earlier, writer/director John Hughes knew it when creating John Candy's "Meet the Flintstones" sing-along scene in 1987's *Planes, Trains, and Automobiles*. In the trailer, the scene was strategically positioned right before the words, "Paramount Pictures Presents." Joe Barbera sometimes gave people cash if they could sing all the words, including "through the courtesy of Fred's two feet."

"It was Kathleen's idea to use 'Meet the Flintstones' in trailers for *The Flintstones* movie, played in theaters right before *Jurassic Park*, which was huge," said Flintstones director Brian Levant. "Everyone knows it, but just in case, they put the words on the screen, so the whole theater could sing along."

This positive association with the aspects of what made audiences love the original property drove them into the theater to make it one of the year's box-office hits. Based on the song mix, MCA Records skewed the target age to teens and adults for *The Flintstones*, a little higher than the tween target for *Jetsons the Movie*. The overall sound rocked harder than the TV cartoons did, creating what MCA believed could sell as a pop soundtrack compilation in the nineties. The idea of asking the B-52s to become the "B.C. 52's" is a clever gag befitting the original show and its spinoffs. A short suite of background music by composer David Newman closes out the album. (In the CD era, pop compilation soundtracks began the general practice of putting instrumental suites at the end.)

On his 2001 talk show *Dinner for Five,* host Jon Favreau mentioned how he and other actors who fit the physical description of Fred Flintstone were tested for the lead role. Spielberg personally asked John Goodman (*Roseanne, Monsters, Inc.*) to play Fred, with Elizabeth Perkins (*Big*) as Wilma, and Rick Moranis (*SCTV, Honey, I Shrunk the Kids*) as Barney.

The movie's Betty Rubble, Rosie O'Donnell, suggested that the film include "The Bedrock Twitch" from the 1962 episode. "When we met, Rosie started singing all the songs from the show," said Levant. "She was a huge fan and knew all kinds of things about it. The song is in there because of her." It's one of the first songs heard in the movie, in addition to Hoyt Curtin's "Rise and Shine," which was incorporated into the score but is not on the album.

"Hoyt Curtin is one of the superstars of Hanna-Barbera," said Levant to Gilbert Gottfried and Frank Santopadre on their *Amazing Colossal Podcast.*

"We shout him out on this show often," said Santopadre.

Also notable in the soundtrack is a cover version of "Rock with the Caveman," a 1956 hit in Britain for Tommy Steele, a pop star before he transitioned to the musical stage with *Half a Sixpence* on London's West End and Broadway and the screen films like *The Happiest Millionaire*. MCA gave the album, titled

The Flintstones: Music from Bedrock, a substantial promotional campaign with a party for the cast and artists, captured in a video on the DVD release. A promotional CD called *Kave Radio Bedrock* was also distributed to radio stations with a fifteen-minute simulated radio show, songs from the album, and a few "drop-ins" dialogue samples from the soundtrack. The B.C.-52's version of "Meet the Flintstones" was also released internationally as a CD single.

▴▾▴▾▴▾

Rhino Records, which began as a unique Los Angeles record store, blossomed into the most innovative and eclectic pop culture audio and video company of the late twentieth century. In the nineties, it was also the foremost producer of Hanna-Barbera recordings. It is not an exaggeration to recount the rejoicing among Flintstone enthusiasts when Rhino Records released *The Flintstones: Modern Stone-Age Melodies—Original Songs from the Classic TV Soundtrack*. For the first time, an audio collection of the "real" show songs and music was gathered on one CD or audio cassette. These were not cover versions, bootlegs, or easy pickups from random film prints or videos.

Each selection was lovingly curated by historian Earl Kress from the finest sources available, carefully edited, and remixed. When some Rhino staffers expressed doubts about including Hoyt Curtin's underscore as well, Kress got their permission to add a cue or two after most of the songs, doubling a lot of the tracks. Most selections are from soundtracks, but a few were found without dialogue and sound effects, like the LP version of "Laugh Laugh" by the Beau Brummels, the single release of "Open Up Your Heart" by Pebbles and Bamm-Bamm, and an extended cut of James Darren's "Surfin' Craze." Kress also located the stereophonic edition of *The Man Called Flintstone* HBR studio album and included the theme, plus the soundtrack promo LP track of "They'll Never Split Us Apart" with Marty Paich's Orchestra from *Alice in Wonderland* with Fred and Barney as the two-headed, song-and-dance caterpillar.

▴▾▴▾▴▾

The Flintstones' recording career saw a dramatic resurgence in the nineties. Even before the movie and the Cartoon Network, the USA Network had been broadcasting an abundance of cartoons from Hanna-Barbera and other studios.

At this point, there were a handful of *Flintstones* revivals being seen in addition to the 1960–1966 series. Henry Corden's Fred was becoming more familiar to audiences, though Alan Reed would always be cherished as the original Fred. Corden had gradually developed his own interpretation of Fred as time went on. He stayed closer to his own voice and strove less toward sounding like Reed. The first album headlined by Corden with Jean Vander Pyl as Wilma was 1993's *The Flintstones Present "A Christmas in Bedrock"* on Rhino Records, with Frank Welker as Barney and B. J. Ward as Betty.

Back in the Hanna-Barbera Cartoon Series record days, Jean Vander Pyl voiced Wilma and Pebbles with Alan Reed on a few albums but never worked with Corden. On Rhino Records, Vander Pyl and Corden perform a "talk-sing" tune together called "The Flintstone Way." Hearing the two of them giving a sincere impression of having fun is a rare gem, as well as their only commercially released duet on recordings. At the very end, Vander Pyl can be heard gently reacting to the experience as the song fades, saying, "That was fun!" While the entire cast is given the chance to sing and talk through the album of mostly original songs, Corden's singing range is very much in evidence. However, it is B. J. Ward who gives Betty Rubble her first chance to take center stage as a singer since another B. J.—Baker—sang for Bea Benederet in the original series. Classically trained, Ward makes her presence known in each song that includes Betty without upstaging the other cast members, but her solo in "Buffalo Christmas Dance" is one of those tracks worth repeating. Her voice adds poignancy to the finale tune, "Noel All's Well," sung by the whole cast.

A Christmas in Bedrock is the only album featuring this particular cast singing songs together. However, all four did return to provide dialogue for a 1996 Christmas R&B compilation album called *A Flintstone Motown Christmas*. It's a collection of classic Motown R&B holiday hits with the Flintstones and Rubbles speaking between the songs. The adventure is described on the package in this way: "It's Christmas and the Flintstones plan to spend this Christmas in New Rock City . . . but along the way, they get lost and are guided by a star to that magic, musical town of Motown where they discover the true spirit of Christmas." The artists include Diana Ross and the Supremes, Smokey Robinson and the Miracles, The Jackson 5, and The Temptations. In addition to the two stone-age couples, Pebbles and Bamm-Bamm are also along for the ride. Russi Taylor, voice of Minnie Mouse, Strawberry Shortcake, Martin of *The Simpsons*, and many more, is heard in a rare Hanna-Barbera album appearance as Pebbles. Taylor was the third teen Pebbles in the eighties on *The Flintstone Comedy Show*, but here she voices a baby Pebbles.

▲▼▲▼▲

Earl Kress arguably did more to bring the music and audio of Hanna-Barbera, commercially and officially, to the public than anyone else in the 1990s. There is one Rhino Records project in particular that bears the stamp of his knowledge, research, writing, and acting talent like no other. *The Flintstones Story: Meet the Flintstones in the First Authorized Biography of the Modern Stone-Age Family* (1994) stars Henry Corden, Jean Vander Pyl, Frank Welker, and B. J. Ward again in the leads, re-creating moments from the lives of the modern stone-age family. Kress plays one or two small roles and filled the background with Hoyt Curtin music and classic sound effects.

Kress managed this by adapting sequences from series scripts and original sections that could have taken place during the ABC prime-time run. The recording offers a humorous explanation of how Bedrock got its name worthy of early H-B writer and pun master Charles Shows. There are also sequences about the meeting of Wilma and Betty as youngsters, Fred and Barney in school, and stories about

Fred, Wilma, Barney, Betty, and the kids take a holiday road trip, set to the music of Motown.

the Flintstone and Rubble marriages. Kress adapted "Bachelor Daze" by Ralph Goodman and Herbert Finn, in which the foursome work at a posh resort pretending to be affluent; "Dress Rehearsal" aka "The Blessed Event" by Harvey Bullock and R. S. Allen; describing the circumstances surrounding Pebbles's birth, and the final Flintstones episode about Grandpa Flintstone, "The Story of Rocky's Raiders" by Joanna Lee. This audio production was released only on cassette.

For a Hanna-Barbera children's educational video called *Rappin' and Rhymin'* (1991), Corden and Welker overdubbed early Fred and Barney clips, along with Greg Burson as Yogi and Don Messick as Boo-Boo. Veteran stage musical director and album producer Bruce Kimmel directed a talented cast of young adults and children in songs that taught simple lessons through rap and hip-hop music arranged in a vari-

ety of energy levels. No companion album resulted despite the variety of songs cowritten by Norman Martin, who worked on projects for TV, stage, and records for Shari Lewis, Dinah Shore, the Muppets, and Ben Vereen.

In 1997, Pebbles and Bamm-Bamm appeared in a Public Television series for young children called *Cave Kids*. They were toddlers again this time, but able to speak to animals and fanciful creatures. Along with Dino, the two characters were restored somewhat to their original design, but placed in imaginary playtime adventures with gentle lessons. Each of the eight episodes ended with a song, visualized with animated graphics and snippets from the adventure—the sort of thing Hanna-Barbera had been doing since the '60s but became known as a "music video." Instead of "yabba dabba doo" or the teen Pebbles's "yabba dabba doozy," the Cave Kids said, "Ugga bugga boo!"

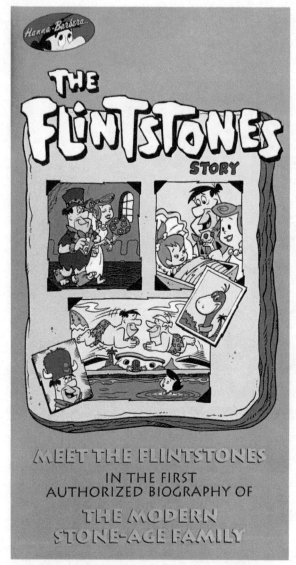

The back stories of the characters and the wedding of Fred and Wilma are chronicled on this album, set to Hoyt Curtin's original Hanna-Barbera background music.

Coincidentally or not, this was the lodge phrase that opened every episode of Mel Blanc's 1946 radio sitcom ("Ugga bugga boo, everybody!").

The Kid Rhino children's label released an audio cassette with sing-along lyrics for the series. It included the theme and six songs, four of which were heard on the show. Aria Curzon (*The Land before Time* videos, *Adventures in Odyssey*) voices Bamm-Bamm.

E. G. Daily (*Rugrats*, *Powerpuff Girls*) sings for Pebbles. (Daily also dubbed in the voice of Bamm-Bamm for *The Flintstones* 1994 live-action film.) *Cave Kids* had the potential for more than a mere eight episodes, but PBS opted for a more economical heavy repeat cycle. Three home videos were also released.

▲▼▲▼▲

According to director Brian Levant, two additional sequels to the first Flintstone live-action theatrical movie were about to be filmed at the same time, presumably with the same cast. Levant said that Goodman did not refuse to return as Fred while the next two films were in prep mode. However, as Levant explained: "After everybody in every airport he ever went to said, 'Yabba dabba doo!' to him, he went to Steven and I can just hear him say, 'Please don't make me do any more of these.' We had been prepping to do, like *Back to the Future*, two and three, back to back, so that threw a wrench in that."

Six years passed before the modern stone-age family returned to the big screen in live-action in 2000's *The Flintstones in Viva Rock Vegas*. Sequels to hit movies also command higher salaries for their actors. Some might contend that the cast of *The Flintstones in Viva Rock Vegas* was even better suited to the roles than the first. Because they were primarily from stage and television they also came at a reduced budget. This time, Fred was played by British actor Mark Addy (*Game of Thrones*), with Stephen Baldwin (*The Usual Suspects*) as Barney; Kirsten Johnson (*Third Rock from the Sun*) as Wilma; and Jane Krakowski (*30 Rock*) as Betty. A prequel of sorts, the movie found the characters younger and explained how they met and married. It was loosely based on the episodes "Bachelor Daze" and "The Gambler."

The Flintstones in Viva Rock Vegas soundtrack album on Hip-O Records has a light, festive tone in its selection of pop tunes, befitting the film's increased comedic approach and colorful design. Almost all the songs have a theme of fun and celebration. The album opens with the closing finale of the movie—the cast singing

"Meet the Flintstones" and "Viva Rock Vegas," a parody of Doc Pomus and Mort Shulman's theme from the 1964 Elvis movie. Ann-Margret added another page to her Flintstone history by recording the "Viva Rock Vegas" version that closes the album.

"It was great to go to her house . . . ," said Levant of meeting Ann-Margret. "She had a cel [from her *Flintstones* episode], prominently displayed."

According to Earl Kress, Ann-Margret's absence from the Rhino *Flintstones* compilation was due to her feeling that her early singing did not meet the standards she later preferred. European rights issues being different, Bear Family Records in Germany was able to release "The Littlest Lamb" and "Ain't Gonna Be a Fool" on a 1998 CD boxed set called *Ann-Margret 1961–1966*.

Universal licensed *The Flintstones in Viva Rock Vegas* to Disney's Buena Vista Records to produce a read-along book and recording set featuring the original cast dialogue with stock music from Walt Disney Records' read-along library. It is the only recording with genuine Hanna-Barbera characters and sound effects produced and released by the Disney in-house label. While the sequel comes across as less opulent and more intimate than the first, it also offers more direct references to the TV series and allows more screen time for Wilma and Betty. But too much time had passed since the first film. In the interim, reunion TV movies and revivals were becoming less of an event. *Viva Rock Vegas* was also denied the massive marketing campaign, promotional tie-ins, and broadcast marathons accompanying the first movie.

Harvey Korman was the only actor who was seen and/or heard in both live-action features, as well as the original series and the first animated feature. He voiced the Dictaphone Bird in *The Flintstones* and played Wilma's father on camera in *Viva Rock Vegas*. Although actor Alan Cumming played the Great Gazoo, Korman did reprise the role at the production read-through. Mel Blanc, who had passed before both films, is heard as Dino by way of archival audio. Bill Hanna and Joe Barbera appear briefly in both movies. Jean Vander Pyl appears as a party guest

Walt Disney Records' Buena Vista label produced and released *The Flintstones in Viva Rock Vegas* read-along set, featuring soundtrack dialogue and genuine Hanna-Barbera sound effects for the page-turning signal.

in the first film. John Stephenson is the voice of a showroom announcer and the minister, played on screen by Walter Gertz, in *Viva Rock Vegas*.

▲▼▲▼▲▼

Even though they supposedly "lived in the past," the Flintstones proved their resilience and consistent ability to stay relevant and current. Part of this flexibility was musical. No matter the trend, the characters could embrace a genre and stand the test of time because it would end up "in the stone age" anyway, whether Fred imitated Elvis or KISS.

Yogi, Huck, and pals found themselves disco dancing when the craze was in full swing, especially on NBC's *Galaxy Goof-Ups*, where they boogied to sequences in which even "Eep Opp Ork" was set to a disco beat. H-B-related records were generally story-driven during the disco era. When rap and hip-hop became popular with kids, however, the Flintstones hopped on the rap wagon as did most characters from other studios.

The H-B characters themselves didn't do the rapping and singing in the aforementioned *Rappin' and Rhymin'* video, but they did on Rhino's *The Flintstones Present Bedrock Rocks!* (1994). Henry Corden comfortably handled the most complicated wordplay as "Funky Fred." B. J. Ward returned as Betty, but in this case, Barney was voiced by Jeff Bergman and Wilma by Susan Boyd.

Rap music was something deeply personal to one of this album's key consultants, Carlton Zapp. Carlton's story is a book in itself, but it began with a chance meeting with Hanna in front of the building and discussing the flowerbeds. Hanna was so unpretentious, Zapp didn't realize who he was until later in the conversation, after which Hanna suggested an opportunity. With time and hard work, Zapp became Hanna and Barbera's assistant, remaining close to both families long after the partners passed away.

One of many highlights that Zapp recalled is attending the *Bedrock Hop* voice sessions. "Henry Corden was made for this," Zapp said. "He's so over the top anyway. He had that gift for it."

Rhino combined a hip-hop version of "Meet the Flintstones" with the eighties and nineties pop hits by Brandy, the Knack, All-4-One, and others with the original *Pebbles and Bamm-Bamm Show* theme for an album called *Bedrock Rocks!* It was distributed as three slightly different CDs sold through Post Pebbles cereals. Each disc contained slightly different artists. Often advertising agencies distribute alternate items to measure responses, so the versioning may have been a research component of the marketing campaign.

Such enterprises are usually only conducted with major characters and brands. *The Flintstones* had become both, a level only a few creations have reached. "One of the longest-running cartoon series, in a sense, was all those Pebbles commercials, where Barney was tricking Fred out of his Fruity or Cocoa Pebbles," said Scott Shaw, who directed countless installments.

Tom and Jerry and *The Flintstones* made high-profile comebacks in the nineties, but they were not alone among Hanna-Barbera characters. The nineties were a boom time for new and classic animation-related home entertainment. It had never been easier for consumers to access past and present favorites on audio and video. The smartest companies provided the widest selections of both and made sure the public knew it was available.

Hanna-Barbera enthusiasts could finally find music and stories with original soundtracks and authentic voices, beautifully restored and mastered. As for finding previous Hanna-Barbera records, there was a new online auction service suddenly making it more feasible to collect vintage H-B records from sellers around the world. In *Flintstones* terminology, the website might have been called "RockBay."

Chapter 26

H-B'S COAST-TO-COAST
POWERPUFF LABORATORY

~~~~~~

**Being a Powerpuff Girl isn't about getting your way . . .
it's about using your own unique abilities to help people
and the world we all live in.**
—BLOSSOM (CATHY CAVADINI)

The early nineties began as a period of bounteous discoveries and long-awaited treasures from the vast corners of Hanna-Barbera Productions. By the end, it would be the bridge to the next age of television animation.

When Fred Siebert became president of Hanna-Barbera, Ted Turner was primarily interested in the "content" from the library. Siebert arrived at a studio that in some ways had seen better days but was still alive with possibilities. Siebert was renowned for developing the MTV logo and the endless variations seen on the music channel. He also cocreated the Nick at Nite block on cable's Nickelodeon channel—which did not simply "dump" vintage shows on cable but rebranded and marketed them with identities and elaborate campaigns as if they were new shows. It was wildly successful, drawing not only longtime fans but the elusive youth market, blending kindhearted kitsch with nostalgia. Siebert was wise and secure enough to realize that learning from experts was good for himself and his business, so he sought out genuine specialists in what Hanna-Barbera did, why it worked, and what could be done with it.

"When Fred first arrived, we had a meeting because he didn't have a lot of capital to work with right away," said Earl Kress. "He wanted ideas about what he could do NOW with materials that Hanna-Barbera had that had not really been used enough. I told him how many people loved the music and would be hungry for ways to access the themes and songs. That's when it started."

Rhino Records became the leader in releasing classic and original Hanna-Barbera recordings in the nineties and early 2000s. Their H-B output rivaled even the HBR label in its authenticity, though it was sadly too late to bring in all the original actors for new material. Nevertheless, the volume was greater than that of Peter Pan, Golden, or any other label. Audio and video producers like George Feltenstein, Robyn Frederick, and E. J. Dick worked with H-B staffers like music supervisor Joanne Miller and Bodie Chandler for new material while Kress combed the reels and stock areas for everything he could find from the past. Just because he found it did not mean it could be released, of course. There would still have to be product approvals and business affairs issues.

▲▼▲▼

The first release was a compact disc or cassette packaged in an elaborate gift box with a lyric folio called *Hanna-Barbera's Christmas Sing-A-Long*. Festive, eclectic, but all-too-brief, the ten-song album contains five soundtrack songs from Hanna-Barbera Christmas specials of the seventies and eighties never released on disc or audio cassette before. Boo-Boo (Don Messick) sings "Hope" from *Yogi's First Christmas*, and a chorus of elves join Fred and Barney (Henry Corden and Mel Blanc) for "A Brand New Kind of Christmas Song" from *A Flintstone Christmas*. Beautifully sung by a studio choir, the first six tracks are from the soundtrack of the eponymous thirty-minute Hanna-Barbera home video, in which some are accompanied by scenes from H-B's *Greatest Adventure: Stories from the Bible* video series.

Bill Hanna and Joe Barbera appeared on screen in this made-for-video special with a companion soundtrack album on Rhino Records.

The video is hosted by Bill and Joe themselves with assorted children, helping to decorate in the setting of a cozy home. The duo was becoming more visible in later years, including a highly scripted introduction to the Universal theme park ride and a 1989 song-and-dance on their fifteenth anniversary TV special. Hanna-Barbera Home Video, an in-house division, released a series of "Personal Favorites" cartoon episodes with introductions by Hanna and Barbera, reminding the public that they were "hands-on" with their company's output. While they had been on camera occasionally since the 1964 *Magilla Gorilla* promo film, the 1965's *Atom Ant/Secret Squirrel Show* special,

and some talk and game shows, neither was afforded sufficient avenues to hone their skills at becoming more familiar TV faces, like Rod Serling, Alfred Hitchcock, or Walt Disney. With Barbera focused on development and Hanna meeting deadlines, little time was prioritized for onscreen personas.

Seibert appreciated this need and set about defining the Hanna-Barbera "brand," including changing "productions" to "cartoons" at the end of their company name to define their specialty. "Walt Disney was a visionary," said Siebert. "Bill and Joe were craftsmen. That's a great thing, too, it's just different and needed to be defined and clarified."

▲▼▲▼

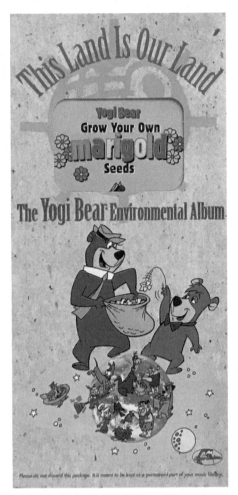

Bill Mumy and Robert Halmer of Barnes and Barnes produced this musical reunion with classic H-B characters.

The Yogi Bear Environmental Album was coproduced by actor composer/musician Bill Mumy, whose following increases with new generations for his young roles in *Lost in Space* and *The Twilight Zone*. Mumy and his coproducer Robert Halmer formed the novelty group Barnes and Barnes, beloved to Barry "Doctor Demento" Hansen radio fans for the listener favorite, "Fish Heads." Mumy and Halmer created original songs and included three standards: Yogi and Boo-Boo's interpretation of "Sunshine on My Shoulder," Huckleberry Hound crooning "Rocky Mountain High," and all the characters singing "This Land Is Your Land."

▲▼▲▼▲▼

Rhino Records also partnered with Turner on releasing classic movie soundtracks for home audio. Turner's ownership of the MGM film library enabled Rhino to access extremely rare and often neglected audio elements from hundreds of films. Producers like Marilee Bradford worked carefully but swiftly to get these materials into album form before the elements had degraded beyond repair. "When we were doing the transfer work for Gigi," she recalled, "I saw some of the tracks disintegrate just after we managed to send them through the machines. That's how urgent this all was."

George Feltenstein produced a six-disc boxed set called *That's Entertainment: The Ultimate Anthology of MGM Musicals* that included Gene Kelly and Sara Berner performing "The Worry Song" from *Anchors Aweigh*. After fifty years, the actual soundtrack was now available in crystalline audio on a retail album. The following year, the track was included on another Rhino set called *Gene Kelly at Metro-Goldwyn-Mayer: S'Wonderful*.

Throughout the nineties, Earl Kress restored and compiled hours of H-B music and songs, most for the first time. He worked tirelessly on behalf of the Hanna-Barbera legacy, while writing cartoons for H-B, Disney, DePatie-Freleng and Warner, for which he also helped create bonus features for Hanna-Barbera DVD sets.

The first original Rhino Hanna-Barbera musical album was *This Land Is Our Land: The Yogi Bear Environmental Album*. The 1993 audio cassette-only release was the first featuring classic characters that sang and spoke together on records since the Colpix albums. No previous album combined these particular characters. Yogi, Huckleberry Hound, Quick Draw McGraw—who had recorded an anti-litter Golden Record in 1961—and George Jetson are all played by Greg Burson. Other characters include Fred Flintstone (Henry Corden); Barney Rubble (Frank Welker); Ranger Smith and Boo-Boo (Tony Pope, a Daws Butler protégé); and even Penny Singleton as Jane Jetson.

Hanna-Barbera Classics, Volume One was Rhino and Kress's first compilation of themes and music from the early days of the studio. This required legal approvals from various owners and estates of music libraries that would consent to include "needle-drop" cues used between 1957 and 1959 before Hoyt Curtin's Loopy DeLoop scores began taking their place. Kress included as many as feasible. The forty-five tracks covered 1957 through 1969, opening with the world premiere soundtrack recording of the *Ruff and Reddy* open and closing themes. There was just enough of a mix—*The Flintstones, Yogi Bear, Magilla Gorilla, Wally Gator, Scooby-Doo*—to provide an overview as well as a tantalizing tease to those yearning for a second volume or more. Kress was also able to provide a generous supply of underscores to this disc. Nowhere is the impact of the Loopy DeLoop music on the H-B sound more evident than here, unless one watches the cartoons themselves. There is also a suite of Jack de Mello and Curtin pieces from the *Magilla Gorilla/Peter Potamus* shows, representing the mid-sixties comedy sound. Rather than reuse the earlier Tee Vee Toons tracks, Kress created brand-new mixes and edits of every theme song. Whenever possible, sub-themes (accompanying title cards) and bumpers were also included. Stereo versions of *Top Cat* and *The Jetsons* were like revelations to eager listeners.

▲▼▲▼▲▼

Another collection, *Hanna-Barbera Cartoon Sound FX*, allowed retail consumers to enjoy either listening or finding ways to use the iconic noises that became integral to millions of TV watchers. It's impossible to calculate all the home videos, school projects, and community events that were enhanced by these sound effects. The disc also includes H-B character greetings for answering machines and a "top ten" of greatest sound effects. These and other effects were used in tandem for revised Hanna-Barbera end logos later that decade, one for comedies and one for action/adventure shows.

Previously, Hanna-Barbera Productions released its own collection of sound effects on vinyl record sets for the entertainment industry. The Sound Ideas company later offered the H-B sounds on compact discs and digital downloads, but they were still intended for professional use. *Hanna-Barbera Cartoon Sound FX* was the first H-B sound effects collection sold to the general public—again, mostly due to the efforts of Earl Kress.

One of the connoisseurs of Hanna-Barbera sound effects is animation director J. J. Sedelmaier. Among the animation director's acclaimed projects are *Saturday Night Live* "TV Funhouse" segments and hundreds of commercials, often affectionately parodying classic cartoons, e.g., the spot-on *Speed Racer* Volkswagen ads. Sedelmaier cites editor Tom Pompasello as a key influence during this time as well. "Tom was a big part of the whole MTV Nickelodeon networks group," said Sedelmaier. "He was a blues musician . . . he was a big part of making that transition from the old days to the new, having such a big background in music, how to repackage and repurpose stuff."

Pompasello constantly found ways to use the H-B sound effects. "It made the work very smart because those sound effects were in our DNA," said Sedelmaier. "When you see something that isn't an H-B cartoon, and you hear these effects, you go, 'Woo! Somebody's talking my language!' There had never been anything like that done before. You hardly ever heard those sounds out of context." Since then, the influence of Hanna-Barbera's sound effects is impossible to measure.

In 1997, Rhino released the most comprehensive H-B soundtrack collection as of this writing. *Hanna-Barbera's Pic-A-Nic Basket of Cartoon Classics* is a four-disc set boxed to resemble a basket with an attached handle and a book filled with interviews, some sourced from *The Cartoon Music Book*. Three of the discs were previously released: *Modern Stone-Age Melodies, Hanna-Barbera Classics, Volume One*, and *Hanna-Barbera Sound Effects* with new CD case designs to match the box set. The fourth disc, *Hanna-Barbera Classics, Volume Two*, was created

Space Ghost turned from interstellar crime fighting to zany celebrity chat, resulting in several Rhino albums and this promo comedy CD for radio stations.

exclusively for the boxed set and never released separately. Kress and Rhino's goal was to make *Classics, Volume Two*, the new booklet, and the clever packaging substantial enough to convince those already owning the first three discs to still buy *Pic-A-Nic Basket*. It was indeed a treasure trove, including themes and background music from *Top Cat, Jonny Quest*, and *The Jetsons*, as well as several previously unreleased themes.

▴▾▴▾▴▾

The Hanna-Barbera library proved to be a gold mine largely untapped when the creative minds at Turner figured out that there was much that could be done beyond the series and films. The music and the sounds were an asset unto themselves. So were individual cartoon snippets and specific dialogue phrases.

Hanna-Barbera offered mountains of material that could be isolated and repurposed to create new forms of entertainment.

One such cluster of animation elements transformed late-night television into an evening of irreverent animation for teens and adults. By creating composites of animation elements from the series and live-action videos, Adult Swim producer Mike Lazzo built a series around H-B's first superhero, Space Ghost, as the last thing anyone would have dreamed he would be in 1966: a talk show host. The Gary Owens–like voice-over wit of George Lowe was added to the restructured animation clips. The crudeness only added to the bizarre attraction.

Deconstructive talk shows that poke holes in the established form, like *Late Night with David Letterman*, sketch comedies like *Saturday Night Live*, and electronic characters in the form of Max Headroom created a ready audience for *Space Ghost Coast-to-Coast*. Suddenly some of the hippest guests appeared on his show, starting at the beginning when Jim Carrey promoted *The Mask*. Zoe Saldana used an appearance with Space Ghost to promote *Avatar*.

Throughout the nineties, Space Ghost became a guest star himself on other programs and made commercial endorsements. Just as Hanna-Barbera Records did in 1965, Cartoon Network distributed a disc of "drop-ins" to radio stations to add comedy and promote the show along with jazz artist Sonny Sharrock's theme song, "Hit Single." Entitled *Yeah, Whatever . . .*, the 1995 disc held over ninety 15-second gags, old jokes, and "affirmations." In addition to having an affinity for reciting "I'm a Little Teapot," Space Ghost makes one affirmation that would take on a different meaning in the wake of COVID: "Greetings! I'm Space Ghost! Are you ready for today's daily affirmation? (*A-a-a-ahem*.) Wear a surgical mask when grocery shopping."

Former villains were also culled from the earlier series, irritated by their punitive roles and resentful of Space Ghost. Zorak (C. Martin Croaker) is the bandleader of "The Real Way-Outs," and Moltar (Croaker) is the producer/director. There's also the loud, over-the-top Brak (Andy Merrill), who was destined for his own bizarre star turn.

Rhino gathered music and comedy selections from the show as well as new material on *Space Ghost's Musical Bar-B-Que* (1997) and *Space Ghost's Surf & Turf* (1998). The albums are best enjoyed by those who can access episodes of the series to get some of the running gags and in-jokes, but on their own, both discs are great examples of fine-tuned novelty music madness. One highlight is when Brak sings the relentlessly catchy "Song That Doesn't End," which originated with beloved TV ventriloquist Shari Lewis and her little puppet, Lamb Chop.

The characters appeared in another block featuring Hanna-Barbera cartoons and other comedy materials called *Cartoon Planet*. In 2000, Brak starred in his own special, *Brak Presents the Brak Show Starring Brak*. The special, spoofing TV variety shows, featured animated guests like Wally Gator and Grape Ape and live-action guests including singer Monica, the Chieftains, and Freddie Prinze Jr., who would soon play Fred in the first two live-action Scooby-Doo films. It was followed up by a second special, then a full series spoofing TV sitcoms called *The Brak Show*. Soundtrack albums of the special and the series were released by Kids' WB! Music.

▲▼▲▼▲▼

Kids' WB! was the name of a children's programming block on the WB! Cable network. Kids' WB! Music was a label at Rhino Records, which also became a division of Warner. Hanna-Barbera was also included in the portfolio, as was all of Turner Entertainment, Cartoon Network, and the MGM library. "The success of Adult Swim and *Space Ghost Coast-to-Coast* opened up a new avenue of satire for H-B characters," said archivist Matt Patterson. "Series like *Harvey Birdman: Attorney-At-Law* and *Sealab 2022* found the premises turned on their heads."

Perhaps the most dramatic and long-ranging creative decision made in the nineties was when Fred Siebert launched the "What a Cartoon!" project, an artist-driven program to develop cartoons for television in the traditional model, to create fresh, original characters and premises. The trade publications were awash in articles and ads inviting animation artists to submit storyboards. One ad in *Animation Magazine* showed Bill and Joe's shoes, asking who could fill them. Space Ghost hosted "World Premiere Toon-In" and the results spoke for themselves, as several became household names, including *Powerpuff Girls*, *Dexter's Laboratory*, *Courage the Cowardly Dog*, *Cow and Chicken*, and *Johnny Bravo*. After "What a Cartoon!" the Cartoon Network brand represented all the cartoons created under its umbrella as well as Hanna-Barbera in some cases, like merchandise and publishing. Plans were underway to revive classic characters in new ways.

As to recordings, Rhino released several compilations of themes and original cast songs, starting

Oscar-winning composer Paul Williams makes a guest appearance in this musical comedy story.

with 1999's *Cartoon Network Cartoon Medley*. Two of these shows, in particular, generated a considerable number of recordings.

Dexter's Laboratory inspired two completely different albums. The first was *The Musical Time Machine*, an original story told like an operetta, not unlike a Looney Tunes cartoon or Animaniacs episode, plus songs from a few episodes including one featuring guest artist Paul Williams ("The Rainbow Connection"). A much bigger fuss was made over Dexter's second album, *The Hip-Hop Experiment*, which was released as a CD and on green vinyl. Produced with Atlantic Records, it features well-known rap and hip-hop artists like Coolio and will.i.am, whose songs—"Dexter (What's His Name?)" and "Secrets," respectively—were made into videos. The album was advertised before the theatrical release of 2002's *Powerpuff Girls Movie*.

The first Powerpuff Girls' audio release was a read-along book and cassette produced by Phil Baron, former music and comedy partner with Will Ryan as "Willio and Phillio," frequent stars of hit Disney albums. *The Powerpuff Girls: Mojo Jojo's Rising* (1999) is an origin story explaining how the villainous Mojo Jojo came to be and how Blossom, Bubbles, and Buttercup gained their superpowers.

The frantic, driving pace of *The Powerpuff Girls* theme and each cartoon's melodramatic state of urgency cried out for fast-paced, full-bodied, kid-friendly rock, the kind that was on the rise on radio services aimed at young people in the nineties. *The Powerpuff Girls: Heroes and Villains* is a collection of original songs about the characters, sung by artists like DEVO, the Apples in Stereo, and Cornelius. A follow-up album, *The Powerpuff Girls: Power Pop*, features such artists as No Secrets, Cherish, and

Several recordings starred the Powerpuff Girls, including this album showcasing the series' inventive music.

Jennifer Ellison. *The City of Soundsville (Music from "The Powerpuff Girls")* is a soundtrack score album with snippets of dialogue from various episodes. Except for the read-along, which describes the actual cartoon, this album most fully captures the essence of the actual series and allows a rare showcase for the music of James L. Venable. Signature phrases and amusing lines abound from Cathy Cavadini as Blossom, Tara Strong as Bubbles, E. G. Daily as Buttercup, Tom Kenny (best known as Spongebob Squarepants's voice) as narrator and the mayor, Tom Kane as the Professor and Him, and Roger L. Jackson as Mojo Jojo. Also heard are Jennifer Hale, Jeff Bennett, Kevin Michael Richardson, Jim Cummings, and Chuck McCann, who over thirty-five years earlier voiced Yogi Bear, Huckleberry Hound, and other characters for Colpix's *Wake Up, America!* album.

Rhino almost always used the original cast voices and/or soundtracks. The Cartoon Network logo bumper music was also usually heard before the albums began.

▲▼▲▼▲▼

The Real Adventures of Jonny Quest was the third iteration of the 1964 action series. This one would introduce computer animation to series TV, at least in "Quest World" sequences. Computer generation (CG) was still relatively new on the film and TV landscape—*Toy Story* was only four years old as a pioneering CG feature. Introducing modern story lines and some CG to a highly regarded TV classic was highly touted. The publicity was heavy. Jonny Quest could be a merchandising bonanza, so all the business units were focused on the project. Perhaps too much. Early computer graphics look like what they are, early graphics, without a reason to exist. Backstage issues were in abundance, so much so that there was a staff change for the second season, which is immeasurably improved, but after the hoopla had subsided.

Rhino released a narrated soundtrack audio cassette of one of the first season's best episodes, *Return of the Anasazi*. The story works beautifully in audio, with the absence of a "Quest World" sequence speaking for itself. It is a good example of the difference between viewing an artistic work and hearing the same work without the image. Ably stepping in the shadows of John Stephenson and Don Messick is George Segal (*Who's Afraid of Virginia Woolf*, *The Goldbergs*) who brings his distinctive intensity to Dr. Quest. Some enthusiasts were disconcerted by the southern accent of Race Bannon, but Robert Patrick (*Terminator 2: Judgement Day*) brings personality and acting skills to it. The complex, troubled production saw the recasting of all the main characters except Frank Welker as Bandit.

This would not be the last "vision" of Jonny Quest. Tom and Jerry, the Flintstones, Yogi Bear, Scooby-Doo, or even the hundreds of other Hanna-Barbera characters would transition into the next millennium, in their original films, shows, and formats as well as in new configurations. There were also still a lot more Hanna-Barbera records, discs, and digital files to come in the new millennium.

Chapter 27

MODERN MILLENNIUM-AGE HISTORY

~~~~~~~~~~~~~~~~~~~~~~~~~~~~~~~~~~~~

Yabba dabba doo.

—HOMER SIMPSON (DAN CASTELLANETA), AUGUST 6, 2010

In 1982, "Bruce Springstone" recorded "Meet the Flintstones" for a seven-inch and ten-inch single released with a caricature of "The Boss" in Flintstonian garb on the cover. The novelty recording, sung by John Ebersberger, was especially well received on the "Dr. Demento" syndicated radio show. Rhino included *Bruce Springstone, Live from Bedrock* in a disc of celebrity impressionists singing TV themes called *Rerun Rock*.

"Bruce Springstone" enjoyed a lot of airplay with his rocking rendition of the famous theme song.

The real Bruce Springsteen never performed on a *Flintstones* album or special. Nonetheless, there is a significant Hanna-Barbera musical connection. Max Weinberg, drummer in Springsteen's "E"-Street Band and renowned big bandleader, was given rather unusual instructions when he became the musical director of NBC's *Late Night with Conan O'Brien.* Weinberg shared this history with the author:

After talking my way into an audition (with a band that I had yet to organize), and following a series of meetings during the spring of 1993 with Conan O'Brien and his start-up team, most importantly writer and producer Robert Smigel for the new post-Letterman "Late Night" broadcast, I was tasked to present five types of musical ideas. Chief among these snippets of what I would do if given the shot was, in Conan's own description: ". . . a cartoony, 1960's-era fast, swinging, and 'funny' instrumental. Something like *The Jetsons*, or *The Flintstones*, you know, *Scooby-Doo*."

The Hanna-Barbera music was the soundtrack in many ways to Conan's life as he was born in 1963. My musical partner and I, Jimmy Vivino knew exactly what Conan was getting at.

The group I quickly assembled was sort of a "little" big band—seven players featuring a tight horn section. Excellent musicians all, with a keyboardist, Scott Healy, who could do anything—pianistic gymnastics I called it! The 'funny' came with our use of the xylophone riding on top of everything else. Trills, slides, dissonant voicings occasionally, the xylophone was quirky, and certainly, no one on late-night television in the early '90s was using that sound. And like the great television big bands behind the scenes, like Hoyt Curtin for H-B, we swung everything rather than use a rock beat as our foundation. That was different from everything else you heard on non-animated television back then and it set our approach apart from the other shows.

Bruce Springsteen's drummer Max Weinberg and his Max Weinberg 7 brought the Hanna-Barbera/Hoyt Curtin–style sound of *The Flintstones*, *The Jetsons*, and *Scooby-Doo* to late-night TV, as requested by *Late Night* host Conan O'Brien. Photo by Christopher Sikich. (CC-BY-SA-2.0, Wikimedia Commons.)

Jimmy Vivino was so important to that idea. He and I understood Broadway and TV underscore and so-called legitimate music—we had a common vocabulary—almost a telepathy, really. And Jimmy's a great arranger, writer, and multi-instrumentalist who wrote charts like some people type—fast and clean. I did a lot of humming out an approach and editing. A great collaboration and one of my greatest musical memories was the work on that show from 1993 to 2010.

But—it all started when Conan said to ". . . play something FUNNY."

▲▼▲▼▲▼

David Letterman often used cues and sound effects from Hanna-Barbera discs to punctuate comedy segments and graphics on his *Late Show* talk show on CBS. One evening, Letterman became so flustered at one point by a particular abundance of these effects, he remarked on the air, "Have we become Hanna-Barbera?"

Within walking distance of Letterman's studio in the Ed Sullivan Theater, former "Harry Potter" star Daniel Radcliffe was appearing in the 2011 revival of the Pulitzer Prize–winning musical *How to Succeed in Business without Really Trying*.

"The goal was to recharacterize what the original did for the 1962 audience in a way that makes sense for the audience of today," explained arranger/conductor David Chase (Broadway's *The Music Man*, *Frozen*, and *Elf*). "Doug Besterman, our orchestrator, brought up Marty Paich. We started with Marty Paich, who had worked with Ella Fitzgerald and so many other great singers."

As mentioned earlier, Marty Paich worked often with Hanna-Barbera. The decision was made to give *How to Succeed* the sound of early sixties television and records, a bold brassy sound with exotic flavor, jazz, and guitar. Chase drew upon his lifelong affection for the early stereo records of Esquivel, Martin Denny, Arthur Lyman, and others of the era. Chase found the early Hoyt Curtin/Hanna-Barbera musical styles to also be an influence.

"Listening to *The Flintstones* and *The Jetsons* scores and realizing that was the same composer—coming across the whole Hoyt Curtin legacy—that is something I didn't know anything about, other than obviously knowing the theme songs." Chase's "Pirate Dance" arrangement in this score of *How to Succeed* could easily have come from a classic episode of *Jonny Quest*, but it played to packed houses on Broadway.

The world lost Bill Hanna in 2001 and Joseph Barbera five years later. Many of the now-immortal talents who worked with them have also passed on. Several of them were animation veterans who spent their last days working at the studio. The Hanna-Barbera studio, actually a complex of three structures, still stands at 3400 Cahuenga Boulevard in North Hollywood. Designed by Arthur Froelich, it has been designated historically protected by the Los Angeles Conservancy. While Hanna-Barbera cartoons and records are no longer produced at 3400 Cahuenga, there has

been no shortage of interest in either of them, both new and classic, in the new millennium. In some cases, it deepened and expanded beyond expectations.

Such was the case in 2017 when *Jonny Quest* was the focus of a massive soundtrack assembly, organization, and restoration project. Serious recognition was due for the Hanna-Barbera scores of Curtin, Nichols, de Mello, and others, with the *Jonny Quest* music at the top of the list. Jon Burlingame, whose acclaimed books chronicle works of film and television's finest composers and lyricists, wrote the liner notes for the two-disc *Jonny Quest: Original Television Soundtrack* set, produced for La-La Land Records by Nik Ranieri, Lukas Kendall, and Taylor White. Ranieri, master animator behind such characters as Lumiere in Disney's *Beauty and the Beast*, Hades in *Hercules*, and on 20th Television Animation's *The Simpsons*, also credits classic Hanna-Barbera as an artistic influence on his life and work. Kendall, one of Hollywood's most successful and inventive producers of new and classic soundtracks, set about restoring and remastering the original tracks.

Organizing seemingly random cues of various lengths and repetitions that were never designed for a cohesive album was a daunting labor of love for Ranieri and his associates. He told the author:

> I created a template of ten-second increments for the full twenty-three minutes of each episode which cue was being used, how long it was, and so on, for all twenty-six episodes. Once I did that, I looked at how often each cue was used, what episode it was used in, and how often. That's how I decided what pieces went with what episodes.
>
> I broke the rule for an iconic cue that belongs in an episode like "Curse of Anubis," even if a longer version was in another episode. Some patterns emerged. I gave the templates to Jon Burlingame for the liner notes. You know the famous one, "Avalanche?" Once they recorded it, they used it from episode 13 through the end of the series in its full form or a small part of it. I guess they did another recording session after the

Hoyt Curtin's Hanna-Barbera music provided inspiration for this 2011 Broadway revival starring Daniel Radcliffe.

thirteen episodes and again at the very end, they added some of the de Mello cues for the last two or three episodes.

The cues originally did have titles. We did everything we could to assure they were accurate despite the passage of time by researching information from packages, boxes, and lists. There are names on the boxes, some hard to see because the copies aren't clear. What you see in the liner notes are the actual names. I also found things like "Pasha's Theme" and "Jade's Theme," which weren't always used.

▲▼▲▼▲▼

Many of the concepts that made *Josie and the Pussycats* a TV success in 1970 and 1972 were brought to the big screen in 2001. The film was a Universal/Sony production in association with Archie Comics. Rhino

wisely leveraged the attention drawn to the new film by releasing a new disc filled with music from the original series. *Stop, Look and Listen: The Best of Josie and the Pussycats* included the Capitol album, the Kellogg's singles, and several bonus tracks. It was released on the Rhino Handmade label, designed for the collectors' market.

In the feature film, Hanna, Barbera, and Curtin's *Josie and the Pussycats* theme song played over the end title outtake sequence. The lyrics were changed to reflect the band and show business rather than the *Jonny Quest*–style adventure premise of the TV series, which the comics also avoided. However, the feature film itself owes the concept of Josie and friends as a female rock band (and the existence of Valerie) to the animated series that originated in 1969 with Fred Silverman, CBS, Hanna-Barbera, and Archie Comics as a follow-up to *The Archies*.

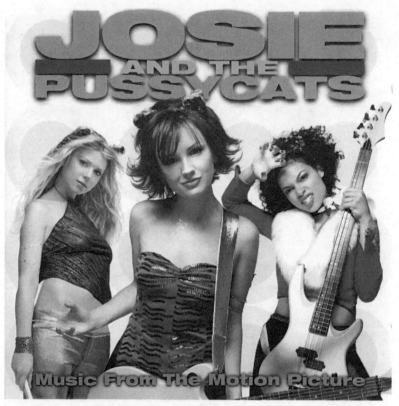

The big-screen version of *Josie and the Pussycats* has amassed a loyal fan following long after its first release.

Written and directed by Deborah Kaplan and Harry Elfont, co-screenwriters of *Viva Rock Vegas*, the movie is a satire of media and marketing manipulation with a veneer of campy farce. The filmmakers overdid the product placement as a self-reflexive joke and overplayed the evil as science fiction. The film was not initially a huge success. Some audiences interpreted the intent as "wealthy Hollywood" telling the masses how easily they can be duped, while the film itself was heavily hyped at the time in order to sell it. Over time, it has gained admiration for its female-driven story, creative approach, casting, and music. Now freed from its previous hype, the message hits harder than ever and beyond expectations.

The *Josie and the Pussycats* feature soundtrack album included songs worthy to stand among their contemporary charting peers. It was released on actor Tom Hanks's and producer Gary Goetzman's label,

Playtone Records, in association with Epic and Sony. Beyoncé might have been on this album as one of the Pussycats, but after auditioning for the film, she was considered "too quiet and shy."

In 2017, the album was reissued on vinyl. The three stars—Rachel Leigh Cook (*The Baby-Sitters Club*, *Batman Beyond*); Rosario Dawson (*Daredevil*, *The Mandalorian*); and Tara Reid (*American Pie*, *Sharknado*)—participated in what was, in effect, the second *Josie and the Pussycats* reunion (after the voice cast reunion). They were as enthusiastic about promoting the album and Blu-ray releases as they were to see what a huge following the film has gained over the years. Cook, Dawson, and Reid reunited again in 2021 for the film's twentieth anniversary. "I love how the songs are *songs*," said Rosario Dawson in a Universal Pictures Zoom video. "We're not still trying to be tongue-in-cheek and silly. They're proper, awesome, fun songs."

▵▿▵▿▵▿

Scooby-Doo's recording career took off at the turn of the new millennium, starting with *Scooby-Doo's Snack Tracks*, a compilation from Kid Rhino that was almost to *Scooby* fans what *Modern Stone-Age Melodies* was to Flintstone fans. Some may not associate Scooby-Doo with music and songs, but there has been a steady stream of them that continues to the newest series and films. *Snack Tracks* started from seasons one and two, included the never-released Austin Roberts "chase" songs, all the Curtin/Hanna/Barbera tunes from *Scooby Goes Hollywood*, and even the relentless "Pretty Mary Sunlite" by Jerry Reed and "I Can Make You Happy" by Davy Jones. A shortened version of the album was made available by mail order from Franco-American Spaghetti-O's.

The boom in direct-to-video animated films slowed down for some studios, but never really for Scooby-Doo, Tom and Jerry, the Flintstones, the Jetsons, or Jonny Quest, all of which pop up regularly in new releases on whatever platform is current. Scooby-Doo continues to lead the pack, though, with a new film or series almost every year. There was a move toward introducing "real" monsters in the Scooby films, starting with *Scooby-Doo on Zombie Island*. Rhino released soundtrack albums from the second and third of these films that also included original material.

The main artists of *Scooby-Doo and the Witch's Ghost* are the Hex Girls, a sort of ghoulish version of Josie and the Pussycats who made subsequent appearances in Scooby adventures. The soundtrack to *Scooby-Doo and the Alien Invaders* adds extra comedy with sci-fi novelty songs, many sung by Scooby and Shaggy, voiced at this point by New Orleans radio personality Scott Innes. Among them are "Vacuum Cleaner Hoses" by Phil Baron and "Slime Creatures from Outer Space" sung by Weird Al Yankovic.

▴▾▴▾▴▾

The "hybrid" feature film, combining live-action and animation in the manner of *Who Framed Roger Rabbit*, became a standard form of feature filmmaking, especially when reviving classic characters. Pixar also revolutionized animated features with a long run of hit computer-generated features starting in 1995 with *Toy Story*. The Warner Looney Tunes characters struck gold with basketball star Michael Jordan in 1996's *Space Jam*. Twenty-five years later, Bugs Bunny and friends teamed again for *Space Jam: A New Legacy*—this time with Warner's Hanna-Barbera characters, also in CG, cheering on basketball star LeBron James from the sidelines.

It helps that the characters in question are constantly in view on current broadcast, cable, or initiative-marketed streaming. Among the reasons 2000's *The Adventures of Rocky and Bullwinkle* did not succeed was the virtual absence of Jay Ward cartoons on broadcast TV at the time of the film's promotion. For *Scooby-Doo*, this was not a problem as he and Mystery Incorporated were solving capers on almost every form of media, nearly 24/7. Director Raja Gosnell's *Scooby-Doo* trotted onto movie screens in 2002 with a young cast eager to promote the film. Freddie Prinze Jr. sincerely told one talk-show host that the original series was "one of the best TV shows ever made."

A computer-animated Scooby partnered with a live-action Shaggy—embodied so completely by Matthew Lillard that he joined the animation voice cast. The aforementioned Prinze (*I Know What You Did Last Summer*) was cast as Fred, with Sarah Michelle Gellar (*Buffy the Vampire Slayer*) as Daphne, and Linda Cardellini (*ER*, *Mad Men*) as Velma.

The script by James Gunn (*Guardians of the Galaxy*) took advantage of the success of affectionate, nostalgic sendup revival films like 1996's *The Brady Bunch Movie* and included "meddling kid" references to the delight of most audiences that had only to watch a handful of episodes to get the jokes. Like the *Brady* films, the *Scooby-Doo* feature carried out the difficult task of celebrating the series for those who loved it and poking fun at it for those who felt otherwise.

Scooby-Doo 2: Monsters Unleashed unearthed familiar creatures from the original series to come alive and seek revenge on the gang. Like *The Flintstones in Viva Rock Vegas*, the second film did not make the same impact but in some ways paid more tribute to its source material.

Both films generated pop compilation albums. The first *Scooby-Doo* movie soundtrack included songs related to the characters and their familiar situations. In addition to the *Where Are You?* theme by reggae artist Shaggy and punk band MxPx, there's "It's a Mystery" by rappers Little T and One Track Mike and "Scooby D" by Baha Men ("Who Let the Dogs Out?"). A suite of David Newman's underscore closes out the album. For the *Scooby-Doo 2: Monsters Unleashed* music soundtrack, the songs were assembled but less directly tied to specific Scooby lore, plus there was no score suite. Especially notable is Imagination Studio's story version of *Monsters Unleashed*, an audiobook based on the Random House novelization. Four fine (uncredited) actors read a chapter at a time in their roles as Shaggy, Fred, Velma, and Daphne.

Scooby-Doo continued to be a powerhouse property with new made-for-TV/home video features and new series premiering regularly. Original songs took on importance depending on the film. In 2009 *Scooby-Doo and the Goblin King* featured four original songs; and a comical pop chase occurred in *Curse of the 13th Ghost*, a 2019 sequel to the acclaimed ABC series with Vincent Price. The wildly outfitted group KISS teamed with Scooby and the gang for 2015's *Rock and Roll Mystery*, in which the band members provided sweet, harmonious vocals as "The Ascot Five" for a delightfully out-of-character song called "Don't Touch My Ascot." And to reward the devoted Scoobyphiles, director and longtime Scooby-Doo fan Scott Jeralds brought back several Ted Nichols music cues and the original voice of Nicole Jaffe as Velma for *The Monster of Mexico* and *The Legend of the Vampire*.

Tony Cervone, who along with animator/directors Spike Brandt and Darrell Van Citters, directed highly regarded "comeback" theatrical shorts, direct-to-video and TV feature films with Bugs Bunny and the Looney Tunes, the Flintstones, the Jetsons, Jonny Quest, and Tom and Jerry, brought a fully CG-animated Scooby-Doo to theaters and streaming in 2020.

SCOOB! is an origin story filled with Scooby and Hanna-Barbera in-jokes and classic characters like Blue Falcon and Dick Dastardly. With COVID a worldwide concern, Warner made the feature available for streaming at home. In its first three weeks, SCOOB! was the most-watched digital title, becoming the third-highest on-demand movie of the year.

SCOOB! also generated two soundtrack albums. *SCOOB! The Album* is a pop/rap compilation and *SCOOB! The Original Motion Picture Score* presents forty-seven minutes of instrumental background music from the film by Dutch composer Tom Holkenborg (*Justice League*, *Sonic the Hedgehog*, *Godzilla vs. Kong*). Before the movie was released, a fourteen-year-old dancer promoted the film on the TikTok social media platform. On May 8, 2020, the *Deadline* blog reported that "The #ScoobDance challenge, with original music from Movers+Shakers, has accumulated 2.1 billion global views to date, and it's still climbing. In just over three days, views on the #ScoobDance challenge reached 1 billion."

▲▼▲▼▲▼

In the year 2011, there was a box-office battle between Smurfs, Indiana Jones, and James Bond. *The Smurfs*, a big-screen comedy combining CG Smurfs with live-action actors in New York City, opened the same weekend as *Cowboys and Aliens* starring Harrison Ford and Daniel Craig. The results were so close that, depending on whom one asks, the competition was smurfed. The 3-D feature costarred Neil Patrick Harris (*How I Met Your Mother*, *Doogie Howser, M.D.*) and Jayma Mays (*Glee*) as a New York couple who befriend the Smurf-out-of-water, and Hank Azaria (*The Simpsons*) as a live-action Gargamel. Voice actors Jonathan Winters (Papa Smurf) and Frank Welker (Azrael) participated in the TV series as well as the movie. The *Smurfs* TV theme song was heard several times in the feature and its status as a relentless "It's a Small World"–like earworm was used as a running gag. The music score to *The Smurfs* by Heitor Pereira (*Despicable Me*, *Space Jam: A New Legacy*) was given a limited release on the Madison Gate label.

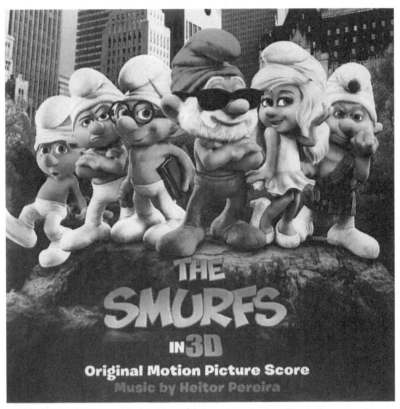

Little blue Smurfs battled Harrison Ford and Daniel Craig to conquer top box-office results.

The success of the first Smurfs movie surprised some insiders, but no one was taking any chances for the sequel, which sent the characters to Paris, forty-seven years after the Flintstones and Rubbles' theatrical movie visit. Raja Gosnell directed the first two Smurf features, just as he had done for Scooby-Doo. Everything about the 2013 sequel was more ambitious, including the investment in music. Two soundtrack albums were released. *The Smurfs 2: Original Motion Picture Score* contained Heitor Pereira's music, this time widely distributed by Varese Sarabande Records. *The Smurfs 2: Music from and Inspired by the Motion Picture* on RCA's Kemosabe label was a pop compilation with some original songs, including Britney Spears's "Ooh La La," which was released as a single and music video. The band Right Said Fred contributed a spoof of their hit "I'm Too Sexy" called "I'm Too Smurfy." Another pop idol, Katy Perry, is the

speaking voice of Smurfette in both films but is not featured as a singing star.

Demi Lovato, whose career also began with teen fame, voices Smurfette in the fully CG-animated third feature, *Smurfs: The Lost Village* (2017). Directed by Kelly Asbury (*Spirit*, *Shrek 2*), the film is dedicated to Jonathan Winters, the voice of Papa Smurf in the first two films, and in this film voiced by Mandy Patinkin. Lovato does no pop singing on the Sony Classical soundtrack which features two songs by Canadian singer Shaley Scott and the full *Smurfs: The Lost Village* background score by Christopher Lennertz. This was the composer's second Smurf project after a "Christmas Carol" featurette included on the DVD release of the first Smurfs feature.

Lennertz collaborated with composer Jay Gruska (*Charmed*, *Beverly Hills 90210*) to keep the score true to the Ted Nichols sound in the critically acclaimed

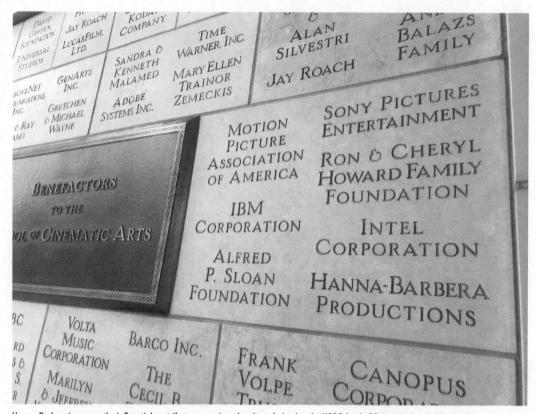

Hanna-Barbera is among the influential contributors prominently acknowledged at the USC School of Cinematic Arts in Los Angeles

2017 "Scoobynatural" episode, directed by Spike Brandt for the TV series *Supernatural*. "We recorded it at Capitol Records," Lennertz recalled. "The producers got to license the master of the *Scooby* theme, but we couldn't use it within the score. If we did, every time we used the melody it would cost a ton of money. So we did Scooby-inspired supernatural music without actually quoting the theme, which they only used once."

This explains why some of the beloved music heard in classic films, shows, and cartoons is not always used in reboots and remakes. It might be approximated or changed completely, but every cue and theme incurs a budgetary expense and sometimes earlier cues can drive up the budget. Music licensing is fraught with often-costly challenges. Quite often new projects have to move on to other options unless the originals are just too iconic to leave out.

Christopher Lennertz would soon compose for a highly successful theatrical feature connected to Hanna-Barbera, unexpectedly bringing his career as a top film composer full circle.

Chapter 28

POSSIBLE IMPOSSIBLES

~~~~~~

**Bill Hanna and Joe Barbera have not only made
animation history, they *are* animation history.**
—JERRY BECK

Hanna-Barbera imagery is on display in the Museum of Modern Art and at the
Smithsonian Institution. Every time an enduring favorite like *The Flintstones* or
The Jetsons returns, it generates a fascinating blend of warm familiarity and fresh
insights. New and recent projects featuring Hanna-Barbera characters, stories,
and music seem to be on the rise as well.

Yabba Dabba Dinosaurs showcased Pebbles and Bamm-Bamm in witty adventures with regular appearances by Wilma, Betty, Fred, and Barney. *Scooby-Doo:
Mystery Incorporated* refuted the claim that there's nowhere to go with the formula
when the formula itself is part of the appeal. *The New Scooby-Doo Movies* of 1972
was revived in 2019 as *Scooby-Doo and Guess Who?* Two of the original guest stars
returned—Cher and Sandy Duncan—and even the *Scooby-Doo* voice cast was given
a chance to be guest stars. A series like *Jellystone!* filled a city with characters like
Winsome Witch, the Hair Bear Bunch, the Biskitts, and Granny Sweet in addition
to Yogi, Cindy, and Mayor Huckleberry Hound, which gives the spotlight to the
many unsung H-B greats waiting to be rediscovered.

There is still much to be discovered or recovered from the past. Some of the
vintage Hanna-Barbera recordings have been made available since the millennium,
even as compact discs have given way to digital platforms, and vinyl keeps defying
predictions of obsolescence.

Rhino and its subsidiary labels reissued elements from earlier Hanna-Barbera
and Cartoon Network compilations. Target Stores sold a special three-disc set
from Rhino called *Cartoon Classics and Wacky Sounds by Hanna-Barbera*. Musician
Evan Jolly's versatility is featured on the 2011 Silva Screen EP, *The Theme Tunes
of Hanna-Barbera*. *Top Cat*, *Smurfs*, *The Jetsons*, and others have been carefully
orchestrated to sound authentic.

A test pressing from the planned Hanna-Barbera Records soundtrack album for *The Impossibles* in 1967.

After years of requests and negotiations, Varese Sarabande reissued the soundtrack album to *Charlotte's Web* on compact disc in 2017. A year later the vinyl version was also reissued, replicating the Paramount album without the gatefold, along with a digital edition.

▲▴▾▴▾

Among the most cherished recordings for vintage collectors are the thirty-eight 1965–1967 Hanna-Barbera Records Cartoon Series albums. Discussions are ongoing about possible ways to reissue them in some way. The first HBR Cartoon Series album that was officially reissued on CD appeared on Warner's Water Tower label. *Pebbles and Bamm-Bamm Singing Songs of Christmas* is beautifully packaged, with respect to the original art, and even the HBR label design. Two of its twelve songs are presented in stereo for the first time. A website was created to promote the album. This CD was marketed as a children's album, and no further Cartoon Series reissues have yet resulted. Perhaps a different title from the series might have been better as a first reissue. Delightful as this album

is, it does not offer the story, comedy, pop sound, and H-B music cues that make the Cartoon Series so special. These were unusual records, even in their day. The references and in-jokes on most of the albums are part of their era, in the manner of a vintage cartoon or movie. The album art makes them a natural for vinyl reissues and Record Store Day promotions.

There are also several "lost" HBR records. There are several unreleased Hanna-Barbera Cartoon Series record albums that, if reissued, could be considered "world premieres." Great names like Daws Butler and Don Messick star in never-before-heard productions. These are essentially brand-new albums featuring classic characters and legendary artists.

In a 1967 *Billboard* article about upcoming children's record releases, Eliot Teigel reported that six new albums were about to be released by Hanna-Barbera Records. "These include 'Don Quixote' as told by Yogi Bear and Huckleberry Hound," Teigel wrote, "and the following new characters: 'Dino Boy,' 'Frankenstein, Jr.,' 'Space Cadets,' [sic] 'The Impossibles,' and 'Aladdin and His Magic Lamp' starring Lippy the Lion." (Teigel also mentioned Gene Kelly's Jack and the Beanstalk album, which did get an LP release.)

There is documentation to support that the following unreleased Hanna-Barbera Cartoon Series albums exist on quarter-inch master tapes:

HLP-2058	*Yogi Bear and Boo-Boo: The Star-Spangled Banner*
HLP-2059	*Ruff and Reddy: Gulliver's Travels*
#1000	*Quick Draw McGraw: Gun Slingers of the Old West*
[no number]	*Yogi Bear: The Snow Witch*
[no number]	*Space Kidettes: Million Dollar Mutt*
[no number]	*Frankenstein Jr.*
[no number]	*The Impossibles: Songs from the TV Series*

While the HBR *Quick Draw McGraw* album has not been released as of this writing, one of the songs, "Billy the Kid," was included on the HBR album *Golden Cartoons in Song, Vol. II*. Fourteen songs from

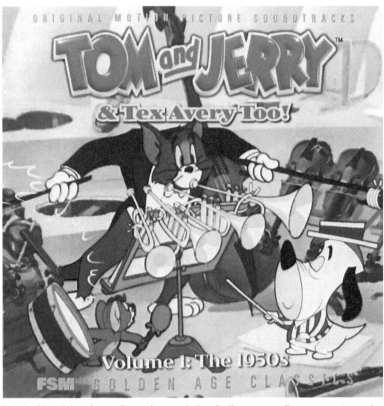

La-La Land Records brought crystalline quality scores by Scott Bradley to compact discs, some even in stereo!

The Impossibles album are contained on another master reel. Two of them have been verified on a ten-inch test record pressing: "Hiddy Hiddy Hoo" and "She Couldn't Dance."

"I remember the *Ruff and Reddy Gulliver's Travels* record," said Joe Bevilaqua. "Daws gave me a copy. I don't remember listening to it, but I distinctly recall seeing it, so maybe they made a few and gave them to him."

HBR was also planning to release earlier Cartoon Series albums in stereo editions. That does not necessarily mean that the music cues or dialogue were recorded in stereo, but there is a good chance that everything recorded for the label, specifically music, and songs, was done in mono and stereo as home systems were gradually shifting to stereo, even children's record players. Some or all of the material on such albums like *The Flintstones: Flip Fables, Monster Shin-*

dig, The New Alice in Wonderland, or What's a Nice Kid Like You Doing in a Place Like This?, and *The Man Called Flintstone* would be a vivid new experience in stereo.

The existence of these stereo editions is evidenced by producer Earl Kress managing to reissue the title song from the stereo master of the HBR studio LP recording of *The Man Called Flintstone*. It was heard for the first time in stereo on Rhino's *Modern Stone-Age Melodies*. The author was also able to premiere the stereo version of "Tickle Toddle" (with the opening verse missing from the LP) as the producer of a Kid Rhino compilation album called *Billboard Presents Family Lullaby Favorites*.

Is a world-premiere release of "The Impossibles" soundtrack album still possible? Why not? When the series aired, few if any enthusiasts dreamed that the whole series would be available in an instant. No one watching *The Flintstones, The New Adventures of*

Huckleberry Finn, or *The Atom Ant Show* would have believed how accessible they have become.

▲▼▲▼▲▼

The Film Score Monthly label again proved that anything is possible in 2006 when it released a two-disc set of Scott Bradley cartoon music soundtracks—many in stereo. *Tom and Jerry & Tex Avery Too!* (2006) combined fifteen Hanna and Barbera Tom and Jerry cartoon scores, two Spike and Tyke scores, and eight Tex Avery cartoon soundtracks, three starring Droopy. Lukas Kendall executive produced this album with George Feltenstein, who created the highly successful Warner Archive DVD and Blu-ray project—now a wise business model benchmarked by other companies to effectively market classic material. Coproducer is Daniel Goldmark, a professor of film music, specializing in animation.

In a way, Tom and Jerry ultimately survive as a symbol of a creative entity that excelled after being underestimated, bounced back after being dismissed, and endured in the face of constant trends, technology, and upheavals. In terms of H-B creations, the cat-and-mouse duo are second only to Scooby-Doo in popularity in direct-to-video and streaming specials and features. The creatives behind the films—including Earl Kress, who scripted *Tom and Jerry Meet Sherlock Holmes*—developed a way to position them in a variety of extended storylines without adding their voices or changing their dynamics. The solutions can be traced to classic story principles involving other great comedy teams. Two good examples are Abbott and Costello and Laurel and Hardy. They were inserted into an original or famous story. While they participated, they also stood on the periphery, providing a reactive link to the audience and laughs when needed. Suddenly, Tom and Jerry didn't seem incongruous when inside the world of *The Wizard of Oz* or *Willy Wonka and the Chocolate Factory*.

The films also manage a high-quality production level combining the work of overseas artists with that of major Hollywood animation artists. For a standout animation showcase like Slugworth's song in *Willy Wonka*, Windsor McCay award winner Dale Baer (*The Lion King, Frozen, The Bob's Burgers Movie*) provided the animation. The songs are also the work of top stage and screen talents. Spike Brandt and Tony Cervone's *Tom and Jerry: Back to Oz* (2016) featured original songs by Benj Pasek and Justin Paul (*La La Land, Dear Evan Hansen*).

▲▼▲▼▲▼

In 2021, Tom and Jerry proved their astounding staying power perhaps more effectively than ever. With half the movie theaters closed, Warner announced the option of streaming new tentpole features on HBOMax at no additional fee or choosing to see new films in theaters while observing COVID guidelines. The new feature, titled simply *Tom and Jerry*, used CG in a technique suggesting a slick forties animation style. Tom and Jerry, as well as Spike and other animal characters, were animated in a live-action New York City background. The tone was complete escapism, something all ages seemed to crave because Tom and Jerry achieved big numbers at the box office as well as in homes.

The Tom and Jerry Soundtrack album was released for download or streaming on the Water Tower label. Composer Christopher Lennertz and director Tim Story were highly respectful of the Scott Bradley sound when approaching the musical score, though the score couldn't resemble an MGM cartoon completely for several reasons, as Lennertz explained to the author:

> The Scott Bradley music didn't come with the Tom and Jerry movie rights, so we couldn't use any of the original scores. I love the Scott Bradley stuff, so when I discussed this with Tim Story, he said, "I would love to take the jazz elements and the classical elements that he uses and import them into our modern-day live-action New York, where we pay homage to them

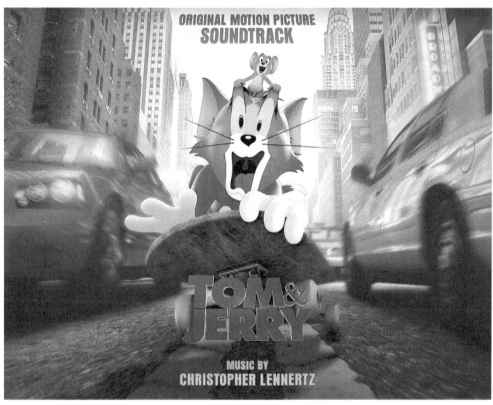

Almost twenty years after visiting a session for Henry Mancini's 1992 *Tom and Jerry: The Movie* score, Christopher Lennertz provided the score for the highly successful 2021 *Tom & Jerry* feature as a top Hollywood composer himself.

as a style and as a genre and blend it with our young live human leads."

That was our challenge from the get-go, to make our own sound but use these elements so that everyone's ears will say, "Oh, I get it, these people love Tom and Jerry. They understand that their language is based on classical music and thirties and forties jazz, so that's what we went after. There are cues where we had the orchestra but we also had others with modern elements of New York, like drum beats and sort of "record style production." Tim was interested in having a cool factor to it, to sound sort of like "Lizzo meets Scott Bradley."

We recorded a big band brass section at Abbey Road in London. We ran the tracks through effects to make them sound like vinyl records, so

it felt not only like a big band, but like an actual big band record that was sampled to put on a new record, mixed with the classical orchestra, and also recorded in Abbey Road.

So it really was a hybrid; we created our own "new old jazz." Depending on which cue it was and how much it involved Tom and Jerry, it became more jazzy or less jazzy. If you listen as the two of them are plotting against each other, that's when you hear the stand-up bass, which I always associate with the early days. Making Jerry laugh with a clarinet and violin rather than having him actually laugh—we did that specifically as an homage to a lot of the shorts. Tim felt very strongly about that—the soul of what Scott Bradley did even without using the exact notes, a creative way to get around a challenge.

Composing the score for 2021's *Tom and Jerry* was a homecoming for Christopher Lennertz. It connected back to a life-changing experience when he was studying music in college, never imagining he would work in movies and television. He continued:

> I was playing a lot of jazz on guitar, a lot of Pat Metheny, jazz fusion, and things like that. I had been to recording sessions, but the first orchestral film scoring session I had ever been to was the 1992 *Tom and Jerry* with Henry Mancini. He's a hero of mine. A teacher said to me, "You should check this out. Maybe it's something you want to do."
>
> He introduced me to a session pianist named Ralph Grierson, one of the best that ever lived. He said, "The music that Chris writes feels very filmic." I'd grown up with the music of John Williams and Jerry Goldsmith. As a favor to my teacher, Ralph let me sneak in. I pretended to be his roadie and sat next to him. Two minutes later, in walked Mancini and Ralph introduced me. Mancini said, "Call me Hank." At that point, I was thinking, "Oh you gotta be kidding me!" So I watched this whole session.
>
> Joe Barbera was there. I watched as Henry—or Hank—wrote. There were two great cues they had recorded in the morning but they wanted to change them. They said they needed more energy. So he rewrote those cues! In one of them, the style changed completely! They re-recorded them in the afternoon on the same day. He had written them on the piano during the break and they were brilliant. The original was brilliant and then it was a totally different approach, also brilliant. I remember everyone being so happy and loving it.
>
> But it was watching Mancini rewrite those cues that made me want to be a film composer because I was such a fan of so many different styles of music. That's probably why I love early cartoon music. It went from jazz to classical and things like that. Here was this situation where somebody was able to be versatile and explore different genres. Very few did it as well as Henry Mancini. I walked out of there with my eyes wide, my head was spinning and I changed my major the next morning to film composition and that was it.
>
> I made that decision at the *Tom and Jerry* session in 1992, and almost 30 years later, I was able to score the 2021 *Tom and Jerry*. I'm also dear friends with Felice, Hank's daughter because we worked on the Mr. Holland's Opus Foundation together. To take my own spin on *Tom and Jerry* brings it full circle. Back when I was in that studio watching Hank Mancini and Joe Barbera working on the earlier *Tom and Jerry* movie, it literally changed the course of my whole life.

▲▼▲▼

"I didn't know Bill Hanna that well, but I got to know Joe Barbera very well," said actor Pamelyn Ferdin. "He was so devoted to the cartoons and so proud of the studio. He had framed pictures and cels on the walls of his office. Even though it doesn't show in the credits, he directed the voice cast of *Charlotte's Web* himself. He loved all the H-B characters, loved the creation process, and loved the voice actors. It certainly wasn't a cartoon factory."

"Historians of the future will view and assess the incredible body of work that bears the co-credit of William Hanna," Mark Evanier wrote on his blog. "My guess is they'll find it wildly variable, including some of the best and worst animation of its day.

"But I hope they'll also give a little weight to the staggering number of people who bought homes and groceries for 30-some-odd years working for Bill. And I hope they'll give him some credit for an entire generation of us who got into writing and/or drawing because, back when we were small, we loved watching *The Flintstones*."

And at the heart of it all is a definite "Hanna-Barbera" musicality—in the themes, songs, and scores, and also in the voices, sound effects, and editing. It is inherent in the musical timing Hanna cemented into the production system and Barbera infused with his knack for story and vocalization.

"This is crucial to why Hanna-Barbera cartoons worked so well," said Stacia Martin. "Bill Hanna was a musician and songwriter. Joe Barbera understood that the differences in the tonal qualities of the voices are very musical and therefore very pleasing and compelling to the ear.

"Sometimes we are hearing what we see without realizing it, just as our sense of smell tells us about a food's taste. Hanna-Barbera would often make what we watched and heard seem simple. Simplicity is a technique of some of the world's finest artists."

Acknowledgments

Many thanks to those who provided information, interviews, and insight over the years, including the following:

Sherry Alberoni Van Meter, Trey Alsup, Billy Ayres, Brian Bakerman, Devon Baxter, Michael Bell, Noah Bell, Greg Berg, Peter Berk, Joe Bevilaqua, Lyle Blosser, Chris Bracher, Marilee Bradford, Spike Brandt, Steve Burstein, Kevin Butler, David Chase, Christopher Cook, Carolyn Copeland, Mark Christiansen, Jim Cleveland, Christopher Curtin, Evelyn Dana, Jon de Mello and the Mountain Apple Company, Andy Decker, Shawn Degenhart, Ron Dias, E. J. Dick, Herb Duncan, Ben Edge, Jerry Eisenberg, Jim Engel, Hal Erickson, Sam Ewing, Shannon Farnon, George Feltenstein, Sandy Fries, June Foray, Robyn Frederick, Fred Frees, Craig Fuqua, Lee Gambin, Kathy Garver, Neil Gold, Kathy Gori, Barry Grauman, Maurice Gravelle, Margery Gray, Earl Hamner, Barry Hansen, Bruce K. Hanson, Kirk Hanson, Sheldon Harnick, Kerry Heafner, Ted Herrmann, Ron Hicklin, Michael Hopkins, Scott Hopkins, Jackie Joseph, Jason Hollifield, Clark Holloway, Kirk Honeycutt, Danny Hutton, Phyllis Tucker Vinson Jackson (Phyllis Middleton), Patricia Ward Kelly, Lukas Kendall, Jay Kenton, Kevin Kern, Thad Komorowski, Judy Gail Krasnow, J. Lee, Ruta Lee, Christopher Lennertz, Bob Leszczak, June Lockhart, Dave Madden, Michael Mallory, Tim Matheson, Mark McCray, Jack Mendelsohn, Don Messick, Tom Minton, Anthony Miranda, Kate Mishkin, Jeff Missinne, Paul Mular, Bob Nelson, Cary O'Dell, James E. Parten, Brandon Pierce, Jerry Rees, Debbie Reynolds, Glenn Romano, Tom Ruegger, Judy Saffer, J. J. Sedelmaier, Fred Seibert, John Semper, Jr., Charles Galen Shows, Chris Sobienak, Mark Stein, Ralph Stein, Roger Stephenson, Janet Waldo, Jackie Ward, Max Weinberg, Taylor White, and Kevin Wollenweber. Several people contributed information through my "Animation Spin" column at cartoonresearch.com series and on Facebook using their online names: bigg3469, kc, öh, rdten1, rnigma, robgems6, Randy, acountryfan, Martin, Matt, DBenson DC Hampton Jacobs, DGM, EugaenOhnland, It's So Hanna-Barberaesque, progrockasaurus, Ross, S Carras, Uncle Wayne, Top Cat James.

For all their support, friendship, and expertise, I wish to thank Jeff Abraham, Steve Anderson, Chris Anthony, Mark Arnold, Phil Baron, Jerry Beck, Tony Benedict, Bob Bergen, Steve Beverly, James Bohn, Heather Boyd, Beth Burns Bramlett, Tom Brooks, Charles "Chas" Butler, Sheila Butler, Brian Campbell, Andrea Canny, Dennis Chalifour, Lori, Chris and Alex Chapman, Cheryl Chase, Tom Chen, Becky Cline, Jesse Cohen, John Cole, the Cordell family, Bill and Carol Cotter, John Debney, Jonathan David Dixon, Janice Douma Lange, Peter Emslie, Tom Farley, Pamelyn Ferdin, D. W. Ferrante, Jorge Finkelman, Will Finn, Richard Foos, June Foray, Deborah Fox, David Frankham, Will Friedwald, Bill Funt, David Gerstein, Didier Ghez, Daniel Goldmark, Howard Green, Steve Heise, the Henton family, Barry Hill, Jim Hollifield, Tim Hollis, Wesley Hyatt, Willie Ito, Vinny Jaey, Mindy Johnson, Ron Jones, the Joseph family, Donald Kasen, Jeanine Kasun, J. B. Kaufman, Mark Kausler, Bruce Kimmel, Lee Kitchen, Jim Korkis, Chris Korman, Nic Kramer, Earl and Denise Kress, Jeff Kurtti, Beth Leahey, Katie Leigh, Svea Macek, Jymn Magon, Leonard, Alice, and Jessie Maltin, Jeff Marquis, Stacia Martin, Tim Matheson, Cathy Matthews, Gary Miereanu, Kelsie Milburn, Walt Mitchell, Dale Moore, Sue Moore, Bill Morgan, Kliph Nesteroff, Nicolasa Nevarez, Cary O'Dell, Ben Ohmart, Alyssa Padia Walles, Matthew Patterson, Hans Perk, Les Perkins, Jim Pierson, Herbie J. Pilato, Ray Pointer, Chase Pritchard, David Pruiksma, Nik Ranieri, Alex Rannie, Steve and Virginia Reeser, Linda Rolls, Joanna Romersa, Will Ryan, Kevin Sandler, Nick Santa Maria, Frank Santopadre, Mike Schlesinger, Keith Scott, Scott Shaw!, Robert Sher, Gregg Sherman, Jeffrey Sherman, Laurie Sherman, Richard M. Sherman, Robert J. Sherman, Stuart Shostak, Laura Simpson, Tom Sito, Bill Smith, Brit Sommers, Kamden Spies, Sandy and Bob Stein, George Stewart, Randy Thornton, Darrell Van Citters, Michael Vargo, Janet Waldo, Brian AR Washington, Frederick Weigand, Tyler Williams, John Wilson, Carlton Zapp, and Lori Zide. Many, many thanks also to anyone else I overlooked, including the thousands who created happiness at Hanna-Barbera.

Special thanks to Jon Burlingame, Mark Evanier, Michael Lyons, Tony Milch, Bambi Moé, Rick Stockton, and Don Yowp for reviewing the manuscript or substantial sections; to Ed Robertson for advice and public support; and to the extraordinary staff of University Press of Mississippi, particularly to Craig Gill for years of enthusiasm, kindness, and friendship. Many thanks to Joey Brown, Pete Halverson, Courtney McCreary, Shane Gong Stewart, Katie Turner, Deborah Upton, and everyone else at UPM who helped guide this labor of love to being a dream come true (sorry for the clichés but they're true).

To Katie and Colin Ehrbar—thanks for being there to inspire Dad! And to my wife, Suzanne, who "read it and fixed it and marked it with an 'H-B,'" I am not exaggerating when I say this book could never have happened without you, who said often, "This story needs to be told—so get over there and write!"

Notes

1: Tom and Jerry and Bill and Joe

1. "The mouse was named 'Pee Wee' in studio publicity for *Puss Gets the Boot*," said animation historian David Gerstein. "The name 'Jinx' is often mentioned too, cited as possibly appearing on a model sheet." Gerstein surmises the news of the selected names must have taken a while to fully circulate through the studio. "In early publicity for the cartoon *Midnight Snack*, Jerry has his final name but Tom is still Jasper," he noted. "Also that year, a prototype for Butch the Bulldog is simultaneously present in *The Alley Cat*, with his original model sheet name of . . . Tom."

2. Disney, in its early history, was a small independent without a music publishing company or cartoon budgets for outside songs, so they relied primarily on public domain music until the song "Minnie's Yoo Hoo" initiated in-house original songs.

3. Gene Kelly reenacted the "chain dance" for Hanna-Barbera in 1967's *Jack and the Beanstalk* with two animated Woggle-Birds.

4. In 1965, Bret Morrison was the singing voice of the fox in Universal's animated feature *Pinocchio in Outer Space*, produced by Filmation cofounder Norm Prescott at the Belvision studio in Brussels. As American film studios increased the number of foreign films for distribution in the US, Morrison was frequently called upon to perform English language dialogue.

5. Leroy Holmes was also the musical director for *The Tonight Show* in the mid-fifties. Holmes eventually signed with United Artists Records as a recording artist himself, conducting studio versions of *Citizen Kane* and *The Ten Commandments*. He continued working on children's records, arranging and conducting a "Song and Picture Book" album of *Chitty Chitty Bang Bang* with cosongwriter Richard Sherman singing with Lola Fisher (Miss Tickle on Filmation's *Mission: Magic*), as well as composing and conducting for Golden Records.

6. Regarding Jack Nicholson's early MGM days, Jerry Beck was told in 1994:

BARBERA: He was the office boy at MGM.
HANNA: He has often talked about us. As a matter of fact, he recently quoted me telling him not to quit at MGM. He said I told him, "Don't be a fool. You have your chance here to become something. Stay with it."
BARBERA: He used to bring us Cokes, he'd wheel in the cart, go into the offices and ask, "What do you want today?" So years later I'm standing in the Polo Lounge, and I hear this voice in my ear say (Joe doing a wicked Jack Nicholson impression) "Mr. Bar-ber-a."—I respond, "I'll have a Coke and two milks." (Laughs.)

2: Ruff and Reddy Get H-B Set

1. Both Hal Roach and Walt Disney moved into television early, while the major studios were resistant, either unable or unwilling to make the new medium work into their business models.

2. One of the other trailers that did not show any clips was for RKO's *The Bishop's Wife* (1947), which cleverly pitched the romantic holiday fantasy as a film for all audiences by having its stars discuss it while strolling through the movie studio.

3. On the establishment of their company, Hanna said, "We financed ourselves with the pension money that we accumulated at MGM. And we never did have to go in debt to borrow to make Hanna-Barbera work. We were able to use the money that we had, make the first cartoon, and get compensated for it in a very short time."

4. Arthur Shimkin left Golden Records in the late sixties and developed children's records for the Columbia label. In 1970 he added *Sesame Street* recordings to the line.

When Columbia discontinued the children's division in the mid-seventies, Shimkin founded Children's Records of America (CRA), which reissued selected Columbia and Sesame Street titles. CRA became Sesame Street Records and the generic Columbia children's titles were discontinued. Sesame Street became one of the most popular and award-winning children's labels in the seventies.

3: Huckleberry Hound Goes to College

1. The original *Time for Beany* puppet series, created by Warner Bros. cartoon director Bob Clampett, featured the talents of Daws Butler, who puppeteered with Stan Freberg, and writer Charles Shows, both of whom worked on Hanna-Barbera's earliest cartoons. *Time for Beany* was revived as the animated *Beany and Cecil Show*.

2. One of the album selections is "Sheriff Huckleberry" (aka "Dinky Dalton and the Showdown at Hoedown Corral"). It contains another amusing organ music cue underlining the clever writing in this "courteous" exchange between Huck, outlaw Dinky Dalton, and the listeners:

> HUCK: (to listeners) It's safer over the phone when you're talkin' to an outlaw like Dinky.
> DINKY: Hellooooo?
> HUCK: Is this the Dalton residence?
> DINKY: Yeeehhhhs!
> HUCK: Is this Dinky Dalton?
> DINKY: This is heeee!
> HUCK: (to home audience) Ya know what? This feller's got a right nice voice on the telephone! (into phone) Y'all sure this is Dinky Dalton?
> DINKY: Yehhhhhs!
> HUCK: Hold the phone a second, will you?
> DINKY: Love to!

4: Quick Draws and Loopy Loops

1. From Super Snooper and Blabber Mouse's track comes one of their wittiest cartoons, with this dialogue sending up radio and TV's *Dragnet*. The Fairy Godmother is one of the early Hanna-Barbera vocal appearances by Jean Vander Pyl (the future Wilma Flintstone), as budgets limited previous female roles to being played by Messick or Butler:

> GODMOTHER: Yeeah, I remember her. She ordered the whole woiks. White mice, pumpkin, glass slipper, ya know. The whole woiks.
> SNOOPER: Yes, ma'am.
> GODMOTHER: I want you to know I run a respectable place here. I want you to know that.
> SNOOPER: Yes, ma'am.
> GODMOTHER: I use an honest wand in my woik. I want you to know that.
> SNOOPER: Ma'am, yes.
> GODMOTHER: I don't want any trouble with the police.
> SNOOPER: Who does? By the way, could you tell us where she lives?
> GODMOTHER: With an ugly sister down at the waterfront.
> SNOOPER: Thanks. I'll just mark this wand "Exhibit A" and return it later. Hold on to Exhibit A, Blab.
> BLABBER: Right, Snoop.
> SNOOPER: Oh uh, by the way, I needn't precaution you about leavin' town.
> GODMOTHER: I'm stayin' right here. I hate to travel. Ask anybody. "She hates to travel," they'll tell ya.
> SNOOPER: Yes, ma'am.

2. Before his passing in 2016, Howard Berk and his son Peter published the science fiction novel *Time Lock* based on their movie script.

3. "Robin Hood Yogi" contains a line (and a story device) that anticipates a future Hanna-Barbera record, perhaps by coincidence. Yogi tells Boo-Boo, "We'll rob tidbits from the rich and give them to the poor, namely us," an almost word-for-word line that Top Cat says twice on his own *Robin Hood* album six years later.

4. A substantial amount of early TV scoring was composed, recorded, and repurposed. A composer might write music for one or more episodes of a series and the music could be reused in subsequent episodes. For example, Oscar-winner John Williams wrote the *Star Wars*–like background music for only four episodes of *Lost in Space*. As the series progressed, his cues were reused from 1965 to 1968. Some episodes had fresh scores by other composers and others relied completely on existing music. Both *Lost in Space* and *Daniel Boone* also reused cues from the 1947 classic *Miracle on 34th Street*. *The Outer Limits* picked up the theme song from *One Step Beyond* in its second season, a theme that originated on *The Loretta Young Show*.

5. In the thirties, Walt Disney used this device to introduce early Silly Symphony cartoons under the banner, "Mickey Mouse Presents," to connect the lesser-known film series with a familiar character.

6. In their initial release, Loopy's Golden recordings gave some Hanna-Barbera enthusiasts their first inkling about the origins of some H-B background music. Unless they had watched Loopy DeLoop films in theaters, they would have had no idea they were hearing his theme song in other H-B cartoons until they were shown years later on television.

5: The Flintstones Rock the World

1. The end of "I Flipped" has one of the most familiar orchestral "outros" in *The Flintstones* cue library, though the end of "Split Level Cave" certainly rivals it in use by the Hanna-Barbera editors.

2. Jim Timmens moved along with producer Arthur Shimkin from Golden Records to the Columbia, CRA, and Sesame Street record labels. Timmens edited albums at all these labels and occasionally arranged and conducted.

6: Top Cat's Big City Blues

1. In a scene from "Top Cat Falls in Love," Top Cat is unaware that he is speaking with expectant fathers in a maternity ward. T. C. thinks they're talking about their lady friends instead of babies, in a scene rather sophisticated for most cartoons of the day.

T.C.: You don't seem so happy, sir.
MAN: I just hope this isn't like the last one.
T.C.: Why? What was wrong with her?
MAN: Nothing but a problem. She'd take a bottle at eight o'clock and polish it off, then at two in the morning, yell her head off for another one!
T.C.: Boy, what a swinger! She'd drink them all by herself, huh?
MAN: Just like that, every drop. And keep the whole neighborhood awake.
T.C.: Yeah, you mean singing and playing the piano and breaking things, eh?
MAN: Mostly with her loud crying.
T.C.: Oh, that kind, yeah. Oh, they're the worst, the worst!
MAN: And then, crawling all around on her hands and knees.
T.C.: Well, after two bottles who wouldn't?
MAN: Oh, it's been awful. I haven't had a decent night's sleep in two years.
T.C.: Yeah, but what parties?! What parties?!

8: Jonny Quest and Ann-Margrock

1. By sheer coincidence the same year, one of the jokes was also told by Dick Van Dyke and Ed Wynn in Walt Disney's *Mary Poppins*: "I know a man with a wooden leg named Smith." "Really? What's the name of his other leg?"

10: Enter, Stage Left: Hanna-Barbera's Record Company

1. As an example of the HBR Cartoon Series humor, this is an excerpt from the *Cinderella* album in which "Cindy" races in her hot rod dragster from the ball at midnight and is stopped for speeding:

CINDERELLA: Uh-oh. The cycle fuzz.
POLICEMAN: All right, let's see your registration papers.
CINDERELLA: Registration papers? But I don't have any!
POLICEMAN: Okay, who owns this heap?
CINDERELLA: Well . . . I guess I do.
POLICEMAN: You guess you do? Where'd you get this rail?
CINDERELLA: Well, there was this fairy godmother, and she had like uh, you know, uh, a magic wand . . .
POLICEMAN: Never mind all that malarkey about fairy godmothers and magic wands. Where'd this heap come from? I mean, who tooled this rig?
CINDERELLA: Well you see officer, my fairy godmother made this rod out of a big old pumpkin.
POLICEMAN: A pumpkin, huh? And a fairy godmother, huh? Oh boy, how come I run into all of you kooks? All right, let me see your driver's license.
MR. JINKS: But uh, just coincidentally at that second, the clock in the church steeple ding-donged of midnight ... and exactly at midnight, a very peculiar thing happened. I mean, the chromey dragster turned back into a pumpkin.
POLICEMAN: Well, I still wanna see your driver's license!
CINDERELLA: So who needs a driver's license to drive a pumpkin?

2. In the 1970s, disco also was not included on major children's labels until it gained more mainstream acceptance. The exception was Peter Pan Records, which got a three-year jump on disco ahead of Disney; and two years ahead of Sesame Street's record label.

11: The Gruesomes Have a Monster Party

1. Something else is also mixed up on this Yogi Bear album. A pressing or text error was made, flipping the two sides of the original album. What is labeled "side two" is

actually the start of the album with the "Yogi Bear" song, the introduction, and "Jack and the Beanstalk." It concludes with "Little Red Riding Hood."

2. SPOILER ALERT: Yogi's version of *Jack and the Beanstalk* ends with a bizarre twist. When Jack returns home, his mom has a surprise that few if any other storybook "Jacks" have encountered. Yogi (Allan Melvin) narrates the following and does the voices:

"I knew you'd be hungry after all that work, Jack, so I fixed you a quick supper."

"Crazy!" said Jack. "What's to eat?"

"We've got your favorite dish. Chicken and dumplings."

"Wild!" said Jack. "But where did you get the chicken, Ma?"

"Whaddaya mean, 'Where did I get a chicken?' You just brought a big ol' chicken home with you, don't you remember?"

"Ohhh, no! Not my magic hen!"

"Don't worry," said his mother. "There's nothing wrong with your magic hen. In fact, it's delicious."

"But ma," explained Jack, "That hen could lay golden eggs!"

Yogi continues: "That chicken dinner cost Jack about a million dollars. But somehow, he didn't enjoy it."

3. In another standout comic sequence and vocal performance, Allan Melvin delivers a lengthy comic monologue as the Big Bad Wolf, who is representing himself in court. Seeing this in print does not do it justice, especially without H-B's funniest mock-sorrowful music cues and the sound of tweeting birds:

Your honor, it all started when I was walking through the woods, on my way to take some warm soup to a sick friend. I'm always doin' good deeds like that—it's just the way I am. When the plaintiff, Miss Red Riding Hood, came along, and I noticed she was crying. Well, I never could stand to see a woman cry. I politely asked her if I could be of any help. Well, she tells me a phony story about a sick granny and all that jazz. Well, I felt so sorry for the poor dear that I went home and made a nice pot of soup, and took it to her ailing granny.

Well, you can imagine my surprise when I walked into Granny's house and the two of them jumped me! I screamed for help, but nobody heard me. It seems the plaintiff, a Miss Red Riding Hood, and her so-called Granny were running a phony fur coat racket! They were gonna tan my hide, dye it grey, and sell it as a mink stole! Can you imagine that?

Red accuses him of lying, so the Wolf says, "May lightning strike me if that's not the truth." True to the old joke, lightning strikes him!

12: Pebbles and Bamm-Bamm Go to Hollyrock

1. Just a few samples of Shows's (and perhaps Butler's) clever lines for Snagglepuss on *The Wizard of Oz* album include:

- "The unfunny, funnel-shaped cyclone lifted the tiny house into the air, Watutsi-ed it around and around, and slowly lifted it into the sky, like a giant balloon even! If you can imagine a square balloon. Heavens to Morpheus!"
- "Dorothy couldn't believe her eyes! She thought her eyes were tellin' lies! Fibs, even!"
- "So they walked up to a big, *GREEN* gate and rang a *GREEN* bell. A tiny guard appeared, dressed in—what else? Purple. Fooled ya, didn't I? Actually, it was green."
- "And at once, her big pack of ferocious wolves came running to the castle from every direction! North! South! East! West! And I forget the other one!"

2. On this album, "If I Only Had a Brain" is a different song from the one Ray Bolger sings in the MGM movie. The uncredited singer is most likely Ron Hicklin, in the same "goofy" voice he would later employ for "I Wan'na Be Like You" for Disneyland Record's "Jungle V.I.P." edition of *The Jungle Book*. It could also be Lynn Bryson, or possibly Leo DeLyon of *Top Cat*, who was doing vocal work for H-B and Disney. *The Man Called Flintstone* was in production, for which he sang a song, and he appears on an HBR *Top Cat* LP, so he was probably available.

3. Here is an amusing exchange (with a serious undertone) between Touché Turtle and Smokey the Dragon, whose vivid personality as played by Daws Butler reminds the author of his aunt Sadie. The "Lookita dragon! Lookita dragon!" nods to the cartoon "Yogi's Big Break," also written by Charles Shows, in which Yogi tires of tourists saying "Lookita bears! Lookita bears!"

SMOKEY: There was a time when dragon slaying was quite the thing to do.
TOUCHE: Oh you poor soul.
SMOKEY: But then, after a while, the brave knights had slain—or is it slew—nearly all the dragons. There were only a few of us left.
TOUCHE: Um, hmm.
SMOKEY: The handsome ones.
TOUCHE: Ah, yes.

SMOKEY: Well, being a peace-loving dragon, I just couldn't stand the idea of fighting a knight or anyone, so I hid in this deep cave, hundreds of feet underground.

TOUCHE: My, my.

SMOKEY: For many years it was quite peaceful down here. But then, when they started shooting off those bombs underground, I couldn't stand all that noise. So I came up to the top.

TOUCHE: Well uh, what do you do out here all day, Smokey?

SMOKEY: Well, there isn't a lot to do, ya know. I work crossword puzzles, make fudge brownies, but I keep busy, ya know?

4. Top Cat and his friends prepare for what they think is their movie debut:

CHOO-CHOO: Gee, I hope they photograph me from the left. It's my best profile.

T.C.: I don't see our producer around. Oh, there he is, across the street hiding in that alley. Oh boy, what an actor! He looks like a real crook!

BRAIN: Duh, is my make-up on straight?

13: Mary Poppins and James Bond

1. In another instance of working around story copyrights, David Seville and the Chipmunks recorded seven songs from 1967's *Doctor Dolittle*. Like the *Flintstone/Poppins* album, this LP did not tell the entire story either. Dave asked the Chipmunks questions about elements of the story—the equivalent of showing promotional clips.

2. Mel Blanc did not voice Barney with Corden as Fred on HBR discs except in the *Alice in Wonderland* TV cast album. It may have been a matter of budget or availability.

3. One-liner jokes abound as Barney Rubble narrates Hansel and Gretel's encounter with the wicked witch at her candy house:

BARNEY: Hansel and Gretel were so frightened, they ALMOST stopped eating!

WITCH: Well, bless my broomstick.

BARNEY: . . . said the little old lady.

WITCH: Two nice, plump—uh, healthy kiddies. Eh, who are you?

HANSEL: I'm Hansel and she's Gretel.

BARNEY: . . . mumbled Hansel, with his mouth full of strawberry shingles.

WITCH: Well, Hansel and Gretel. Welcome to Grandma Grizzly's Goodyland. Won't you—heh, heh, heh, heh—step into my dining room, and

we'll have a dinner that won't quit. Ha, ha, ha, ha, ha, ha, ha, ha, ha!

BARNEY: Hansel and Gretel were afraid, but after all, a free lunch is a free lunch! So the creepy old lady led them inside the strange house.

WITCH: You look like a couple of yummy—uh, good kids.

BARNEY: . . . said the little old woman.

WITCH: But you need to be fattened up a little. Mweh heh, heh, heh, heh, heh, heh, heh, heh!

HANSEL: What's with that crazy laugh?

BARNEY: . . . whispered Hansel.

HANSEL: Her lines are not that funny!

4. Super Snooper and Blabber Mouse, aboard James Bomb's flying Rolls-Royce, start tossing out items to lighten the load in a scene that is pure audio magic, with gags that are much funnier in one's imagination than if literally shown.

BOMB: We'll just have to lighten our weight. Snooper, you grab the baby grand piano and toss it overboard.

SNOOP: Aye aye, 007!

(*Musical crashes.*)

BOMB: Blab, you tear out the snack bar and jettison it.

BLAB: Right!

(*More crashes.*)

BOMB: Now toss out the pool table, Snooper.

(*More crashes.*)

SNOOP: Pool table overboard!

BLAB: We've thrown out everything but the kitchen sink, 007!

BOMB: Well, throw the kitchen sink out! It was full of dirty dishes anyway!

(*Dishes smash and glass tinkles.*)

14: Atom Ant, Secret Squirrel, and The Way-Outs

1. The *Atom Ant* album contains one of the slyer examples of political humor on the HBR Cartoon Series, Chief Mildew (Daws Butler) calls "LBJ" for help in dealing with the killer ants. The other two voices are by Messick and Butler, respectively:

CHIEF: Is this the boss?

LBJ: You wanted to speak to the boss? One moment, please. (*yells away from the receiver*) Oh, Lady Bird! Telephone!

CHIEF: But—but sir, I wanna speak to you. You are the President, aren't you?

LBJ: That is right, Sir. What can I do for you?

CHIEF: This here is the chief of police of Possum Corners, and we're in a mess a' trouble!

LBJ: Trouble, eh? Now, do not worry about a thing, Chief. I will send you a whole wagonload of money. Where shall I have it delivered?

CHIEF: Oh, Mr. President! We don't need money!

LBJ: Don't need money? So what are you, a Republican?

CHIEF: But sir! We're being invaded from outer space!

LBJ: Invaded from outer space?! That's different. I'll have the Air Force up in the wild blue yonder before you can say, "All the way with LBJ!"

2. The TV title cards read "Precious Pupp," but the record album cover adds Granny Sweet to the title since she is featured prominently on side one, with Precious taking center stage on side two.

15: Fred, Barney, Sammy, and Alice in Wonderland

1. Veteran story artist Tony Benedict rendered sketches of both Hanna and Barbera's offices. True to their differences in personalities, each office reflects their interests and personal style, but both are equipped with stereo turntable systems.

16: Laurel and Hardy and The Three Stooges

1. A wider range of choices, extending to early films and television through endless platform access, proves this true today more than ever. A marketing study presented by the Dentsu McGarry-Bowen advertising agency asserted that millennials do not care when something was produced, they like it because it is interesting to them. A statement to that effect was, "They like to drive forward but look in the rear-view mirror."

2. Media composers are sometimes given footage with a "scratch track" to use as a guide from those who offer an idea of what is requested. This track might have temporary voices as well as established music, which will be removed after the composer creates a fresh score based on the general idea.

3. Here is an example of the comic repartee between Fred, Barney, and José aboard the time machine rocket:

FRED: Barney, we've been in a lot of trouble in our day, but this time we're in a real mess. Here we

are thousands of miles above the Earth, in a pilotless rocket driven by a nut from outer space.

BARNEY: It could be worse, Fred.

FRED: How could it possibly be worse, Barn?

BARNEY: Well, we could be up here without the rocket. (Hee-heee-heee-heee!)

FRED: Barney, how can you laugh at a time like this? We're going thousands of miles an hour, and we don't even know where we're going!

BARNEY: I hadn't thought of it like that, Fred. Just where are we going, José?

JOSE: Where are we going? I don't even know where we've been!

FRED: You think this rocket is going back to Cape Kennedy, José?

JOSE: Oh, I hope so. I left my car double-parked.

4. The HBR *G.I. Joe* album is the only Hanna-Barbera record to use Ted Nichols's "Spy Chief" soundtrack cue from *The Man Called Flintstone*. The HBR album version of that film score is a studio re-creation.

17: The Avengers, Elvis, and the Beanstalk

1. SPOILER ALERT! The face of Jack's mother, played by former Miss America Marian McKnight, is not seen until the end of the story when Jeremy (Gene Kelly) asks her name, and she looks and sounds like the animated Princess Serena. Janet Waldo is dubbing McKnight's voice. McKnight receives album credit even though she is not heard on the soundtrack, but Dick Beals, singing for Bobby Riha, is uncredited.

18: Banana Splits and Cattanooga Cats

1. Ron Hicklin, Al Capps, and Stan Farber, along with singer Carol Lombard, sang cover songs from *The Jungle Book* in 1967 as "The Jungle V.I.P.'s." This was the first Disneyland album to adopt a pop sound, two years after the Hanna-Barbera Cartoon Series.

2. The final albums created by Ross Bagdasarian Sr., *The Chipmunks See Doctor Dolittle* (1967) and *The Chipmunks Go to the Movies* (1969), were released as Sunset Records and not under the brand of parent label Liberty.

3. *The Three Musketeers* and *Arabian Nights* cartoons of 1968 are forerunners of the Australian-made API and Hanna-Barbera literary adventure specials of the seventies.

4. Al Alsup, who was general counsel of the Arlington, Texas, park, would become president of the World of Sid and Marty Krofft indoor theme park in Atlanta, now CNN.

19: Scooby-Doo, Where Are Your Records?

1. The following are a few examples from "What a Night for a Knight" in which Ted Nichols's music cues actually fit the action: In the museum scene, there is a xylophone section for a gag in which Scooby knocks over a skeleton and throws it in the air; it reassembles itself to the melody of the public domain song, "Dry Bones." An off-key string tune plays when Scooby dresses as an artist and pretends to paint the Black Knight's portrait. Rhythmic drum beats accompany Shaggy and Scooby as they hide under a bear rug. One of the most directly underscored scene is one in which Shaggy and Scooby attempt escape in a vintage prop airplane to the tune of the US Air Force song, "Off We Go into the Wild Blue Yonder."

2. Disney read-alongs of the late '70s and '80s used a script format, with the character's name and a colon for each line in the text. Peter Pan did not indicate the speaker in the Scooby-Doo read-along books.

20: Making Tracks with Josie and the Pussycats

1. Dante's anonymity as The Archies' lead singer was such that even a *Miami Herald* feature writer was unaware. When a reader asked about The Archies in the Sunday *Tropic* magazine's entertainment column, the reply stated that "the fellow who does the voice of Archie" was the singer. Archie's speaking voice was Dal McKennon, who did not sing for Archie on the albums. McKennon recorded the dialogue in California, while the music and vocals were produced at RCA's New York studios.

2. CBS retooled *In the Know* into *In the News*, which condensed current events and feature stories into brief Saturday morning segments. It was hosted by Christopher Glenn.

3. Bob Engelmann attended Brigham Young University and helped raise hundreds of thousands of dollars for the school and football stadium.

4. Filmation redesigned the TV images of the characters while Hanna-Barbera adapted their images directly from Archie artist Dan DeCarlo's Josie character designs.

5. According to *Harlem Globetrotters* voice actor Nancy Wible, who played Granny, Los Angeles disc jockey Eddie Anderson played Bobby Joe. It is not Eddie "Rochester" Anderson of *The Jack Benny Program*, as is sometimes incorrectly listed.

21: Charlotte, Wilbur, Bill, Joe, Bob, and Dick

1. Paul Lynde was also a popular imitation for impressionists, including John Byner in DePatie-Freleng's 1969 *Ant and the Aardvark* cartoon, "Technology, Phooey."

22: The Funtastic, Radiant, Humble Seventies

1. The Columbia albums that compiled material that HBR released on 45 rpm records sound as if they were not accessed from the master tapes, but instead transferred directly from the discs. The giveaway is the "groove echo" present on some of the HBR 45 rpm pressings. This is a condition caused when the grooves on a record are cut so close that the listener can hear the sounds occurring before and after the specific groove being played.

23: Smurfs Heard 'Round the World

1. Belvision studios also produced the 1965 theatrical feature, *Pinocchio in Outer Space*, which was helmed by screenwriter/producer Norm Prescott, who established Filmation Associates with Lou Scheimer and Hal Sutherland. One of Filmation's earliest endeavors, *Journey Back to Oz*, was brought briefly to Belvision for animation work. Pinocchio was impressive enough for Prescott to present as his calling card for his potential clients. A year later, CBS hired Filmation for *The New Adventures of Superman*, the foundation of Filmation's emergence as one of Hanna-Barbera's primary rivals on Saturday morning TV. Filmation developed its own style to reduce animation costs, particularly by compiling a stock library of animation drawings that could be used in multiple episodes, enabling the studio to offer competitive bids to networks.

2. Since the opening of Kings Island, another park with a Happy Land of Hanna-Barbera ride opened in 1975, Kings Dominion in Virginia. Other Hanna-Barbera-themed areas opened in theme parks around the world, years before Disney began to build resorts and parks outside the US. Once again, Hanna-Barbera was ahead of the industry in maximizing in-person access to its characters.

24: Heidi Sings and the Jetsons Fly Again

1. Heidi's vocal in the song, "A Christmas-sy Day," is credited to singer Sandie Hall. Perhaps a new vocal track with Gray was not created, so Hall's vocal remained in the finished film.

Hanna-Barbera Discography by Label

To date, this is the most complete listing of recordings relating in some way to Hanna-Barbera, its characters, and productions ever published. Of course, there are always "surprises" as records pop up unexpectedly.

Each category—LP, 45 rpm, 78 rpm, cassette, compact disc, and digital—is organized by record companies and catalog numbers. Original releases are included with most reissues. Some titles are listed because they relate to Hanna-Barbera in some way. Some entries represent a few examples of promotional discs, international releases, educational products, and other recordings worthy of further research. Every effort was made to assure the recordings listed are legally produced, commercial recordings and not bootlegs.

Some recordings are related to the history of Hanna-Barbera by their artists or other connections. These are noted and/or explained elsewhere in this book. These are intended as starting points, such as albums by The Eligibles, Bill Lee, and other artists who have made other records that could not be listed here. Selected principal recording artists for a given movie or TV series are listed with the original release but not for reissues for space reasons.

Certain catalog numbers with two prefixes (e.g., "HLP/HST") indicate that mono and stereo versions were available. An asterisk (*) indicates a recording that is not specifically Hanna-Barbera but related to the studio, characters, and/or artists; there are more but much too numerous to include.

KEY:

OC: Original Cast
MOC: Includes Members of the Original Cast
TST: TV Soundtrack
MST: Movie Soundtrack
SC: Studio Cast
VAR: Various Artists

Original casts are based on who was playing the roles in the cartoons and shows when the recordings were made. For example, the 1965 *Flintstones* recordings with Henry Corden as Fred Flintstone are "SC," but recordings made after he replaced Alan Reed are "OC."

33 1/3 RPM 12" LP

AA (Golden)

AR-60 **Huckleberry Hound for President** (1960 SC)

AUTUMN

LP-104 **The Beau Brummels Volume 2—You Tell Me Why / Don't Talk to Strangers** (1965)*
Back cover art of the band is caricatured by H-B artists in "Flintstone" style. There is no H-B-related material on the record itself.

BLANCO Y NEGRO (Spain)

MXLP-540   **Los Picapiedra Mix (The Flintstones Mix)**
(1994 VAR)
Pop dance songs with a pop version of *The Flintstones*
theme in Spanish.

BOARDWALK

SW-36880   **Popeye** (1980 MST)*
Theatrical feature that opened with Hanna-Barbera animation and premiered while the H-B series was a Saturday
morning hit on CBS.

CBS (Canada)

PFC-90591   **Nos amis del al Télé (Our Friends of the
TV)**: Hanna-Barbera's Mightor, Hong Kong
Phooey, Scooby-Doo, Great Grape Ape, and
Captain Caveman; Pierre Douglas and French
Canadian Cast (1979 SC).

CAPITOL

ST-1310   **The Eligibles: On the Trail** (1960)*
ST-1411   **The Eligibles: Love's a Gamble** (1960)*
Vocalists Ron Hicklin, Stan Farber, Bob Zwirn, and Ron
Rolla, with personnel variations, became The Hanna-
Barbera Singers, The Way-Outs, The Impossibles, and sang
in countless H-B songs and themes.
ST-667   **Josie and the Pussycats**—Patrice Hollo-
way, Cheryl Ladd, Cathy Dougher (1970 TST)

CAPITOL LIBRARY MUSIC SERVICES
(sample listing; many more released)

RB-2157/58 **High-"Q" Series Reels L-7 & 8***
HB-2261/62 **High-"Q" Series Reels L-51 & L-52***
YB-2406/7   **High-"Q" Series Reels L-107 & L-108***

CAPITOL CUSTOM

L-277   **Alice in Wonderland, or What's a Nice
Kid Like You Doing in a Place Like This?**
(1966 *TST*)
E. H. Morris Publishing Company promo.

CATHEDRAL FILMS (Filmstrips)

GT-13   **Christopher Mouse** (1959)*
Bill Hanna worked on this filmstrip and recording set
sometime during the transition from MGM to Hanna-
Barbera.

CHILD WORLD (Peter Pan)

GT-13   **Pound Puppies: Jingle Bells** (1985 SC)

COLPIX

CP-201   **Ruff and Reddy: Adventures in Space**
(1958 TST)
CP-202   **Huckleberry Hound: The Great Kellogg's
TV Show** (1959 TST)
CP-203   **Quick Draw McGraw** (1960 TST)
CP-205   **Yogi Bear and Boo-Boo** (1961 TST)
CP-207   **Here Comes Huckleberry Hound** (1961
TST)
CP-208   **Mr. Jinks, Pixie and Dixie** (1961 TST)
CP-210   **Huckleberry Hound and the Ghost Ship**
(1962 OC)
CP-211   **Quick Draw McGraw and the Treasure of
Sarah's Mattress** (1962 OC)
CP-212   **Top Cat** (1962 TST)
CP-213   **The Jetsons** (1962 TST)
CP-302   **The Flintstones** (1961 TST)
CP/SCP-45   **Yogi Bear and His Friends: Wake Up,
America!** (1965 SC)
CP/SCP-474 **Hey There, It's Yogi Bear** (1964 MST)
CR-905   **Yogi Bear Speaks for Summer Safety**
(Radio Public Service Announcements; 1964
OC)

COLUMBIA

P2–15024   **Gene Kelly: Songs and Stories for Chil-
dren** (1979 MOC)
Includes 1945's *The King Who Couldn't Dance*
C-32413   ***Charlotte's Web* and Other Children's
Favorites**—Ray Conniff (1973 SC)
"Charlotte's Web" is sung by The Ron Hicklin Singers.

COLUMBIA SPECIAL PRODUCTS

JL-8010   **The House That Wouldn't / The King Who
Couldn't Dance / The Cuckoo Who Lived
in a Clock**—Gene Kelly (1949 MOC)

COLUMBIA SPECIAL PRODUCTS / THE FUNTASTIC WORLD OF HANNA-BARBERA

(1977 Reissues of 1965–1966 Hanna-Barbera Cartoon Series albums unless otherwise noted.)

P-13829 **Huckleberry Hound with Stories & Songs of Uncle Remus** (SC)

P-13830 ***Alice in Wonderland* Starring Magilla Gorilla** (MOC)

P-13831 **Hansel & Gretel as Told by the Flintstones** (OC)

P-13855 **The Flintstones Favorite Stories** (OC)

P-13856 **Yogi Bear & Huckleberry Hound Present: Jack and the Beanstalk / Little Red Riding Hood / Uncle Remus** (SC)

P-13864 ***Robin Hood* in Story & Song with Top Cat** (MOC)

P-13865 **Yogi Bear & Boo-Boo: Jack and the Beanstalk / Little Red Riding Hood** (SC)

P-13903 **The Jetsons: First Family on the Moon** (MOC

P-13904 **Snagglepuss and *The Wizard of Oz*** (OC)

P-13905 **Doggie Daddy & Augie Doggie Tell the Story of *Pinocchio*** (MOC)

P-13906 **Wilma Flintstone Tells the Story of *Bambi***

P-13907 **The Flintstones Meet the Orchestra Family**
Reissue of 1968 Sunset/Liberty release.

P-13908 **Magilla Gorilla: *Alice in Wonderland* / Pixie & Dixie: *Cinderella* / Top Cat: *Robin Hood*** (MOC)

P-13909 **Snagglepuss: *The Wizard of Oz* / Wilma Flintstone: *Bambi* / Doggie Daddy & Augie Doggie: *Pinocchio*** (MOC)

P-13910 **Kiddie Klassics** (SC)
Reissue of *Golden Cartoons in Song, Volume 1*

P5–13934 **Fred Flintstone Presents All-Time Favorite Children's Stories and Songs** (Five-Record Set; MOC)

COLUMBIA PICTURES

SP-2341 **Hey There, It's Yogi Bear**—Radio Spot Announcements (1964)

CORAL

CRL-57137 **Bill Lee: My Port of Call** (1957)
Singing voice of Yogi in *Hey There, It's Yogi Bear*, Christopher Plummer in *The Sound of Music*, John Kerr in *South Pacific,* and more.

CRICKET

CR-31 **Kiddie TV Themes** (1959 SC)
New York studio vocalist Steve Clayton sings light jazz versions of the *Huckleberry Hound* and *Yogi Bear* themes.

DECCA

DL-75075 **We're the Banana Splits** (1968 TST)

DISCHI (Italy)

CGLPD-30 **Un Felice Natale con le più belle canzoni di Bimbolandia** (1986 SC)
Includes *Smurfs* theme.

DISCOVERY

DS-357 **Marty Paich—What's New** (1982)
One of many instrumental albums by the arranger/conductor of the songs in *Hey There, It's Yogi Bear*, *The Man Called Flintstone*, and *Alice in Wonderland*.

DISNEYLAND STORYTELLER

3811 **Dicken's Christmas Carol**—The Walt Disney Players (1975 SC)*

3825 **Mickey's Christmas Carol** (1983 Reedited 1983 Edition) (MOC/MST)*
Written by Alan Young and H-B associate producer/voice director Alan Dinehart with many Hanna-Barbera voice talents, several making their sole appearance on commercial Disney records, like Janet Waldo and Walker Edmiston.

DOT

DLP-9009 **The Nina, the Pinta, and the Santa Maria**—Eddie Albert and Cast (1958)*
Original musical for records; later animated and released by Hanna-Barbera home video)

DRUM (EMI / Australia)

DRUM-8223 **Songs from The First Family on the Moon Starring the Jetsons** and Other Hanna-Barbera Songs & Stories (MOC)

DRUM-8224 **Little Red Riding Hood Starring Yogi Bear** and Other Hanna-Barbera Songs & Stories (SC)

More exist in this series; some are complete albums, others are compilations of material from 45 rpm Cartoon Series records.

ELBA PRODUCTIONS

C-32412   **The Night Before Christmas** with the Norman Luboff Choir (1968 TST)*
TV special produced by neighboring studio Playhouse Pictures with Hanna-Barbera artists like Iwao Takamoto, and actors including Olan Soulé, giving it an H-B look and sound.

EVEREST

SDBR-1071   **The Randy Van Horne Singers: Rollin' West** (1960)*
SDBR-1089   **The Randy Van Horne Singers: Our Magic Moments** (1961)*
This vocal group sang the theme songs for classic H-B shows from *Ruff and Reddy* to *The Jetsons*.

51 WEST (Columbia)

Q-16001   **Gene Kelly: The Happiest Birthday in the World** (1979 MOC)
Includes 1945's The King Who Couldn't Dance.
Q-16101   **Gene Kelly in *Jack and the Beanstalk*** (1979 TST)
Reissue of 1967 HBR album in mono sound.

FORWARD

ST-F-1018   **Cattanooga Cats**—Michael Lloyd, Peggy Clinger (1969 TST)

GAMMA (Mexico)

GX-01 01338   **El Gran Espectaculo do Don Gato y su Pandilla** (The Great Show of Top Cat and His Gang) (1983 SC)

GENERAL FOODS

L-10   **Linus the Lionhearted**—Sheldon Leonard, Carl Reiner, Ruth Buzzi, Gerry Matthews, Jesse White, Bob McFadden (1964 OC)
Hoyt Curtin provided music for this animated series from Ed Graham Productions.

GOLDEN / WONDERLAND (A. A. Records)

LP-51   **Quick Draw McGraw and Huckleberry Hound** (1959 SC)
LP-55   **Howl Along with Huckleberry Hound and Yogi Bear** (1960 SC)
LP-66   **Songs of the Flintstones** (1961 OC)
LP-70   **Songs of Yogi Bear and All His Pals** (1961 SC)
LP-90   **Yogi Bear: How to Be Better Than the Average Child without Really Trying!** (1962 SC)
LP-98   **The Jetsons** (1962 SC)
LP-120   **Magilla Gorilla and His Pals** (1964 OC)
LP-124   **2 Songs from Hey There, It's Yogi Bear and Many Other Songs of Yogi, Huck, and Quick Draw** (1964 SC Compilation)
LP-285   **Cartoon Favorites** (1972 OC/SC Compilation)

HANNA-BARBERA

A-101   **Hanna-Barbera Drop-ins, Volume 1**
1965 Broadcast Promo with Daws Butler as Huckleberry Hound. No additional volumes were released.
HLP-8500/HST-9500 **A Swingin' Summer**—Raquel Welch, The Righteous Brothers, and Others (1965 MST)
HLP-8501/HST-9501 **Gloria Tracy: Gloria A-Glo** (1965)
HLP-8502/HST-9502 **The Golden Hits of Louis Prima** (1966)
HLP-8503/HST-9503 **The Five Americans: I See the Light** (1966)
HLP-8504/HST-9504 **The New Renaissance Society: Baroque 'n Stones** (1966)
HLP-8505/HST-9505 **Jean King Sings for the In Crowd** (1966)
Member of the vocal group, The Blossoms, and vocalist on numerous HBR Cartoon Series albums.
HLP-8506/HST-9506 **Laurie Johnson and His Orchestra: The Avengers** (1966)
The first official recording of the theme released in the US.
HLP-8507/HST-9507 **T. V. and the Tribesmen: Barefootin'** (1966)
HLP-8508/HST-9508 **Earl Gains: The Best of Luck to You** (1966)
HLP-8509/HST-9509 **The Dynatones: The Fife Piper** (1966)
HLP-8511/HLP-9511 **Gene Kelly in *Jack and the Beanstalk*** with Bobby Riha, Marni Nixon, Janet Waldo, Ted Cassidy, Cliff Norton, Chris Allen, Leo DeLyon, Dick Beals (1967 TST)

HANNA-BARBERA (Pye/England)

HLP-9   **The New Alice in Wonderland, or "What's a Nice Kid Like You Doing in a Place Like This?"** (TV Special) (1966 MOC)

HLP-10   **Pixie & Dixie with Mr. Jinks Tell the Story of Cinderella** (1965 SC)

More exist in this series.

HANNA-BARBERA CARTOON SERIES

HLP-2020   **Monster Shindig Starring Super Snooper & Blabber Mouse** (1965 SC)

HLP-2021   **The Flintstones: Flip Fables** (1965 OC)

HLP-2022   **Huckleberry Hound Tells Stories of Uncle Remus** (1965 SC)

HLP-2023   **Yogi Bear Tells Boo-Boo the Stories of Little Red Riding Hood / Jack and the Beanstalk** (1965 SC)

HLP-2024   **Magilla Gorilla Tells Ogee the Story of Alice in Wonderland** (1965 MOC)

HLP-2025   **Pixie & Dixie with Mr. Jinks Tell the Story of Cinderella** (1965 SC)

HLP-2026   **Snagglepuss Tells the Story of The Wizard of Oz** (1965 OC)

HLP-2027   **Wilma Flintstone Tells the Story of Bambi** (1965 OC)

HLP-2028   **Doggie Daddy Tells Augie Doggie the Story of Pinocchio** (1965 MOC)

HLP-2029   ***The Reluctant Dragon* Starring Touché Turtle & Dum-Dum** (1965 MOC)

HLP-2030   **Jonny Quest in 20,000 Leagues Under the Sea** (1965 OC)

HLP-2031   **Robin Hood Starring Top Cat** (1965 MOC)

HLP-2032   **Merry Christmas**—The Hanna-Barbera Organs & Chimes (1965)

HLP-2033   **Pebbles and Bamm-Bamm Singing Songs of Christmas** (1965 OC)

HLP-2034   **Gemini IV: Walk in Space / Gemini V: Eight Days in Space**—A Hanna-Barbera "Real Life" Documentary (1965)

HLP-2035   **Fred Flintstone & Barney Rubble: Songs from Mary Poppins** (1965 SC)

HLP-2036   **James Bomb Starring Super Snooper & Blabbermouse** (1965 OC)

HLP-2037   **The Jetsons in First Family on the Moon** (1965 MOC)

HLP-2038   ***Hansel & Gretel* Starring the Flintstones** (1965 OC)

HLP-2039   **Treasure Island Starring Sinbad, Jr.** (1965 OC)

HLP-2040   **On the Good Ship Lollipop Starring Pebbles and Bamm-Bamm** (1965 OC)

HLP-2041   **Atom Ant in Muscle Magic** (1965 OC)

HLP-2042   **Winsome Witch in It's Magic** (1965 OC)

HLP-2043   **Squiddly Diddly's Surfin' Surfari**—The Hanna-Barbera Singers (1965)

HLP-2044   **The Hillbilly Bears in Hillbilly Shindig** (1965 OC)

HLP-2045   **Precious Pupp & Granny Sweet in Hot Rod Granny** (1965 OC)

HLP-2046   **Secret Squirrel & Morocco Mole in Super Spy** (1965 MOC)

HLP-2047   **The Flintstones in S.A.S.F.T.P.A.E.O.G.O.F. B.O.T.S.** (1966 SC)

HLP-2048   **Golden Cartoons in Song, Vol. I**—The Hanna-Barbera Singers

HLP-2049   **Golden Cartoons in Song, Vol. II**—The Hanna-Barbera Singers

HLP-2050   **Yogi Bear and The Three Stooges Meet the Mad, Mad, Mad Dr. No-No** (1966 OC)

HLP-2051   **The New Alice in Wonderland, or "What's a Nice Kid Like You Doing in a Place Like This?"** (1966 MOC)

HLP-2052   **The Flintstones & José Jiminez in The Time Machine** (1966 MOC)

HLP-2053   **Golden Cartoons in Song, Vol. III**—The Hanna-Barbera Singers

HLP-2054   **Golden Cartoons in Song, Vol. IV**—The Hanna-Barbera Singers

HLP-2055   **The Man Called Flintstone** (1966 Movie Score with Soundtrack Vocals)

HLP-2056   **Edgar Allan Poe's The Tell-Tale Heart**—William Castle (1966)

HLP-2057   **G.I. Joe: The Story of the Green Beret**

BN-819   **The Impossibles: Hey You (Hiddy Hiddy Hoo) / She Couldn't Dance** (10" Test Pressing) (TST 1967)

HANNA-BARBERA PRODUCTIONS

[no number] **Hanna-Barbera Library of Sounds** (1986 Box Set)

HAPPY TIME (Pickwick International)

HT-1012   **TV and Movie Favorites for Children** (1962 SC)

Revised reissue of Cricket Records' 1959 *Kiddie TV Themes* including *Huckleberry Hound* and *Yogi Bear* themes.

ISP (England)

ISP-1001   **The Yogi Bear Show** (1973 British Stage Show Cast)

HARMONY (Columbia)

HL-9552   All-Star Children's Album, Vol. 1 (1965)
Includes 1945's The King Who Couldn't Dance.

IMPERIAL

LP-9097   The Happiest Band in the Land—Jimmie
Haskell Orchestra Featuring The Eligibles
LP-9270   Fantastic Baggys—Tell 'Em I'm Surfin'
(1964)
Includes "Surfin' Craze" from *The Flintstones* episode,
"Surfin' Fred."
LP-12351   The Love Generation
**LP-12364   The Love Generation: A Generation of
Love**
LP-12408   The Love Generation: Montage
Members of The Eligibles and The Love Generation were
often heard in Hanna-Barbera films and records.

JELLYBEAN PRODUCTIONS

157   We Think the World Is Round (1971)
Based on the earlier LP, *The Nina, the Pinta, and the Santa
Maria*; the audio on this album was animated and released
on Hanna-Barbera Home Video; also broadcast as a Disney
Channel special.

JELLY STONE PARK CAMPGROUND

**4062–12   Sing Along or Listen While "PAT" Sings
Your Favorite Song***
Live performer at Yogi Bear's Jellystone Park in Orlando.

KAPP

**KS-3367   Do-Re-Mi Children's Chorus: Marching
Along Together**
Includes "Ash Can Parade" from *Hey There, It's Yogi Bear*,
reissued on MCA Coral Records CB-20040.

KELLOGG'S

**22980/22985 A Kellogg Concert of Best Cereal Sellers:
The H. O. T. Tunes for 1965**
Hanna-Barbera characters appear in an orchestra on the
cover.

KID STUFF

KSR-5018   The Amazing Musical Monchhicni Album
(1982 SC)
KSS-5029   Pac-Man Christmas Parade (1982 SC)
KSS-5023   The Amazing Adventures of Pac-Man
(1982 SC)
KPD-6012   The Pac-Man Album (1982 SC; Picture Disc)

KIRSHNER

KES-108   The Globetrotters (1971 TST)

K-TEL

NU-5310   Heidi's Song (1982 MST)
NU-5320   Heidi's Song (Picture Disc) (1982 MST)

LION

L-70074   Tom and Jerry Cartoon Favorites
1958 compilation of single MGM stories.

MCA

MCAP-13302 Charlotte's Web (1973 MST Picture Disc)
MCA-6431   Jetsons: The Movie (1990 MST)

MFP—MUSIC FOR PLEASURE LTD. (England)

MFP-50086   Scooby Doo and the Snowmen Mystery
(1973 SC)

MGM

E-3450   Tom & Jerry Story Time (SC)
1957 compilation of MGM stories from 78 rpm discs.
**SE-3720   The Randy Van Horne Singers: Sing a
Song of Goodman***
MG-1–5301   That's Entertainment, Part 2 (1974 MST)*
The film included an animated movie star sequence pro-
duced by Hanna-Barbera; no H-B material on the album.
SE-4664   Danny Hutton: Pre-Dog Night (1969)
Includes HBR's "Roses and Rainbows" and "Monster Shin-
dig Part 2."

MGM CHILDREN'S SERIES / LEO THE LION

**CH-1000   MGM's Tom and Jerry—Four Musical
Adventures of TV's Favorite Cat and
Mouse**

1966 compilation of single MGM stories to tie into CBS network broadcast; cover art depicts Chuck Jones designs and incorrectly credits Fred Quimby as the creator of the characters.

CH-1033 **Curious George**—Jimmy Blaine and Cast (1967)*

Blaine hosted the live-action segments of NBC's original *Ruff and Reddy Show.*

LES-903 **Connie Francis and the Kids Next Door** (1967)

Francis appears on front cover surrounded by generic plush animals, except for Tom prominent on the top right; no material on the recording references Tom and Jerry or other MGM cartoons.

MASTER CONTROL RADIO

45/46-87 **Salute to Hanna-Barbera** (Weeks of November 6 & 13, 1987)

Inspirational radio program transcription; one of the few, if only, vinyl records with the voices of Hanna and Barbera; also features Daws Butler.

MERCURY

SR-60710 **The Eligibles: Mike Fright***

MODE

LP-126 **Delightful Doris Drew** (1957)*

Singing voice of Alice in Hanna-Barbera's *Alice in Wonderland.*

PARACHUTE

422–811–109–1-M-1 **Richie Rich: 4 Great Stories** (1983 SC)

422–811–110–1-M-1 **Richie Rich: Mysteries of the Deep!** (1983 SC)

812–576–1 **Richie Rich: The Merry Adventures of Richie Hood** (1983 SC)

814 233–4 M-1 **Richie Rich: Double Trouble!** (1983 SC)

422–812 577–1 M-1 **Richie Rich: Surprise Party!** (1983 SC)

PARAMOUNT

PAS-1008 **Charlotte's Web** (1973 MST) (L-34837 Australia)

PAS-6058 **The Brady Bunch Phonographic Album** (OC 1973)

Includes "Zuckerman's Famous Pig" and "Charlotte's Web."

PARKER BROTHERS MUSIC

PB-7214 **A Cabbage Patch Christmas** (SC)*
PB-7216 **Cabbage Patch Dreams** (SC)*

Both include original songs by the Sherman brothers.

PETER PAN

1107 **Fangface** (Ruby-Spears TV Cartoon Stories)

The first series from Joe Ruby and Ken Spears's company.

1113 **Popeye: Spinach on the Spanish Main / Popeye in the Movies / Gold Fever / Who's Afraid of a UFO?** (1980 MOC)

Released during the CBS run of H-B's *The All-New Popeye Show.*

8001 **A Musical Trip to the Magic Land of Allakazam** (1962 VAR)*

Peter Pan recordings introduced by magician Mark Wilson; ties into the CBS/ABC TV series that reran H-B short cartoons; LP contains no H-B material.

8018 **Laurel & Hardy: This Is Your Laff** (1963 MOC)*

Prototype for what would become Hanna-Barbera's 1966 cartoon.

8101 **Hanna-Barbera's The Funky Phantom** (1972 SC)

8102 **Hanna-Barbera's The Hair Bear Bunch** (1972 SC)

8105 **Hanna-Barbera's The Flintstones** (1972 SC)

8157 **The Flintstones: Ghost Chasers / Even Steven** (1975 SC)

8181 **Laurel & Hardy** (1976 Reissue) (MOC)

8183 **Scooby-Doo—3 Stories** (1977 MOC)

8214 **Exciting Christmas Stories with Scooby-Doo and Friends** (1978 OC)

8222 **Scooby-Doo and His Friends: 2 All-New Adventures!** (1978 OC)

BR-521 **Fun-Filled Adventures with Scooby-Doo and His Friends**

Two stories from #8183 with a book.

PD-203 **Scooby Doo**

"Picture Disk" identical to #8183 on picture disc.

PICKWICK

SPC-5168 **Eustace, the Useless Rabbit**—Frank Welker*

Children's story with H-B voice veteran Frank Welker in multiple roles.

PICKWICK (Baker-Rhodes Marketing)

BRMC-1   **Hear-See-Do: Hanna-Barbera Record of Safety** (MOC)

POLY (Polygram / Germany)

2961 009   **Tom and Jerry 1 (Original Version)**—Ilse Werner (SC 1976)

PS-343   **Tom and Jerry 2 (Original Version)**—Ilse Werner (SC 1976)

Narrated stories in German based on short TV episodes from the 1975 *Tom and Jerry Show.*

POLYDOR (Canada)

PDM 1 6401 **Hello, We're the Snorks** (SC)

Songs inspired by the TV characters.

2417–317   **La Flûte à six schtroumpfs (The Smurfs and the Magic Flute)**—Music by Michel Legrand (MST)

RCA VICTOR

LSP-1751   **Randy Van Horne & His Swinging Choir—Clef Dwellers** (1958)*

RCA VICTOR (England)

SF-8153   **The Globetrotters** (TV Soundtrack, 1971)

RCA VICTOR (México)

SF-8073   **Popeye—Musica Original de la Serie de T.V.—Superbanda**

Includes stories in Spanish based on short episodes from H-B's *The All-New Popeye Show* including background music.

ROYAL HAWAIIAN RECORDS—HAWAII'S GOLDEN HERITAGE SERIES

[no number] **The Adventures of Coconut Willie and Pukahead—The Magic Menehune*** (Library of Congress Catalog Number #98701112)

Produced by Jack de Mello with music cues from H-B cartoons.

SCREEN GEMS

[no number] **The Flintstone Baby Contest** (1962, promotional)

The original cast in radio spots asking listeners to guess the baby's weight and gender.

[no number] **"The Hopperoo" song** (1964, promotional)

Studio group vocal tying in with the introduction of Hoppy to the show.

SESSIONS

ARI-1018   **Smurfing Sing Song**

ARI-1022   **The Smurfs All Star Show**

ARI-1027   **The Smurfs: Best of Friends**

ARI-1028   **Father Abraham in Smurfland**

ARI-1029   **Smurfing Sing-Along** (Picture Disc)

Songs about the characters recorded in Holland.

SMALL WORLD (England)

SW-1   **The Snorks** (SC)

SOUNDTRACK

MFA-1024   **Hollywood Directory—Songs about Hollywood**—Hoyt Curtin (1965)

Includes songs by Hoyt Curtin, Liz Curtin, Bill Hanna, Joe Barbera, and Others

STARLAND MUSIC

S-1036   **The Smurfs Party Time** (SC)

SUNSET (Liberty)

SUS-5325   **Santa and the Three Bears** (MST)

A theatrical feature written and directed by H-B story artist Tony Benedict with several H-B artists. Benedict pitched this as a TV special called Yellowstone Cubs, but Joe Barbera thought it lacked a villain and passed.

SH-6060   **The Flintstones Meet the Orchestra Family** (OC)

SH-6061   **Shazzan and the Evil Jester of Masira** (OC)

TAFT ATTRACTIONS

CSPS-2229 **The Best of Broadway** (Canada's Wonderland Stage Show)*

Theme park included The Happy Land of Hanna-Barbera; no H-B material on the disc.

206066-XB Kings Island Celebration (1982)
Kings Island theme park 10th anniversary festivities including Hanna-Barbera 25th Anniversary Salute.

TEE VEE TOONS / TVT

TVT-5005 Jane, Get Me Off This Crazy Thing! / *The Jetsons* Theme (TST 1986; 12" Single)
Dance mix combining H-B themes with other TV show soundtracks.

TEMPO (England)

TMP-9001 Spin a Magic Tune—20 Fantastic New Songs about Your Favourite Cartoon Characters (1973 SC)
Includes songs inspired by *Scooby-Doo*, *Space Kidettes*, *It's the Wolf!*, *Penelope Pitstop*, and *The Hair Bear Bunch*.

TRADING PLACES

TDP-54012 Introducing the Beau Brummels
2019 Reissue of 1965 Release includes "Laugh, Laugh" from *The Flintstones* episode, "Shinrock a Go-Go."

UNITED ARTISTS (England)

UAS-29290 Lucky Luke (1971 MST)
Music from this feature became the theme to the 1984 H-B series.

VANGUARD

STV-81260 Clark Terry and His Jolly Giants (1975)
Jazz album opens with "Meet the Flintstones."

VARESE SARABANDE

STV-81260 Return to Eden—Music by Brian May (1985 TST)
Hanna-Barbera Australian live-action TV soap opera.
302–067–512–1 Charlotte's Web (2017 Reissue of 1973 Vinyl LP)

WARNER BROS.

WS-1616 Inside Daisy Clover (1965)*
Jackie Ward sings for Natalie Wood one year after singing for Cindy Bear.

YOGI BEAR JELLYSTONE CAMPGROUND

NR-11912 The Brand L's Live from Yogi Bear "Jellystone" Camp Resort*

---

7 INCH LLPs

COLPIX

CR-6010 Hey There, It's Yogi Bear!—Story and Song from the Feature (1964 OC)

DISNEY STORIES (Brazil)

HD-48 A Ilha Das Maravilhas (The Island of Wonders)*
This Disney character read-along, and presumably others in the series, contains H-B background music.

K-TEL BOOK & RECORD

KS-075 Heidi's Song—Read-Along Record and Book (1982 MST; also on cassette)

KELLOGG'S

SCP-83 Snap, Crackle Pop Tunes (1983)*
Songs about the Kellogg's Rice Krispies characters sometimes animated by H-B.

KID STUFF BOOK AND RECORD (all SC)

KSR-264	**Smurfing in the Air** (1984)
KSR-265	**Smurf's Daydream** (1984)
KSR-299	**Pink Panther & Sons: The Rainbow Panthers' Carnival** (1985)
KSR-300	**Pink Panther & Sons: Pinky Saves the Beach Bullies** (1985)
KSR-589	**The Pac-Man Christmas Story** (1982)
KSR-616	**Baby Pac-Man Goes to the Market** (1982)
KSR-617	**The Adventures of Super Pac-Man** (1982)
KSR-995	**Pac-Man: Run for Fun** (1983)
KSR-996	**Pac-Man Picnic** (1983)
KSR-997	**Pac-Man Goes to Playland** (1983)
DBR-205	**Pac-Man and the Ghost Diggers** (1985)
DBR-206	**Ms. Pac-Man's Prize Pupil** (1985)
DBR-997	**Pac-Man and the Ghost Chasers** (1985)

MOVIE WHEELS

MW-1002 **Huckleberry Hound / Yogi Bear** (1960 SC)

PARACHUTE BOOK & RECORD

814-936 **The Biskitts: Trouble in the Tunnel!** (1984 SC/TST)
814-937 **The Biskitts: As the Worm Turns** (1984 SC/TST)

PETER PAN

2323 **Laurel and Hardy: Chiller Diller Thriller** (1976 Reissue MOC)

SHOW 'N TELL PROGRAMS
(Child Guidance / All SC)

53401 **Shirt Tales: The Lost Scent** (1982)
53402 **Shirt Tales: Challenge the Storm** (1982)
53403 **Shirt Tales: Guardians of the Gate** (1982)
53404 **Shirt Tales: Mission: Save the Moose** (1982)
54936 **The Flintstones: Fred Learns to Share** (1983)
54937 **The Flintstones: Fred's Tall Tale** (1983)
54938 **Scooby-Doo Visits Outer Space** (1983)
54952 **The Pink Panther & Sons: The Best Biker in Town** (1984)
54953 **The Pink Panther & Sons: To Be a Star** (1984)

STARLAND BOOK & RECORD (All SC)

S-2003 **A Winter's Smurf** (1983)
S-2004 **The Smurf Champion** (1983)
S-2005 **There's a Smurf in My Soup** (1983)
S-2006 **The Smurf-Eating Bird** (1983)

SOUNDSHEETS AND SPECIAL RECORDS

HANNA-BARBERA EDUCATIONAL DIVISION

11972T **Fred Flintstone Talks about Educational Filmstrips** (OC)

KENNER PLAY 'N' SHOW TALKING COLOR SHOWS

No. 2658 **The Flintstones: The Fisherman and His Wife** (MOC)
No. 126–273–02 **The Flintstones: Beauty and the Beast / Yogi Bear: Goldilocks and the Three Bears** (MOC)

TALKING VIEW MASTER

AVB553 **Scooby-Doo: That's Snow Ghost** (1972 SC)

ELECTRONIC TALKING VIEW MASTER

4411 **Scooby-Doo: That's Snow Ghost** (1983 TST)

45 RPM

B-H (Barbera-Hanna)

BH-61-001 **Fred Flintstone and His Orchestra: Quarry Stone Rock / A Night in Bedrock Forest**—Hoyt Curtin
The use of "B-H" is unique in that Hanna's name always came first after the two reportedly agreed to decide with a coin toss.

BION

122 **Johnny Selph's Yogi Bear Record** (Jellystone Park Campgrounds)
Original song inspired by Yogi Bear.

CAPITOL (Retail)

2967 **Josie and the Pussycats: Every Beat of My Heart / It's All Right with Me**
3025 **Josie and the Pussycats: Stop, Look and Listen / You've Come a Long Way Baby**

CAPITOL CREATIVE PRODUCTS (Kellogg's Mail Order)

CP-58 **Josie and the Pussycats: Letter to Mama / Inside, Outside, Upside Down**
CP-59 **Josie and the Pussycats: Josie (Theme) / With Every Beat of My Heart**

CP-60 **Josie and the Pussycats: Voodoo / If That Isn't Love**

CP-61 **Josie and the Pussycats: I Wanna Make You Happy / It's Gotta Be Him**
Unreleased songs: "Dreammaker," "Clock on the Wall," "Together / The Time to Love / I Love You Too Much / Dreaming"

CLEAN CUTS

CC-1202 **Meet the Flintstones—Bruce Springstone Live at Bedrock**—John Ebersberger (1982 12" and 7" Singles)

COLPIX

J-4-181 **From Hey There, It's Yogi Bear: Yogi Bear March / Whistle Your Way Back Home**—Billy Costa and His Orchestra (1964)

PX-11035 **Little Eva: Makin' with the Magilla** (1964 TVS)

GOLDEN (all SC unless otherwise noted; six-inch 78 rpm versions were also released with an "R" prefix)

FF-550 **Huckleberry Hound and Yogi Bear** (1959)
FF-558 **Ruff and Reddy / Professor Gizmo** (1959)
FF-589 **Quick Draw McGraw & Baba Looey** (1959)
FF-591 **Huckleberry Hound Presents Boo-Boo Bear & Mr. Jinks** (1959)
FF-592 **Yogi Bear Introduces Loopy De Loop / Let's Have a Song, Yogi Bear** (1960)
FF-593 **Quick Draw McGraw: El Kabong! / Ooch Ooch Ouch!** (1960)
FF-610 **Huckleberry Hound Presents Pixie and Dixie / Iddy Biddy Buddy** (1962)
FF-625 **Huckleberry Hound Presents Snuffles & Augie Doggie** (1962)
FF-646 **Quick Draw's A-Comin' (and Baba Looey Too) to Clean Up Your Town** (1961)
FF-643 **Yogi Bear Presents Cindy Bear and Snooper & Blabber** (1960)
FF-650 **Have a Hap-Hap-Happy Christmas with Yogi Bear** (1961)
FF-660 **Huckleberry Hound Presents Hokey Wolf & Ding-A-Ling** (1961)
FF-663 **Yogi Bear TV Theme** (1961)
FF-665 **Quick Draw McGraw's Pals: Snooper & Blabber** (1961)
FF-674 **Huck, Yogi & Quick Draw Safety Song** (1961)

FF-680 **Songs of the Flintstones** (1961 OC)
FF-689 **Top Cat Theme Song** (1961)
FF-700 **Touché Turtle & Dum-Dum** (1962)
FF-701 **Wally Gator / Lippy the Lion & Hardy Har Har** (1962)
FF-739 **The Flintstones: Dino the Dino** (1963 OC)
FF-740 **Fred Flintstone: Lullaby of Pebbles**—Alan Reed (1963)
FF-720 **The Jetsons: Theme Song / Eep Opp Ork** (1962)
FF-748 **Laurel and Hardy: One Together Is Two (Theme Song)** (1963)
FF-755 **The Jetsons: Push Button Blues / Rama Rama Zoom** (1962)
FF-768 **The Presidential Campaign Songs of Yogi Bear & Magilla Gorilla** (1964)

GOLDEN 3-ON-1

EP-570 **Huckleberry Hound and His Friends** (1959)
EP-571 **Ruff & Reddy and Their Friends** (1959)
EP-601 **Huckleberry Hound Presents Quick Draw McGraw** (1961)
EP-624 **Yogi Bear and Huckleberry Hound and Quick Draw McGraw and Snooper and Blabber Present Loopy de Loop** (1960)
EP-637 **Bill Hanna & Joe Barbera's Musical Songfest (Hokey Wolf / Snuffles / Cindy Bear)** (1960)
EP-653 **Songs of the Flintstones** (1961 OC)
EP-654 **Yogi Bear's Friends (Yakky Doodle / Fibber Fox / Major Minor / Snagglepuss)** (1961)
EP-692 **The Best of Hanna-Barbera** (Touché Turtle & Dum-Dum / Hardy Har Har & Lippy / Top Cat / Wally Gator) (1962)
EP-742 **The Jetsons** (1962)
EP-749 **The Flintstones Featuring Pebbles** (1963)

HANNA-BARBERA (1965–1966)

HBR-440 **The Creations IV: Dance in the Sand / Little Girl**
HBR-441 **The Bompers: Do the Bomp / Early Bird**
HBR-442 **Shorty Rogers and the Giant: Theme from Jonny Quest / Vacation**
HBR-443 **Billy Bossman: Up the Road** (Vocal & Instrumental)
HBR-444 **Roger & Lynn: Baby, Move In / Summer Kind of Song**
HBR-445 **The Bats: Big Bright Eyes / Nothing at All**

HBR-446   The Guilloteens: I Don't Believe / Hey You

HBR-447   Danny Hutton: Roses and Rainbows / Monster Shindig

HBR-448   Corky Wilkie Band: Little by Little / Something Swinging

HBR-449   Pebbles and Bamm-Bamm: Open Up Your Heart / The Lord Is Counting on You

HBR-450   Jean King: Something Happens to Me / Nicest Things Happen

HBR-451   The Guilloteens: Don't Let the Rain Get You Down / For My Own

HBR-452   Louis Prima & Gia Maione: See That You're Born an Italian / Wonderland by Night

HBR-453   Danny Hutton: Monster Shindig Part 2 / Big Bright Eyes

HBR-454   The Five Americans: I See the Light / The Outcast

HBR-455   Charles Christy: Cherry Pie / Will I Find Her

HBR-456   Les Baxter Orchestra & Singers: Little Girl Lonely / Michelle

HBR-457   The Dartells: Clap Your Hands / Where Do We Stand

HBR-458   Gerri Diamond: Mama, You Forgot / Give Up on Love

HBR-459   The Pop-Ups: Candy Rock / Lurking

HBR-460   The Chains: Carol's Got a Cobra / Hate to See You Crying

HBR-461   George Chambers: The Ribbon / These Things You'll Never Know

HBR-462   Art Grayson: Be Ever Mine / When I Get Home

HBR-463   Jean King: Watermelon Man / The In-Crowd

HBR-464   Anne Christine: Kitty Up Go / I'd Fight the World

HBR-465   DeWayne and the Beldettas: Tennessee Stud / I'd Walk Along

HBR-466   Gloria Tracy: I'd Never Known / Out in the Street

HBR-467   Louis Prima: I'm Gonna Sit Right Down & Write Myself a Letter / Civilization

HBR-468   The Five Americans: Evol—Not Love / Don't Blame Me

HBR-469   Murray's Monkeys: Gipsy / I'll Be There

HBR-470   The Laurie Johnson Orchestra: Theme from The Avengers / Minor Bossa Nova

HBR-471   Bobby Loveless: Baby No More / Nite Owl

HBR-472   Dale and Grace: Let Them Talk / I'd Rather Be Free

HBR-473   Charles Christy & the Crystals: In the Arms of a Girl / Young and Beautiful

HBR-474   Billy Storm: Please Don't Mention Her Name / The Warmest Love

HBR-475   Bob and Kit: Autumn Too Long / You've Gotta Stop

HBR-476   Scatman Crothers: What's a Nice Kid Like You Doing in a Place Like This? / Golly Zonk! (It's Scat Man)

HBR-477   The Dimensions: She's Boss / Penny

HBR-478   The Packers: Pink Chiffon / Boondocks

HBR-479   The Plunkers: Hippy Lippy Goosey / Night Time to Love

HBR-480   The Epics: Blue Turns to Grey / Goes to Show

HBR-481   Earl Gains: It's Worth Anything / The Best of Luck to You

HBR-482   The Tidal Waves: Farmer John / She Left Me All Alone

HBR-483   Pebbles and Bamm-Bamm: Good Times / The Losing Game

HBR-484   The Five Americans: Daddy / The World Is Full of Joys

HBR-485   The Riot Squad: I Take It We're Through / Working Man

HBR-486   The Guilloteens: I Sit and Cry / Crying All the Time

HBR-487   Simon T. Stokes: Truth Is Stranger Than Fiction / Big City Blues

HBR-488   Ron Gray: Hold Back the Sunrise / The Shake

HBR-489   Robbie and Robyn: Cradle of Love / Dreamin'

HBR-490   Paul Frees: A Girl / Portrait of a Fool

HBR-491   Peter Harcourt (Paul Frees): Sneaky Pete / Someone's in Love Again

HBR-492   The Thirteenth Floor Elevators: You're Gonna Miss Me / Tried to Hide

HBR-493   TBD

HBR-494   The Dynatones: The Fife Piper / And I Always Will

HBR-495   Scotty McKay: I'm Gonna Love Ya / Waikiki Beach

HBR-496   Jimmy James: Hi Diddly Dee Dum Dum / Don't Wanna Cry

HBR-497   Jean King: Don't Say Goodbye / It's Good Enough for Me

HBR-498   The Abbey Tavern Singers: Off to Dublin in the Green / The Gallant Forty Twa'

HBR-499   Larry Butler: Almost Persuaded / Green Green Grass

HBR-500   Positively 13 O'Clock: Psychotic Reaction / 13 O'Clock Theme for Psychotics

HBR-501   The Tidal Waves: Big Boy Pete / I Don't Need Love

HBR-502	George Chambers: Flood of Tears / Don't Make Me Go
HBR-503	TBD
HBR-504	TBD
HBR-505	Porter Jordan: Untouchable Woman / Nobody's Boy
HBR-506	DeWayne and the Beldettas: Hurtin' / Big Time
HBR-507	W. C. Fields Memorial Electric String Band: Hippy Elevator Operator / Don't Lose the Girl
HBR-508	The New Breed: Want Ad Reader / One More for the Good Guys
HBR-509	The Four Gents: Soul Sister / I've Been Trying
HBR-510	Earl Gains: I Have Loved and I Have Lived / Don't Take My Kindness for a Weakness
HBR-511	The Hogs: Loose Lips Sync Ships / Blues Theme
HBR-512	Rainy Day People: Junior Executive / I'm Telling It to You
HBR-513	Sunny Lane: Tell It Like It Was / Trollin'
HBR-514	The Unrelated Segments: It's Unfair / Story of My Life
HBR-515	The Tidal Waves: Action! (Speaks Louder Than Words) / Hot Stuff
HBR-516	The Time Stoppers: I Need Love / Fickle Frog

HANNA-BARBERA CARTOON SERIES (1965)

CS-7020	Super Snooper & Blabber Mouse: Monster Shindig (MOC)
CS-7021	Flintstones: Goldi-Rocks and the Three Bearosauruses (OC)
CS-7022	The Flintstones Favorite Songs—The Hanna-Barbera Singers
CS-7032	Jonny Quest: 20,000 Leagues Under the Sea (OC)
CS-7033	Top Cat: Robin Hood (MOC)
CS-7034	Snagglepuss: The Wizard of Oz (OC)
CS-7035	Wilma Flintstone: Bambi (OC)
CS-7036	Doggie Daddy & Augie Doggie: Pinocchio (MOC)
CS-7037	Touché Turtle & Dum-Dum: The Reluctant Dragon (MOC)
CS-7038	Songs from Robin Hood—The Hanna-Barbera Singers
CS-7039	Songs from The Reluctant Dragon—The Hanna-Barbera Singers
CS-7040	Songs from The Wizard of Oz—The Hanna-Barbera Singers

CS-7041	Songs from Bambi—The Hanna-Barbera Singers
CS-7042	Songs from Pinocchio—The Hanna-Barbera Singers
CS-7043	Favorite Songs of Jonny Quest—The Hanna-Barbera Singers
CS-7044	Pebbles Bamm-Bamm: Songs of Christmas (featuring "Little Drummer Boy")
CS-7045	Pebbles Bamm-Bamm: Songs of Christmas (featuring "I Saw Mommy Kissing Santa Claus")
CS-7046	Merry Christmas (featuring "Jingle Bells")
CS-7047	Merry Christmas (featuring "Carol of the Bells")
CS-7048	Songs from Mary Poppins—The Hanna-Barbera Singers
CS-7050	Songs from Treasure Island—The Hanna-Barbera Singers
CS-7051	Songs from Hansel & Gretel—The Hanna-Barbera Singers
CS-7052	Pebbles & Bamm-Bamm—On the Good Ship Lollipop (Featuring "Animal Crackers")
CS-7053	Songs from James Bomb—The Hanna-Barbera Singers
CS-7054	Pebbles & Bamm-Bamm: On the Good Ship Lollipop (Featuring "Good Ship Lollipop")
CS-7056	Super Snooper & Blabbermouse: James Bomb (OC)
CS-7057	Fred Flintstone & Barney Rubble in "Songs from Mary Poppins" (SC)
CS-7059	The Flintstones: Hansel & Gretel (OC)

HANNA-BARBERA SINGERS CARTOON SERIES (1966; the H-B characters appear in the picture sleeve art

C-101	Atom Ant Presents: Happy Birthday / A Busy Day
C-102	The Hillbilly Bears Present: Old Mac Donald
C-103	Secret Squirrel Presents: Alphabet Song
C-104	Precious Pupp Presents: Brahms Lullaby / Little Rag Doll
C-105	Precious Pupp Presents: The Lord's Prayer
C-106	Precious Pupp Presents: Mary Had a Little Lamb / Skip Rope
C-107	Atom Ant Presents: I've Been Working on the Railroad / When I Grow Up
C-108	Secret Squirrel Presents: Children's Marching Song / Yo Yo Song
C-109	Precious Pupp Presents: Row, Row, Row Your Boat

C-110	**Secret Squirrel Presents: Three Blind Mice / The World Is Full of Things**
C-111	**Winsome Witch Presents: Alouette / Space Dream**
C-112	**Winsome Witch Presents: Ba Ba Black Sheep / A Dog Is Your Best Friend**
C-113	**Atom Ant Presents: London Bridge / It Puzzles Me**
C-114	**The Hillbilly Bears Present: Blue Tail Fly / I've Got a Pony**
C-115	**The Hillbilly Bears Present: Skip to My Lou / Hide and Seek**
C-116	**Winsome Witch Presents: Old King Cole / Circus Life**
C-117	**Squiddly Diddly Presents: Jack & Jill / Riddles**
C-118	**Squiddly Diddly Presents: Mulberry Bush**
C-119	**Atom Ant Presents: Yankee Doodle / Little Soldier**
C-120	**Squiddly Diddly Presents: Sing a Song of Six Pence / The World Is Full of Joy**
C-121	**Squiddly Diddly Presents: Looby Lou**
C-122	**Winsome Witch Presents: Pop Goes the Weasel / The Word Game**
C-123	**The Hillbilly Bears Present: Farmer in the Dell / No No World**
C-124	**Secret Squirrel Presents: Little Bo Peep / Dolly with the Golden Hair**

HANNA-BARBERA PREMIUM DIVISION
(Kellogg's Mail Order; 1968 TST)

34578	**The Banana Splits Sing'n Play "The Tra-La-La Song"**
34579	**The Banana Splits Sing'n Play "Doin' the Banana Split"**

KENNER TALKING SHOW PROJECTOR

[no number] **Scooby-Doo / Josie and the Pussycats / Lassie / Superman**—Norma Macmillan, Janet Waldo, Ginny Tyler, Gary Owens, Mel Blanc (MOC 1971)

MARK 56

[no number] **Huck Yogi & Quick Draw's Magic Record** (1961 SC Promo Giveaway)

MERRI

M-6011	**Huck "Ringo" Hound: Bingo Ringo! / Clementine**—Daws Butler (1964)

MFP—MUSIC FOR PLEASURE LTD. (England)

FP-50086	**Where Are You, Scooby Doo? / Mystery Incorporated**

Songs from the 1973 SC album, Scooby-Doo and the Snowmen Mystery.

PARAMOUNT

PAA-0205	**The Brady Bunch: Zuckerman's Famous Pig / Charlotte's Web** (1973)
PAA-0220	**Debbie Reynolds: Charlotte's Web** (Single Version) / **Mother Earth and Father Time** (1973 OC/MVS)

PETER PAN

PP-1093	**The Funky Phantom: Friends to the End** (1972 SC)
PP-1094	**The Hair Bear Bunch: Hair Cuts Out** (1972 SC)

PETER PAN BOOK & RECORD
(all SC unless otherwise noted)

1961	**The Flintstones Zoo Adventure**
1962	**Huckleberry Hound at the Firehouse**
1963	**Fred & Barney: Circus Fun**
1964	**Fred Flintstone the Magician**
1971	**Yogi Bear and His Jellystone Friends**
1977	**The Flintstones: Pebbles and Bamm-Bamm and the Friendly Witch**
1978	**Fred Flintstone and Good, Old, Unreliable Dino**
1984	**Scooby Doo: The Mystery of the Sticky Money** (MOC)
1985	**Scooby Doo: The Mystery of the Strange Paw Prints** (MOC)
1986	**Scooby Doo: The Mystery of the Ghost in the Dog House** (MOC)
1987	**Scooby Doo The Mystery of the Rider without a Head** (MOC)
2014	**Tom and Jerry: Astrocat & Mouse**

PHILIPS (Sweden)

433 413 PE	**Owe Thörnqvist: Wilma!**

ROMAR (MGM)

RO-703   **The Sundance Kids featuring Butch Cassidy: Little Miss Magic / Blue** (1973)
RO-717   **The Sundance Kids featuring Butch Cassidy: Rosie Was a Good Old Girl / De De Dinah** (1973)

SHELL

45-720   **The Ivy Three: Yogi / Was Judy There**

SPIN / ZIN-A-SPIN

SRC-6   **Huckleberry Hound Theme Song**—The Scarlet Combo

---

78 RPM 10"

CAPITOL

CASF-3162   **Dinky Pinky**—Stan Freberg (1953; also 45 rpm)*
Original story written by Charles Shows.

COLUMBIA

J-25   **From *Anchors Aweigh*: The King Who Couldn't Dance**—Gene Kelly (1945 MOC; includes storybook)

MGM (all SC)

51A   **Tom and Jerry at the Circus** (1950, includes storybook)
L-17   **Tom and Jerry—Johann Mouse** (1951)
S-18   **Tom and Jerry Meet Santa Claus** (1951)
S-19   **Tom and Jerry and the Fire Engine** (1951)
S-20   **Tom and Jerry and the Rocket Ship to the Moon** (1952)
S-21   **Tom and Jerry in the Wild West** (1952)
S-22   **Tom and Jerry Down on the Farm** (1952)
S-23   **Tom and Jerry Find Aladdin's Lamp** (1952)
S-24   **Tom and Jerry and Charlie & the Choo-Choo Train** (1952)
S-25   **Tom and Jerry and Old MacDonald's Barnyard Band** (1952)
S-26   **Tom and Jerry Meet Robin Hood** (1952)
S-27   **Tom and Jerry and the Texas Rangers** (1952)
S-28   **Tom and Jerry and the Tugboat** (1952)

CASSETTES

BUENA VISTA BOOK AND CASSETTE

60471-4   **The Flintstones in *Viva Rock Vegas*** (MST)

COLUMBIA SPECIAL PRODUCTS

BT-13910   **Kiddie Klassics: Golden Cartoons in Song**
Other titles in the 1977 "Funtastic World" reissue series were also released on audio cassette.

HANNA-BARBERA PRODUCTIONS EDUCATIONAL DIVISION (All MOC)

Library Set #1   **The Flintstones: Barney Borrows a Book / Barney Returns a Book**
59210   **Flintstones Driving Guide: Driving Controls**
59220   **Flintstones Driving Guide: Gauges & Safety Controls**
59310   **Flintstones Driving Guide: Common Driving Hazards**
59320   **Flintstones Driving Guide: Emergency Procedures**
Many additional titles were issued in various educational series.

KID RHINO

R4-71423   **This Land Is Our Land: The Yogi Bear Environmental Album** (1993 OC)
R4-71627   **The Flintstones Story** (1994 OC)
R4-72523   **Pebbles & Bamm-Bamm: Cave Kids Sing-Along** (1997 TST)
R4-72525   **Jonny Quest, the Real Adventures: Return of the Anasazi** (TST 1996)

KID RHINO BOOK AND TAPE

R4–76728   **The Powerpuff Girls: Mojo Jojo's Rising** (2001 OC)

PETER PAN READ & LISTEN (all SC)

C-257–39   **The Paw-Paws: The Northern Arrow**
C-258–40   **The Paw-Paws: The Golden Canoe**
C-267   **The Jetsons: Big Boy & His Giant Pooch**
C-268   **The Jetsons: Frogman & the Mermaids**
C-269   **The Flintstones: Stop That Gorilla**
C-270   **The Flintstones: Treasure Hunt**

SOUNDTRACK

[no number] **The Jetsons (and Friends)**—Hoyt Curtin and the Hanna-Barbera Orchestra (Promo; 1985 TST)

COMPACT DISCS

BLACKSTONE PUBLISHING

9781482-930832 **Yabba Dabba Doo! The Alan Reed Story**—Alan Reed Jr., Bill Marx, Joe Bevilacqua (2013)

9783455-115785 **Daws Butler: Characters Actor**—Joe Bevilacqua (2016)

CARTOON NETWORK

SGCTC2CD **Space Ghost Coast to Coast: Yeah, Whatever . . .** (Radio Promo / 1995)

CASTLE MUSIC (England)

CMDDD-231 **Those Pesky Kids! Children's Classics & Toddler TV Themes of the 60s & 70s** (2001)

COLUMBIA (Nippon-Columbia / Japan)

COCC-11654 **We Love Hanna-Barbera Vol. 1**
Original songs about H-B characters in Japanese.

DECCA BROADWAY

B0015645-02 **How to Succeed in Business without Really Trying**—Daniel Radcliffe and 2011 Broadway Cast*
The arrangements in this version were inspired in part by Hoyt Curtin's Hanna-Barbera music.

DRG

CMDDD-231 **Gene Kelly: When We Were Very Young / Nursery Songs & Stories** (MOC 2019)
Includes *The King Who Couldn't Dance.*

EMI (England; all SC)

7243 8 38289 2 0 **The Smurfs Go Pop!** (1996)
7243 8 59738 2 6 **The Smurfs Go Pop! Again** (1997)

7243 8 94195 2 0 **The Smurfs Greatest Hits** (1998)
7243 8 83505 2 5 **The Smurfs—Your Christmas Wish** (1996)
72438-53873-2-6 **The Smurfs Christmas Party** (1996)

EMI

E2-99939 **The Fantastic Baggys: Tell 'Em I'm Surfin'** (1992 Reissue)

ENCORPS

EP-001 **The Future of Corps** (*Epcot* Future Corps Brass)
Includes *The Jetsons* theme, as played outside Spaceship Earth.

FILM SCORE MONTHLY SILVER & GOLDEN AGE CLASSICS

FSM Vol9No17 **Tom and Jerry & Tex Avery Too!**—Scott Bradley (MGM Cartoon Soundtracks; 2006)

FLASHBACK

R2–75636 **Cartoon Network Groovin' Toons** (1999 TST)
R2–75637 **Cartoon Network Toon-A-Rama** (1999 TST)

FOX

07863–66286–2 **Once Upon a Forest**—Michael Crawford, Andrae Crouch (1993 MST)

HALLMARK (Pickwick / England)

711512 **Here Comes Huckleberry Hound** (2012 Reissue of 1961 Colpix LP)
711982 **Yogi Bear and Boo-Boo** (2012 Reissue of 1960 Colpix LP)

HIP-O

314 541 989-2 **The Flintstones in *Viva Rock Vegas***—Ann-Margret, B. B. King, Bill Haley and His Comets, and others (2000 MST)

IMAGINATION STUDIO (Random House)

157   **Scooby-Doo 2: Monsters Unleashed**
        (Movie Story; 2004 SC)

JOHN DEBNEY

JDCD-01   **Jetsons: The Movie / Jonny's Golden
          Quest** (1992 MST)

KID RHINO

R2-7442   **Bedrock Rocks!** (Themes & Pop Artists)
           (1999)
PR-7512   **Your Own Bedrock Rocks! Music CD** (Pebbles Cereals) (2000)
PR-7513   **Your Own Bedrock Rocks! Music CD** (Pebbles Cereals) (2000)
PR-7514   **Your Own Bedrock Rocks! Music CD** (Pebbles Cereals) (2000)

The three above releases have slight variations in song selections, most likely for test marketing purposes.

R2-70450   **Hanna-Barbera's Christmas Sing-A-Long**
           (1991 TST)
R2-71238   **The Flintstones: A Christmas in Bedrock**
           (1993 OC)
R2-71625   **The Flintstones: Bedrock Hop** (1994 OC)
R2-72171   **Billboard Presents Family Christmas
           Classics** (VA)

Includes "Comin' Up Christmas Time" from Yogi's First Christmas & Casper's First Christmas.

R2-72290   **Hanna-Barbera's Pic-A-Nic Basket of
           Cartoon Classics** (1996 TST)
R2-72554   **Billboard Presents Family Lullaby Classics** (VA)

Includes "Tickle Toddle" from The Man Called Flintstone, first time in stereo with opening verse.

R2-72752   **Toon Tunes: 50 Favorite Classic Cartoon
           Theme Songs** (1997 TST)
R2-72876   **Space Ghost's Musical Bar-B-Que** (OC)
R2-74336   **Toon Tunes: Funny Bone Favorites** (2001
           TST)
R2-74337   **Toon Tunes: Action-Packed Anthems**
           (2001 TST)
R2-75693   **Cartoon Network Cartoon Medley** (1999
           TST)
R2-79870   **Scooby-Doo and the Alien Invaders** (2000
           TST)

KIDS' WB! MUSIC

R2 75277   **Dexter's Laboratory: The Musical Time
           Machine** (1998 OC)
R2-75487   **Space Ghost's Surf & Turf** (OC)

LA-LA LAND

LLLCD-1400 **Jonny Quest**—Music by Hoyt Curtin and
           Ted Nichols (TST)

LAVA (Atlantic)

07567-83543-2   **Scooby-Doo** (2002 MST/ VAR)

MADISON GATE

B005AKHZS0   **The Smurfs**—Music by Hector Pereira
             (2011 MST)

MCA

MCAD-10721   **Tom and Jerry: The Movie** (Movie
             Score: Henry Mancini)
MCAD-6431   **Jetsons: The Movie** (1990 MST/VAR)
MCAD-11045   **The Flintstones: Music from Bedrock**
             (1994 MST/ VAR)
MCAD-11348   **Saturday Morning Cartoons' Greatest
             Hits** (1995 SC/VAR)

MCA (England)

MCSTD-7986   **The B.C.-52s: Meet the Flintstones**
             (1994 CD Single)

MILAN (BMG)

73138-35635-2   **Tex Avery** (1993)
Six Scott Bradley soundtrack scores from MGM short cartoons.

MUSIC CLUB (England)

MCCD-279   **Tunes from the Toons: The Best of**
           Hanna-**Barbera** (1996 TVS)

PSM (Polygram Special Markets)

314 520 380-2   **A Flintstones Motown Christmas**
                (1996 OC/VAR)

PLAY-TONE / RIVERDALE (Epic/Sony)

LK-85683   **Josie and the Pussycats** (2001 MST)

POLTRONISSIMA (Italy)

JVM-1207-CD   **Scooby-Doo! Live on Stage** (2007 Italian Cast)

QUALITY SPECIAL PRODUCTS

RSP-190   **Smurfin'!—10th Anniversary Commemorative Album** (1989 SC)

R-KIVE MUSIC / RHINO

R2-72528   **Toon Tunes** (1996 TVS/SC)

RHINO

R2-7405   **Best-O-Scooby-Doo!** (1998 TVS)
(Spaghetti-O's)

R2-70199   **Rerun Rock: "Superstars" Sing TV Themes** (1989)
Includes "Bruce Springstone Live from Bedrock."

R2-71649   **The Flintstones: Modern Stone-Age Melodies** (1994 TST)

R2-71886   **Hanna-Barbera Classics, Vol. 1** (1995 TST)

R2-72434   **Gene Kelly at Metro-Goldwyn-Mayer: 'S Wonderful** (1996 MST)
Includes "The Worry Song" from the *Anchors Aweigh* soundtrack

R2-75505   **Scooby-Doo's Snack Tracks** (1998 TST)

R2-75709   **Scooby-Doo and the Witch's Ghost** (1999 TST)

R2-75848   **The Powerpuff Girls: Heroes & Villains** (2000 OC)

R2-78131   **Dexter's Laboratory—The Hip-Hop Experiment** (2002 OC/VAR)

R2-79772   **Brak Presents the Brak Album Starring Brak** (2000 OC)

R2-72182   **That's Entertainment! The Ultimate Anthology of MGM Musicals** (1995 MST)
Includes music from *Anchors Aweigh* and *Dangerous When Wet*.

R2-73897   **The Powerpuff Girls: Power Pop** (2003 TST/VAR)

R2-74330   **The City of Soundsville: Music from the Powerpuff Girls**—James L. Venable (2001 TST)

RHINO HANDMADE

RHM2-7783   **Josie and the Pussycats: Stop. Look & Listen—The Capitol Recordings** (2001 TST)

RHINO SPECIAL PRODUCTS

R2-79808   **Cartoon Classics and Wacky Sounds by Hanna-Barbera** (2001 TST; Target Stores)

ROCK AND ROLL (Scotti Bros BMG)

72392-75493-2   **Weird Al Yankovic: The T. V. Album** (1995)

SILVA SCREEN

SILCD-807   **Battle of the Planets**—Music by Hoyt Curtin and Bob Sakuma (2004 TST)*

SONY CLASSICAL

88985441292   **Smurfs—The Lost Village**—Music by Christopher Lennertz (2017 MST)

KEMOSABE (RCA)

88883 74167 2   **The Smurfs 2** (2013 MST/VA`)

SOUND IDEAS

885686833865 HB-01/02/03/04 **Hanna-Barbera Studio Effects Library** (TST 1993)

STEMRA (England)

96318   **Merry Christmas from the Smurfs** (Reissue)

SUNSET / SUNSET BLVD

SBR-7985   **Ron Dante's Funhouse** (TST 2020)
Includes songs from *The Amazing Chan and the Chan Clan*.

TEE VEE TOONS / TVT

TVT-1100-2   **Television's Greatest Hits** (1985 TVS/SC)

TVT-1200-2   **Television's Greatest Hits, Vol. 2** (1986 TVS/SC)

TVT-1300-2 **Television's Greatest Hits, Vol. 3: 70's & 80's** (1987 TVS/SC)

TVT-1400-2 **The Commercials: Over 50 Original TV Jingles** (1989 TVS/SC)

TVT-1600-2 **Television's Greatest Hits, Vol. 4: Black and White Classics** (1996 TVS/SC)

TVT-1700-2 **Television's Greatest Hits, Vol. 5: In Living Color** (1996)

TVT-1600-2 **Television's Greatest Hits, Vol. 7: Cable Ready** (1985)

TVT-1958-2 **Sci-Fi's Greatest Hits, Vol. 4: Defenders of Justice** (1999)

All of the above include H-B material; only volume 6 in the series does not; TVT-1600–2 *Television's Greatest Hits, Remote Control* (1996).

TOSHIBA (Japan)

TOCT-8498•99 **Hanna-Barbera Theme Songbook** (TVS/SC 1994)

UNIVERSE PRODUCTIONS

96319 **The Smurfs All Star Show** (Reissue)

VARESE SARABANDE

VSD-5535 **Bubblegum Classics, Vol. 1** (1995)
Includes "Captain Groovy."

VSD-7775 **Bubblegum Classics, Vol. 2** (1995)
Includes "With Every Beat of My Heart" by Shawn.

VSD-5719 **Bubblegum Classics, Vol. 3** (1996)
Includes "I Enjoy Being a Boy (In Love with You)" by The Banana Splits.

VSD-5858 **Prime Time Musicals: Great Songs from Musicals Written for Television** (1997 VAR)
Includes "One Starry Moment" from *Jack and the Beanstalk*.

3020672118 **Smurfs 2**—Music by Hector Pereira (2013 MST)

WARNER / SUNSET / REPRISE

48654-2 **Scooby-Doo 2—Monsters Unleashed** (MST/VAR)

WATER TOWER

WTM-39197 **The Music of DC Comics: 75th Anniversary Collection** (2020 MST/TVS)
Includes *Super Friends* and *The All-New Super Friends Hour*.

DIGITAL AUDIO

ATLANTIC

B088BCFH8W **SCOOB! The Album** (MST/VAR)

HOLOGRAM MUSIC

[no number] **Cartoon Rocket**—London Music Works Featuring Evan Jolly (2011 SC)

SILVA SCREEN

[no number] **The Theme Tunes of Hanna-Barbera**— Kids Superstars (SC 2019)
Includes *Yabba Dabba Dinosaurs*.

WATERTOWER MUSIC (Warner)

B0891RT9VM **SCOOB!**—Music by Tom Holkenborg (2020 MST)

[no number] **Tom and Jerry**—Music by Christopher Lennertz

[no number] **Space Jam: A New Legacy**—Music by Kris Bowers (2021 MST)*

Hanna-Barbera characters appeared in the film; no H-B material on the album.

Selected Bibliography

Books

Adams, T. R. *The Flintstones: A Modern Stone-Age Phenomenon*. Atlanta: Turner Publishing, 1994.

Baldwin, Gerard. *From Mr. Magoo to Papa Smurf: A Memoir*. Austin: Neighborhood Publishers, 2013.

Barbera, Joe. *My Life in 'toons: From Flatbush to Bedrock in Half a Century*. Kansas City: Andrews and McMeel, 1994.

Barrier, Michael. *Hollywood Cartoons: American Animation in Its Golden Age*. New York: Oxford University Press, 1999.

Beals, Dick. *Think Big*. Self-published, 1992.

Beck, Jerry. *Hanna-Barbera Treasury: Rare Art & Momentos from Your Favorite Cartoon Classics*. San Rafael, CA: Insight Editions, 2007.

Burlingame, Jon. *Music for Prime Time*. New York: Oxford University Press, 2023.

Collier, Kevin Scott. *Jonny, Sinbad, Jr. & Me*. New York: Cartoon Research, 2017.

Cooper, Kim, and David Smay, eds. *Bubblegum Music Is the Naked Truth*. Los Angeles: Feral House, 2001.

Foray, June, Mark Evanier, and Earl Kress. *Did You Grow Up with Me, Too? The Autobiography of June Foray*. New York: Bear Manor Media, 2009.

Garner, Joe, and Michael Ashley. *It's Saturday Morning! Celebrating the Golden Era of Cartoons 1960s–1990s*. Dallas: Taylor Publishing, 1996.

Goldmark, Daniel. *Tunes for 'Toons: Music and the Hollywood Cartoon*. Los Angeles: University of California Press, 2005.

Goldmark, Daniel, and Yuval Taylor, eds. *The Cartoon Music Book*. Chicago: A Capella Books, 2002.

Hanna, William, with Tim Ito. *A Cast of Friends*. Dallas: Taylor Publishing, 1996.

Hanna, William, Joseph Barbera, and Hoyt Curtin. *Hanna-Barbera Songbook*. Milwaukee: Hal Leonard, 1996.

Holbrook, Tom, and Friends. *The Bozo Chronicles*. Self-Published, 2010.

Hollis, Tim. *Toons in Toyland*. Jackson: University Press of Mississippi, 2015.

Hollis, Tim, and Greg Ehrbar. *Mouse Tracks: The Story of Walt Disney Records*. Jackson: University Press of Mississippi, 2006.

Johnson, Jimmy. *Inside the Whimsy-Works: My Life with Walt Disney Productions*. Edited by Greg Ehrbar and Didier Ghez. Jackson: University Press of Mississippi, 2014.

Krasnow, Judy Gail. *Rudolph, Frosty, and Captain Kangaroo: The Musical Life of Hecky Krasnow, Producer of the World's Most Beloved Children's Songs*. Santa Monica: Santa Monica Press, 2007.

Lawson, Tim, and Alisa Persons. *The Magic Behind the Voices*. Jackson: University Press of Mississippi, 2004.

Lenburg, Jeff. *William Hanna and Joseph Barbera: Sultans of Saturday Morning*. New York: Chelsea House, 2011.

Lenburg, Jeff, Joan Howard Maurer, and Greg Lenburg. *The Three Stooges Scrapbook*. Secaucus: Citadel Press, 1982.

McCray, Mark. *The Best Saturdays of Our Lives*. Bloomington, IN: Universe, 2015.

McParland, Stephen J. *It's Party Time: A Musical Appreciation of the Beach Party Film Genre*. Los Angeles: PTB Publishing, 1992.

Mallory, Mike. *Hanna-Barbera Cartoons*. Fairfield, CT: Hugh Lauter Levin Associates, 1998.

Maltin, Leonard. *The Disney Films*. New York: Crown, 1973.

Miller, Johnny Ray. *When We're Singin': The Partridge Family and Their Music*. Los Angeles: When We're Singin' LLC, 2016.

Mitenbuler, Reid. *Wild Minds: The Artists and Rivalries That Inspired the Golden Age of Animation*. New York: Atlantic Monthly Press, 2020.

Muldavin, Peter. *The Complete Guide to Vintage Children Records*. Paducah, KY: Collector Books, 2007.

Murray, Matt. *The World of Smurfs*. New York: Abrams Image, 2011.

Norman, Floyd. *Animated Life: A Lifetime of Tips, Tricks, Techniques, and Stories from an Animation Legend*. Indianapolis: Routledge/Taylor & Francis, 2013.

Oldham, Todd, and Michael Graves. *Bedrock City*. New York: Ammo Books, 2008.

Scott, Keith. *The Moose That Roared: The Story of Jay Ward, Bill Scott, a Flying Squirrel, and a Talking Moose*. New York: Thomas Dunn, 2000.

Scott, Keith. *Cartoon Voices of the Golden Age, 1930–70, Volumes 1 and 2*. Orlando: Bear Manor Media, 2022.

Sennett, Ted. *The Art of Hanna-Barbera: Fifty Years of Creativity*. New York: Viking Penguin, 1989.

Sherman, Robert B. *Moose: Chapters from My Life*. Bloomington, IN: AuthorHouse, 2013.

Shows, Charles. *Walt: Backstage Adventures with Walt Disney*. LaJolla: Communication Creativity, 1980.

Stevens, Sally. *I Sang That: A Memoir from Hollywood*. Austin: Atmosphere Press, 2022.

Strouse, Charles. *Put on a Happy Face: A Broadway Memoir*. New York: Union Square Press, 2008.

Swanigan, Michael, and Darell McNeil. *Hanna-Barbera's World of Super Adventure*. Austin: Atmosphere Press, 2022.

Takamoto, Iwao. *My Life with a Thousand Characters*. Jackson: University Press of Mississippi, 2009.

Weinman, Jaime. *Hammers, Anvils, and Dynamite: The Unauthorized Biography of Looney Tunes*. Toronto: Sutherland House Books, 2021.

Articles

Amidi, Amid. "The #ScoobDance Campaign on TikTok Has Generated 3 Billion Views in a Week." cartoonbrew.com, May 10, 2020. https://www.cartoonbrew.com/advertising/the-scoobdance-campaign-on-tiktok-has-generated-3-billion-views-in-a-week-191428.html#.

Ankeny, Jason. Arthur Shimkin Artist Biography. https://www.allmusic.com/artist/arthur-shimkin-mn0000932487/biography.

Beck, Jerry. "Q&A with H&B." *Animation Magazine*, March/April 1994.

Coate, Michael. "Yabba Dabba Doo! Remembering 'The Flintstones' on Its 60th Anniversary." thedigitalbits.com, November 19, 2020. https://thedigitalbits.com/columns/history-legacy-showmanship/flintstones-60th.

Dylan, Bob. "Theme Tune Radio Hour Archive, Episode 89: Cats." themetimeradio.com, 2014. https://www.themetimeradio.com/episode-89-cats/.

Giddins, Gary. "Sweet Smell of Success: The Fantastic Falco" *Sweet Smell of Success* Criterion DVD/Blu-ray essay, February 22, 2011.

Global Dog Productions, Inc. "45 Discography for Hanna-Barbera Records." globaldogproductions.com, 2005.

Global Dog Productions, Inc. "Facts and Figures about Hanna-Barbera 1966." January 5, 2019.

Helbig, Don. "A Look Back at 50 Years of Fun and Memories at King's Island." visitkingsisland.com, April 11, 2022. https://www.visitkingsisland.com/blog/2022/april/a-look-back-at-50-years-of-fun-and-memories-at-kings-island.

Jones, Tom. "The Flight (and Fights) of Apollo 7," smithsonian.com, October 2018. https://www.smithsonianmag.com/air-space-magazine/02_on2018-forgotten-apollo-7-mission-180970365/.

Karpinski, Gary. A Conversation with Hoyt Curtin. classicjq.com, 1999. http://www.classicjq.com/info/hoytcurtininterview.aspx.

Lawrence. Guy. "Yogi Bear's Nuggets: A Hanna-Barbera 45's Guide." spectropop.com, https://spectropop.com/HBR/.

Mallory, Michael. "Hoyt Curtin's Jug Band Session." Animationmagazine.com, March 15, 2012. https://www.animationmagazine.net/2012/03/hoyt-curtins-jug-band-session/.

MeTV Staff. "7 Facts about Yogi Bear to Make You Smarter Than the Average Fan." metv.com. November 12, 2019. https://www.metv.com/lists/7-facts-about-yogi-bear-to-make-you-smarter-than-the-average-fan.

MeTV Staff. "The Story Behind the Flintstones' Most Rocking Song." metv.com, March 17, 2020. https://www.metv.com/stories/the-story-behind-the-flintstones-most-rocking-song.

Miller, Chuck. "Hanna-Barbera Records: The Other Side of Bedrock," no longer available at this writing.

Miller, Chuck. "K-Chuck Radio: Flintstone Rock, or When Hanna-Barbera Made Rock and Roll Records!" chuckthewriter.blog, February 23, 2012. https://chuckthewriter.blog/2012/02/25/k-chuck-radio-flintstone-rock-or-when-hanna-barbera-made-rock-and-roll-records/.

Nesteroff, Kliph. "Hanna-Barbera: The Vinyl Side of Bedrock." *Billboard*, 2006.

Nesteroff, Kliph. "Wall of Sound to Huckleberry Hound: The Weird History of Hanna Barbera Records." www.classicshowbiz.blogspot.com. December 1, 2016. https://blog.wfmu.org/freeform/2007/08/the-vinyl-side-.html.

Novak, Matt. "50 Years of the Jetsons: Why the Show Still Matters." Smithsonian.com, September 19, 2012. https://www.smithsonianmag.com/history/50-years-of-the-jetsons-why-the-show-still-matters-43459669/.

Runtagh, Jordan. "Beatles' Sgt. Pepper at 50: How a Corn Flakes Ad Inspired 'Good Morning, Good Morning.'" rollingstone.com, May 30, 2014. https://www.rollingstone.com/music/music-features/beatles-sgt-pepper-at-50-how-a-corn-flakes-ad-inspired-good-morning-good-morning-127336/.

Simmons, Rick. "The Brief, Unknown Recording Career of Meadowlark Lemon." rebeatmag.com, 2016. http://www

.rebeatmag.com/the-brief-unknown-recording-career-of
-the-late-meadowlark-lemon/.

Vilas-Boas, Eric, and John Maher. "The 100 Sequences
That Shaped Animation." vulture.com. October 5, 2020.
https://www.vulture.com/article/most-influential-best
-scenes-animation-history.html.

Wolters, Larry. "TV to Get Fine New Cartoon." *Chicago Tribune*, September 29, 1958.

Yowp, Don. "An Interview with Hoyt Curtin." *YOWP: Stuff
about Early Hanna-Barbera Cartoons*, August 22, 2022.
yowpyowp.blogspot.com. (Many other articles from this
website were instrumental in researching this book.)

Liner Notes

Barbera, Joe, David Burd, Bill Burnett, Hoyt Curtin, Bill
Hanna, Earl Kress, Barry Hansen, Marty Pekar, and Fred
Siebert. *Hanna-Barbera Pic-A-Nic Basket of Cartoon Clas-
sics*. Rhino Records, Compact Disc Set, R2-72290, 1996.

Janssen, Danny, and Sue Sheridan. *Josie and the Pussycats:
Stop, Look and Listen*: The Capitol Recordings. Rhino Handmade, RHM2-7783, 2001.

Magazines

Billboard: May 23, 1953; January 16, 1965; February 13, 1965;
March 20, 1965; April 3, 1965; May 8, 1965; May 13, 1965;
May 15, 1965; August 21, 1965; October 16, 1965; October
23, 1965; November 6, 1965; December 4, 1965; January
15, 1966; January 29, 1966; May 7, 1966; June 4, 1966; July
16, 1966; June 15, 1968.

Hollywood Reporter: December 11, 1987 (Hanna-Barbera Anniversary Issue).

Variety: March 2, 1965; March 9, 1965; August 26, 1965; May
4, 1967.

Websites

45cat.com
45worlds.com
animationscoop.com
cartoonbrew.com
cartoonresearch.com
classicmoviehub.com
Discography of American Historical Recordings: https://
adp.library.ucsb.edu/index.php
discogs.com
Hanna-Barbera Wiki: Hanna-barbera.fandom.com
Mark Evanier's blog: newsfromme.com
radiothen.blogspot.com

secondhandsongs.com
Stu's Show: stusshow.com
themoviedb.com
TV Confidential: tvconfidential.net
Yowp: Stuff about Early Hanna-Barbera Cartoons: yow
pyowp.blogspot.com

Video

Daws Butler: Voice Magician. (Documentary) Sabado Productions, Ltd. 1987.

Joseph Barbera Interviews with Leonard Maltin, Archive of
American Television.

Hanna-Barbera collections on Warner Home Video DVD
and Blu-ray: *Tom and Jerry Spotlight Collections*; *Loopy
DeLoop*; *The Huckleberry Hound Show*; *The Yogi Bear Show*;
The Flintstones; *Top Cat*; *The Jetsons*; *Wally Gator, Lippy the
Lion and Hardy Har Har*; *Jonny Quest*; *The Magilla Gorilla
Show*; *The Peter Potamus Show*; *Hey There, It's Yogi Bear*; *The
Atom Ant Show*; *The Secret Squirrel Show*; *Frankenstein, Jr.
and The Impossibles*; *The Man Called Flintstone*; *Space Ghost
and Dino Boy*; *Space Kidettes and Young Samson*; *Birdman
and the Galaxy Trio*; *Herculoids*; *Shazzan*; *Moby Dick and
Mighty Mightor*; *The New Adventures of Huckleberry Finn*;
Wacky Races, The Perils of Penelope Pitstop; *Dastardly and
Muttley in Their Flying Machines*; *Scooby-Doo, Where Are
You?*; *Where's Huddles?*; *Josie and the Pussycats*; *The Pebbles
and Bamm-Bamm Show*; *Help! It's the Hair Bear Bunch!*;
The Funky Phantom; *Wait Till Your Father Gets Home*; *The
Amazing Chan and the Chan Clan*; *The Roman Holidays*;
Sealab 2020; *Josie and the Pussycats in Outer Space*; *Speed
Buggy*; *Butch Cassidy and the Sundance Kids*; *Yogi's Gang*;
Super Friend; *Goober and the Ghost Chasers*; *Inch High,
Private Eye*; *The Addams Family*; *Hong Kong Phooey*; *Devlin*;
Valley of the Dinosaurs; *Wheelie and the Chopper Bunch*;
Korg: 70,000 B.C.; *The Scooby-Doo/Dynomutt Hour*; *Clue
Club*; *Jabberjaw*; *Laff-a-Lympics*; *Captain Caveman and
the Teen Angels*; *Heidi's Song*; *The All-New Super Friends
Hour*; *Challenge of the Super Friends*; *Casper and the Angels*;
The Super Globetrotters; *Scooby-Doo and Scrappy-Doo*; *The
World's Greatest Super Friends*; *Drak Pack*; *Richie Rich*; *Space
Stars*; *The Kwicky Koala Show*; *Smurfs*; *Pac-Man*; *Shirt Tales*;
The Dukes; *Monchhichis*; *The Biskitts*; *Snorks*; *Challenge of
the Go-Bots*; *Super Friends: The Legendary Powers Show*;
Paw Paws; *Galtar and the Golden Lance*; *The 13 Ghosts of
Scooby-Doo*; *The New Adventures of Jonny Quest*; *The Flint-
stone Kids*; *Sky Commanders*; *A Pup Named Scooby-Doo*; *The
Completely Mental Misadventures of Ed Grimley*; *Paddington
Bear*; *Tom and Jerry Kids*; *The Pirates of Dark Water*; *The
Real Adventures of Jonny Quest*; *Best of Warner Bros, 25
Cartoon Collection: Hanna-Barbera*; plus numerous made-
for-TV movies and specials.

Hanna-Barbera streamed series and features: *Flintstone Funnies* (*The Flintstone Comedy Show*); *Yogi's Space Race*; *Galaxy Goof-Ups*; *The New Fred and Barney Show*; *Yogi's Treasure Hunt*; *The New Yogi Bear Show*; *Yo Yogi!*; *Droopy, Master Detective*; *Cave Kids*; *Jeannie*; *Partridge Family 2020 A.D.*; *Jetsons: The Movie*; *Be Cool, Scooby-Doo*; *Shaggy and Scooby, Get a Clue*; *Scooby-Doo: Mystery Incorporated*; *Scooby-Doo and Guess Who?*; *Yabba Dabba Dinosaurs*; *Jellystone!*; *SCOOB!*; *Tom and Jerry*; *Space Jam 2: A New Legacy*.

Other Hanna-Barbera home video DVDs: *Charlotte's Web*; *Fonz and the Happy Days Gang*; *Laverne and Shirley*; *Tom and Jerry: The Movie*; *Once Upon a Forest*.

Walt Disney Studios Home Entertainment: *The Boys: The Sherman Brothers' Story*.

Index